I · N · S · O · L · V · E · N · C · Y

General Editor: Dr L. S. Sealy

Administrative Receivers
and
Administrators

I should like to dedicate this book to my
mother and father, to Gillian and to Fiona.

*Gordon Stewart*
1987

I·N·S·O·L·V·E·N·C·Y

General Editor: Dr L. S. Sealy
*Fellow of Gonville and Caius
College and Lecturer in the
University of Cambridge*

# Administrative Receivers and Administrators

**Gordon Stewart MA(Oxon), Solicitor**
*Partner in Allen & Overy*

## CCH Editions Limited
TAX, BUSINESS AND LAW PUBLISHERS

Published by CCH Editions Limited
Telford Road, Bicester, Oxfordshire OX6 0XD
Tel. (0869) 253300, Facsimile (0869) 245814.

| | |
|---|---|
| USA | Commerce Clearing House, Inc., Chicago, Illinois |
| CANADA | CCH Canadian Limited, Toronto, Ontario. |
| AUSTRALIA | CCH Australia Limited, North Ryde, NSW. |
| NEW ZEALAND | Commerce Clearing House (NZ), Auckland. |

This publication is designed to provide accurate and authoritative information in regard to the subject-matter covered. It is sold with the understanding that the publisher is not engaged in rendering legal or other professional services. If legal advice or other expert assistance is required, the services of a competent professional person should be sought.

## Ownership of Trade Marks

The Trade Marks

COMPUTAX and **COMMERCE, CLEARING, HOUSE, INC.,** are the property of Commerce Clearing House Incorporated, Chicago, Illinois, U.S.A.

Stewart, Gordon
  Administrative receivers and
  administrators.——(Insolvency).
  1. Receivers—England
  I. Title   II. Series
  344.206'78     KD2155.R

  ISBN 0-86325-140-4
  ISBN 0-86325-085-8 Pbk

First published 1987
Reprinted 1991

PO 2940

First printed by Page Bros (Norwich) Ltd.
Reprinted in Great Britain by Hartnolls Ltd., Bodmin, Cornwall

# General Editor's Preface

One of the most important and far-reaching reforms of the 1980s has been the radical transformation of insolvency law. The first step was the publication in 1982 of the report of the Review Committee on Insolvency Law and Practice, chaired by Sir Kenneth Cork, CBE. This report made recommendations for the improvement and modernisation of virtually every aspect of the subject, and for bringing together and assimilating the rules and practice governing what had previously been regarded as the separate topics of individual bankruptcy and corporate insolvency.

The Insolvency Act 1985, enacted after much debate and controversy, implemented many of the reforms which the Cork Committee had advocated, sweeping away outdated provisions from the Victorian era, introducing professional qualifications and standards for insolvency practitioners, launching the new phenomena of voluntary arrangements, administrators and administrative receivers, and tightening up the rules and sanctions governing delinquent directors. Finally, the Insolvency Act 1986 and the Company Directors Disqualification Act 1986 were passed, to consolidate the 1985 Act with related parts of the Companies Act; and these consolidating Acts, together with the voluminous Insolvency Rules 1986 and other subordinate legislation, now constitute a wholly new and modern insolvency regime, which has been in force since 29 December 1986.

In the present volume Gordon Stewart provides an informed and comprehensive account of the new law on administrative receivers and administrators, with a particular emphasis on the practical aspects of these subjects and on recent judicial rulings (including a number that have not been reported). This book will be a most useful and invaluable guide not only to insolvency practitioners and their legal advisers, but also to their commercial clients – whether companies, their directors and employees, banks and other charge-holders, or creditors generally.

*L. S. Sealy*
Gonville and Caius College, Cambridge
May 1987

v

# About the Publisher

CCH Editions is part of a world-wide group of companies that specialises in tax and law publishing. The group produces a wide range of books and reporting services for the accounting, business and legal professions. The Oxfordshire premises are the centre for all UK and European operations.

All CCH publications are designed to provide practical, authoritative references and useful guides, and are written by CCH's highly qualified and experienced editorial team and specialist outside authors.

CCH Editions Limited publish bound books and loose-leaf reporting services specific to the United Kingdom, as well as distributing the publications of the overseas affiliate companies.

# Acknowledgement

The provisions of the Insolvency Act 1986 and the Company Directors Disqualification Act 1986 set out in Appendixes 1 to 3 and 5 and 6 of this book, and the forms set out in Appendix 4 are reproduced with the kind permission of the Controller of Her Majesty's Stationery Office.

# Author's Preface

The recent insolvency legislation – The Insolvency Acts 1985 and 1986 and the Company Directors Disqualification Act 1986 – is the first full-scale attempt at reform of insolvency law for over 80 years. It marks the beginning of a new era of insolvency law and practice.

Reform was long overdue. The recessions which hit British industry and business in the 1970s and 1980s dramatically increased the volume of insolvency work, and the fact that it has become big business has necessitated modern statutory regulation.

The work of insolvency practitioners, lawyers and accountants, has always had a large commercial or practical streak to it. This will no doubt continue. However, the increase in the demand for insolvency services was noticed and met by the very largest firms of accountants, some of which had not previously specialised in this field. The technical departments of these firms have ruthlessly sought the 'right' answers in the insolvency field, just as they have done in other fields, and we are to be grateful to them for that. As a result, the last 15 years has seen an upsurge in the number of insolvency cases coming to court and these cases have, themselves, produced a new body of law.

This book deals, first, with corporate administrative receivers and, secondly, with corporate administrators. Fixed-charge receivers and receivers appointed out of court are more than adequately covered elsewhere (*Kerr*, *Picarda*, etc.) and it is fair to say that the administrative receiver is, and will be, the receiver most commonly encountered.

The treatment of the subject matter in this work, within the headings of 'administrative receivers' and of 'administrators', is chronological, in an attempt to give an impression of the way in which a receivership or an administration progresses in practice.

I am indebted to a number of people who have assisted me in producing this book. First, I would like to thank Peter Beirne of Grant Thornton, and Maurice Withall also of Grant Thornton and chairman of the technical committee of the Insolvency Practitioners Association, for reading and commenting on parts of the manuscript. The tax chapters of the book were contributed by my partner Peter Hewes and I am most grateful to him for his efforts. For assistance with other topics, my thanks are due to my colleague Brian Cain. Thanks are also due to Barney Hearnden and the many other articled clerks of my firm who carried out the thankless task of checking and cross-checking and correcting references, quotations, etc., and to the two Maureens for their cheerful help in typing and retyping (and re-re-typing, etc., etc.) the manuscript. Writing the book would have been much more difficult without the help, encouragement and ready willingness to discuss all manner of points of my partners Peter Totty and Nick Segal, and I am grateful to them. Finally, my thanks go to Fiona for her constant support and encouragement throughout this project.

If this book is to be considered worthwhile, then this is due in no small part to those to whom thanks are now proffered, but responsibility for the text and errors and inaccuracies is mine alone.

The law is stated as at 30 April 1987.

*Gordon Stewart*
30 April 1987

# Introduction

The text deals almost exclusively with the new law introduced by the Insolvency Act 1986 and the Insolvency Rules 1986. The old law, however, does still apply, generally speaking, to insolvency occurring before 29 December 1986 and to transactions entered into before that date. The text makes reference to the old law but not by way of exposition, first, because the old law has a finite life span, and, secondly, because there are many worthwhile works on the old law to which reference can be made. Appendix 1 to this book contains the specific transitional provisions set out in Schedule 11 to the Insolvency Act 1986. The text assumes the new law is of application. On the other hand, many of the basic principles of insolvency law remain unchanged and, when in point, old authorities are cited in the text.

The text deals only with the law of England and Wales. The Insolvency Act 1986 and the Insolvency Rules 1986 do contain provisions affecting the law of Scotland and these are not dissimilar in effect to those introduced in England and Wales, taking into account the existing differences between English and Scots law, but reference should be made to an appropriate textbook on Scots law. In general, the Act and Rules do not extend to Northern Ireland (see s. 441 of the Insolvency Act). There are new provisions requiring co-operation between those courts exercising an insolvency jurisdiction in the various constituent parts of the UK in respect of the cross-border operation of receiverships. These provisions are set out in Appendix 2 to the book. Cross-border insolvencies can give rise to problems of some complexity but these are outwith the remit of this work.

In accordance with the recommendations of the Cork Report, the recent insolvency legislation has utilised the concept of the 'connected person' in a number of areas. The concept had already been used in a limited way in other areas of company law – see s. 346 of the Companies Act 1985. In certain situations, the onus of proof is placed upon a connected person when it would not have been if he had been unconnected and, further, transactions involving a connected person may be vulnerable to review for a longer period than would have been the case if no such person had been involved (see, for example, transactions at an undervalue and preferences, discussed at ¶1016). The relevant provisions of the Insolvency Act 1986, setting out who is a connected person, are contained in Appendix 3 to this book, to which reference should be made when the phrase 'connected person' is used in the text. The new definition of 'administrative receiver' is discussed at ¶301.

The various forms relating to voluntary arrangements, administrations and administrative receivers and miscellaneous proxy forms contained in Pts. 1, 2, 3 and 8 of Sch. 4 to the Insolvency Rules 1986 are set out in Appendix 4 to this work.

# Abbreviations

In references, the following abbreviations are used:

CA      Companies Act 1985
CDDA    Company Directors Disqualification Act 1986
IA      Insolvency Act 1986
IR      Insolvency Rules 1986
LPA     Law of Property Act 1925

In the text, 'the Taxes Act' is used to describe the Income and Corporation Taxes Act 1970. The following abbreviation is also used:

The Cork Report (and      Insolvency Law and Practice – Report of the
hence the Cork Committee)  Review Committee (Chairman Sir Kenneth
                          Cork CBE) (Cmnd. 8558, 1982)

# Contents

| | Page |
|---|---|
| General Editor's Preface | v |
| About the Publisher | vi |
| Acknowledgement | vi |
| Author's Preface | vii |
| Introduction | ix |
| Abbreviations | x |

## Part I – Licensing of Insolvency Practitioners

**1  Background** — 3
THE CORK REPORT — 3
¶101  Nefarious conduct — 3
THE INSOLVENCY LEGISLATION — 3
¶102  Solutions — 3

**2  Details of Licensing Requirements** — 5
RESTRICTION — 5
¶201  Acting 'as an insolvency practitioner' when unqualified — 5
QUALIFICATION — 5
¶202  Prohibition — 5
¶203  Recognised professional bodies — 6
¶204  Competent authorities — 7
¶205  Authorisations by competent authorities — 7
INSOLVENCY PRACTITIONER'S BONDING — 9
¶206  Detailed requirements — 9

## Part II – Administrative Receivers

**3  Appointment of an Administrative Receiver** — 13
INTRODUCTION — 13
¶301  Definition of 'administrative receiver' — 13
CHARGES — 14
¶302  General — 14
¶303  Floating charges — 15
¶304  Fixed charges and mortgages — 17
¶305  Charges on future book debts — 18

| | | Page |
|---|---|---|
| APPOINTMENTS | | 20 |
| ¶306 | When they occur | 20 |
| ¶307 | The right to appoint | 21 |
| ¶308 | Demands generally | 27 |
| ¶309 | Checklist for appointments | 29 |
| ¶310 | Appointments | 31 |
| ¶311 | Acceptance of appointments | 33 |
| ¶312 | Formalities subsequent to appointment | 34 |
| ¶313 | Invalid appointments | 35 |

**4 Nature, Capacity, Powers and Duties of an Administrative Receiver** 37

| AGENCY | | 37 |
|---|---|---|
| ¶401 | Nature and extent | 37 |
| ¶402 | Conflict of interest | 39 |
| ¶403 | Responsibilities | 39 |
| ¶404 | Effect of liquidation | 39 |
| PROPERTY COVERED BY THE APPOINTMENT | | 41 |
| ¶405 | Contractual position | 41 |
| ¶406 | Third-party property and contractual rights | 41 |
| ¶407 | Specific third-party rights | 48 |
| ¶408 | Prohibitions on charging | 66 |
| ¶409 | Better than his principal? | 67 |
| POWERS OF AN ADMINISTRATIVE RECEIVER | | 68 |
| ¶410 | Contractual provisions | 68 |
| ¶411 | Additional statutory powers | 68 |
| ¶412 | Limitations on powers | 69 |
| ¶413 | Exercise of powers in joint appointments | 71 |
| ¶414 | The administrative receiver as 'office holder' | 71 |
| DUTIES OF AN ADMINISTRATIVE RECEIVER | | 72 |
| ¶415 | To report on unfit directors | 72 |
| ¶416 | Duties owed to the company and others | 75 |
| ¶417 | To make distributions | 79 |
| ¶418 | Notification | 79 |
| ¶419 | Statement of affairs | 80 |
| ¶420 | Report to creditors | 80 |
| ¶421 | Meetings of creditors | 81 |
| ¶422 | The creditors' committee | 82 |
| ¶423 | Enforcement of duties | 83 |

**5 Fulfilling the Purpose of the Receivership** 84

| THE EARLY DAYS | | 84 |
|---|---|---|
| ¶501 | Preliminary steps | 84 |
| ¶502 | Establishment of procedures | 85 |

| | | **Page** |
|---|---|---|
| TRADING | | 86 |
| ¶503 | To trade or not to trade? | 86 |
| ¶504 | Hiving-down | 87 |
| ¶505 | Set-off | 88 |
| TRADING AND OTHER LIABILITIES | | 89 |
| ¶506 | Reservation of title | 89 |
| ¶507 | Other statutory and tortious liabilities | 89 |
| ¶508 | Rates | 91 |
| ¶509 | Rent | 93 |
| ¶510 | Concept of the receivership expense | 94 |
| EMPLOYEES | | 96 |
| ¶511 | The supposed mischief of Nicoll v Cutts | 96 |
| ¶512 | Meaning of 'adoption' | 96 |
| REALISATION OF ASSETS AND PROPERTY | | 99 |
| ¶513 | Sale documentation | 99 |
| ¶514 | Negotiating the deal | 99 |
| ¶515 | Common areas of concern | 100 |
| ¶516 | Conveyancing questions | 109 |
| ¶517 | Power to sell charged property | 111 |
| ¶518 | Duties regarding price | 111 |
| ¶519 | Considerations for purchasers | 112 |
| **6 Payments and Distributions** | | 114 |
| PREFERENTIAL CREDITORS | | 114 |
| ¶601 | Who are they? | 114 |
| ¶602 | From what assets are they paid? | 115 |
| ¶603 | Content of duty to pay | 115 |
| ¶604 | Surplus of fixed-charge realisations | 118 |
| ¶605 | Crown set-off | 118 |
| ORDER OF PAYMENTS | | 119 |
| ¶606 | General principles | 119 |
| CONTRIBUTION BETWEEN CO-GUARANTORS | | 120 |
| ¶607 | Introduction | 120 |
| ¶608 | Co-guarantors' rights | 121 |
| ¶609 | Receiver's power and duty to allocate funds | 124 |
| REMUNERATION | | 125 |
| ¶610 | Generally | 125 |
| **7 Termination** | | 129 |
| METHODS OF TERMINATION | | 129 |
| ¶701 | Repayment of secured debt: duty to cease to act | 129 |

| | | Page |
|---|---|---|
| ¶702 | Dismissal | 129 |
| ¶703 | Resignation | 130 |
| ¶704 | Death | 130 |
| ¶705 | Vacation of office | 130 |
| INDEMNITIES | | 131 |
| ¶706 | Statutory provisions | 131 |
| ¶707 | Relationship with appointor | 132 |
| ¶708 | Relationship with administrator | 133 |
| ¶709 | Relationship with a liquidator | 133 |
| ACCOUNTS | | 134 |
| ¶710 | Abstract of receipts and payments | 134 |

**8  Tax** — 136

| EXISTING LIABILITIES | | 136 |
|---|---|---|
| ¶801 | General rule | 136 |
| ¶802 | Preferential payments | 136 |
| ACCRUING LIABILITIES | | 139 |
| ¶803 | Value added tax accruing | 139 |
| ¶804 | Tax liabilities incurred during the receivership | 140 |
| ¶805 | Obligations to deduct | 143 |
| ¶806 | Value added tax | 144 |
| ¶807 | Value added tax: bad debt relief | 146 |
| ¶808 | Hive-downs | 148 |
| REVENUE POWERS | | 152 |
| ¶809 | Distress | 152 |
| ¶810 | Section 62 of the Taxes Management Act 1970 | 153 |

*Part III – Administrators*

**9  Appointment of an Administrator** — 157

| INTRODUCTION | | 157 |
|---|---|---|
| ¶901 | Rationale of the administration process | 157 |
| ¶902 | Outline of the procedure | 158 |
| APPLICATION FOR AN ADMINISTRATION ORDER | | 160 |
| ¶903 | Details of the application | 160 |
| ¶904 | Consequences of application | 169 |
| ¶905 | Attitudes of secured creditors | 175 |
| ¶906 | The hearing of the application | 177 |
| ¶907 | Notice of the order | 179 |
| ¶908 | Consequences of order | 180 |
| ¶909 | Invalid appointments | 181 |

|  |  | Page |
|---|---|---|
| **10** | **Nature, Capacity, Powers and Duties of an Administrator** | 182 |
| INTRODUCTION | | 182 |
| ¶1001 | Comparison with other office-holders | 182 |
| ¶1002 | Purpose of appointment | 182 |
| AGENCY AND POSITION | | 183 |
| ¶1003 | Nature and extent | 183 |
| ¶1004 | Officer of the court | 183 |
| ¶1005 | Officer of the company | 184 |
| PROPERTY COVERED BY THE APPOINTMENT | | 185 |
| ¶1006 | Apparent entitlement | 185 |
| ¶1007 | Third-party property | 185 |
| ¶1008 | Charged property | 186 |
| POWERS OF AN ADMINISTRATOR | | 187 |
| ¶1009 | Statutory list of powers | 187 |
| ¶1010 | Directors of the company | 187 |
| ¶1011 | Information and powers as 'office-holder' | 188 |
| ¶1012 | Limitations on powers and their exercise | 192 |
| ¶1013 | Exercise of powers in joint appointments | 192 |
| DUTIES OF AN ADMINISTRATOR | | 192 |
| ¶1014 | Purposes of the appointment | 192 |
| ¶1015 | Reporting on unfit directors | 193 |
| ¶1016 | Investigating antecedent transactions | 193 |
| ¶1017 | Miscellaneous requirements | 204 |
| ¶1018 | Duties owed to the company | 204 |
| ¶1019 | Duties owed to the creditors and members? | 205 |
| **11** | **Fulfilling the Purpose of the Administration** | 206 |
| THE EARLY DAYS | | 206 |
| ¶1101 | Preliminary steps | 206 |
| ¶1102 | Establishing procedures | 207 |
| ADMINISTRATOR'S PROPOSALS | | 207 |
| ¶1103 | Formal requirements | 207 |
| ¶1104 | Examples of possible proposals | 208 |
| ¶1105 | Revision of proposals | 211 |
| MEETINGS | | 212 |
| ¶1106 | Creditors' meetings | 212 |
| ¶1107 | Creditors' committee | 219 |
| ¶1108 | Members' meetings | 223 |
| PROTECTION OF CREDITORS AND MEMBERS | | 224 |
| ¶1109 | Unfairly prejudicial management and acts | 224 |
| ¶1110 | Court orders and time limits | 227 |

|  |  | Page |
|---|---|---|
| SCHEMES | | 228 |
| ¶1111 | Voluntary arrangement scheme | 228 |
| ¶1112 | Section 425 schemes | 242 |
| TRADING | | 242 |
| ¶1113 | Considerations for administrators | 242 |
| ¶1114 | Hiving-down | 243 |
| TRADING AND OTHER LIABILITIES | | 243 |
| ¶1115 | Concept of the administration expense | 243 |
| ¶1116 | Liability in tort | 247 |
| ¶1117 | Suppliers of utilities | 247 |
| ¶1118 | Existing contracts | 247 |
| ¶1119 | Employees | 248 |
| REALISATION OF ASSETS AND PROPERTY | | 248 |
| ¶1120 | Considerations for administrators | 248 |
| ¶1121 | Conveyancing questions | 248 |
| ¶1122 | Power to deal with charged and third-party property | 249 |
| **12** | **Remuneration and Termination** | 251 |
| REMUNERATION | | 251 |
| ¶1201 | Pre-order | 251 |
| ¶1202 | Creditors' committee | 251 |
| ¶1203 | Applications to court | 252 |
| TERMINATION | | 253 |
| ¶1204 | Discharge of administration order | 253 |
| ¶1205 | Vacation of office | 255 |
| ¶1206 | Resignation | 255 |
| ¶1207 | Death | 256 |
| ¶1208 | General considerations on termination | 256 |
| ¶1209 | Expenses and floating charges | 257 |
| ¶1210 | Accounts | 257 |
| ¶1211 | Release | 257 |
| **13** | **Tax** | 259 |
| BEFORE THE ORDER | | 259 |
| ¶1301 | Corporation tax | 259 |
| ¶1302 | Preferential debts in an administration | 261 |
| ¶1303 | Value added tax accruing | 262 |
| AFTER THE ORDER | | 262 |
| ¶1304 | Corporation tax as an administration expense | 262 |
| ¶1305 | Value added tax | 264 |
| ¶1306 | Hive-downs | 265 |
| ¶1307 | Revenue powers | 265 |

|                                                                 | Page |
|-----------------------------------------------------------------|------|
| **Appendix 1: Transitional Provisions**                         | 267  |
| **Appendix 2: Co-operation between courts exercising jurisdiction in relation to insolvency and cross-border operation of receivership provisions** | 272  |
| **Appendix 3: Connected Persons**                               | 274  |
| **Appendix 4: Relevant Forms**                                  | 276  |
| **Appendix 5: Powers of an Administrator or an Administrative Receiver** | 330  |
| **Appendix 6: Badges of Unfitness for Directors**               | 332  |
| **Case Table**                                                  | 335  |
| **Legislation Finding List**                                    | 341  |
| **Index**                                                       | 347  |

# PART I
# LICENSING
## OF
# INSOLVENCY
# PRACTITIONERS

# 1  Background

## THE CORK REPORT

### ¶101  Nefarious conduct

One of the objectives of the new insolvency legislation is to ensure that those persons who are responsible for the management of a company's affairs in an insolvency context, whether as administrator, administrative receiver, liquidator, trustee in bankruptcy or supervisor under a voluntary arrangement, have '. . . the confidence and respect, not only of the courts and of creditors and debtors, but also of the general public . . .' (Cork Report, para. 732). It was not unknown for unscrupulous individuals acting as receivers, liquidators or trustees to have more regard to their own interests and those of the officers of the company over which they were appointed than to those of the company's creditors at large.

## THE INSOLVENCY LEGISLATION

### ¶102  Solutions

The Cork Report recognised the public's dissatisfaction with the type of conduct described at ¶101 and recommended the introduction of minimum standards of qualification for any person wishing to act as an 'insolvency practitioner' (Cork Report, para. 758). The recommendations of the Cork Report formed the basis of the provisions relating to insolvency practitioners which can be found in Pt. XIII of the Insolvency Act 1986. Briefly, an insolvency practitioner needs to hold a licence to act, whether granted by or through the Secretary of State or by a recognised professional body of which he is a member, and he also needs to provide security for the proper performance of his functions. The idea behind the scheme is that misbehaviour by a practitioner should lead to withdrawal or non-renewal of the practitioner's 'ticket' or licence to act. A great deal will depend on how robust a line is taken by the professional bodies with those who behave badly. Practitioners will be well advised to avoid committing offences under the Insolvency Act or Rules – as what might previously have been shrugged off as merely a technical breach may now be the subject of investigation or adverse comment when licences come up for renewal. A summary of the provisions relating to insolvency practitioners is given in Chapter 2.

# 2 Details of Licensing Requirements

## RESTRICTION

### ¶201 Acting 'as an insolvency practitioner' when unqualified

Section 389 of the Insolvency Act 1986 makes it a criminal offence (punishable by a fine and/or imprisonment) for a person to act as an insolvency practitioner in relation to any company or individual at a time when he is not qualified to do so.

By virtue of s. 388(1) of the Insolvency Act 1986 (and see also s. 230), a person acts as an insolvency practitioner in relation to a company by acting as its:

(1) liquidator; or

(2) provisional liquidator; or

(3) administrator; or

(4) administrative receiver; or

(5) supervisor of a voluntary arrangement.

A receiver or manager, other than an administrative receiver, is not caught and so, for example, a surveyor can still be appointed under a fixed charge to collect the income of a property owned by a company, as was often the practice prior to the recent legislation, without needing to be qualified as an insolvency practitioner.

## QUALIFICATION

### ¶202 Prohibitions

Only an individual may qualify to act as an insolvency practitioner (IA, s. 390(1)). Furthermore, if at the relevant time the individual concerned:

(1)   has been adjudged bankrupt; or

(2)   has had a sequestration award made against his estate; or

(3)   is subject to a disqualification order made under the Company Directors Disqualification Act 1986; or

(4)   is a patient within the meaning of Part VII of the Mental Health Act 1983 or s. 125(1) of the Mental Health (Scotland) Act 1984,

he is not qualified to act as an insolvency practitioner (IA, s. 390(4)).

Assuming none of the above prohibitions are applicable, a person will be qualified to act as an insolvency practitioner if (IA, s. 390(2) and s. 392) he has provided the requisite security and either:

(1)   he is a member of a recognised professional body and that body's rules allow him to act; or

(2)   the Secretary of State, or a 'competent authority' designated by him, grants an authorisation to act.

Earlier versions of the Insolvency Bill contained restrictions on the taking of appointments where there was a conflict of interest. These were later dropped and the system relies upon the rules of the recognised professional body, or competent authority, to cover this area.

## ¶203   Recognised professional bodies

The Secretary of State may designate a body as a 'recognised professional body' if it maintains and enforces rules for securing that its members, who are permitted under its own rules to act as insolvency practitioners, are fit and proper persons and meet acceptable requirements as to education and practical training and experience (IA, s. 391).

At the time of writing, the Secretary of State has designated the following organisations as recognised professional bodies (The Insolvency Practitioners (Recognised Professional Bodies) Order 1986 (SI 1986 No. 1764)):

(1)   The Chartered Association of Certified Accountants;

(2)   The Insolvency Practitioners Association;

(3)   The Institute of Chartered Accountants in England and Wales;

(4)   The Institute of Chartered Accountants in Ireland;

(5)   The Institute of Chartered Accountants in Scotland;

(6)   The Law Society; and

(7)   The Law Society of Scotland.

## ¶204   Competent authorities

An individual who wishes to act as an insolvency practitioner, but who is not a member of any of the recognised professional bodies (or is not able to get a licence from that body), may seek to obtain an authorisation to act as an insolvency practitioner from a 'competent authority' (IA, s. 392).

Section 392(2) of the Insolvency Act 1986 states that the 'competent authority' to whom an application for authorisation must be made will be either:

(1)   the person or body designated by the Secretary of State in relation to specified types of cases; or

(2)   the Secretary of State himself where no such designation has been made.

At the time of writing no competent authorities have been designated by the Secretary of State, so all applications must be made to him.

The application must be made in the form prescribed by the competent authority and the applicant can be required to provide such further information as the competent authority considers desirable (IA, s. 392(4)). A fee of £200 must accompany the application (reg. 7 of the Insolvency Practitioners Regulations 1986 (SI 1986 No. 1995)).

## ¶205   Authorisations by competent authorities

A competent authority may grant or refuse an application (IA, s. 393(1)). Section 393(2) of the Insolvency Act 1986 provides that: 'The authority *shall* grant the application . . .' (emphasis supplied), from which it would seem that the authority must grant the application if it appears to it from the information furnished by the applicant, and having regard to such other information as it may have, that the applicant:

(1)   is a fit and proper person to act as an insolvency practitioner; and

(2)   meets the prescribed requirements with respect to education and practical training and experience.

The Insolvency Practitioners Regulations 1986 (SI 1986 No. 1995) give details of the required educational qualifications and practical experience (see regs. 5 and 6). In general terms, it seems unlikely that this qualification route will be seen as an easy way to become qualified. Regulation 4 of the Regulations gives some guidance as to what matters may be taken into consideration in determining whether an applicant is a fit and proper person. For example, one such matter is whether the applicant 'has engaged in practices in the course of carrying on business appearing to be deceitful or oppressive or otherwise unfair or improper, whether lawful or not, or which otherwise cast doubt upon his probity or competence' (reg. 4(c)).

Any authorisation granted by a competent authority may continue in force for no longer than three years from the date upon which it was granted (reg. 8).

An authorisation of a competent authority may be withdrawn if, as provided by the Insolvency Act 1986, s. 393(4) and (5):

(1)  the holder is no longer a fit and proper person; or

(2)  he fails to comply with any of the provisions of Part XIII of the Insolvency Act 1986 (Insolvency Practitioners) or any regulations made thereunder or under the Rules; or

(3)  he furnishes a competent authority with false, misleading or inaccurate information; or

(4)  the holder requests or consents to the withdrawal.

If a competent authority intends to refuse an application or withdraw an authorisation, it must give the applicant/holder written notice of its intention to do so, setting out the grounds upon which it intends to refuse or withdraw the authorisation (IA, s. 394(2)). Within 14 days of the date of service of such notice the applicant/holder may make written representations to the competent authority commenting upon the intended course of action. The competent authority must then have regard to any such representations in determining whether to refuse the application or withdraw the authorisation (IA, s. 395).

An individual upon whom a competent authority has served a notice of refusal or withdrawal may give written notice to the authority requiring his case to be referred to the Insolvency Practitioners Tribunal (IA, s. 396(2)). In accordance with s. 396(2), the individual must serve such notice on the authority either:

(1)  within 28 days of the service upon him by the authority of the initial notice of intention to refuse or withdraw the authorisation; or

(2)  at any time after he has made representations to the competent authority and before 28 days after the authority has served a further notice on him that it does not propose to alter its decision as a result of those representations.

Once an individual has required his case to be referred to the Insolvency Practitioners Tribunal, the authority must refer the matter to the Tribunal (assuming that the authority has not decided to grant the application or agreed not to withdraw the authorisation (IA, s. 396(3)).

The Tribunal is comprised of experienced insolvency practitioners and barristers, advocates or solicitors of not less than seven years' standing (IA, Sch. 7, para. 1). On a reference, the Tribunal investigates the case and makes a report to the competent authority stating what would, in their opinion, be the appropriate decision in the matter and giving their reasons for such opinion. The competent authority must then decide the matter in accordance with the Tribunal's report, a copy of which is sent to the applicant/holder (IA, s. 397).

## INSOLVENCY PRACTITIONER'S BONDING

### ¶206   Detailed requirements

The Cork Report recommended (paras. 763–7) that all insolvency practitioners should be covered by insurance and bonding against all types of fraud, dishonesty and professional negligence. It has already been noted that an individual is not qualified to act as an insolvency practitioner unless (in addition to having a licence to act) at the relevant time there is in force security, in the prescribed form, for the proper performance of his functions (see ¶201–2 and IA, s. 390(3)).

The Insolvency Practitioners Regulations 1986 (reg. 10) require an insolvency practitioner to:

(1)   obtain a general bond in the sum of £250,000 to cover the proper performance by the practitioner of his duties and obligations under the insolvency legislation and the rules made thereunder; and

(2)   obtain a certificate of specific penalty[1] under that general bond (as soon as is reasonably possible after the practitioner's appointment) in respect of any particular individual or company.

In the case of an insolvency practitioner other than an administrative receiver, the 'specific penalty sum' must be not less than the value of the individual or company's assets as estimated in accordance with Sch. 2 of the Regulations, or £5,000, whichever is the greater. In the case of an administrative receiver the specific penalty sum will be the estimated value of the company's assets which, at the date of appointment, would appear to be available for unsecured creditors (including those with preferential claims) if the company were in liquidation at the date of the appointment (see Sch. 2 of the Regulations).

---

[1] This requires registration at Companies House within 14 days of receipt in the case of an administrative receiver or voluntary liquidator (reg. 12(1)).

# PART II
# ADMINISTRATIVE RECEIVERS

# 3 Appointment of an Administrative Receiver

## INTRODUCTION

### ¶301 Definition of 'administrative receiver'

Section 29(2) of the Insolvency Act 1986 defines an 'administrative receiver', for the purposes of Pt. III of Ch. 1 of the Act, as follows:

'(*a*) a receiver or manager of the whole (or substantially the whole) of a company's property appointed by or on behalf of the holders of any debentures of the company secured by a charge which, as created, was a floating charge, or by such a charge and one or more other securities; or

(*b*) a person who would be such a receiver or manager but for the appointment of some other person as the receiver of part of the company's property'.

The second limb covers the case of a receiver under a second charge who is not receiver of a company's assets and property because there is a receiver appointed under the prior charge.

Another definition of 'administrative receiver' is provided by s. 251 of the Insolvency Act 1986 and applies throughout Pts. I–VII of the Act (except where the context otherwise requires). This definition is as follows:

'(*a*) an administrative receiver as defined by section 29(2) in Chapter I of Part III, or

(*b*) a receiver appointed under section 51 in Chapter II of that Part in a case where the whole (or substantially the whole) of the company's property is attached by the floating charge'.

Limb (*b*) is a receiver appointed under the law of Scotland (IA, s. 50).

In short, the term 'administrative receiver' is no more than a new way of describing what was formerly known as a 'receiver and manager' under an all-embracing (fixed and) floating charge debenture. (The term excludes, for example, all court-appointed receivers.) The new definition is simply for the purposes of the Insolvency Act 1986 and there is no requirement that the phrase should be used for all purposes when one is referring to a receiver and manager over substantially all the assets of a company. Although comparatively rare, it is possible to have a receiver and manager of only part of a company's assets. Where one division of a company operates out of one factory and the property and assets of that division are charged by way of a fixed and floating charge and the charge gives power to a receiver and manager to run the business operated from those premises as agent for the company he will not be an administrative receiver (unless the one division constitutes substantially all the assets of the company) but he will still be recognisable as an 'ordinary' receiver and manager in respect of that division. Chapter I of Pt. III of the Insolvency Act 1986 must be carefully examined in each case to ascertain whether any particular provision applies only to an administrative receiver as defined or to any receiver and manager.

# CHARGES

## ¶302  General

An administrative receiver is appointed over the assets of a company included in the security under which the appointment is made and he has certain powers in relation to the company (as its agent until liquidation – IA, s. 44(1)(a)) largely to the exclusion of the powers of the directors (see, for example, *Re Emmadart Ltd* [1979] Ch. 540).

The security document is crucial and forms the basis of the administrative receiver's authority. His agency for the company relates to the property over which he has been appointed. Where, for example, an item of property has been released from a charge, a receiver appointed under that charge is not able to exercise his powers as agent for the company, such as the power of sale, in respect of that property (cf. *Byblos Bank SAL* v *Rushingdale Limited SA and Others* (1986) 2 BCC 99, 509).

As regards assets of the company situated abroad, the law of the relevant jurisdiction will decide the priority of competing interests in the assets. For example, it may be possible for an execution creditor (or the equivalent) in another jurisdiction to gain rights over assets of the company in that jurisdiction in priority to the holder of the English charge. Where, however, the receiver manages to repatriate the asset (for example, where he collects a book debt from a foreign debtor) the English courts will uphold the charge on the asset under English law (see *Re The Anchor Line* [1937] Ch. 483). Therefore, a debt collected from a debtor in a foreign jurisdiction which does not recognise the concept of a fixed charge on book debts should still be treated by a receiver in England as subject to any fixed charge created in England.

## ¶303 Floating charges

### (1) Advantages
The floating charge is a device peculiar to the common-law jurisdictions, having been recognised by the courts towards the end of the last century. The floating charge gives unique and unrivalled flexibility to both the chargor and the chargee. It constitutes present security but leaves the chargor free to deal with its assets in the ordinary course of business. In recognition of its merits, it was introduced into Scots law by statute (see Companies (Floating Charges) (Scotland) Act 1961 and Companies (Floating Charges and Receivers) (Scotland) Act 1972, but note also the reservations of Scottish academics and lawyers referred to in 'Floating Charges: The Scottish Experience' [1984] JBL 255, criticisms which might strike those more used to this form of security as born of unfamiliarity).

In addition to the advantages of the floating charge as a form of security prior to its enforcement, when finally enforced it can facilitate the preservation of going concerns by enabling an appointed receiver and manager to trade and sell the business to a purchaser, all without the need for the involvement of the court. The rehabilitation process in the United States – the 'Chapter 11' procedure – is court-based.

The Cork Committee supported the continued existence of the floating charge:

'**1525.** The floating charge has the advantage of simplicity, convenience, and above all, flexibility . . . its importance as a security for the provision of short and medium term finance for commerce and industry must not be underestimated.

**1526.** The floating charge affords the creditor, by a single instrument, an effective and comprehensive security upon the entire undertaking of the debtor company and all the assets comprised therein and yet at the same time leaves the company free to deal with its assets and pay its trade creditors in the ordinary course of business without reference to the proprietor of the charge. . . .

**1527.** . . . On the continent, it is unknown, or known only in a very limited form. . . .

**1529.** The [Cork] Advisory Committee emphasised the importance of floating charges to the commercial community in the United Kingdom, and considered it undesirable that the EEC Bankruptcy Convention, if adopted, should in any way prejudice their validity. . . .

¶303

**1531.** We are satisfied that the floating charge has become so fundamental a part of the financial structure of the United Kingdom that its abolition cannot be contemplated. . . .'

## (2) Disadvantages

The criticism of the charge was and is that in some ways it operates too effectively on behalf of the secured creditor, to the detriment of unsecured creditors. The Cork Committee's suggested solution was to set aside a fund for unsecured creditors comprising ten per cent of realisations under the charge, but this idea did not take root.

## (3) Elements of a floating charge

The elements of a floating charge were described by Romer LJ *Re Yorkshire Woolcombers Association Limited* ([1903] 2 Ch. 284) when he said (at p. 295):

'(1) It is a charge on a class of assets of a company present and future; (2) that class is one which, in the ordinary course of business of the company, would be changing from time to time; and (3) . . . by the charge it is contemplated that, until some future step is taken by or on behalf of those interested in the charge, the company may carry on its business in the ordinary way as far as concerns the particular class of assets I am dealing with.'

What Romer LJ was saying was that if the charge contained all three characteristics then it was of necessity a floating charge; he said he could conceive of floating charges which contained some but not all of these three characteristics. The third characteristic described by the judge has proved to be the key element and the object of most analysis (see ¶305).

## (4) Crystallisation

In certain circumstances the charge is said to crystallise and converts into a fixed charge. Crystallisation occurs in the following circumstances:

(1)   when a receiver is appointed under the floating charge;

(2)   on the company going into liquidation;

(3)   on the company ceasing to carry on its business; and

(4)   by agreement between the parties that certain events shall cause the charge to crystallise or by agreement that the chargee may serve a notice causing the charge to crystallise.

(See, generally, *Re Woodroffes (Musical Instruments) Limited (In Liquidation)* [1985] 2 All ER 908 and *Re Brightlife Limited* [1987] 2 WLR 197; (1986) 2 BCC 99, 359.)

¶303

The form of crystallisation described at (4) has been the subject of extensive debate, being described, somewhat misleadingly, as 'automatic' crystallisation. The best view seems to be that the parties to the charge, the chargor and the chargee, are free to agree as a contractual matter that the charge shall crystallise on a specific event occuring. The effect that the crystallisation has on the rights of third parties is, however, a different matter (see the arguments in Goode, *Legal problems of credit and security*, p. 35 et seq.). The point is that, by taking only a floating charge, the chargee allows the chargor to represent to the world at large that it has authority to deal with its assets in the ordinary course of business without reference to the chargee. A purchaser from a company who purchases after an automatic crystallisation but without notice that such a crystallisation has occurred should take free of the crystallised charge (see the discussion in Goode as mentioned above and in particular the comments about 'overkill' at p. 40).

It remains to be seen whether, in the absence of an express stipulation to this effect in the security document, the making of an administration order in respect of a company will operate to crystallise a floating charge given previously by the company.

## ¶304   Fixed charges and mortgages

In a famous comment made in the case of *Illingworth* v *Houldsworth* ([1904] AC 355 at p. 358), Lord MacNaghten distinguished between fixed and floating charges in this way:

> 'A specific charge, I think, is one that without more fastens on ascertained and definite property or property capable of being ascertained and defined; a floating charge, on the other hand, is ambulatory and shifting in its nature, hovering over and so to speak floating with the property which it is intended to affect until some event occurs or some act is done which causes it to settle and fasten on the subject of the charge within its reach and grasp.'

Unlike a floating charge, the effect of a fixed charge or mortgage[1] is that the chargor is not free to dispose of the charged assets in the ordinary course of business but requires the consent of the chargee. Further, the preferential debts of the company must be paid out of the assets caught by a floating charge in a receivership and in a winding up (IA, ss. 40 and 175(2)(*b*), and see ¶601), but this is not the case with assets caught by a fixed charge.

Much of the heat has been taken out of the debate about 'automatic' crystallisation by changes introduced by the recent insolvency legislation. One

---

[1] Note the argument of Professor Goode that the distinction between a charge and a mortgage on a debt may have important consequences: 'The effect of a fixed charge on a debt' [1984] JBL 172.

of the reasons for having charges capable of crystallisation on notice being given was to give a debenture holder the opportunity of converting his charge into a fixed charge so that, on the subsequent appointment of receiver or liquidator, the charge would not be a floating charge but already a 'fixed' (that is, crystallised) charge and the preferential creditors would not have to be paid by the receiver or liquidator out of the proceeds of sale of such assets (see CA, ss. 196 and 614(2)(*b*) prior to amendment and *Re Brightlife Limited* [1987] 2 WLR 197).

A 'floating charge', as now defined by s. 251 of the Insolvency Act 1986, means:

'. . . a charge which, *as created*, was a floating charge' (emphasis supplied)

and the effect as regards all receivers is spelled out specifically in s. 40 of the Act, although this double explanation is not repeated for liquidators in s. 175(2)(*b*). It was never intended that the rights of preferential creditors should be affected by the fact that crystallisation had been brought about by some event prior to the appointment of a receiver or a winding up and the original 'defect in the drafting' highlighted by *Re Griffin Hotel Company Limited* ([1941] Ch. 129) has now been put right (per Hoffmann J in *Re Brightlife Limited* [1987] 2 WLR 197, at p. 203; (1986) 2 BCC 99, 359, at p. 99, 364).

## ¶305   Charges on future book debts

The search to improve the security of creditors has led to more and more assets of companies being made the subject of fixed, rather than floating, charges. Book debts, that is 'receivables', inevitably constitute an attractive target.

A debt may be described as a monetary sum payable by one party to a contract to another party pursuant to the terms of that contract (but note also judgments debts etc.). There is little conceptual difficulty in taking a charge or assignment of an existing debt or specific income stream. There was formerly doubt about whether a fixed charge on future book debts of, for example, manufacturing companies could be taken as these are debts which constitute a class of assets revolving in the ordinary course of business (see Romer LJ's third element of a floating charge referred to in ¶303).

The efficacy of a fixed charge on future book debts was, however, accepted in *Siebe Gorman & Co Ltd* v *Barclays Bank Limited* ([1979] 2 Lloyd's Rep. 142) which has since been followed by the Supreme Court in Dublin[1] in *Re Keenan Brothers Ltd* ([1986] 2 BCC 98,970). The factors which led Slade J in

---

[1] The Supreme Court decision has effectively been overturned by statute in Ireland – see s. 115 of the Finance Act 1986.

*Siebe Gorman* to conclude that the 'fixed' charge before him was in fact a fixed charge were that:

(1)   the debenture concerned contained a covenant by the chargor to pay the proceeds of the book debts into the chargor's bank account with the bank;

(2)   the debenture contained a provision prohibiting the mortgagor from charging or assigning the debts without the consent of the bank; and

(3)   there was a covenant requiring the mortgagor to execute a formal legal assignment of book debts on the bank's request.

In the *Keenan Brothers* case the bank concerned had set up a special account into which proceeds were to be paid and this was a particularly tight form of control over collected proceeds of book debts. It is the 'control' exercised by a chargee over the debt caught by the charge which supports the claim that the charge is fixed. On the facts of the *Keenan Brothers* case, transfers of credit balances in the special account were made from time to time to the company's trading account, with the consent of the bank. Of this arrangement, Macarthy J commented as follows:

'I do not accept that an elaborate system set up to enable the company to benefit by the collection of such debts detracts from its qualifying as a specific fixed charge.

[The] purpose was to give the bank a degree of control over exceptional transactions, but was far from directing the company to carry on its normal business, rather to trade subject to the express terms of the debenture with the provision for a cash flow set up by the bank in which the inflow of cash would go directly to the bank.'

Some doubts have been expressed about the decision in *Siebe Gorman* (see, for example, Lingard, *Bank security documents*, paras. 8.32–45), but there seems no reason to think that it will not be followed in the English courts. One point that is sometimes made is that it is impossible (or very difficult) to take a fixed charge on a company's stock because of its revolving nature and it should be similarly difficult to take a fixed charge on book debts. Book debts are not like stock, however, in that they are much more easily controlled, partly via their proceeds, and any analogy with stock would be false.

Where a charge lacks the relevant control provisions, the charge may be held only to be floating (*Re Armagh Shoes Ltd* [1984] BCLC 405) and the difficulties facing a trade creditor attempting to take a fixed charge when (inevitably) not operating banking facilities for the chargor are illustrated by *Re Brightlife Limited* ([1987] 2 WLR 197; (1986) 2 BCC 99, 359).

¶305

A charge on 'book and other debts' was considered in *Re Brightlife Limited* ([1987] 2 WLR 197; (1986) 2 BCC 99, 359). Hoffmann J did not consider that this phrase covered a credit balance at a bank. He said:

'It is true that the relationship between banker and customer is one of debtor and creditor. It would not therefore be legally inaccurate to describe a credit balance with a banker as a debt. But this would not be a natural usage for a businessman or accountant. He would ordinarily describe it as "cash at bank"'.

He was strengthened in this view by other references in the security document to debts being 'got in' and 'realised' and he felt these were terms lacking a sensible meaning as regards a credit balance at a bank.

The following further points should be noted in connection with charges on debts:

(1) A distinction may have to be drawn (for example for the purposes of registration under CA, s. 395) between a charge on a debt and a charge on a contingent right to payments under a contract (see *Re Brush Aggregates Ltd* (1983) 1 BCC 98, 904).

(2) For a case where a supposed 'lien' turned out to be a (registrable) charge on book debts see *Re Welsh Irish Ferries Limited (In Liquidation)* [1986] Ch. 471; (1985) 1 BCC 99, 430.

(3) A charged debt is held on trust for the chargee (*Barclays Bank plc* v *Willowbrook International Ltd, The Times,* 5 February 1987, CA).

# APPOINTMENTS

## ¶306   When they occur

Administrative receiverships are almost always an indication of insolvency of some description or, at the very least, of financial difficulties. It would, in theory, be possible for a lender to lend moneys (repayable on demand), take security, make demand and then, within a very short time, appoint a receiver, whatever the state of solvency of the borrower. The period between the demand and the appointment of a receiver need not be long enough to allow a company otherwise solvent to pursue a programme of realisations to effect repayment (see ¶307). In practice, there are many reasons why demands followed by appointment of a receiver do not occur in the absence of insolvency: lenders are in the business of lending and there is usually no point commercially in calling in a loan to a company well able to pay interest and repay capital in due course, and there is also the question of the lender's reputation which would be badly damaged by capricious enforcement of security.

Prior to the recent insolvency legislation, if lenders were worried about the financial stability of a borrower they would often require the borrower to commission a report on the borrower's financial position for the lender's benefit. This would no doubt be carried out by a reputable firm of accountants. Decisions on whether to lend more or to appoint a receiver would often be made on the basis of such an investigation and report (subject always to the question of contractual entitlement to make demand and appoint a receiver). The report might recommend changes to the company's business or practices with a view to resolving the company's problems. With the increased risks of personal liability and/or disqualification which face directors under the new legislation, earlier action may now be taken by companies themselves, whether by requesting a lender to appoint a receiver or by applying to the court for the appointment of an administrator – a move which in many cases will precipitate the appointment of an administrative receiver in any event. This theme is discussed below (at ¶901 and ¶905).

## ¶307   The right to appoint

### (1)   Contractual and statutory powers

A modern, properly drafted debenture or charge will give an express contractual power to the chargee to appoint a receiver. There is no need to obtain a court order appointing the receiver. Even without specific power to appoint in the charging document, s. 101 of the Law of Property Act 1925 gives a chargee under a deed the limited power to appoint a receiver 'of the income of the mortgaged property'. By s. 109(1) of that Act, the appointment must be in writing and may be under hand.

It is sometimes implied that the powers of a chargee under the Law of Property Act 1925 apply only in the case of fixed and not floating charges. It is submitted that this is an unjustifiably restricted view of the Act (see Pennington's Company Law (5th edn) pp. 550–1). Many cases proceed on the basis that the provisions of the Act apply to floating-charge receivers (see, for example, *Re John Willment (Ashford) Ltd* [1980] 1 WLR 73).

### (2)   Appointment on invitation of the borrower

Sometimes security documentation contains a provision entitling a chargee to appoint a receiver on the invitation of the borrower. While in these circumstances a receiver appointed will not be a trespasser it is still important to trigger the liability to repay the secured debt (for example, by making demand), as a receiver in office without a debt to repay is in a strange position.

There may be an argument that he is not able to exercise his powers of sale where there is no outstanding indebtedness (but consider *Re Fosters & Rudd* ((1986) 2 BCC 98, 955) which held that a chargee may hold on to his security where it secures a contingent debt which has not yet matured into an actual liability).

**(3)   Construction of loan and security documentation**
Where the secured debt consists of moneys lent under a facility letter or other form of loan document and it constitutes a term loan[1] only repayable on demand where an event of default or acceleration has occurred and been declared, but the security document contains a convenant to repay on demand, the rule is that both documents must be read together (*Cryne* v *Barclays Bank plc*, 31 July 1985, CA; Lexis). If, on the true construction of the documents, the bargain between the parties is that the moneys are not repayable on demand, then it is not safe for the lender to rely on the covenant to repay on demand in the security document. The *Cryne* case is also of interest in stating that there is no inherent right for a debenture holder to appoint a receiver out of court on the basis that its security is in jeopardy, in the absence of an express contractual provision entitling them to appoint in those circumstances. The Court of Appeal limited the decision in *Re London Pressed Hinge Co. Limited* ([1905] 1 Ch. 576) to appointments of receivers by the court.

**(4)   Limited duties of a mortgagee**
In recent years two linked questions have been considered by the courts in a number of cases. First, does a debenture holder owe any duty to a borrower or others in exercising a contractual or statutory right to appoint a receiver and, if so, what is the extent of the duty? Secondly, where moneys are expressed to be payable on demand (whether simpliciter or pursuant to default by the borrower) what does 'on demand' mean in these circumstances and how soon after demand can the debenture holder appoint a receiver?

The basic rule is that a mortgagee enforcing his security when contractually entitled to do so owes no duty to the company (or, for example, to guarantors) to exercise his powers in any particular way. As Hoffmann J said in *Shamji & Others* v *Johnson Matthey Bankers Limited & Others* ([1986] 2 BCC 98,910, at p. 98,916), in a passage specifically approved by the Court of Appeal:

'The appointment of a receiver seems to me to involve an inherent conflict of interest. The purpose of the power is to enable the mortgagee to take the management of the company's property out of the hands of the directors and entrust it to a person of the mortgagee's choice. That power is granted

---

[1] The moneys borrowed being, for example, repayable over a period in tranches.

¶307

to the mortgagee by the security documents in completely unqualified terms. It seems to me that a decision by the mortgagee to exercise the power cannot be challenged except perhaps on grounds of bad faith. There is no room for the implication of a term that the mortgagee should be under a duty to the mortgagor to "consider all relevant matters" before exercising the power. If no such qualification can be read into the security documents, I do not think that a wider duty can exist in tort.'

He drew on the judgment of the Court of Appeal in *Cuckmere Brick Co Limited & Another* v *Mutual Finance Limited* ([1971] Ch. 949), when he added:

'It is clear, however, that in a case of a conflict between the interests of the mortgagor and the mortgagee, any duty of care which the mortgagee owes to the mortgagor is subordinated to his right to act in the protection of his own interests. As Salmon LJ said in the *Cuckmere Brick Co.* case at p. 965H: "if the mortgagee's interests, as he sees them, conflict with those of the mortgagor, the mortgagee can give preference to his own interests . . . ".'

The Court of Appeal in *Shamji* (at p. 98,916) approved this statement also.

A similar question came before Hoffmann J in the case *Re Potters Oils (No. 2) Limited* ((1985) 1 BCC 99, 593; [1986] 1 All ER 890). This case involved an application by a liquidator under what is now s. 36 of the Insolvency Act 1986 to fix the remuneration of a receiver appointed under an instrument out of court.

The facts were that the lender concerned had lent money for the company to purchase a specific item of plant to be used in its business and the general debenture given as security included a fixed charge on the specific item of plant. In fact the money forwarded by the lender was not used by the company to pay the supplier of the plant. The plant having been delivered in March 1983, in November 1983 the supplier issued proceedings against the company. In December 1983 another trade creditor presented a petition to wind the company up. The company entered a defence to the claim of the supplier in January 1984 while the petition was pending. The company was wound up on 23 January 1984 and a liquidator was appointed on 22 February 1984. Also in that February the supplier obtained leave of the court to continue with its action against the company notwithstanding the winding-up order, and it issued a summons applying for leave to amend its statement of claim to permit it to argue that the defence entered amounted to a repudiation of the contract. The summons also requested immediate delivery up of the plant. The lender at this stage decided to protect its interest by appointing a receiver, which it did on 6 April 1984. In the event, the plant was sold back to the supplier for a sum which, as the judge put it, 'was much higher than either the liquidator or receiver had dared to hope'. The sale was effected by the liquidator with the consent of the receiver and the proceeds of sale went, first, to pay a third party which claimed reservation of title to the trailer to which the plant had been attached, secondly, to pay the receiver's remuneration, costs and expenses, thirdly, the principal and interest owing to the lender with, finally, the surplus being passed to the liquidator.

The liquidator's action was not to suggest that the sum claimed by the receiver was excessive but that the entire remuneration should be disallowed because the appointment of the receiver was unnecessary. Hoffmann J rejected the claims of the liquidator and made the following comments (99, 595 at pp. 99, 597–598; 891 at p. 894):

'The liquidator says that the appointment of the receiver was unnecessary because he, the liquidator, was doing all that could be done to protect the interests of [the lender] and the appointment of the receiver only caused duplication of effort and unnecessary expense. I think that there are two answers to this submission. The first is that [the lender] was contractually entitled to appoint the receiver to protect its own interests. As between [the lender] (by its receiver) and the company, the former had the prior right to possession of the plant. Since the liquidator was an officer of the court and already in possession the receiver could not exercise his right to possession without the leave of the court. But he would be entitled to that leave as of right: see *Re Henry Pound, Son and Hutchins* (1889) 42 ChD 402. It would be no answer that the property could be realised by the liquidator more cheaply and no less effectively. The debenture holder is under no duty to refrain from exercising his rights merely because doing so may cause loss to the company or its unsecured creditors. He owes a duty of care to the company and this duty is qualified by being subordinated to the protection of his own interests. . . .

A second answer is that in this case I think that [the lender] was justified in thinking that its own interests would best be served by the appointment of a receiver to assert a right to possession of the plant. . . .'

The judge took the view that, first, the chargee had an unfettered right to appoint a receiver, but in any event on the facts of the case the chargee was in his opinion correct in its view that its interests could be best protected by appointing a receiver.

Where the right of a chargee to appoint a receiver is disputed, what remedies are available to the company and its directors? In particular, can they prevent the receiver taking office by injunction? The principles applicable in such a situation were considered by the Court of Appeal in *Byblos Bank SAL* v *Rushingdale Limited SA and Others* ((1986) 2 BCC 99, 509). On the facts, it appeared that the charges had not been properly sealed by the chargor in that, instead of the company seal being affixed and witnessed, the documents had simply been signed by one director of the company. The chargee appointed a receiver under the charges and the company attempted to injunct the receiver claiming, *inter alia*, that the charges were not binding on it. The chargee contended that the one director had authority to bind the company and the documents took effect, at least in equity, as effective charges on personalty. The court felt that there were clearly serious arguable issues raised by both sides and then turned to the question of whether *on the balance of convenience* injunctive relief should be granted to restore the status quo ante. One complicating factor was a doubt about the extent of the receiver's powers to enter the company's premises and take possession of the 'charged' assets. The main point considered by the court was, however, the adequacy of damages as a remedy to either side (citing *American Cyanamid Co.* v *Ethicon Ltd* [1975] AC 396). Although there might be difficulty in calculating the company's damages, Dillon LJ thought this: 'the sort of task . . . the courts can readily undertake and satisfactorily discharge' (at p. 261). The plaintiffs were forced to concede that there was no doubt about the ability of the bank to meet any claim against it, having arranged a guarantee of its liabilities from a clearing bank. On the other hand, there were doubts about the ability of the company to meet its cross-undertaking in damages. In view of these facts, and taking into account also evidence regarding the jeopardy to the bank's security at the date of the receiver's appointment, the court came down firmly against displacing the receiver pending trial of the issues (and see, also *Watts* v *Midland Bank plc* [1986] BCLC 15).

There may be an argument that a chargee owes a duty of care to the borrower in the selection of a receiver and a chargee should, therefore, exercise care to select someone of reasonable competence. In view of the new licensing scheme, it may be more difficult for a borrower to complain about a particular choice where the chargee selects (as he ought to) a licensed insolvency practitioner. The effect of licensing may be to raise a presumption of competence and probity.

### (5) 'On demand'

What is meant by moneys being repayable 'on demand'? In *R. A. Cripps & Sons Ltd* v *Wickenden* ([1973] 1 WLR 944) the facts were that a demand was made on the borrower at around 10.50 a.m. and at around 12.30 p.m., the demand not having been complied with, the bank appointed a receiver. Goff J had little difficulty in concluding that sufficient time had been given to the borrower. The company argued that it had to be given 'a reasonable time' to enable payment to be made. In particular, two days before the appointment the bank had written to the company, upon hearing that negotiations for a takeover of the company by a third party had broken down, to express concern at the current position and asking for proposals 'as soon as possible'. Goff J commented (at p. 955):

' it was said that [the Bank manager] never really gave the company any chance to put up proposals in answer to the letter of August 6, but in my judgment, that is not the point. The question is whether he gave such time as the law requires if the money is payable on demand, and the cases show that all the creditor has to do is to give the debtor time to get it from some convenient place, not to negotiate a deal which he hopes will produce the money. . . .

It is abundantly plain that Cripps had not got the money and had no convenient place to which they could go to get it . . . In my judgment therefore, the plaintiffs cannot object on the grounds that they were not given time to find the money or that the interval of time between 11 o'clock or shortly before, when the demand was made, and 12 o'clock or later when the receiver was appointed, was too short.'

The trend of cases in certain Commonwealth countries has given rise to some speculation that in certain circumstances borrowers must be given more than a minimum amount of time to meet a demand (see Hubert Picarda, 'Receivers and on demand debentures', BLR, April 1984, p. 105). The trend of cases in Canada points in this direction (see *Ronald Elwyn Lister Ltd* v *Dunlop Canada Ltd* [1982] 1 SCR 726 and an interesting discussion by John R. Varley in 'Recent Developments and emerging trends in the enforcement of security – the receiver besieged', Ontario Law Society Special Lectures (1985) 181 at pp. 190 et seq.).

The approach of the court in *Cripps* v *Wickenden* has, however, been confirmed, and the Commonwealth authorities rejected, in the case of *Bank of Baroda* v *Panessar and Others* ((1986) 2 BCC 99, 288; [1986] 3 All ER 751). Walton J explained that the true test, as exemplified by *Cripps* v *Wickenden*, was what he called 'the mechanics of payment test', i.e., that the amount of time which need be given after demand is that necessary for the debtor to implement the mechanics of payment, and (99, 288 at p. 99, 297 and 751 at p. 760):

'he must . . . arrange for such mechanics of payment as are, under modern conditions, available for the transfer of the money to his creditor, and as is well known in these days of telex, fax, and other methods of communication and transfer of money, the time required for that is exceptionally short. . . .

It appears that a slightly different approach has been adopted by a number of Commonwealth authorities. In these the amount of time to be allowed for the debtor to comply with the demand has been stated in a number of cases to be a "reasonable time". The difficulty inherent in this formulation

¶307

is that the test of reasonableness is left wholly imprecise: reasonable for doing what? . . . as a commercial matter (and a debenture is very much a commercial matter), it appears to me that a time limited to the implementation of the mechanics of payment, a short but adequate period, is to be preferred to the test of a "reasonable time depending on all the circumstances of the case", as this would appear to be wholly imprecise, and the danger of underestimating the period from the creditor's point of view would be considerable. Moreover, it would appear to be wholly unfair to the creditor that the period should depend on all the circumstances of the case, since he may very well not know, and have no means of knowing, all such circumstances.'

On the facts of the case, there were demands made on two companies. One was served at 9.45 a.m. on the morning of the appointment at the registered office of that company. The second was delivered between 10 a.m. and 10.15 a.m. at the principal place of business of the other company. Appointments were accepted by receivers shortly after 11 a.m. that morning. The judge found that these time intervals were quite sufficient.

## ¶308 Demands generally

### (1) Form of the demand

Receivers and their advisers should not only be careful to ensure that a demand has been served giving time for the mechanics of payment to be implemented prior to appointment but they must also check that sufficient care has gone into preparation of the demand. The cases of *Fox* v *Jolly* ([1916] 1 AC 1) and *Bunbury Foods Pty Ltd* v *National Bank of Australasia Limited* ((1984) 54 ALJR 199, discussed below) may be authority for the proposition that a demand made for a sum greater than that actually owing may still be a good demand if at least part of the sum demanded is actually due and owing. Caution, however, suggests that care should be taken to ensure that the demand is not excessive. Wherever there is doubt as to whether sums are owing, the prudent course would seem to be to make the demand for a sum excluding the uncertain amounts because, for the purposes of the appointment of a receiver, what is important is that *some* of the secured moneys should have become payable. It should be possible for a lender to make further demands once the true position regarding the uncertain amounts is known.

Where the security instrument secures 'all moneys owing' it is possible simply to make demand in those terms rather than to specify a particular sum. The authority for this is *Bank of Baroda* v *Panessar and Others* ((1986) 2 BCC 99, 288; [1986] 3 All ER 751) where Walton J reasoned that, as the covenant in the charge was to pay all moneys owing, a demand which required repayment of all moneys owing was accordingly sufficient. The judge found persuasive the decision of the High Court of Australia in *Bunbury Foods Pty Limited* v *National Bank of Australasia Limited* ((1984) 54 ALJR 199). The court in that case pointed to the fact that in certain instances the ascertainment of the amount due might, as they put it, 'require the resolution over time of complex issues of fact and of law'. It is respectfully submitted that this is correct: for example, what if the bank suspects that one of the company's accounts with a credit balance is in fact a trust account? There may not be time to ascertain what may be a difficult question (see for example the cases mentioned at ¶407(4)) before making a demand prior to enforcing security – a procedure often implemented with some degree of urgency. The Australian Court in *Bunbury* went on to state that even where a demand stated the wrong amount it was not invalid and cited a number of Australian and New Zealand authorities. On this point Walton J commented (99,288 at p. 99, 296 and 751 at p. 759):

'As the High Court [of Australia] points out, it would seem stupid that the creditor could put in, without imperilling the validity of the notice, an entirely wrong sum, and that is much more likely to give rise to confusion and difficulty than is the form of the notice adopted in that and the present case'.

If the borrower required more information on receiving a demand for an indefinite sum, the judge felt that an immediate reply to the demand by way of a request for a more precise sum should be sent and it would seem that the creditor must provide the information requested. Where, however, there is no realistic likelihood that the borrower can meet a demand it would seem that the courts are not going to strike down demands on technicalities.

### (2)   Method of service

How should a demand be served? Where the security *permits* a particular method of service, it is safe to follow the contractually agreed route. Where the debenture *requires* a particular method of service, then that method should be followed. Many debentures have a clause which states that if the demand is sent by pre-paid first class post it shall be deemed to have been served at 10 a.m. on the following day (no doubt barring a Sunday). Alternatively, the clause may provide that service may be made personally at a particular address or by giving it to one of the directors of the borrower. It is usual to provide that the relevant address should be the registered office of the company or one of its principal places of business.

If the charging document is silent on the method of service, there are three legal rules which may be of assistance, as follows:

(1)   By s. 725 of the Companies Act 1985 a document may be served on a company by leaving it at, or sending it by post to, the company's

registered office. By s. 744 of that Act, 'document' is defined to include 'summons, notice, order, and other legal process, and registers' which would seem to include demands for repayment of borrowings. It is suggested in *Pennington's Company Law* (5th edn) at p. 26 that, where the idea is simply to bring something to the attention of a company, it is possible to serve a document on the company by leaving it with its directors or managing director or even by simply giving it to a director or company secretary. The authority given is *Houghton Co. v Nothard, Lowe & Wills Ltd* ([1928] AC 1).

(2)    Section 196 of the Law of Property Act 1925 (as amended) provides for 'notices required to be served by any instrument affecting property' to be sufficiently served if sent by post in a registered letter or by recorded delivery addressed to the mortgagor at its last-known place of abode or business in the UK, if the letter is not returned by the Post Office undelivered. Service in these circumstances is deemed to be made at the time at which the letter would in the ordinary course be delivered.

(3)    Per Walton J in *Bank of Baroda* v *Panessar and Others* ((1986) 2 BCC 99, 288, at p. 99, 299; [1986] 3 All ER 751, at p. 762):

> '[a]debenture is a commercial document intended to have commercial validity. I cannot imagine a better place at which to serve a notice intended to reach those in control of the company's affairs than at its one and only place of business, being the sole address for the company given on its notepaper . . .'

and accordingly in certain circumstances it may be possible as a simple matter of commercial law properly to serve a demand on a company by delivering it or sending it to its principal place of business.

## ¶309   Checklist for appointments

In addition to the areas concerning the right to appoint already discussed, an administrative receiver and his advisers will wish to check the following points to ensure that any appointment is not invalid:

(1)    Was the charging document properly executed? That is, if the document is a deed, was the company seal properly affixed in accordance with the memorandum and articles of association? In this connection, receivers and their appointors may often be able to rely on s. 74(1) of the Law of Property Act 1925 which provides as follows:

'(1) In favour of a purchaser a deed shall be deemed to have been duly executed by a corporation aggregate if its seal be affixed thereto in the presence of and attested by its clerk, secretary or other permanent officer or his deputy, and a member of the board of directors, council or other governing body of the corporation and where a seal *purporting to be the seal of a corporation has been affixed to a deed,* attested by persons *purporting* to be persons holding such offices as aforesaid, the deed shall be deemed to have been executed in accordance with the requirements of this section, and to have taken effect accordingly' (emphasis supplied).

A mortgagee is a purchaser for these purposes provided that he acts in good faith (LPA, s. 205(1)(xxi)). Good faith would seem to be destroyed by notice of a defect or wilful blindness to it (see generally *TCB Limited* v *Gray* [1986] Ch. 621; (1986) 2 BCC 99, 044 and Lingard, *Bank security documents*, para. 2.5).

(2)   A check should be made that the creation of the security was within the borrower's corporate capacity, i.e. that it was intra vires. There may be protection for the chargee under s. 35 of the Companies Act 1985, and this section may also be of assistance under (1) above.

(3)   Was the chargee on notice of any abuse of the powers of the directors of the company in creating the charge – for example was the chargee on notice of any lack of commercial justification? (See *Rolled Steel Products (Holdings) Limited* v *British Steel Corporation and Others* [1986] Ch. 246.) Similarly, was the transaction one at an undervalue (IA, s. 238, and see ¶1016(2))?

(4)   Did the board of directors or other appropriate organ of the company effectively resolve to create the security? Good practice when taking security is to ensure that an adequate board minute is prepared by the chargor evidencing the decision to create the security. In certain circumstances, the 'internal management' rule laid down in the case of *Royal British Bank* v *Turquand* ((1855 5 E&B 248) may come to the aid of the chargee, as may s. 35 of the Companies Act 1985.

(5)   Where the security was taken as part of a larger transaction involving the purchase of shares in the chargee or its holding company, was there any breach of s. 151 of the Companies Act 1985 which might render the security void? That is, did the creation of the security by the company involve the giving of financial assistance for the purpose of the purchase of the company's shares? This is often a potential problem in management buy-outs.

(6)   Has the security been registered at Companies House as required by s. 395 of the Companies Act 1985? If not, the security is void against the company's creditors and any liquidator appointed, although valid against the company itself.

¶309

(7) Could the security (or any guarantee which it might support) constitute a preference (IA, s. 239, see ¶1016(3)) or, in the case of transactions entered into before 29 December 1986, a fraudulent preference (CA, s. 615)?

(8) Is the floating charge vulnerable under s. 245 of the Insolvency Act 1986, e.g. because it was created within the last 12 months (or two years if the mortgagee is a connected person) and no moneys were advanced at the time of, or subsequent to, the creation (see ¶1016(6))? Note, however, that the security (and hence the receiver) is only vulnerable when the company is in liquidation or administration (*Mace Builders (Glasgow) Ltd v Lunn* [1986] Ch. 459).

(9) Are there any charges ranking in priority to that under which the receiver has been appointed? A prior debenture holder has a prior right to possession of the assets caught by that charge, and the receiver under the subsequent charge will have to surrender up the assets under his control to any receiver appointed by a prior debenture holder. Subsequent charges should also be noted as they will have to be considered and dealt with on any realisation of assets.

(10) Pre-1971 charges need to be stamped and, in the event of an appointment under such a charge, a check should be made that the document has been adequately stamped.

## ¶310 Appointments

### (1) Form of appointment

Appointments should be in writing and any particular requirements of the security documents should be observed. Where there is no specific requirement for the appointment to be sealed, it may be under hand. Some commentators support the view that if the receivers are given a power of attorney, the appointment should be sealed, but this seems excessive and the crucial requirement is that the security should be created by deed. This approach is accepted by the Land Registry.

An important new rule, which must be observed when making appointments of more than one administrative receiver, is to ensure that the appointment contains a declaration as to whether acts may be done by each appointee individually or by all of those holding office together (IA, s. 231). It would be usual to provide that each may act individually as the rationale for a joint appointment is to cover the situation where one practitioner is unavailable because engaged on other matters and hence to allow his co-appointee to act effectively on his own.

**(2) Specimen appointment**

A specimen form of appointment is set out below:

## APPOINTMENT OF ADMINISTRATIVE RECEIVERS

DEFINITIONS:

Appointor: _____ Bank plc

Insolvency Practitioners: _____ and _____

_____

of _____ & Co (address)

Company: _____ plc

Security: Mortgage/debenture dated _____ and made between the Company (1) and the Appointor (2)

RECITAL:

The power for the Appointor to appoint [administrative receivers] [receivers and managers] under the Security has arisen

APPOINTMENT:

**1.** Pursuant to the powers conferred by the Security and all other powers enabling whether by statute or otherwise the Appointor hereby appoints the Insolvency Practitioners to be [administrative receivers] [receivers and managers] of all the undertaking property assets and rights of whatever nature charged by the Security.

**2.** The Insolvency Practitioners (and each of them) shall have and may exercise all the powers and authorities conferred by the Security and by statute and otherwise.

**3.** It is hereby declared that any act required or authorised under any enactment or document to be done by the Insolvency Practitioners may be done by either of them individually [and this declaration applies to the persons holding office from time to time as [administrative receivers] [receivers and managers] to the Company under the Security].

**4.** The Insolvency Practitioners are hereby directed to insure the undertaking property assets and rights over which they are appointed in such sum as they may consider appropriate having regard to current prudent commercial practice.

SIGNED:

.......................

(duly authorised signatory for and on behalf of the Appointor) [or otherwise in accordance with the provisions of the Security]

¶310

## ¶311   Acceptance of appointments

The rules regarding acceptance of appointments by administrative receivers
are now governed by statute (IA, s. 33 and IR, r. 3.1, but note that s. 33 applies
to all receivers or managers whereas IR, 3.1 only applies to administrative
receivers). These rules replace the common law rules laid down in cases such
as *R. A. Cripps & Son Ltd* v *Wickenden* ([1973] 1 WLR 944). The new rules
must be followed carefully, and the main points are:

(1)   The appointee must accept the appointment before the end of the
business day (see IA, s. 251) following that on which the appointment
document is *received* by him (IA, s. 33(1)(*a*)).

(2)   In the absence of specific statutory provision, acceptance may be
indicated by telephone or in writing or by facsimile transmission.
Under the normal rules of agency, someone duly authorised can
probably accept on behalf of the appointee. Receipt of the appointment
itself may be by someone acting on behalf of the appointee (IA, s.
33(1)(*a*)).

(3)   Provided that acceptance occurs in accordance with point (1) above,
the appointment is deemed to date from the time of receipt of the
appointment document by the appointee or the person acting on his
behalf (IA s. 33(1)(*b*)).

(4)   The Rules contain an additional concept of confirmation of acceptance.
Where an appointment is accepted, an administrative receiver has to
confirm his acceptance in writing within seven days (IR, r. 3.1(1) and
(2)). It is not clear whether the seven days run from acceptance or
receipt of the document.

(5)   The confirmation must state the time and date of acceptance and the
time and date of receipt of the appointment (IR, r. 3.1(4) – the rule
refers to receipt of 'notice' of appointment but must mean receipt of
the appointment itself as there is no statutory provision requiring the
appointor to give 'notice' to the appointee).

(6)   The confirmation may be given by someone duly authorised by the
appointee (IR, r. 3.1(3)).

(7)   The provisions governing confirmation seem to be different depending
on whether it is a sole appointment or a joint appointment. There
appears to be no sanction for a failure to confirm in the case of a sole
appointment (IR, r. 3.1(1)) but in the case of a joint appointment the
appointment is only 'effective' when all the appointees confirm in the
correct manner (IR, r. 3.1(2)). There is a supposition, made by the
use of the word 'when', that the appointment is only effective *after* both

appointees confirm acceptance. This view conflicts with s. 33(1)(*b*), discussed at (3) above, unless there is meant to be a distinction between an appointment being 'made' and it being 'effective'.

## ¶312   Formalities subsequent to appointment

The following is a check list of the steps to be taken after the appointment of an administrative receiver:

(1)   Notice of the appointment of the receiver must be given by the debenture holder to the Registrar of Companies within seven days of the appointment (CA, s. 405(1)).

(2)   The receiver must forthwith send notice of his appointment to the company (IA, s. 46(1)(*a*)). The notice must contain specific details, and the provisions of the Rules should be followed carefully, not least because failure to comply without reasonable excuse is a criminal offence (see IA, s. 46(4)). The details required by r. 3.2(2) of the Insolvency Rules 1986 are:

(*a*)   the company's name and address;

(*b*)   other corporate names used within the previous 12 months;

(*c*)   any trading name used in the previous 12 months, if 'substantially different' from the corporate name;

(*d*)   name and address and date of appointment of the administrative receiver;

(*e*)   the name of the appointor;

(*f*)   the date and a 'brief description' of the security document; and

(*g*)   a 'brief description' of those assets of the company which are not caught by the appointment (if any).

(3)   The receiver must forthwith publish a notice of his appointment in the *London Gazette* and in one other newspaper chosen with a view to bringing the appointment to the attention of creditors (IA, s. 46(1)(*a*) and IR, r. 3.2(3)). This notice must give the details listed above at points (*a*)–(*e*) in para. (2) above (IR, r. 3.2(4)).

(4)   Within 28 days of his appointment (save where the court directs otherwise) the receiver must send a notice to all the creditors of the company to the extent that he is aware of their addresses (IA, s. 46(1)(*b*)). This notice must give the same details as the notice to the company.

(5)   On pain of a fine, all invoices, orders for goods, and business letters must state that a receiver or manager has been appointed (IA, s. 39

and, in a similar vein, where there is also a liquidation, note IA, s. 188).

(6)   The receiver must comply with the bonding requirements discussed at ¶206.

There are specific exemptions from compliance with the rules set out in paras. (1)–(4) above in the case of replacement or additional administrative receivers (IA, s. 46(2)).


## ¶313   Invalid appointments

### (1)   Effect of invalidity

Subject to any statutory relief, the basic rule is that where a receiver is invalidly appointed as a result of a defect in his appointment or as a result of a defect in security he will be a trespasser and liable accordingly (*Re Simms ex parte Trustee* [1934] Ch. 1). His appointor will also be liable in damages (see, for example, *R. A. Cripps & Son Ltd* v *Wickenden* [1973] 1 WLR 944 at p. 957). The possibility most worrying to the receiver in these circumstances is a claim in respect of damage to the goodwill of the business. There may be difficulties in assessing damages but these difficulties do not make the damages unquantifiable (*Byblos Bank SAL* v *Rushingdale Ltd SA and Others* (1986) 2 BCC 99, 509 at p. 99, 517). It may be possible for the receiver and the chargee to show that no loss has been suffered where the company was demonstrably insolvent at the time of the receiver's appointment and he has achieved the best price reasonably obtainable for the assets he has sold.

There are a number of further points to note. In particular:

(1)   Where the security is null and void the receiver is liable to repay his professional fees plus interest (*Rolled Steel Products (Holdings) Ltd* v *British Steel Corporation and Others* [1986] Ch. 246).

(2)   If a receiver has not been validly appointed because the demand is defective, the company may be stopped from denying that the receiver has been validly appointed where it acquiesces in his appointment (see *Bank of Baroda* v *Panessar and Others* (1986) 2 BCC 99, 288; [1986] 3 All ER 751 in which Walton J cited as authority for this proposition *Habib Bank Limited* v *Habib Bank AG* [1981] 1 WLR 1265, *Taylors Fashions Limited* v *Liverpool Victoria Trustees Co. Limited* [1982] QB 133 and *Save (Acoustics) Limited* v *Pimms Furnishing Limited*, 11 January 1985, unreported).

(3)   If a receiver is not validly appointed, he will not necessarily be the agent of the mortgagee merely because he is not the agent of the

mortgagor (*Bank of Baroda* v *Panessar and Others* (1986) 2 BCC 99, 288; [1986] 3 All ER 751). The reasoning is that the existence of a statutory indemnity (IA, s. 34, see below) denies the existence of a principal/agent relationship because, were there such a relationship, a statutory indemnity would be unnecessary as the law implies an indemnity in any event.

### (2)  Statutory validity

An administrative receiver's acts are valid notwithstanding any defect in his appointment or qualifications (IA, s. 232). It is not clear how wide the relief offered by this provision actually is. A distinction will be drawn between a defective appointment and a case where there is no appointment at all. In *Morris* v *Kanssen* ([1946] 1 All ER 586 at p. 590) Lord Simonds summarised the purpose of a similar provision covering the appointment of directors as follows: '. . . being designed as machinery to avoid questions being raised as to the validity of transactions where there has been a slip in the appointment . . . cannot be utilised for the purpose of ignoring or overriding the substantive provisions relating to such appointment'.

### (3)  Indemnities

It is often not possible for a proposed administrative receiver or his legal advisers to go through the type of checklist given above (¶309) prior to accepting appointment – there may not be sufficient time available. The insolvency practitioner may, in such circumstances, be justified in requesting a full indemnity to protect him in the event that his appointment should later prove defective. This indemnity can be anything from a strict deed to a form of comfort letter (or even an oral assurance), depending on the commercial realities.[1]

There is now a right for any receiver or manager to seek an order of the court that he be indemnified by his appointor where he has been invalidly appointed (whether because the document of appointment is invalid, or otherwise) against any liability arising 'solely' because of the invalidity of his appointment (IA, s. 34). Presumably, although a decision of the court must be awaited, where the invalidity of the appointment is such that the receiver is only a purported receiver, he will still be able to seek an order for indemnification from the court.

---

[1] That the 'commercial realities' of receivership work are sometimes misunderstood was illustrated to the author by the comment of a purchaser of a business from a receiver at the conclusion of a deal, which had admittedly involved somewhat arduous and lengthy negotiations, to the effect that the receiver would no doubt 'not want another receivership in a hurry'!

¶313

# 4  Nature, Capacity, Powers and Duties of an Administrative Receiver

## AGENCY

### ¶401  Nature and extent

Prior to the Insolvency Act 1986, it was normal for the security to provide that a receiver, when appointed, would be the agent for the company in carrying out his functions. In the case of an appointment of a receiver of income under the Law of Property Act 1925, the receiver was (and is) deemed to be agent of the company (LPA, s. 109(2)). The principal reason for the appointment of a receiver as the means by which a mortgagee enforces his security is that the mortgagee avoids the consequences of being a mortgagee in possession.[1] This aim would be defeated if the receiver were to be the mortgagee's agent and hence the device of making the receiver the agent of the mortgagor was adopted.

An administrative receiver is now deemed by the Insolvency Act 1986 to be the agent of the company (IA, s. 44(1)(a)). This agency continues until such time as the company may go into liquidation (IA, s. 44(1)(a)). The introduction of this provision exemplifies the main approach of the new legislation to receiverships which is to codify in statutory form what had hitherto been the norm in contract or good practice.

The effect of the agency is that the acts of the agent are those of his principal, that is the company, and are not his own acts or, indeed, those of the chargee. This agency is, however, different to a normal agency in a number of respects. First, an administrative receiver will, unlike most agents, be personally liable on contracts entered into by him unless he expressly excludes that liability under the contract, and he will in any event be personally liable on contracts of employment 'adopted' by him in carrying out his functions

---

[1] There are potentially onerous duties such as accounting, waste and maintenance – see Fisher & Lightwood's *Law of Mortgage* (9th edn) p. 348 et seq.

(IA, s. 44(1)(*b*) and see ¶511–12).[2] Secondly, the agent's principal (the company) is not able to dismiss him, as is the case in the normal agency. Further, as Hoffmann J put it in *Gomba Holdings UK Limited and Others* v *Homan and Another* ((1986) 2 BCC 99, 102 at p. 99, 106; [1986] 3 All ER 94 at p. 98):

> 'It cannot simply be assumed that his obligations are the same as those of an ordinary agent who owes a duty of undivided loyalty to his principal'.

To an extent, the ordinary law of agency will apply to an administrative receiver. For example, he is, notwithstanding his agency, potentially personally liable for torts committed by him (see *Bowstead on Agency* (15th edn) at p. 490 and see ¶506–7 below).

As agent for the company, the receiver displaces the board of directors from its management function. As Hoffmann J said in the *Gomba* case (99, 102 at p. 99, 106; 94 at p. 98):

> 'There are, I think, certain principles which can be deduced from what the parties may be supposed to have contemplated as the commercial purpose of the power to appoint a receiver and manager. The first is that the receiver and manager should have the power to carry on the day to day process of realisation and management of the company's property without interference from the board. As Lord Atkinson said in *Moss Steamship Co. Ltd* v *Whinney* [1912] AC 254, 263, the appointment of a receiver:
>
> > "entirely supersedes the company in the conduct of its business, deprives it of all power to enter into contracts in relation to that business, or to sell, pledge, or otherwise dispose of the property put into the possession, or under the control of the receiver and manager. Its powers in these respects are entirely in abeyance."'

A simple illustration of the effect of a receiver managing a company's affairs as its agent can be given by considering a purchase of goods. The receiver will place the order as agent for the company and he may exclude his personal liability. In the event that he does not put the company in funds to meet the debt incurred, a supplier would merely have a right of action in damages against the company (*Nicoll* v *Cutts* (1985) 1 BCC 99, 427). Normally, in such a situation, a receiver will pay for the supply of goods as a receivership expense because otherwise he would not be able to pursuade suppliers to supply him (see ¶510) and there is always in the background the undefined limits of the receiver's potential liability for fraudulent trading (IA, s. 213).

---

[2] He is however, entitled to an indemnity out of the assets of the company in respect of any such liability (IA, s. 44(1)(*c*)).

¶401

## ¶402   Conflict of interest

The somewhat artificial nature of the administrative receiver's agency can be thrown into relief by recalling that the receiver is appointed by the holders of security to attempt to obtain repayment of the secured debt of his appointor, usually by realising the property and assets caught by the charge. As Lord Evershed MR noted in *Re B. Johnson & Co. (Builders) Limited* ([1955] 1 Ch. 634 at p. 664):

> '. . . it is quite plain that a person appointed as receiver and manager is concerned, not for the benefit of the company but for the benefit of the mortgagee bank, to realise the security; that is the whole purpose of his appointment; and the powers which are conferred upon him . . . are . . . really ancillary to the main purpose of the appointment, which is the realisation by the mortgagee of the security (in this case, as commonly) by the sale of the assets.
>
> All that is perhaps elementary . . .'

## ¶403   Responsibilities

An administrative receiver does have certain duties which he owes to the mortgagor. Few would pretend that all the consequences of the tension (see ¶402) caused by his dual role have been fully argued and analysed. The conflict was noted by Hoffmann J in *Gomba Holdings UK Limited and Others* v *Homan and Another* ((1986) 2 BCC 99, 102; [1986] 3 All ER 94) when considering a receiver's duty to provide information to the directors of the company and he said (99, 102 at p. 99, 107; 94 at p. 99):

> 'I think that the receiver's duty to provide . . . information must be subordinated to his primary duty not to do anything which may prejudice the interests of the debenture holder'.

An administrative receiver's duties generally, including the duty to provide information, are considered below (see ¶416 et seq., and ¶416 (2) in particular).

## ¶404   Effect of liquidation

It seems clear that liquidation effectively ends an administrative receiver's agency for the company (IA, ss. 44(1)(*a*) and 247(2) and *Gosling* v *Gaskell* [1897] AC 575). The rationale for what is a statutory codification of a common law rule is that the insolvency code provides that a company's (free) assets are to be used on a winding-up in settlement of the company's liabilities *at that date 'pari passu'* (IA, s. 107) and it should not be possible for the receiver to add to those liabilities as agent for the company after the commencement of the winding-up. It is important to note that the termination of the agency prevents the creation of new debts on the company's behalf by the receiver but does not prevent the receiver continuing to realise assets caught by the security (see ¶412 and ¶516(5)). This can lead to an exception to the rule that the receiver may not create further liabilities on behalf of the company after the commencement of the winding-up, as where a receiver realises property after the commencement of liquidation at a price which gives rise to a corporation tax liability in respect of a chargeable gain, that charge to tax is a liability of the company and, further, must be paid as an expense of the liquidation, in priority even to payment of the liquidator's remuneration (*Re Mesco Properties* 54 TC 238, and see ¶1301).

What is the position of an administrative receiver after liquidation? *Thomas v Todd* ([1926] 2 KB 511) is authority for the proposition that, in the absence of anything further, the receiver is personally liable for his acts after the date of liquidation. As Wright J put it (at p. 518):

'I . . . think that the contract which the [receiver] made with the plaintiff after the commencement of the voluntary winding up is binding on him personally. . . . I think the position is that a contract was made by the [receiver] at a time when he had no principal in fact, when he did not purport to be acting for any principal, and when he was not thought by the plaintiff to be acting for any principal. . . . It follows, I think, that the [receiver], and the [receiver], alone is personally liable.

In two subsequent cases, *Re Courts (Emergency Powers) Act (1939)* (65 TLR 141) and *Re S Brown & Co (General Warehousemen) Limited* ([1940] 1 Ch 961), Bennett J made certain comments which, although they have to be read in the light of the 1939 Act referred to in the title of the former case, suggest that the normal position was that after liquidation receivers became agents for their debenture holders. *Thomas v Todd* ([1926] 2 KB 511) does not appear to have been cited. In the case of *Re Wood's Application* ([1941] 1 Ch. 112), however, Moreton J thought that there must have been 'special facts' in the *S. Brown & Co.* case which led the judge to conclude that the receivers were the debenture holders' agents and he indicated that the position was open.

A recent clear statement of the true position can be found in the judgment of Mann J in the case of *American Express International Banking Corporation v Hurley* ((1986) 2 BCC 98, 993 at p. 98, 997; [1985] 3 All ER 564 at p. 568) where the judge stated:

'If the mortgagor is put into liquidation then the agency terminates (see *Gosling v Gaskell and Grocott* [1897] AC 575). If the receiver continues to act he does not automatically become the agent of the mortgagee (see *Re*

*Wood* [1941] Ch. 112) but he may become so if the mortgagee treats him as such. In this case I find that after the liquidation . . . the bank constituted the receiver its agent. Counsel for the bank did not seriously contend to the contrary. He could not do so. There was constant communication between the bank and the receiver and the latter sought the former's approval to such actions as he proposed to take.'

If he is to avoid being held to be the agent for his debenture holder, it seems that a receiver must tread a narrow path between on the one hand keeping his appointors informed of progress in the administration in a proper professional manner and, on the other hand, being seen to be acting on the instructions of, or for ever seeking the approval of, his debenture holder.

# PROPERTY COVERED BY THE APPOINTMENT

## ¶405 Contractual position

An administrative receiver is not appointed 'to a company' but is appointed over the assets of the company charged by the security under which he is appointed. In this his position is to be contrasted with the position of a liquidator or an administrator who is appointed to the company itself.

To ascertain the extent of the administrative receiver's appointment, it is necessary to look closely at the property and assets which are effectively charged by the security, but, by definition, the assets caught will be all or substantially all the assets of the chargor (IA, s. 251).

Where property is released from a charge and sold by the chargor but later re-acquired there may be arguments that the property, on being re-acquired, is not caught by a charge in the security on future-acquired property.

## ¶406 Third-party property and contractual rights

### (1) General principles

Where property of a company is subject to a fixed charge, the company does not have actual or ostensible authority to deal with the asset free from the rights of the holder of the charge and, therefore, third parties cannot acquire rights in the charged property ranking in priority to the rights of the fixed chargee. (This briefly summarises a very complicated area of the law – see Goode, *Legal problems of credit and security*, pp 22–27, particularly at p. 24.)

The question of the creation of third-party rights over company property is most often encountered where the security in question is a floating charge because, in such a case, the company has authority to deal with the assets in the ordinary course of business. Here the question of priority which most often arises is the relative priority of the third-party rights and the equitable assignment effected by the crystallisation of the floating charge on the appointment of a receiver (*N.W. Robbie & Co. Limited* v *Witney Warehouse Co. Limited* [1963] 1 WLR 1324). Another category of third-party rights is made up of those cases where the company did not ever receive title to the property or assets in question and, therefore, the company is not in a position to give an effective charge to the chargee. These third-party rights may arise where title is retained by a third party (whether pursuant to a leasing or hire-purchase agreement or a retention of title provision) or where the property is held on trust by the company for the third party. Specific heads of third-party rights, such as set-off, lien and title retention, are considered at ¶407.

## (2)   Rights in property and mere contractual rights

Questions of third-party rights are part of a wider question: to what extent is a receiver able to deal with property which is, or appears to be, property of the company, free of third-party rights and claims? To answer this question it is necessary to consider not just third-party proprietory claims and rights as a matter of contract, but also a receiver's personal position in tort. Although claims framed in contract and tort are conceptually distinct, and often considered separately as a result, they are here considered together to assist in answering the above question – which is the question faced by a receiver in practice.

A principle which may assist in analysing third-party claims to assets caught by the crystallised floating charge under which a receiver has been appointed is that mere contractual rights, in contradistinction to interests in property, are ineffective as against the crystallised floating charge and hence the receiver appointed under it. The distinction is one well-recognised in liquidations but it is also, it is submitted, applicable in the case of receiverships. Professor Goode formulates the rule (in discussing liquidations) slightly differently. He talks of the 'real rights' which survive liquidation (see Goode, *Proprietory rights and insolvency in sales transactions,* pp. 1–11) and one of these rights is possession, lawfully held. This is not to suggest that mere possession defeats receivers' and liquidators' claims. Such an assertion, if true, would, for example, do away with the need to have common law rules of lien. It is more that in certain circumstances the fact that a third party does not have a legal or equitable interest in the property of the company, does not prevent him asserting contractual or common law rights in respect of the goods where the third party is entitled to, and has, possession. The classic example is where the company grants a lease of a chattel to the third party – say a vehicle is hired out for a term of 12 months. A lease of a chattel does not create a legal estate in the goods in the same way that a lease of land creates a legal estate (see LPA, s. 1). It is submitted that, where possession of the machine has been given to the third party prior to the appointment of an administrative receiver, the receiver is not able to require the third party to deliver up the machine to him until expiry of the 12-month term (subject to the terms of the lease). The floating charge crystallises on the machine subject to the third party's 'real right to possession' (see Goode, *Proprietory rights and insolvency in sales transactions*, p. 5). On the other hand, it is submitted that, where a company agrees, prior to the appointment of the receiver, to lease the machine for the same term but possession is not given to the third party, the mere contractual right to the 12-month hire is not enforceable against the receiver. The absence of the 'real right' of possession is fatal. (There appears to be no authority directly in point but the cases considered below do not contradict this approach.)

**(3)   Judicial consideration**
It is submitted that the distinction between mere contractual rights and interests in property (or 'real rights') enables a number of decisions, reached on apparently differing grounds, to be reconciled. Before turning to a consideration of specific areas where third parties have rights effective against receivers, there follow a number of examples of cases in which the general principles outlined above have been discussed.

*(a)   Freevale Limited* v *Metrostore (Holdings) Limited*
Where, before the commencement of receivership, a company has contracted to sell land but a receiver is appointed prior to completion of the sale, the court will protect the equitable interest of the purchaser in the property and will order specific performance of the contract for the sale (*Freevale Limited* v *Metrostore (Holdings) Limited* [1984] 1 Ch. 199). As Donald Rattee QC (sitting as a Deputy High Court Judge) put it (at p. 203):

> 'In my judgment, the real question raised in the present case is, "Does the appointment out of court of a receiver in respect of a company vendor of land somehow destroy the equitable interest in the land which was vested in the purchaser prior to the appointment of the receiver by virtue of the subsisting valid contract for its sale and purchase, or does the appointment of a receiver alternatively somehow prevent the court perfecting that equitable interest by making an order for specific performance?"'

He answered both questions in the negative. The report of the case does not reveal whether the debenture under which the receiver was appointed contained a fixed charge on the land in question but one would presume it did not. If the property was subject to a fixed charge, the purchaser could not

take free of the charge without redeeming it, and therefore on completion of
the purchase would buy subject to the charge under which the receiver would
still have been in office.

### (b)   Airlines Airspares Limited v Handley Page Limited and Another

The case of *Airlines Airspares Limited* v *Handley Page Limited and Another*
([1970] 1 Ch. 193) accords with the principle enunciated above, although some
of the comments in the judgment suggest a different basis for the decision.
Prior to the appointment of the receiver (and indeed prior to the creation of
the debenture) the company had entered into a contract whereby it undertook
to pay a commission to a third party, K, in respect of every aircraft the
company sold. K later assigned the benefit of that agreement to K Ltd. When
the receivers were appointed their plan for realising the assets of the company
was to hive-down the business into a subsidiary and to attempt to sell that
subsidiary to American purchasers. K Ltd sought an injunction to prevent the
receivers carrying out this plan (although at the date the hearings took place
the hive-down had already occurred). K Ltd argued that if the company itself
was not permitted by law to put itself in a position where it could not honour
its contractual commitments (and authority was cited in support of that
proposition), then it was not open to the receiver to cause the company so to
do. He should be prevented therefore, from hiving-down and selling the hive-
down company and, instead, should make satisfactory provision for the
payment of the commission in the future. Counsel for the receivers put the
view, as one of a number of arguments, that K Ltd had no rights in property
as such and therefore its claim should be rejected. The judge felt that to be
an unhelpful analysis and chose to decide the case on a different ground.
Graham J said (at p. 198):

> '. . . it is said that to merit the grant of an injunction, the acts complained
> of must threaten an invasion of the plaintiffs' legal rights and the relief
> asked for must relate to those rights. Here, the relief asked for relates to
> the transfer of shares in [the hive-down subsidiary], and if that be so the
> plaintiffs must show that they have some legal rights in respect of the shares
> in question, and no such right has been shown. This argument seems to me
> to beg the real question the answer to which, in my judgment, determines
> the issue in this case. That question may be stated as follows: is a receiver
> and a manager, appointed by debenture holders, in a stronger position,
> from the legal point of view, than the company itself, in respect of contracts
> between unsecured creditors and the company?'

He answered that last question in the affirmative. The judgment suggested
that the decision might have been different if failure to honour the contract
might have resulted in damage to the goodwill of the company. There are two

¶406

considerations which suggest that this is not a relevant factor. First, the cases dealing with damage to goodwill of the company (such as *Re Newdigate Colliery Limited* [1912] 1 Ch. 468) relate to court-appointed receivers, where the considerations are quite different. That these considerations do not apply to receivers appointed out of court by a debenture-holder is made clear in *Re B. Johnson & Co. (Builders) Limited* ([1955] 1 Ch. 634, discussed above at ¶401). Secondly, if the receiver fails to carry out a contract which is profitable, or if he achieves less on a realisation of the assets of the business by damaging goodwill, then he may be in breach of his duty to the company, but that is a duty to be enforced by the company or a liquidator and does not give rights to a third party to insist that the contract is performed (see generally *Lawson (Inspector of Taxes)* v *Hosemaster Co. Limited* [1966] 1 WLR 1300 and the principles discussed at ¶415(1)).

*(c)   Hemlata Lathia v Dronsfield Brothers Limited and others*
One argument for the plaintiffs in the *Airlines Airspares Limited* case was that the receivers were liable in tort for inducing the company to breach its contract with the plaintiffs. This argument was impliedly rejected by the decision of the judge. A similar question fell to be considered by Sir Neil Lawson in *Hemlata Lathia* v *Dronsfield Brothers Limited and others* ([1987] BCLC 321). The statement of claim alleged that the company had, before the start of the receivership, entered into a contract to sell an item of equipment to company X which, in turn, was going to sell the equipment, by way of hire purchase, to the plaintiffs. The claim was against the receivers personally for having sold the equipment to a third party. On those facts, the plaintiffs would not appear to have any interest in the item of equipment itself and the judge agreed to strike out the claim as disclosing no cause of action. The judge commented (at p. 326):

'All the authorities establish that a receiver (in the circumstances of this case) is immune in actions for breach of contract and procurement of a breach of contract unless he did not act bona fide or in the course of his authority. The receiver's authority is to effect the best realisation of assets in the interests of the debenture holder. . . .

He also commented that:

'A lack of bona fides is concerned with fraud or improper motive'.

The judge appeared to base his reasoning on the fact that the receiver was agent for the company. He said (at p. 324):

'It is not suggested that the company went into liquidation, at any material time . . . the receivers can adopt or decline to adopt a contract which the company has entered into and which is unexecuted. It follows from this, and the agency clause [in the debenture], that the agent is personally immune from claims for damages for breach of contract or procurement of breach of contract. The agent has an immunity for a claim for inducing breach of contract unless he has not acted bona fide or acted outside the scope of his authority, i.e. had not acted as agent.'

This leaves open the question of the position of a receiver after liquidation (see (*e*) below).

*(d)    Telemetrix plc* v *Modern Engineers of Bristol (Holdings) plc and Others*

This whole area was given consideration in the recent case *Telemetrix plc* v *Modern Engineers of Bristol (Holdings) plc and Others* ([1985] BCLC 213). The point at issue was one of liability for the costs of an action and whether the receivers were personally liable for them. The question which fell to be decided upon was whether the receivers had been properly joined as parties to the action in question. The facts are not altogether clear from the report, but what appears to have happened is that pre-receivership the company had agreed to assign to the plaintiffs the benefit of an option 'over' certain land. After their appointment, the receivers indicated to the plaintiffs that they did not consider themselves bound by the agreement to assign the option and intended to assign the option to third parties. The plaintiffs successfully prevented the receivers from so doing and sought an order that the option be assigned to them in accordance with the agreement. The receivers finally accepted that they had to assign the option but resisted attempts to make them personally liable for costs. Peter Gibson J found that they had been properly joined as they could have been liable in tort for wrongfully interfering with the 'equitable rights' of the plaintiffs. This decision fits the general principle on the basis that the plaintiffs had rights to property – 'equitable rights' in the option pursuant to the agreement to assign – which the receivers could not ignore. This was one of the lines of argument employed by counsel for the plaintiffs and the judge commented that this was the 'stronger' line, adding (at p. 217):

'[Counsel for the plaintiffs] submits that where there is a threat by a receiver to deal with property in a manner inconsistent with the equitable rights of another that is a threat of tortious conduct such as might make a receiver liable in tort and if he is liable in tort that will, of course, be a personal liability.

When I first saw this matter, it occurred to me that the receivers might be trying to do what was successfully done by the receiver in *Airlines Airspares Limited* v *Handley Page Limited* [1970] Ch. 193 where a receiver was held by Graham J to be in a better position than the company of which he was the receiver and, I would surmise, of which he was the agent too. [Counsel for the receivers] has rightly pointed out that that is a somewhat different case having regard to the nature of the contract in question and [counsel for the receivers] has accepted that, in a case such as the present, where there is an equitable right in the plaintiff, it is not possible for the receiver to ignore the equitable right of the plaintiff: see *Freevale Limited v Metrostore (Holdings) Limited* [1984] 1 Ch. 199.'

In considering the counsel for the plaintiffs' other line of argument, Peter Gibson J touched on the question of the receiver's exemption from liability in tort for inducing a breach of contract because he is an agent. In a case involving a court-appointed receiver, *Re Botibol* ([1947] 1 All ER 26), Evershed J said (at p. 28):

'. . . if a receiver can assert a right, certainly where, as I say there is no constituent behind him, to accept a repudiation so as to terminate the contract, he must have put himself in the position by adoption of being a party to the contract or representing a party. There is a further ground that, even if the receiver could not be sued *ex contractu*, it would not follow that he could not be sued in tort if he had taken steps which effectively prohibited the completion of the contract.'

Peter Gibson J said that a receiver appointed by the Court was not an agent and therefore there was a distinction between that situation and the case where the receiver is an agent, since cases such as *Said v Budd* ([1920] 3 KB 497) and *G. Scammell & Nephew Limited v Hurley and Others* ([1929] 1 KB 419) are authority for the view that a person acting as agent for a principal is immune from liability.

### (e)  An anomaly?

It would be a curious result if there were a set of facts on which a receiver was able to resist claims of a third party as a contractual matter – for example, because the contractual rights do not add up to an interest in property – yet the third party was able effectively to pursue its claims by threatening the receiver with a tortious liability should he act in a manner inconsistent with them (see the reference to the need to equate tortious and contractual liabilities, in a different context, in *Shamji and Others v Johnson Matthey Bankers Limited & Others* [1986] 2 BCC 98, 910 at p. 98, 916).

If the receiver's only immunity arises out of his position as agent, what happens if a company goes into liquidation? In those circumstances would a receiver have to pay heed to existing contractual rights as he would not be immune from actions in tort for causing the company to act inconsistently with them? It may be that this argument could be answered in one of two ways. First, it might be said that the effect of liquidation is to crystallise the third party's rights against the company such that, at the date of liquidation, the third party merely has an unsecured claim and a right to prove. In effect, the receiver would be taking the benefit of the third party's inability to assert against the company in liquidation anything other than an interest in property, except by way of proof of debt. A second argument might be that, after liquidation, the receiver is either personally responsible for his actions or he is agent for his appointor (see ¶404). His acts would, therefore, not be those of the company. This seems a somewhat artificial argument as the property of a company remains its property notwithstanding liquidation and does not in any sense vest in the receiver and, therefore, where a receiver realises assets after liquidation (see ¶412), it is still the company which is the true vendor of its property.

Further, in the *Telemetrix* case (cited above) the receiver's appointor would not have been able to sell the options as mortgagee because the 'equitable interest' of the third party would have been binding on it. This would not be so where the third party had no such interest. It would be strange if there were a set of circumstances where a mortgagee could sell free of contractual claims and a receiver appointed by the mortgagee to enforce the mortgagee's security found himself prevented from so doing because of a potential liability in tort for inducing a breach of contract (for example where liquidation has terminated his agency).

A more realistic approach would be to say that the receiver is immune from suit in tort because the property over which he has been appointed is taken by his appointor free of contractual rights and the purpose of a receiver's appointment is to enforce his appointor's security. Graham J in the *Airlines Airspares* case (cited above) pointed out the problems in a receivership if he did not find for the receiver on the facts before him, when he said (at p. 199):

'. . . otherwise almost unsecured creditor would be able to improve his position and prevent the receiver from carrying out, or at any rate carrying out as sensibly and as equitably as possible, the purpose for which he was appointed.'

## ¶407   Specific third-party rights

### (1)   Liens

It is not intended to give a definitive guide to the law of liens, merely to illustrate its application in the field of receiverships. A detailed analysis can be found in Halsbury's Laws of England (4th edn) Vol. 28.

A lien is a right to retain possession of goods as against their owner as security for an outstanding debt. It is essentially a negative right, but in the case of a contractual lien (and certain statutory liens) the holder may be given a specific power to sell the goods and apply the proceeds against the 'secured' debt.

The first rule is that the holder of a lien can acquire no greater rights to the goods in question than can properly be given to him by the owner. This means that where a company purports to deal with an asset subject to a fixed charge, the third party who might otherwise acquire a lien cannot acquire a right effective against the holder of the fixed charge because the company is not in a position to create such rights (*Smith* v *Chichester* (1842) 2 Dr & War 393).

The position is different with a floating charge where the lien arises in the ordinary course of business, and therefore the critical problems with liens tend to arise in connection with floating charges and their crystallisation on the appointment of a receiver. It seems clear that an effective lien acquired prior to the crystallisation of the floating charge is effective against a receiver (*George Barker (Transport) Limited* v *Eynon* [1974] 1 WLR 462, discussed below, and *Re Diesels & Components Property Limited* [1985] 9 ACLR 825). A more difficult situation may occur where the right to the lien arises out of a contract entered into pre-receivership, but the holder of the lien only obtains possession of the goods after the appointment of the receiver. This was what happened in the *George Barker* case (cited above) and the court held that the lien was effective against the receiver. The critical factor for the carrier in the case was that the lien was a general lien and security not just for the delivery of the goods in question, but also for previous deliveries for which the carrier remained unpaid and for which it would rank, in the absence of the lien, merely as an unsecured creditor. The analysis of the respective rights of the debenture holder and carrier by Edmund Davies LJ (at p. 470) was as follows:

'My conclusion . . . is that the debenture holders could assert their position as assignees of the company's property and contractual rights in the meat [the goods in question] only by themselves recognising and giving effect to the pre-appointment contractual rights of the plaintiffs. These included a general lien, and that became exercisable when the plaintiffs acquired actual possession on September 2, and this none the less because three days earlier the defendant had been appointed receiver'.

And as Sir Gordon Willmer put it in the same case (at p. 475):

'The important and decisive consideration to my mind is that the plaintiffs had acquired a contractual right against the company to exercise a lien if and when they acquired possession and sought to deliver the cartons. That contractual right must be good against an assignee who elects to proceed with the performance of the contract to the same extent as it would have been good against the company had there been no assignment. In these

¶407

circumstances, it seems to me that the date upon which the plaintiffs in fact acquired possession, whether actual or constructive, is not of any relevance'.

What seems clear from this case is that it was important that the person claiming the lien should actually have obtained possession. It is submitted that, had the receiver been able to prevent the carrier from obtaining possession, the carrier would not have been able to demand that the receiver fulfil the contract for carriage by allowing the carrier to take possession of the goods.

### (2)  Set-off

This is one of the more difficult areas of the law relating to administrative receivers. As *Kerr* puts it (*Kerr on Receivers* (15th edn) at p. 309), 'the limits of the doctrine are not easy to discern'.

What follows, therefore, are two particular examples of the legal principles applied to specific facts and then a statement of general rules which, it is submitted, can be derived from the decided cases.

### (a)  The first example

In *Rother Ironworks Limited* v *Canterbury Precision Engineers Limited* ([1974] 1 QB 1) the facts, in chronological order, were as follows:

(1)    Company A granted a debenture containing a floating charge on all its assets and undertaking to a bank.

(2)    Company B supplied goods to the value of £124 to company A and awaited payment for them.

(3)    Company A agreed to deliver goods to the value of £159 to company B.

(4)    After the agreement for the supply of goods for £159, but before their delivery, the bank appointed a receiver to company A.

(5)    After the receiver's appointment the goods were delivered by company A.

The factual position might be illustrated by the following diagram:

¶407

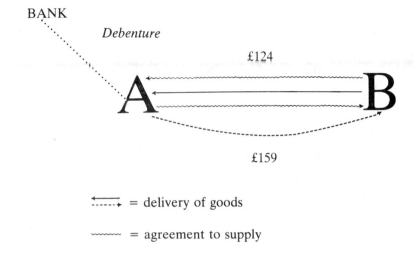

BANK

*Debenture*

£124

A ⟶ B

£159

⟵┄┄➤ = delivery of goods

〰〰〰 = agreement to supply

The continuous arrowed line indicates pre-receivership actions and the broken arrowed lines indicate actions post-receivership.

The receiver sued for the full £159 and company B claimed that it was entitled to set off the £124 and tendered the balance of £35 to the receiver. Perhaps surprisingly in view of the small sums involved the case went to the Court of Appeal and it was decided that company B was entitled to set-off. As Russell LJ summarised his conclusions (at p. 6):

'It is true that the right of [company A] to sue for the debt due from [company B] was embraced, when it arose, by the debenture charge. But if this was because the chose in action consisting of the rights under the contract became subject to the charge on the appointment of the receiver, then the debenture holder could not be in a better position to assert those rights than had been the assignor plaintiff. And if the obligation of the defendant to pay £159 be regarded as a chose in action on its own it never, in our view, came into existence except subject to a right to set off the £124 as, in effect, payment in advance. That which became subject to the debenture charge was not £159, but the net claim sustainable by the plaintiff of £35.'

*(b)  The second example*

The facts in the case of *N. W. Robbie & Co. Limited* v *Witney Warehouse Co. Limited* ([1963] 1 WLR 1324) were as follows (again in chronological order):

(1)  Company X gave a debenture to its bank charging all its undertaking and assets by way of a floating charge.

(2)  Company X sold goods on credit to the value of £95 to company Y.

(3)  Company Z (a subsidiary company of company Y) sold goods on credit to company X to the value of £852.

(4)  Subsequent to the above sequence, a receiver was appointed to company X by the bank.

(5)  Subsequent to the receiver's appointment, further goods were sold on credit by company X to company Y for the sum of £1,251.

(6)  Subsequent to all the above, company Z assigned to company Y the debt owed to company Z by company X, and company Y purported to claim to set off the £852 against the debt of £1,346 (being £1,251 plus £95) owed by it to company X.

The above factual position can be illustrated by the following diagram:

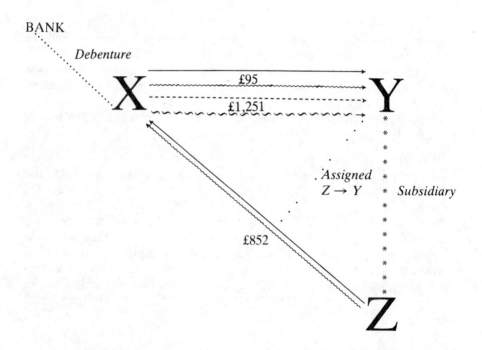

‾‾‾‾‾‾ = delivery

∿∿∿ = agreement to supply

¶407

As previously, the continuous arrowed lines indicates pre-receivership transactions and the broken arrowed lines indicates those that occurred post-receivership.

The Court of Appeal decided that there was no right to set-off in these circumstances. In the *Rother Ironworks* case the essence was that the charge attached to the net position after the set-off but in the *Robbie* case, at the date of the assignment (the date at which the right to set-off might have been thought to have arisen), the assignment of the debt amounting in total to £1,346 had already occurred and company Y was on notice of this. Russell LJ gave the majority opinion of the Court of Appeal and he stated (at pp. 1338–9):

'[The] choses in action [the debts totalling £1,346] belonging to the company became . . . assigned in equity to the debenture holders, at times when the defendants had no cross-claim of any kind against the company and consequently no right of set-off. Before the defendants acquired by assignment this cross-claim the defendants must be fixed with knowledge of this equitable assignment to the debenture holders (by way of charge) of the debt owed by the defendants to the company . . . Just as an assignee of a chose in action takes subject to an already existing right of set-off, so a debtor with no existing right of set-off cannot assert set-off of a cross-claim which he first acquires after he has notice of the assignment of the claim against him. . . .

. . . at the time when [company Y] first acquired the claim for £852, the choses in action sought to be enforced against [company Y] had been assigned to the debenture holders by way of charge, but the £852 claim in no way involved the debenture holders. There was, consequently, at the first moment of assertion of set-off, no identity between the persons beneficially interested in the claim and the person against whom the cross-claim existed. There was, therefore, not that prerequisite of set-off, mutuality. . . .'

It can be seen that notice of the assignment is important.

### (c) The general rules

The above cases involved floating charges on debts, but even if the charges had been fixed (*ab initio*) the results might not have been different, in that the crucial requirement is to establish *when* notice of the assignment was given and, whether the charge is fixed or floating, it will most often be the appointment of the receiver that leads to the giving of notice. The doctrine of constructive notice by registration of the charge at Companies House does not operate in this field as it would not be reasonable to expect a trading company to do a search at Companies House before entering into ordinary trading contracts (see Goode, *Legal problems of credit and security*, at p. 27).

It is submitted that the following principles apply generally to the question of set-off in receiverships,[1] although it has to be stressed that in view of the complexity of the law and in some cases the conflicting dicta in the judgments, any general rules must be carefully examined in the light of particular factual situations:

(1)   The equitable assignment constituted by the charge (whether an assignment *ab initio* in the case of a fixed charge or on crystallisation in the case of a floating charge) is subject to all equities affecting the debt which arise before notice of the assignment is received by the debtor.

(2)   Not all cross-claims or counterclaims give rise to a right to set-off. There are specific rules governing what may be set off, and set-off should be distinguished from counterclaim which is simply a question of procedure. For example, in the *Robbie* case (cited above), company Y might be said to have counterclaimed in respect of the assigned debt of £852 but the critical question was whether company Y had a right of set-off available to it and the use of the term counterclaim does not assist in answering that question.

(3)   What 'equities' are generally available for set-off? First mutual debts, secondly, rights or claims or complaints which reduce or extinguish a debt and, finally, those which equity permits (see *Hanak* v *Green* [1958] 2 QB 9 at pp. 22 et seq.).

(4)   Take, for example, a debt which has accrued due to a company prior to going into receivership and before notice of assignment of the debt is given to the debtor. What set-offs may the debtor claim? First, he may claim to set off debts owed to him by the company which come into existence before he receives notice. Secondly, he may also set off debts or unliquidated damages claims arising either before or after receipt of notice, if they arise out of the same contract or a contract which is inseparably connected with that contract or there is an intention between the parties that they should be set off. In short, the giving of notice is important from the debtor's point of view as regards mutual debts which do not arise out of the same contract (or are otherwise inseparably connected, or are pursuant to some agreement or intention that they should be set off) as they are not capable of set-off after

---

[1] The cases from which these principles can be gleaned are, in addition to the *Robbie* and *Rother Ironworks* cases, the following: *Roxburghe* v *Cox* ([1881] 17 ChD 520), *Hanak* v *Green* ([1958] 2 QB 9), *Parsons* v *Sovereign Bank of Canada* ([1913] AC 160), *Business Computers Limited* v *Anglo-African Leasing Limited* ([1977] 1 WLR 578); and see also the Commonwealth cases: *Rendell* v *Doors & Doors Limited* (*In Liquidation*) ([1975] 2 NZLR 191) and *Aboussafy* v *Abacus Cities Limited* ([1981] 4 WWR 60).

¶407

notice of the assignment has been given. Unliquidated damages claims arising out of different or otherwise unconnected contracts are not capable of set-off whether before or after notice.

## (3)   Reservation of title

### (a)   The concept

As Templeman LJ put it in *Borden (UK) Limited* v *Scottish Timber Products Limited* ([1981] Ch. 25, at p. 42):

> 'Unsecured creditors rank after preferential creditors, mortgagees and the holders of floating charges and they receive a raw deal'.

It was this type of thinking which led to the courts giving a sympathetic reception to what is perhaps certain unsecured creditors' greatest weapon in the insolvency field, that of effectively retaining title to goods supplied for which they have not been paid. Suppliers of services have no such remedy. The basic concept is that s. 19 of the Sale of Goods Act 1979 permits parties to a contract for the sale of goods to decide when property in the goods sold is to pass, and vendors can, for example, stipulate that they retain title to, and the right of disposal of, goods sold until such time as the purchase price is paid. This right to the return of goods is effective against a receiver and liquidator alike as the purchasing company does not own the goods in question. Reservation of title might be thought to constitute something of an exception to the general rule of insolvency which stipulates that all 'unsecured' creditors should be treated alike. The Cork Committee recommended that such clauses should be registered in the same way as charges or else be void against a liquidator and other creditors. They further recommended that there should be a 12-month moratorium on enforcement of rights in respect of reservation of title as against a receiver or an administrator. These recommendations were not followed. An administrator is given effective relief against action by suppliers on retention of title (see ¶904 and ¶908) but this is not so as regards a receiver.

A criticism can be levelled at retention of title clauses on legal/philosophic grounds. The argument runs that words such as 'title', 'property' and 'ownership' are not merely empty terms but descriptions of substantive arrangements. One way of putting it is to say that ownership really consists of a 'bundle of rights' (possession, right to use, right to sell, etc.) and it is, therefore, not possible to retain 'ownership' simply by use of the word – in the same way that in the field of landlord and tenant law a tenancy cannot be made into a licence simply by starting the document 'THIS LICENCE is made the . . . day of . . .' (and note the use of the term 'bundle of rights' by Stamp LJ in *George Barker (Transport) Limited* v *Eynon* [1974] 1 WLR 462 at

¶407

p. 473). The argument continues by asking in what sense ownership or title can truly be said to have been retained by a supplier who has handed over possession and the right to use and (often) the right to on-sell those goods. The artificiality of 'retention of title' in such circumstances is, perhaps, behind some of the limitations imposed upon the concept by the courts since the earliest cases.

Some practical problems posed for receivers by reservation of title disputes are considered below (see ¶506). As a legal matter, the validity or otherwise of a claim decides whether or not a particular asset is an asset of the receivership.

There are three elements to be considered by a receiver in assessing the validity or otherwise of a claim by a supplier in respect of reservation of title. These are: incorporation (of the reservation of title provision in the contract of supply with the purchasing company), identification (of the goods as having been supplied by the supplier) and validity (of the clause as a matter of law in respect of the goods in question).

*(b)    Incorporation*
If the parties did not agree that it was a term of the contract for the supply of the goods that title should be retained by the supplier until payment, then the supplier's claim falls at the first hurdle as the law will not imply such a provision. The following points should be noted in connection with the question of incorporation:

(1)    The usual rules of contract apply. It is necessary for any provision for retention of title (contained, for example, in the standard terms of business of the supplier) to be brought to the attention of the purchaser and accepted by him prior to the contract being made. In general terms, if the contract is made prior to the terms being put forward by the supplier, then these terms will not be incorporated (*Olley* v *Malborough Court Limited* [1949] 1 KB 532). In the case of a one-off contract where the agreement to supply is settled on the telephone, all the pieces of paper which are sent subsequently may properly be regarded as post-contractual and therefore of no legal effect, unless they can be said to amount to an agreed variation.

(2)    The point made at (1) above is often most starkly illustrated where the supplier's terms and conditions, and hence the reservation of title provision, is contained on the back of the invoice which is sent after the goods have been delivered. There may be a difference, however, where the parties have traded over a significant period of time. In such circumstances, the courts may be prepared to infer that the purchaser must have known the basis on which the supplier carried on business as a result of their 'course of dealing' (see *Hardwick Game Farm*

*Limited* v *SAPPA* [1969] 2 AC 31 and *Spurling* v *Bradshaw* [1956] 1 WLR 461). The alternative argument is that if the terms and conditions only ever appeared on the back of the invoice and thus were never even incorporated into one contract (because they were always post-contractual) then a course of dealing argument has no application because for that to apply there must have been at least one contract where the terms were incorporated.

(3) There are further complications where, as is often the case, not only does the supplier have standard terms and conditions of business but the purchaser does also and these conflict. This is often termed the 'battle of the forms'. Although each set of trading circumstances must be looked at individually and on its merits, English law does appear to have accepted the 'last-shot theory' (*Butler Machine Tool Co. Ltd* v *Ex-Cell-O Corpn. (England) Limited* [1979] 1 WLR 401). The sequence of events might be that the purchaser places an order with the supplier and sends his (i.e. the purchaser's) standard-purchase order to the supplier. The supplier responds by sending an acknowledgement of order with his own terms and conditions which may purport to exclude the purchaser's. The analysis of this is that the acknowledgement of order constitutes a counter-offer which will be accepted by the purchaser by his taking delivery of the goods thereafter.

(4) Lord Denning MR once said of an exemption clause that:

'In order to give sufficient notice, it would need to be printed in red ink with a red hand pointing to it – or something equally startling',

(*Thornton* v *Shoe Lane Parking Limited* [1971] 2 QB 163 at p. 170). The courts have stated that as retention of title provisions have become so prevalent, there is no need for a supplier specifically to bring them to the attention of a purchaser in this way (*John Snow and Co. Ltd* v *DBG Woodcroft & Co. Ltd* [1985] BCLC 54). Where the terms are on the reverse of the invoice, it may be important whether the texture of the original document is such that the fact that there is writing on the other side is apparent from looking at the front of the document (see the *John Snow* case cited above).

*(c) Identification*
It is a clear principle that a party claiming proprietary rights must be able to identify the goods to which he claims title. For an interesting example of the difficulties that this can pose see *Re London Wine Company (Shippers) Limited* (decided in 1975 but reported in [1986] PCC 121, discussed at length in Goode,

¶407

*Proprietory rights and insolvency in sales transactions*, at pp. 19–22). The following points should be noted in this area:

(1)   Where a supplier sells to a company goods which are also sold to that company by a number of other suppliers he will need to show, on the balance of probabilities, that any goods to which he claims title were in fact supplied by him and not by the other suppliers.

(2)   A great deal depends on what the retention of title 'secures'. Clauses might readily be divided into three types. First, there is what might be called the 'simple' clause which reserves title to goods until such time as those goods are paid for. A more complicated clause is one which covers a number of supplies all pursuant to one contract (for example) and title to all such supplies is retained until payment is made in full for all the supplies (see, for example, the clause at issue in *Clough Mill Ltd* v *Martin* [1985] 1 WLR 111). Finally there is the full 'all moneys' or 'current account' clause which retains title until the goods are paid for *and* until all sums owed by the purchaser to the supplier on any account whatsoever are settled. At first sight such a clause might appear to bear all the hallmarks of a floating charge but, although it appears that the point has never been fully argued before the court, such 'all moneys' clauses have been upheld, not least in the case which first established that retention of title clauses were effective – *Aluminium Industrie Vaassen BV* v *Romalpa Aluminium Limited* [1976] 1 WLR 676.

(3)   In the case of the 'simple' clause it is necessary for the supplier to relate the goods he identifies as having been supplied by him to specific unpaid invoices since the goods on site at the time of the receiver's appointment might be in fact referable to old invoices which have been paid. Evidence may be adduced regarding the method by which the company used its stocks – for example 'first in first out' or 'last in first out' and the supplier must prove his case on the balance of probabilities. Clear and indelible serial numbers on the goods and on invoices are of great assistance to suppliers under this head of 'identification'.

(4)   In the case of an 'all moneys' clause the supplier has no need to relate the goods to unpaid invoices as title does not pass until all sums owing have been paid. It might be thought that there is an element of commercial nonsense about an 'all moneys' clause in that where there is a running account and there is always a debit balance then the purchaser will never obtain title to any goods, yet that cannot sensibly be said to have been the intention of the parties. The solution is that (in the absence of an express contractual provision to this effect) the

courts will readily imply a licence to on-sell, as they did in the *Romalpa* case itself.

(5) In one situation even a supplier who uses an 'all moneys' clause may have to relate his goods directly to unpaid invoices. Where at some point prior to the receivership the running account reached a nil balance (at which point title to all goods previously supplied will have passed to the purchaser), the supplier may have to show that the goods to which he claims title were supplied after the nil balance was reached and not before. In these circumstances the supplier may find that he has all the difficulties which are encountered by the supplier using a 'simple' clause.

(6) Where goods supplied are mixed with other goods either belonging to the purchaser or to other third parties, there are problems which might be described as problems of identification but which might equally be said to relate to the legal validity of the clause, and they are considered below.

*(d) Legal validity*

The cases have repeatedly stressed that each case must be looked at on its merits, on its own peculiar facts, notwithstanding that there are some general principles which can be gleaned from other cases (see for example the comments of Robert Goff LJ in *Clough Mill Limited* v *Martin* [1985] 1 WLR 111 at p. 114). At one end of the scale there is a case involving goods in their original state and clearly identified and, at the other end, goods which have been irreversibly mixed to form a new product, for example resin soaked into wood shavings and compacted to produce chipboard, upon which set of facts Templeman LJ in *Borden (UK) Ltd* v *Scottish Timber Products Limited* ([1981] Ch. 25 at p. 44) commented, with some feeling:

> 'At some distant date, when the court has unearthed the unearthable, traced the untraceable and calculated the incalculable, there will emerge the sum which it is said belongs to the plaintiffs in equity, a sum which is immune from the claims of Crown and mortgagee, debenture holder and creditor, a sum secured to the plaintiffs by a simple retention of title clause, which referred only to resin but was pregnant with all the consequences alleged in the statement of claim and hidden from the gaze of all other persons who dealt with the defendants'.

Bearing the above in mind, the following points regarding the validity of clauses should be noted:

(1) Assuming that the tests of incorporation and identification can be satisfied, as a matter of legal validity, an appropriately worded clause

¶407

can effectively retain title to goods supplied which remain in their original state and which have not been on-sold by the purchaser. This was confirmed by the Court of Appeal in *Clough Mill Limited* v *Martin* ([1985] 1 WLR 111) overturning the judge at first instance who sought to distinguish the *Romalpa* decision.

(2)   Where the goods supplied have been irreversibly mixed with other goods as part of a manufacturing process, it seems likely that the court will construe any attempt by the supplier to retain or obtain rights in the new product as a charge registrable under s. 395 of the Companies Act 1985 and, if not registered (as in practice is usually the case), void against a liquidator or another creditor of the company. Although the receiver is agent for the company his debenture holder may 'take the section 395 point' (*Re Bond Worth Limited* [1980] Ch. 228). The classic example of the problems which can face a supplier were illustrated by the *Borden* case where a supplier relied on a clause that simply purported to retain title to resin which he knew was going to be, and indeed was, used in the manufacture of chipboard. The attempt by the supplier to claim the proceeds of sale of the new chipboard products failed (Templeman LJ making the comment quoted above).

(3)   Although on the facts before it, it was not necessary for the Court of Appeal in the *Clough Mill* case to comment on cases involving admixture of goods, Robert Goff LJ did so at some length. He started by reciting the argument that a retention of title provision may constitute a charge and considered the decision in *Re Bond Worth Ltd* ([1980] Ch. 228). In that case suppliers failed even in their attempt to retain title to goods in their original state because what they purported to retain was 'equitable and beneficial ownership'. As a matter of property law Slade J felt that the only way such a provision could be construed was by way of a transfer of full legal title to the purchasers with a grant back of rights (of equitable and beneficial ownership) to the supplier. Slade J then made the following general comment (at p. 248):

'In my judgement, any contract which, by way of security for the payment of a debt, confers an interest in property defeasible or destructible upon payment of such debt, or appropriates such property for the discharge of the debt, must necessarily be regarded as creating a mortgage or charge, as the case may be. The existence of the equity of redemption is quite inconsistent with the existence of a bare trustee-beneficiary relationship.'

Robert Goff LJ pointed out that this requires an analysis that title has passed to the purchaser for him to be able to confer an interest in property on the seller. One part of the retention of title provision in the *Clough Mill* case read as follows:

'If any of the material is incorporated in or used as material for other goods before . . . payment the property in the whole of such goods shall be and remain with the seller until such payment has been made, or the other goods have been sold as aforesaid, and all the seller's rights hereunder in the material shall extend to those other goods'.

In a critical passage of his judgment (at pp. 119–20), Robert Goff LJ analysed the effect of this provision and, only with great reluctance, came to the conclusion that it must be construed as a charge:

'Now it is no doubt true that, where A's material is lawfully used by B to create new goods, whether or not B incorporates other material of his own, the property in the new goods will generally vest in B, at least where the goods are not reducible to the original materials: see *Blackstone's Commentaries*, 17th edn (1830) Vol. 2, pp. 404–405. But it is difficult to see why, if the parties agree that the property in the goods shall vest in A, that agreement should not be given effect to. On this analysis, under the last sentence of the condition as under the first [a provision reserving title to goods in their original state], the buyer does not *confer* on the seller an interest in property defeasible upon the payment of the debt; on the contrary, when the new goods come into existence the property in them *ipso facto* vests in the [seller], and [he] thereafter retains [his] ownership in them, in the same way and on the same terms as [he] retains [his] ownership in the unused material. However, in considering the fourth sentence, we have to take into account not only the possibility that the buyer may have paid part of the price for the material, but also that he will have borne the cost of manufacture of the new goods, and may also have provided other materials for incorporation into those goods; and the condition is silent, not only about repaying such part of the price for the material as has already been paid by the buyer, but also about any allowance to be made by the [seller] to the buyer for the cost of manufacture of the new goods, or for any other material incorporated by the buyer into the new goods. Now, no injustice need arise from the exercise of the [seller's] power to resell such goods provided that, having applied the price received from the resale in satisfaction of the outstanding balance of the price owed to [him] by the buyer, [he] is bound to account for the remainder to the buyer. But the difficulty of construing the fourth sentence as simply giving rise to a retention by the [supplier] of title to the new goods is that it would lead to the result that, upon the determination of the contract under which the original material was sold to the buyer, the ownership of the [seller] in the new goods would be retained by the [seller], uninhibited by any terms of the contract which had then ceased to apply; and I find it impossible to believe that it was the intention of the parties that the [seller] would thereby gain the windfall of the full value of the new product, deriving as it may well do not merely from the labour of the buyer but also from materials that were the buyer's, without any duty to account to the buyer for any surplus of the proceeds of sale above the outstanding balance of the price due by the buyer to the [seller]. It follows that the last sentence must be read as creating either a trust or a charge. In my judgement, however, it cannot have been intended to create a trust. Those who insert *Romalpa* clauses in their contracts of sale must be aware that other suppliers might do the same; and the prospect of two lots of material, supplied by different sellers, each subject to a *Romalpa* clause which vests in the seller the legal title in a product manufactured from both lots of material, is not at all sensible. Accordingly, . . . I have come to the conclusion that, although it does indeed do violence to the language of the fourth sentence . . . that sentence must be read as giving rise to a charge on the new goods in favour of the seller.'

The Court of Appeal has thus left open the possibility that a supplier with an appropriate clause can claim title to goods which have become admixed, provided that he deals adequately with what Robert Goff LJ saw as the 'windfall' problem – that is, that if value has been added to the goods supplied by the purchaser, there must be some mechanism for giving credit to the purchaser for that added value, as the court is unlikely to be persuaded that the parties intended the supplier to get the benefit of the additional worth. Where, however, there are a number of suppliers claiming retention of title to a combined product, the task of the suppliers is particularly difficult. As Goff LJ says of such a situation, the 'prospect . . . is not at all sensible'. In a later case coming before the Court of Appeal, *Specialist Plant Services Limited* v *Braithwaite Limited* ([1987] BCLC 1), Balcombe LJ saw *Clough Mill* as a case involving goods in their original state, and in so far as it was authority on admixed goods it was only authority to the effect that simply because one part of a clause attempted to cover admixed goods and was held to be a charge, this did not taint the remainder of the clause and mean that title to goods in their original state could not be effectively retained.

(4)   In attempting to identify where the law draws the line between goods in their original state and goods which have been irreversibly used in a manufacturing process or otherwise lost their identity, two further cases are of interest. In *Hendy Lennox (Industrial Engines) Limited* v *Grahame Puttick Limited* ([1984] 1 WLR 485), the facts were that the supplier had supplied engines intended to be incorporated into generating-sets. One part of the suppliers's claim against the receiver was in respect of an engine which had been attached to a generating-set which had not been on-sold. Having made his now famous comment that 'this area of the law is presently a maze if not a minefield' (at p. 493), Staughton J considered that the suppliers could retake the engine and he said (at p. 494):

> '[I am persuaded] that the proprietory rights of the sellers in the engines were not affected when the engines were wholly or partially incorporated into generator sets. They were not like the Acrilan which became yarn and then carpet (the *Bond Worth* case) or the resin which became chipboard (*Borden's* case) or the leather which became handbags (the *Peachdart* case), . . . They just remained engines, albeit connected to other things.'

Thus, a simple retention of title clause purporting only to cover the goods supplied (and not for example incorporated in a larger product) was sufficient to retain title to an engine which became attached to a generating-set in the context that it was capable of being removed within 'several hours'.

In the case of *Re Peachdart Limited* ([1984] Ch. 131; (1983) 1 BCC 98, 920), Vinelott J had to consider an attempt to reserve title to leather which, at the date of the receiver's appointment, was in three distinct states: first, there was leather in its original form, secondly, leather which had been cut into the shape of handbags and, finally, leather which had been made up into finished and part-finished handbags. Counsel for the receiver conceded that the supplier was entitled to take back the leather in its original state. The supplier failed, however, in respect of the cut leather and the leather made up into handbags. Although the leather remained leather and might therefore be thought to be similar to the engine recovered in the *Hendy Lennox* case, Vinelott J reasoned that the supplier knew the purpose for which the leather was intended and as the leather, once cut, was of little residual value to the supplier (albeit of value to the purchaser for the purposes of his business) it could not have been the intention of the

¶407

parties that, once the manufacturing process had commenced by the leather being cut into shapes, the supplier should retain title.

(5)    A supplier may also wish to recover proceeds of sale of goods which have been on-sold. In the *Romalpa* case, the supplier not only recovered aluminium in its original state but also proceeds of sale of aluminium on-sold by the company prior to the receiver's appointment. There was, however, a critical concession by the counsel for the receiver in that case, in that he conceded that the company held the goods as bailee for the supplier and he therefore effectively conceded that the aluminium was held as fiduciary. From that concession it was easy for the court to say that the proceeds of sale were held on trust for the supplier. That the *Romalpa* case, in this respect, turned on its particular facts was recently reaffirmed in *E. Pfeiffer Weinkellerei-Weinelnkauf GmbH & Company* v *Arbuthnot Factors Limited* (*The Times*, 11 March 1987) where Phillips J said:

> 'It seems to me inappropriate to describe the relationship of a seller and a buyer in possession to whom title has not yet passed as that of a bailor/bailee, for it will not normally have the same incidents as the classic bailment relationship . . . I consider that the normal implication that arises from the relationship of buyer and seller is that if the buyer is permitted to sub-sell in the normal course of business, he will do so for his own account.'

In a succession of cases since *Romalpa*, suppliers have failed to recover the proceeds of sale not only of admixed goods (for example as in *Borden* and *Peachdart* and *Hendy Lennox*) but also goods in their original state as in *Re Andrabell Limited (In Liquidation)* ([1984] 3 All ER 407). From these cases it can be seen that there are a number of points to be borne in mind by a supplier who wishes to recover proceeds of sale. First, it is important to provide specifically in the contract that proceeds of sale belong to the supplier. Secondly, it is important to stipulate that the purchaser takes the goods as fiduciary, and this should be reinforced by an obligation on the purchaser to store the goods separately and clearly marked as belonging to the supplier. Thirdly, the clause ought to stipulate that any on-sale is as agent for the supplier and for the supplier's account. But it is clear from *Hendy Lennox* and *Andrabell* that it will be fatal to a claim for proceeds of sale that there is a fixed credit period offered to the purchaser such that during that credit period the purchaser is free to deal with the goods as it thinks fit. That is, the purchaser can sell the goods yet still not be under an obligation to pay the supplier for them. As Peter Gibson J put it in *Andrabell* (at p. 416): 'It is hard to reconcile this provision with [the supplier's] claim to have an interest in the proceeds of sale'. The supplier's position may be helped by a provision whereby the credit period automatically determines on a resale of the goods. Commercial considerations may militate against the use of such a provision by the supplier. This is true of many other steps a supplier might take to bolster his claims: how many customers will continue to buy from a supplier who insists on separate storage and marking of goods? There is inevitably a tension between the marketing and the credit control aims of suppliers.

(6)   Interesting questions arise when retention of title provisions include a right for the supplier to go on to the land of the purchaser to re-take possession of the goods in certain circumstances. There may be different principles applicable depending upon whether the land is registered or unregistered (see Alexander Hill-Smith, '*The Romalpa Clause in Relation to Land*', NLJ, 4 March 1983, 207).

(7)   It might be asked why the supplier does not attempt to pursue his rights in rem by attempting to recover the goods themselves from a sub-purchaser on the basis that the purchaser could not pass any better title than he has (this is embodied in the Latin maxim: *nemo dat quod non habet*). The answer is usually that the sub-purchaser will not be aware of the rights of the supplier and the purchaser will be in the position of a buyer in possession and therefore able to pass good title to the sub-purchaser under s. 25(1) of the Sale of Goods Act 1979. This principle is confirmed in the case *Four Point Garage Limited* v *Carter* ([1985] 3 All ER 12).

(8)   The proper law of the contract containing the retention of title clause may not be English law and may, for example, be the law of a jurisdiction which gives wider recognition to retention of title clauses. The approach of the court will be to construe the rights of the parties by reference to the proper law of the contract, admitting expert evidence as to the foreign law in question, but ultimately how those rights are to be treated in England will be a matter of English law. Thus where, say, the contract is subject to German law and an attempt has been made to 'retain' title to admixed goods the court will decide, first, what the parties have agreed according to German law. It will, however, go on to decide what effect the agreement of the parties has as a matter of English property law and if German law purports to give the supplier rights over admixed goods the court will say that such rights take effect under English law as a charge (see *Kruppstahl AG* v *Quitmann Products Limited* [1982] ILRM 551).

¶407

**(4)   Trust and other third-party rights**

Where the company holds property on trust for a third party then it is not charged by the debenture and the receiver is unable to realise such property. Trust claims arise in a number of situations and care must be taken by receivers to identify what is and what is not trust property (see for example *Barclays Bank Limited* v *Quistclose Investments Limited* [1970] AC 567, *Carreras Rothmans Limited* v *Freeman Mathews Treasure Limited* [1985] Ch. 207; (1984) 1 BCC 99, 210, *Re Multi Guarantee Co. Ltd* (17 June 1986; Lexis), *Re Chelsea Cloisters Limited* [1981] 41 P&CR 98 and *Re Kayford Limited (In Liquidation)* [1975] 1 WLR 279).

Where the company has, before the start of the receivership, paid money into court in an action, this makes the plaintiff a 'secured' creditor and the receiver is not entitled to recover the moneys paid into court (*W A Sherratt Limited* v *John Bromley (Church Stretton) Limited* [1985] QB 1038).

**(5)   Rights of execution creditors**

The basic rule is that execution creditors must give way to the receiver and the crystallised floating charge unless the execution has been completed before the crystallisation of the charge (*Re Opera Limited* [1891] 3 Ch. 260; cf. *Robson* v *Smith* [1895] 2 Ch. 118). It may be necessary for a receiver to show that he has been validly appointed to defeat the claims of an execution creditor (see *Kasofsky* v *Kreegers* [1937] 4 All ER 374).

A person who obtains a 'Mareva' injunction (see *Mareva Compania Neviera S.A.* v *International Bulk Carriers S.A. Limited* [1975] 2 Lloyd's Rep. 509) does not acquire any property rights against assets within the ambit of the injunction, and therefore the holder of the crystallised floating charge is entitled to have the injunction discharged (*Cretanor Maritime Co. Ltd* v *Irish Marine Management Ltd* [1978] 1 WLR 966).

# ¶408   Prohibitions on charging

What is the effect of a prohibition on charging in a contract, lease or a chose in action? There are two possibilities. First, if the party prohibited does in fact charge the item (say, a contract) that is a breach of the contract giving rise to a right in damages or, possibly, entitling the other party to the contract to terminate it, and the other party cannot be forced to recognise the chargee – but, as between the chargor and chargee, the charge is valid. The alternative theory is that the contract is incapable of being charged and the purported charge is ineffective even as between chargor and chargee. The former view seems more supportable on the ground that, provided the person in whose favour the prohibition operates is not to be affected by the charge and cannot be forced to recognise the rights of the chargee, it should not matter to him that there are contractual relationships affecting only the chargor and chargee.

¶408

Certain comments in *Helstan Securities Limited* v *Hertfordshire County Council* ([1978] 3 All ER 262) seem to support the latter alternative, but these were not necessary for the decision in the case (and see the criticisms of Professor Goode in 'Inalienable Rights?' (1979) 42 MLR 533).

The position in these cases is usually slightly more complicated, in that the provision itself may contain a prohibition on 'assignment' (the *Helstan* case concerned a prohibition on assignment of benefits of a contract) rather than charging as such, and it is often not clear whether this includes assignment by way of security or means simply absolute assignment. When a lender takes security it should ensure, if any particular contract or lease or chose in action is perceived as an important part of the security, that either there is no prohibition or, if there is, consent is given to the charge/assignment.

## ¶409   Better than his principal?

On one view of an administrative receiver's position as agent for the chargor, he can never be in a better position that his principal. There may be exceptions to this rule which highlight the tension between the receiver as enforcer of security for the chargee and 'the administrative machinery' which makes him agent for the chargor. The cases on set-off discussed above (¶407(2)) indicate that the receiver may in a sense act 'in the right of' his debenture holder in collecting debts and refusing to recognise set-offs, even though the set-off might be available as against the company itself of which he is acting as agent (at least until liquidation). As Russell LJ said in *N.W. Robbie and Co. Ltd* v *Witney Warehouse Co. Ltd* ([1963] 1 WLR 1324 at p. 1340):

> 'The argument for the defendants depended very largely on the fact that in this case the receiver and manager was appointed by the debenture holders and that, as is normal, it was provided that the receiver and manager so appointed should be considered to be the agent of the company. Of course the purpose of this agreement between the company and the debenture holders is that the latter should avoid the responsibilities of a mortgagee in possession: but this agency is a reality, as was pointed out in *Gosling* v *Gaskell*. It was, however, accepted that if the receiver and manager had been appointed by the court, the set-off in this case could not have been successfully asserted, because, since such receiver and manager would not have been agent of the company, there would be no "mutuality". It would, I think, be a defect in the law if there was in the present context such a distinction between a receiver and manager appointed by the debenture holders under the common form which makes him agent for the company and a receiver and manager appointed by the court, more especially since at any time the latter may be substituted for the former, and where possible the costs of litigation should be avoided. In both cases the receiver and

manager is a piece of administrative machinery designed to enforce a charge, in the present case (as in most) an equitable charge, on property of the company.'

In the *Airlines Airspares* case (discussed above at ¶406(*b*)) the receiver was held to be in a better position then the company. A similar attitude was taken by Judge O'Donoghue in *Clough Mill Ltd* v *Martin* ([1984] 1 WLR 1067, reversed on appeal on other grounds, see ¶407(3)) when he stated that where a charge was void for want of registration against a liquidator and creditors it was also void against a secured creditor's receiver ([1984] 1 WLR 1067 at p. 1081).

## POWERS OF AN ADMINISTRATIVE RECEIVER

### ¶410    Contractual provisions

Most well-drafted charges or debentures specify the powers that any administrative receiver appointed under it may enjoy and exercise. It is submitted that these powers may not extend beyond the powers which a company could grant to a third party as a matter of contract. For example, as a matter of contract, an adminstrative receiver cannot use the company's corporate seal unless permitted by the Articles of Association of the company, which will stipulate how the company seal may be used (*Industrial Development Authority* v *William T. Moran* [1978] IR 159). Any alteration of the Articles must follow the proper statutory procedure. The same considerations apply to calls of uncalled capital of a company. In general, the Articles of Association will stipulate that the directors should make the call (see Table A, para. 12 – SI 1985 No. 805) and, again, as a contractual matter the power to make a call cannot be given to an administrative receiver.

Often, there will be a wide 'sweeping-up' power in the security. A typical example is:

'Do all such other acts and things as may be considered to be incidental or conducive to any of the matters or powers aforesaid and which the receiver lawfully may or can do as agent for the company.'

This was described as 'an extremely wide power' by Dillon LJ in *Byblos Bank SAL* v *Rushingdale Limited SA and Others* ((1986) 2 BCC 99, 509 at p. 99, 513).

### ¶411    Additional statutory powers

Schedule 1 to the Insolvency Act 1986 sets out certain general powers which are conferred by s. 42 of the Act on administrative receivers. The list is long and widely drawn and will be of particular assistance in cases where, for whatever reason, the security document itself does not give the receiver wide powers.

These statutory powers are identical to those given to an administrator. There is a difference in the manner in which the powers are given to the respective office holders. The administrator is given powers as a matter of statute: 'the administrator of a company . . . has the powers specified in Schedule 1 to this Act . . .' (IA, s. 14(1)). In the case of an administrative receiver, the position is subtly different. Section 42(1) of the Act reads as follows:

'(1) The powers conferred on the administrative receiver of a company by the debentures by virtue of which he was appointed are deemed to include (except in so far as they are inconsistent with any of the provisions of those debentures) the powers specified in Schedule 1 to this Act.'

Thus the powers are given to an administrative receiver as if they were given by contract – that is, as if they were written into the debenture. But, as mentioned above (¶410), as a matter of contract there are certain powers which may not be given to a receiver without altering the Articles of Association of a company (unless the existing wording is wide enough – consider the width of the new Table A, para. 101: SI 1985 No. 805). Power 8 in Schedule 1 is:

'**8.** Power to use the company's seal.'

and power 19 reads as follows:

'**19.** Power to call up any uncalled capital of the company.'

It remains to be seen whether the courts will be able to find a way to give effect to what is clearly the intention of the legislature in the face of what would seem to be an inaccurate way of giving effect to that intention. (The Land Registry is understood to share the author's concern that s. 42 is not as clear as it could be, but has formed the tentative view that an administrative receiver can witness the company's seal as a means of conveying a legal estate in land to a purchaser.) The administrative receiver's power to sell charged property is considered at ¶517 (see IA, s. 15).

## ¶412 Limitations on powers

The general rule is that the powers of the directors of a company to which an administrative receiver is appointed are suspended as against the receiver. It has been called 'a truism' that 'any action which would interfere with the proper discharge of the receiver's function in gathering in the assets of the company, so far as they [are] available, in order to put him in the position to discharge the claims of his appointer [should not be allowed]' (per Shaw LJ in *Newhart Developments Limited* v *Co-Operative Commercial Bank Limited* [1978] 1 QB 814 at p. 819).

Directors do retain certain residual powers. The directors of a company may institute proceedings on behalf of the company against the receiver's appointor (*Newhart Developments Limited* v *Co-Operative Commercial Bank Limited* [1978] 1 QB 814), or against the receiver himself in respect of an improper exercise of his powers (*Watts and Another* v *Midland Bank plc and Others* (1986) 2 BCC 98,961). Further, directors are entitled to receive reasonable information regarding assets and property remaining in a receiver's hands, together with a redemption statement of the secured moneys still outstanding, provided that they are acting in good faith and show to the court an ability to redeem the security (*Gomba Holdings UK Limited and Others* v *Homan and Another* (1986) 2 BCC 99, 102; [1986] 3 All ER 94).

Although it is clear that the effect of liquidation is to terminate a receiver's agency for the company (see ¶404), it is also now clear that liquidation does not prevent the receiver from continuing to act as receiver in order to realise the assets caught by the charge under which he is appointed.[1] The position is succinctly stated by Goulding J in *Sowman* v *David Samuel Trust Limited* ([1978] 1 All ER 616 at p. 623) as follows:

'Winding up deprives the receiver . . . of power to bind the company personally by acting as its agent. It does not in the least affect his powers to hold and dispose of the company's property comprised in the debenture, including his power to use the company's name for that purpose, for such powers are given by the disposition of the company's property which it made (in equity) by the debenture itself. That disposition is binding on the company and those claiming through it, as well in liquidation as before liquidation, except of course where the debenture is vulnerable under [s. 395 of the Companies Act 1985 or s. 245 of the Insolvency Act 1986] or is otherwise invalidated by some provision of law applicable to the winding up.'

The administrative receiver may also bring proceedings in the name of the company notwithstanding liquidation (*Gough's Garages, Limited* v *Pugsley* [1930] 1 KB 615 and *Bacal Contracting Limited* v *Modern Engineering (Bristol) Limited and Others* [1980] 2 All ER 655).

---

[1] *Re Clifton Place Garage Limited* [1970] Ch. 477 does not sit happily alongside the other authorities.

¶412

## ¶413 Exercise of powers in joint appointments

Where two or more administrative receivers are appointed the appointment must state whether anything they are required or authorised to do is to be done by any of them or all of them (IA, s. 231(2), and see ¶310). The more usual arrangement is (for reasons of convenience) that any one office holder is enabled to carry out any acts.

In practice, it is unlikely that two joint appointees, particularly where they are from the same firm, will simultaneously do an act in a manner inconsistent with the act of the other – for example, each selling the same assets to a different purchaser – although the full legal ramifications of such an event have rarely if ever, been the subject of analysis.

## ¶414 The administrative receiver as 'office holder'

Part VI of the Insolvency Act 1986 (ss. 230–46) contains certain 'miscellaneous provisions' which relate to 'office-holders'. These sections should be considered with care as not all of them apply to administrative receivers. Particular points of relevance to administrative receivers are described below.

(1) One problem which used to be faced by a receiver was that monopoly suppliers such as gas boards, electricity boards, etc. would refuse to provide a supply to the company in receivership unless the existing outstanding arrears were settled. A receiver would be reluctant to accord pre-preferential status to such unsecured claims even where there were sufficient funds to pay the arrears. One technique which was used with some success was to hive-down the business to a subsidiary and the subsidiary would make an application for a supply in its own right. This practice did not meet with universal acceptance by suppliers. The need for such arrangements has been removed. Where an administrative receiver requests a supply of gas, electricity, water or telecommunication services, the supplier may not make it a condition of supply that pre-receivership arrears are paid, although the supplier can require a personal guarantee of payment for the supply to be given by the administrative receiver (IA, s. 233).

(2) The administrative receiver may ask the court to require a person who has in his possession or under his control, property, books, papers or records to which the company appears to be entitled to pass these items over to the receiver either forthwith or within a period of time laid down by the court (IA, s. 234(2)).

(3) Certain officers or former officers, employees, former employees and those concerned in the formation of a company, must give the administrative receiver, to the extent reasonably required by him, infor-

mation about the company and its promotion, formation, business, dealings, affairs or property (IA, s. 235(2)–(4)). The receiver can also require such persons to 'attend' on him as he reasonably requires (IA, s. 235(2)(*b*)). The sanction for non compliance by a relevant person is a fine (IA, s. 235(5)), and it is an example of unfit conduct for the purposes of disqualification of directors (CDDA, Sch. 1, para. 10(*g*), and see ¶415).

(4)  Previously, it was only a liquidator in a winding up by the court who could cause those with knowledge about the company's affairs or property to be brought before the court (CA, s. 561), although it was thought that a voluntary liquidator's general right to seek the assistance of the court (CA, s. 602) could be made to operate in a similar manner. By s. 236 of the Insolvency Act 1986, an administrative receiver may apply to the court for an officer of the company or a person who may possess company property or who may have information relating to the company to appear before the court. The court may require an affidavit from that person relating to the matters in question (IA, s. 236(2)–(3)). The court can issue a warrant for the arrest of anyone who, without reasonable excuse, does not appear on a summons or who appears to be about to abscond, and any property in the person's possession may be seized (IA, s. 236(4)–(6)). The court has wide powers to make consequential orders in respect of these matters (IA, s. 237).

# DUTIES OF AN ADMINISTRATIVE RECEIVER

## ¶415   To report on unfit directors

One of the principal weaknesses of the old system for apprehending directors who behaved improperly was that the mechanism for gathering and reporting information was limited. An important part of the new approach is consolidated in the Company Directors Disqualification Act 1986 (formerly s. 12(5) of the Insolvency Act 1985 – the relevant provisions being in force since 28 April 1986), and provides that administrative receivers (and administrators and liquidators) are under a positive duty to report in detail to the Secretary of State for Trade and Industry where they are satisfied that certain directors or shadow directors of the company are unfit to be concerned in the management of the company (CDDA, ss. 6, 7 and 22(5)). The relevant directors or shadow directors are those who were directors or shadow directors of the company, and during or any time after their tenure of office the company became insolvent (CDDA, s. 6(1)(*a*)). 'Insolvency' for these purposes means that the company has gone into liquidation at a time when its assets are insufficient for the payment of its debts, liabilities and expenses of the winding up, or an administration order is made, or an administrative receiver is appointed (CDDA, s. 6(2)).

The disqualification scheme works according to a series of filters. First, it has to appear to the administrative receiver that the unfitness conditions are satisfied. Where this is so he must forthwith submit an adverse report to the Secretary of State (CDDA, s. 7(3)). The Secretary of State has up to two years from the date of the commencement of the insolvency (save where the court gives specific leave) to make an application to the court for a disqualification order (CDDA, s. 7(2)). The Secretary of State makes his application if he considers it 'expedient in the public interest' that a disqualification order should be made (CDDA, s. 7(1)). The court must make the disqualification order where it is satisfied that the person was a director or shadow director of a company which became insolvent and that his conduct as a director of the company, either alone or taking into account other company directorships, makes him unfit to be concerned in the management of the company (CDDA, s. 6(1)).

To bring an element of objectivity into the concept of 'unfitness', the First Schedule to the Company Directors Disqualification Act 1986 details certain 'badges of unfitness' to be taken into account when the question of unfitness is considered (CDDA, s. 9). Schedule 1, which is a non-exclusive list of unfit conduct (CDDA, s. 9(1)), is set out in Appendix 6 below. The Schedule is split into two. There are provisions in the Company Directors Disqualification Act which enable disqualification orders to be made outside the insolvency context, and the matters referred to in Pt. 1 of the Schedule apply to those cases as well as to the insolvency cases. The matters referred to in Pt. 2 of the Schedule apply exclusively to cases where the company has become insolvent. The range of conduct covered is wide and it includes any misfeasance or breach of duty and the extent of the director's responsibility for the company becoming insolvent. A failure by a director or shadow director to cooperate with the administrator, as required by s. 235 of the Insolvency Act 1986, may consititute evidence of unfitness (CDDA, Sch. 1, para. 10(*g*), and see ¶414(3)).

The duty of the administrative receiver is to report 'forthwith' when it appears to him that the relevant conditions are satisfied. Disqualification is a serious matter. The effect of a disqualification order is that, for a specified period, the relevant person may not, without the leave of the court, be a director, liquidator, administrator, or receiver or manager of a company's property or in any way, whether directly or indirectly, be concerned or take part in the promotion, formation or management of a company (CDDA, s. 1(1)). The phrase is very wide in its scope (see *R* v *Campbell (Archibald*

¶415

*James)* [1984] BCLC 83). The minimum period of disqualification is two years and the maximum fifteen years (CDDA s. 6(4)). In view of the seriousness of an allegation of unfitness, it would seem that an insolvency practitioner is entitled to take a reasonable amount of time to examine the evidence before making up his mind, and, in an appropriate case, reporting to the Secretary of State. There will be cases of patent misconduct where an adverse report will be submitted very quickly.

Prescribed forms for the submission of reports are set out in the Schedule to The Insolvent Companies (Reports on Conduct of Directors) No. 2 Rules 1986. The full adverse report form is Form D2 and the 'interim return' (discussed below) is Form D5. The Department of Trade and Industry have issued guidance notes to practitioners regarding the completion of forms ('Disqualification of Directors: Completion of Statutory Reports and Returns'). The statutory forms D2 and D5 (in common with the forms for the other office holders) state at the top 'before completing this form read the DTI guidance notes'. The notes give examples of the types of questions that the practitioner should ask himself when considering the various badges of unfitness in the Schedule to the Company Directors Disqualification Act 1986. That 'unfitness' is to be considered as a reasonably serious allegation is indicated by the Department's advice in the guidance notes that:

> 'In forming a view of conduct which may be considered unfit office holders are asked not to take a pedantic view of isolated technical failures, e.g. the occasional lapse in filing Annual Returns etc., but to form an objective view of the director's conduct. It is also stressed that the officer is required to consider matters of conduct on the basis of information acquired in the course of his normal duties and by reference to the books and records available to him *and is not obliged to undertake investigations which he would not otherwise have considered it necessary to make.*' (Emphasis in the original.)

It is noteworthy that para. 14 of Form D2(B) requires details of the remuneration and other benefits received by the criticised director in the three years prior to the insolvency. Further, para. 11 requires details of the director's 'trade or profession', and for an example of the courts taking a different attitude to non-professionals see *Department of Health and Social Security* v *Evans and Others* ([1985] 2 All ER 471) and compare *Dorchester Finance Ltd* v *Stebbings* ((1977), unreported).

There is a second reporting requirement imposed on office holders by the Conduct Rules. A form of interim return must be submitted in *every* case within six months of the commencement of the receivership. The relevant form, D5, requires the administrative receiver to explain why he has not submitted a report either at all or on some only of the directors. He either has to state that this is because he is not aware of matters which require him to report or that 'sufficient information is not yet to hand'.

Although there is nothing in the Act or Rules to this effect, reports by administrative receivers would appear to be an example of statements which attract qualified privilege and hence, in the absence of malice, a receiver will not be liable in defamation (see *Stuart v Bell* [1891] 2 QB 341). Care should be taken to ensure that the report and any drafts of it are kept confidential and not circulated.

The Act and the Rules do not give guidance on how the rules of natural justice might apply to the reporting requirements. The questions in the DTI guidance notes suggest that it is envisaged that there will have been communication between the receiver and the directors (for example in a number of places the administrative receiver is asked to set out any explanations which have been given by the relevant director). In most cases it is likely that the receiver will have discussed the facts with the directors to ensure that he has a clear picture of events. In some cases the facts will be so clear and/or the directors so unhelpful that such meetings will be unlikely to take place.

As indicated by the extract from the DTI guidance notes set out above, the receiver is not expected to do anything by way of investigation that he would not otherwise do in the ordinary course of his duties. Where in the ordinary course of his duties he comes across matters which excite suspicion, he should clarify such matters by making appropriate enquiries.

## ¶416   Duties owed to the company and others

The general position was summed up by the judgment of Sir Neil Lawson in *Hemlata Lathia* v *Dronsfield Brothers Limited and Others* ([1987] BCLC 321) when he said (at p. 324):

> 'On authority, one must look at the context to determine to whom the duties are owed. Primarily, [receivers] owe a duty to their debenture holders, and also as agents to the company. In my judgment, they do not owe a duty to the general creditors, to contributors, to officers of the company, and members. They also owe a duty to guarantors (see *American Express International Banking Corporation* v *Hurley* [1985] 3 All ER 564). But that is a secondary liability. It is clear on the authorities, and no authority has been cited to the contrary, that the receivers do not owe a duty to the creditors of the company or to contributors.'

An administrative receiver was not formerly considered to be an officer of the company for the purposes of misfeasance proceedings (*Re B. Johnson and*

*Co. (Builders) Limited* [1955] 1 Ch. 634 – but the summary remedy is now available against him (IA s. 212(1)(*b*)). The duty of the receiver to the company must be subordinated to his duty to his debenture holder (see ¶402 and 403). The content of the duty owed to the company may be considered under various heads.

### (1)   Reasonable care in realization

The law in this area was neatly summarised by Mann J in *American Express International Banking Corporation* v *Hurley* ((1986) 2 BCC 98, 993 at p. 99, 000; [1986] 3 All ER 564 at p. 571):

'I propose to proceed on the basis that the following propositions represent the law:

(i) The mortgagee when selling mortgaged property is under a duty to a guarantor of the mortgagor's debt to take reasonable care in all the circumstances of the case to obtain the true market value of that property.

(ii) A receiver is under a like duty.

(iii) The mortgagee is not responsible for what a receiver does whilst he is the mortgagor's agent unless the mortgagee directs or interferes with the receiver's activities.

(iv) The mortgagee is responsible for what a receiver does whilst he is the mortgagee's agent and acting as such.'

The leading case in this area is *Cuckmere Brick Co. Ltd and Another* v *Mutual Finance Limited* ([1971] 1 Ch. 949) where mortgagees were found to have breached their duty of care in exercising a power of sale by failing to obtain a proper price (Cross and Cairns L JJ) or its 'true market value' (Salmon LJ). The breach in this case involved a failure to publicise a planning permission for flats which related to the property sold and a failure to postpone an auction which had been arranged when the failure to publicise the planning permission was pointed out by the mortgagors. Salmon LJ summarised the position as follows (in a passage recently quoted with approval by Fox LJ in *Predeth* v *Castle Phillips Finance Co. Ltd, Estates Gazette*, 27 September 1986):

'I accordingly conclude, both on principle and authority, that a mortgagee in exercising his power of sale does owe a duty to take reasonable precautions to obtain the true market value of the mortgaged property at the date on which he decides to sell it. No doubt in deciding whether he has fallen short of that duty the facts must be looked at broadly, and he will not be adjuged to be in default unless he is plainly on the wrong side of the line'.

¶416

This comment contains an implication that the mortgagee has a discretion as to *when* he sells, provided that the proper value is obtained when he does so.

A receiver owes a duty to the company similar to that of a mortgagee, as is shown by *Standard Chartered Bank Limited v Walker and Another* ([1982] 3 All ER 938) where Lord Denning MR said (at p. 942):

> 'The receiver is the agent of the company, not of the debenture holder, the bank. He owes a duty to use reasonable care to obtain the best possible price which the circumstances of the case permit. He owes this duty not only to the company (of which he is the agent) to clear off as much of its indebtedness to the bank as possible, but he also owes a duty to the guarantor, because the guarantor is liable only to the same extent as the company. The more the overdraft is reduced, the better for the guarantor. It may be that the receiver can choose the time of sale within a considerable margin, but he should, I think, excercise a reasonable degree of care about it'.

Fox LJ commented: 'It is not disputed that a mortgagee can choose his own time for sale but . . . the sale must be a proper sale and must be properly organised.'

The following points should be noted:

(1)   The administrative receiver must take reasonable care to obtain the proper price or market value (which in most cases will amount to the same thing), and will be liable to the company if he does not do so and liable also to any guarantor of the company's debt.

(2)   It is not clear whether the receiver is under a clear duty to delay a sale for any length of time because market conditions are bad. It may be that the comment (given above) of Lord Denning MR concerning the time for sale means that it would not, for example, be appropriate to hold an auction sale on Christmas Day.

(3)   This area of the law most often comes under scrutiny when a lender seeks to enforce a guarantee and the guarantor seeks to set up as a defence and counterclaim the alleged negligence of the lender's receiver. Although the guarantor may have a primary right of action against the receiver, he may not bring into account any negligence of a receiver in an action brought by the lender (as Lord Denning MR put it in *Standard Chartered* at p. 942) '. . . except in so far as [the lender] gives him directions or interferes with his conduct of the realization'.

(4)   The receiver can be negligent for failing to take specialist advice on the valuation of particular types of equipment and for failing to

¶416

advertise in specialist press (*American Express International Banking Corporation* v *Hurley* [1986] 3 All ER 564).

(5)   There is a rule (called the 'fair dealing' or 'self dealing' rule by Peter Gibson J in *Watts* v *Midland Bank plc and Others* [1986] 2 BCC 99,961 at p. 98,968) which imposes special duties where a mortgagee sells to a company in which it is interested. The rule is neatly summarised by the headnote to the Privy Council case *Tse Kwong Lam* v *Wong Chit Sen and Others* ([1983] BCLC 88):

> 'There was no hard and fast rule forbidding a mortgagee from exercising his power of sale to sell the mortgaged property to a company in which he was interested. However, to uphold such a sale, a mortgagee had to show that the sale was in good faith and that he took reasonable steps to secure the best price reasonably obtained at the time of sale, but there was no obligation on a mortgagee to postpone the sale in the hope of obtaining a better price or to adopt a piecemeal method of sale which could only be carried out over a substantial period or at risk of loss. Where mortgaged property was sold to a company in which the mortgagee had an interest, such a sale had to be closely scrutinised, and the onus was on the mortgagee to prove that he acted fairly and used his best endeavours to obtain the best price reasonably obtainable at the time of the sale. Sale by auction in these circumstances did not necessarily prove the validity of the transaction. Normally a mortgagee who wished to secure the sale of mortgaged property to a company in which he was interested would have to take expert advice on the methods necessary to secure the best price obtainable and, if the sale is by auction, on the reserve price.'

Although dealing with a mortgagee's duties, this case may have implications for administrative receivers.

### (2)   Provision of information

The case of *Smiths Limited* v *Middleton* ([1979] 3 All ER 842), as interpreted by *Gomba Holdings (UK) Limited and Others* v *Homan and Another* ((1986) 2 BCC 99, 102; [1986] 3 All ER 94), is authority for the proposition that where a receivership has come to an end, the company is entitled to full accounts from the receiver over and above his statutory duty to file his receipts and payments account (see IA, s. 41 and IR, r. 3.32).

The position is different while the receivership continues, as Hoffmann J explained in the *Gomba* case cited above (99, 102 at p. 99, 107; 94 at p. 99):

> 'During the receivership, the company's right to information beyond the statutory accounts must in my judgment depend upon demonstrating a

"need to know" for the purpose of enabling the board to exercise its residual rights to perform its duties.'

The problems facing directors who do not have control of the company's books and records yet still have duties under the Companies Act as director were discussed in the *Smiths Limited* case by Blackett-Ord V-C who commented as follows (at p. 847):

'During the receivership, the keeping of accounts obviously requires co-operation between the company and the receiver, because although the directors are still, I think, liable technically under s. 147 of the 1948 Act and its successor, clearly they may have to get the necessary information from the receiver . . . it may, not necessarily will, be practically impossible for the directors to keep within their technical obligations without his assistance.'

An administrative receiver's duty to report to creditors, to hold a creditors' meeting, and to provide information to a creditors' committee, are considered at ¶420–22.

**(3)  To cooperate**
An administrative receiver, like an administrator, has a duty to cooperate with the official receiver where the company is being wound up by the court (IA, s. 235).

**(4)  Generally**
Where an administrative receiver discovers a transaction of the company which is to the company's benefit, he may be under a duty to cause the company to fulfil the transaction (*Lawson (Inspector of Taxes) v Hosemaster Co. Ltd* [1966] 1 WLR 1300). This duty was explained by Danckwerts LJ in the *Lawson* case (at p. 1314):

'The whole transaction was so advantageous to the finances of Hosemaster that the receiver of Hosemaster would have been foolish not to adopt and ratify the operations conducted on behalf of Hosemaster . . . and, if he had refused to adopt the transaction, he would, in our opinion, have been in default as regards his duty.'

## ¶417   To make distributions

The distributions of an administrative receiver are considered below in Chapter 6.

## ¶418   Notification

Consideration has already been given to the formalities which must be observed immediately after the appointment of an administrative receiver (see

¶313). In addition, and this applies to every receiver or manager of property of a company, all invoices, purchase orders, and business letters of the company which bear the company's name must state that a receiver and manager has been appointed (IA, s. 39(1)). The company, and anyone who knowingly and wilfully authorises or permits a breach of this provision, is liable to a fine (IA, s. 39(2)).

## ¶419   Statement of affairs

An administrative receiver has a duty to call forthwith on his appointment for a statement of affairs to be prepared and submitted to him (IA, s. 47(1) and Form 3.1). He would seem to have a duty under the Insolvency Act 1986 to call for the statement of affairs, although r. 3.3(1) uses language which suggests that he has a discretion.

The provisions of s. 47 of the Act and rr. 3.3–3.7 (and see Form 3.2) bear a marked similarity to the provisions for the statement of affairs to be submitted to administrators under s. 22 of the Act and rr. 2.11–2.15. For a discussion of those provisions see ¶1011.

## ¶420   Report to creditors

The new legislation has, in many places, given the force of law to what was formerly merely good practice. The responsible receiver generally kept creditors of a company which was in receivership reasonably well informed, and s. 48 of the Insolvency Act 1986 embodies provisions requiring an administrative receiver to produce a written report for the creditors. The report has to be produced within three months of his appointment, or longer if the court allows (IA, s. 48(1)). It has to be sent to the Registrar of Companies (see Form 3.10), trustees for secured creditors, and, to the extent that he is aware of their addresses, to all secured creditors (IA, s. 48 (1)). The report has to cover the events leading up to the receiver's appointment to the extent that he knows about them, his carrying on of the business of the company or disposals or proposed disposals of assets or property, the sums outstanding to his appointor, the amounts payable to preferential creditors, and an estimate of any surplus funds likely to be available for unsecured creditors (IA, s. 48(1)(*a*)–(*d*)).

The unsecured creditors are entitled to see the report. Within three months of his appointment or a longer period allowed by the court the receiver can either send a copy to all unsecured creditors to the extent he is aware of their addresses or else he can publish an address to which unsecured creditors can write for a free copy of the report (IA, s. 48(2)). The address has to be published by way of a notice in the newspaper in which the appointment was advertised (IR, r. 3.8(1)).

The administrative receiver has to call a meeting of the unsecured creditors (on 14-days notice) to consider his report, whether he sends all the creditors a copy or merely gives them the opportunity to write in for one (IA, s. 48(2)).

The administrative receiver may apply to the court for an order that he need not hold a meeting of the unsecured creditors, but there are three points to note in this regard. First, the report has to indicate that he intends to apply for such a direction (IA, s. 48(3)(*a*)). Secondly, the report must be sent or the notice published at least 14 days before the hearing of the application (IA, s. 48(3)(*b*)). And thirdly, the report or the notice must give the time, date and place fixed by the court for the hearing (IR, r. 3.8.(2)).

The receiver's report should include a summary of the statement of affairs submitted to him and any comments he may have on it. A copy of the statement of affairs and any affidavits of concurrence must be attached to the copy of the report sent to the Registrar of Companies (IA, s. 48(5) and IR, r. 3.8(3)). If the receiver has not yet received the statement of affairs or the affidavits by the time he files his report with the Registrar of Companies he is to submit the relevant documents whenever he receives them (IR, r. 3.8(4) and Form 3.3).

The administrative receiver is liable to a fine if he fails, without reasonable excuse, to comply with his obligations in respect of the report (IA, s. 48(8)). There is an important proviso that he is not obliged to put anything in his report which 'would seriously prejudice the carrying out . . . of his functions' (IA, s. 48(6)). What is envisaged is that he should not, for example, be obliged to explain in detail any negotiations with purchasers which might be jeopardised by disclosure. In view of the risk of criminal liability, an administrative receiver might be inclined, in cases of doubt, to seek the directions of the court under s. 35 of the Insolvency Act 1986.

## ¶421   Meetings of creditors

The meeting of creditors (summoned under s. 48(2) of the Act to consider the administrative receiver's report) is a novel concept in receiverships. The Rules envisage one meeting, although there is provision for adjournment (IR, r. 3.14). There will be no creditors' meeting where the company goes into liquidation and the receiver sends the liquidator a copy of his report within seven days of sending it to the Registrar of Companies, etc. (IA, s. 48(4)). Where the company is in liquidation, the liquidator will give information to, and speak for, the unsecured creditors. It may be that, in an appropriate case, an administrative receiver can petition for the winding up of the company (which he has power to do – IA, Sch. 1, para. 21) in order to avoid the cost and expense of a creditors' meeting in the receivership.

Rules 3.9–3.15 set out the details for the meeting and they are not dissimilar to many of the rules governing meetings in an administration (see ¶1106). The meeting would appear to have two purposes only. First, to consider the receiver's report and secondly, if it thinks fit, to establish a creditors' committee (IA, s. 49(1)). The meeting of creditors may elect a creditors' committee and there must be at least three and not more than five members (IR, r. 3.16).

## ¶422   The creditors' committee

The committee's function is to 'assist the administrative receiver in discharging his functions and act in relation to him in such manner as may be agreed from time to time' (IR, r. 3.18(1)). It may be useful to the receiver to use the creditors' committee as a sounding board for any difficult decisions he may have to take, and it will no doubt assist him (should he ever be criticised later by a liquidator for any of his actions) that his decision had the backing of the creditors' committee. The committee is to meet when and where the receiver decides (IR, r. 3.18(2)). The receiver does have a duty to call the first meeting within three months of the committee being established, however, and thereafter within 21 days of a request for a meeting by a committee member or his representative, and to call a meeting on a specific date if the committee had previously resolved to meet on that date (IR, r. 3.18(3)). The receiver is to give seven days written notice of the date, time and place of any meeting, although it is possible for the notice to be waived before or at the meeting (IR, r. 3.18(4)). Many of the rules governing the creditors' committee (IR, rr. 3.16–30 and see Forms 3.4 and 3.5) are similar to those applicable to an administration and these are discussed below (see ¶1107). The only power which the creditors' committee possesses is its ability on seven days' notice to require the administrative receiver to attend before it at some reasonable time and to give it such information relating to his functions as it reasonably requires (IA, s. 49(2)). Where the committee has resolved to require the administrative receivers' attendance it must send a notice to him in writing signed by a majority of the members of the committee or their representatives (IR, r. 3.28(1)). The committee may fix the day for the meeting but the receiver is entitled to determine the time and place (IR, r. 3.28(2)). At this meeting, the committee may elect a chairman instead of the receiver or his nominee (IR, r. 3.28(3), and compare r. 3.19). Should this power be abused by a committee it would seem open to the receiver to ask the court to rule that the committee is not fulfilling its function of assisting him in discharging his functions (IA, s. 35 and IR, r. 3.18). There would appear to be no specific sanction where a receiver fails to comply with the request of the committee.

The committee has a duty to review the adequacy of the administrative receiver's security from time to time (IR, r. 12.8(2)).

## ¶423 Enforcement of duties

The company is the proper plaintiff to bring an action against an administrative receiver for breach of duty and may properly bring such an action during the receivership (*Watts and Another v Midland Bank plc and Others* [1986] 1 BCLC 15, and see ¶412).

# 5   Fulfilling the Purpose of the Receivership

## THE EARLY DAYS

### ¶501   Preliminary steps

It is important that an administrative receiver swiftly takes control of the assets and property of a company over which he has been appointed. He will wish to arrive at the site of the company's business with sufficient staff to ensure that assets remain on site and can be documented. It is also important for him to emphasise that there has been a change in control and that the directors' former powers have ceased. The importance of a smooth assumption of control should not be underestimated. The loss of power can be difficult for directors to accept but any attempt by the directors to prevent the receiver from taking control should be met by an application to court for injunctive relief. The financial difficulties of the company witnessed by the appointment of an administrative receiver will be of great concern to the workforce. It will be important to the receiver to keep the morale of the staff high, both from the point of view of his trading and from the point of view of presenting an attractive package to a potential purchaser.

The steadying effect that the appointment of a receiver can have on a company's position often results in the withdrawal of threats to wind up the company by creditors, and they may instead deal with the receiver on the basis of fresh trading in the receivership.

If the company has a number of locations then the receiver will ensure that members of his staff attend at those locations at the same time as he takes control at the main site, although there are no hard and fast rules in such matters.

The receiver will wish to ensure that no assets leave the premises without his approval. In the event that creditors (for example suppliers with a claim to retention of title to goods) arrive at the company's premises and seek to remove the goods to which they claim title, they are normally refused access, at least until their claim has been investigated. Should the creditors or their representatives seek physically to remove their assets notwithstanding that permission has been refused, the conventional response is immediately to seek the assistance of the police (whose approach in most cases is to preserve the status quo and to require the creditors to pursue their civil remedies in the courts).

An administrative receiver will not wish to seize goods which do not belong to the company and hence are not caught by the security. There is a danger of personal liability in tort for so doing. Section 234 of the Insolvency Act 1986 may be of assistance in an appropriate case. It provides that where an administrative receiver seizes goods which are not the property of the company and believes, on reasonable grounds, that he is entitled to do so, he is not liable for loss or damage resulting from the seizure save where he has been negligent and, further, he has a lien on the property for any costs he may have incurred in seizure (IA, s. 234(3)–(4)). There may be an argument that it will be reasonable for a receiver to assume that assets on the company's premises belong to the company and, if that is so, negligence will only arise where he fails to take reasonable steps to ascertain the true position – which may involve instructing his lawyers promptly. Should the receiver's lawyers negligently advise that the company does own assets, will the receiver be liable for that negligence? In *Cuckmere Brick Co. Ltd* v *Mutual Finance Limited* ([1971] 1 Ch. 949), the Court of Appeal seemed to think that the mortgagee would be liable to the mortgagor where the breach of duty of the mortgagee was caused by the negligence of the mortgagee's agents, and the same principle may apply to negligence of the receiver's lawyer as, otherwise, there might be no remedy for the aggrieved creditor.

Most administrative receivers have arrangements with their insurers whereby they have insurance cover from the instant they are appointed, and the provision of details of the items covered are forwarded in due course. Where there are particular risks against which he seeks cover, the receiver will wish to put his insurers on notice of these at the earliest opportunity.

## ¶502    Establishment of procedures

Most insolvency practitioners have their own checklists, guides and procedures which they will follow in a receivership. A chain of command will be established in order that employees of the company know to whom they are to report and from whom they are to take instructions. It will be normal for employees to be told that no orders are to be placed or agreements entered into or liabilities otherwise incurred on behalf of the company without the express authority of the receiver or a specified member of his staff. In due course authority in these areas may be given to employees as it may be impractical for the receiver or his staff to take every decision, however routine.

At an early stage the administrative receiver may instruct valuers to compile schedules of assets and to assist in the preparation of any sales literature he may want to issue. He may wish to take specific advice from specialist valuers on price and method of sale of specialised items (see *American Express International Banking Corporation* v *Hurley* (1986) 2 BCC 98, 993; [1985] 3 All ER 564).

It is preferable for receivers to have the security and their appointment checked by their lawyers prior to acceptance of the appointment. In practice this may not happen, in which event the receiver should instruct his lawyers to advise as soon as possible after he has taken office.

An administrative receiver will wish to have compiled details of the size and nature of the workforce of the company and their terms and conditions of employment. The potential liabilities of a receiver in respect of employees is discussed below (¶511) and in order that he can assess any potential personal liability he must know who the employees are, precisely what their terms of employment are, what their accrued rights as regards redundancy and unfair dismissal are, and whether there is trade union involvement with the workforce to which the receiver should have regard. It is particularly important to check that there are no employees who are ill, abroad or on holiday and who might otherwise be missed in the census (see *Nicoll* v *Cutts* (1985) 1 BCC 99, 427). The receiver may only have 14 days from his appointment in which to take a number of important steps as regards employees.

An administrative receiver should be conscious of his duty to report unfit directors and shadow directors, and relevant information should be assembled from the first days of the receivership.

As part of the rebuilding of confidence in the business of the company, the receiver will wish to reassure suppliers and customers of the company that (if it is the case) he intends to trade and would hope to sell the business as a going concern.

# TRADING

## ¶503   To trade or not to trade?

The administrative receiver's duty is to realise the assets and property to achieve the best price reasonably obtainable. It is not unknown for companies in receivership to trade so successfully that sufficient profits are generated to pay the secured creditors and indeed to pay the unsecured creditors, such that the company comes out of receivership and is able to carry on trading. There is no necessity that a company should lapse into liquidation or be struck off after it has been in receivership.

In the majority of cases the reason for trading on is that the price which can be realized on a sale of a going concern will be greater than that which can be realized on a break-up basis. The receiver has to weigh against that any losses which may be incurred during the period of receivership trading. The receiver may wish to trade on in order to wind down the business in an orderly manner, perhaps to convert stock and work in progress into debts and to ensure there are no breaches of existing contracts which might prevent the recovery of existing debts from those debtors.

The danger for an administrative receiver is that he may be criticised by preferential creditors for dissipating moneys in trading losses which would otherwise have been available to pay them (see below ¶601–3). The receiver's conduct will be judged in the round. Two extremes might be considered as examples: it is submitted that it is reasonable and not negligent for a receiver to trade at a small loss where he is advised by his valuers that there is every likelihood of selling the business as a going concern and the price thereby achieved is likely to be markedly higher than on a sale at break up. If he fails to sell as a going concern and the trading losses have to be deducted from the forced sale prices achieved for the assets then he should not be liable to the preferential creditors for the reduced amount of their dividend. Alternatively, where trading losses are likely to be large and the possibility of selling the business as a going concern is no more than a hope, the receiver might have difficulty in justifying himself to the preferential creditors in the event that he does trade on and fails to sell as a going concern. Between those extremes, the receiver has to consider his duties carefully.

The above analysis of potential liability for a receiver applies also to his potential liability to his appointor where the preferential creditors are paid in full and hence the loss is suffered by the charge holder under its floating charge. Similarly, he may be liable to the company where both the preferential creditors and the secured creditor are paid in full but the surplus is less than it would have been if the receiver had not been negligent.

## ¶504   Hiving-down

'Hiving-down' has an undeserved reputation. It is sometimes misunderstood as a form of conjuring trick with the company's assets which operates to the detriment of the company's creditors. (See, for example, O'Donovan, *Company Receivers and Managers*, at p. 67 '. . . to allow a receiver and manager to strip the company of its prime assets by transferring them through a subsidiary company appears to be a little harsh on the unsecured creditors.')

Hiving-down is one means of realising a company's assets and is a transfer of assets from the company in receivership to a newly formed subsidiary company.[1] The price for the assets is left outstanding between the subsidiary

---

[1] Employees of the transferor do not follow the undertaking in the case of a hive-down by a receiver, liquidator or administrator as they do on a simple transfer of an undertaking – see reg. 4 of the Transfer of Undertakings (Protection of Employment) Regulations 1981, and ¶515(1) and ¶1114.

and the parent with a provision for it to be certified by an expert in the absence of agreement between the parties (alternatively the assets may be injected in consideration for shares in the subsidiary). Once a purchaser has been found for the business, the price he is prepared to pay is substituted into the agreement in place of the provision for certification and the shares in the subsidiary will be sold to the purchaser. As the company in receivership owns the shares in the subsidiary and in the light of the debt it is owed by the subsidiary, the company may be thought to be in no worse position than it was when it owned the business itself.

There are usually three principal reasons for hiving-down. One is to preserve tax losses of the business (see ss. 252 and 483 of the Taxes Act 1970) but, as discussed below (¶808), the tax advantage has been greatly reduced. Another reason for hiving-down may be to attempt to avoid any personal liability of the receiver. Where the trade is particularly dangerous it may be thought better to trade through a limited company rather than risk any possibility of the receiver incurring liability in his receivership. This is particularly important on the company going into liquidation, as his agency for the company terminates on liquidation and he may be personally liable thereafter (see ¶404). The final reason usually given for hiving-down is to present a going-concern package of the most attractive parts of a business for a purchaser. This might be thought to be a minimal advantage and as regards potential liabilities it is better for a purchaser to buy assets rather than shares.

Considerations which militate against hiving-down are that it may be administratively inconvenient and time-consuming to have to operate two sets of books and records. Should the subsidiary ever become insolvent arguments may be advanced that the receiver is a shadow director of the subsidiary for the purposes of wrongful trading (IA, s. 214). Further, major firms of accountants might feel uneasy to find one of 'their' companies had become insolvent and liability may not, in practice, be as limited as it appears.

## ¶505   Set-off

An administrative receiver should agree with unsecured creditors with whom he trades in the receivership that any possible rights to set-off they may have are expressly excluded. There are arguments available that after the commencement of receivership trading is not 'in the same right' and therefore there is no right of set-off (see for example *Rendell* v *Doors & Doors in liquidation* [1975] 2 NZLR 191) but it is preferable that there should be an express contractual exclusion.

## TRADING AND OTHER LIABILITIES

### ¶506   Reservation of title

An administrative receiver may be liable in tort for interference with goods if he disposes or deals with assets belonging to third parties, such as goods supplied to the company on effective reservation of title terms. There is a statutory exemption from liability for disposal of third-party items in the same terms as that for seizure of goods (IA, s. 234(3)–(4), and see ¶517 and ¶1122 regarding the meaning of 'disposal').

In the case of a manufacturing company, an administrative receiver can be faced with a multiplicity of claims to reservation of title. It may be a difficult task in those circumstances to prevent action by one or more of such suppliers which results in the disruption of production and trading. Suppliers claiming reservation of title may seek an interlocutory injunction to prevent the receiver from dealing with their goods until the trial of the action hearing their claim. In view of the receiver's potential personal liability in tort it should be possible for him to defeat a claim for such an injunction on the grounds that damages would be an adequate remedy for the plaintiff and, save where the sums are particularly large, the receiver will be able to meet the claim (see *American Cyanamid Co.* v *Ethicon Ltd* [1975] AC 396). On the balance of convenience, it may be preferable to let the receiver continue trading and attempt to realise the business on a going-concern basis and leave the plaintiff with his right in damages for conversion. Suppliers who seek interlocutory relief should not underestimate the significance of the cross-undertaking in damages they will have to give the receiver for any loss which may be caused by the injunction, should their claim ultimately not be upheld by the court. The court will consider the likely ability of the plaintiff to comply with that cross-undertaking.

Where reservation of title problems are acute, a receiver may resort to a general policy of telling suppliers that should their claim ultimately prove to be legally valid, he will, as a receivership expense, pay the value of the goods (or, if he wishes to make the offer more attractive, pay the invoice value).

### ¶507   Other statutory and tortious liabilities

An administrative receiver can be liable in tort in certain circumstances, notwithstanding that he is agent for his principal. There may also be circumstances in which the purpose of a particular statute is to ensure that some mischief is prevented, and the person made responsible for preventing the mischief is stated to be the person 'in control'. An administrative receiver has no inherent right to be immune from falling within a relevant statutory definition. There follow examples of potential tortious and statutory liabilities:

(1)     While directors of a company may not strictly be agents for the company they do act on the company's behalf and where they are acting within their authority the principal in respect of those acts will be the company itself. Thus, cases where directors find themselves personally liable for the acts of their companies may suggest potential liability for administrative receivers in the same sets of circumstances. In *C. Evans & Sons Limited* v *Spritebrand Limited & Another* ([1985] 1 WLR 317; (1985) 1 BCC 99, 316), the question before the Court of Appeal was whether, as a preliminary issue, a director of a company could be personally liable in tort where he had authorised, directed and procured an infringement of copyright by the company even where there was no proof that he had acted knowing that the acts were tortious or reckless in this regard. Slade LJ (317 at pp. 329–30; 99, 316 at pp. 99, 325–326), commented as follows:

> '. . . Is it the law of England that a director of a company who has authorised, directed and procured the commission by the company of a tort of the nature specified in s. 1(2) of the Copyright Act 1956 can *in no circumstances* be personally liable to the injured party unless he directed or procured the acts of infringement in the knowledge that they were tortious, or recklessly, without caring whether they were tortious or not? . . .
>
> For my part I have no hesitation in answering this question "No". I can best begin the explanation of my reasons by giving a hypothetical example. Let it be supposed that evidence at the trial reveals that an employee of the defendant company personally manufactured scaffolding components in breach of the plaintiffs' copyrights and that he carried out this operation under the personal supervision and direction of the [appellant] director who was present throughout the operation and told him exactly what to do. Sections 17(2) and 18(2) of the Copyright Act 1956 impose certain restrictions on the remedies of owners of copyright in cases where it is proved or admitted that at the relevant time the defendant was not aware and had no reasonable grounds for suspecting that copyright subsisted. However, subject to any limited defence which he may be able to establish in reliance on either of these subsections, I can see no reason why on the hypothetical facts the employee should not be exposed to personal liability in subsequent proceedings or in these proceedings if added as a party . . .
>
> In my judgment, it would offend common sense if, on the hypothetical facts postulated, the law of tort were to treat the director of the company any more kindly than the servant, who took his orders from the director . . .' (emphasis in the original).

¶507

In a similar vein, in *Mancetter Developments Limited* v *Garmanson Limited* ([1986] QB 1212; (1986) 2 BCC 98, 924), a director was held liable for the tort of 'waste' which had been committed by his company, as he had given instructions for the commission of the tort.

(2)  In *Meigh* v *Wickenden* ([1942] 2 KB 160), a receiver and manager appointed under a debenture was held to be an 'occupier' of a factory for the purposes of the Factories Act 1937 and liable for the absence of proper guards on machinery in the factory. Viscount Caldecote CJ explained the policy behind the Factories Act 1937 (at pp. 164–5):

> 'The occupier's responsibility under the Act does not depend on proof of personal blame or even on knowledge of the contravention. The policy of the Act seems to be to fasten responsibility, in the first instance, on the occupier. The occupier, however, may bring the person who is alleged to be "the actual offender" before the court, and if this person is found to have committed the offence, the occupier may be found not guilty: see s. 137. The Factories Act, 1937, is drastic in its provisions. *It is clearly framed in such a way as to make it certain that someone can be found who can be convicted of an offence in the event of contravention.*' (Emphasis supplied.)

Apart from the strict legal position, an administrative receiver would not wish to be seen to be running a business from a dangerous factory or in breach of statutory regulations covering health or food and drugs. It is thus important for an administrative receiver on his appointment to check with his legal advisers on any statutory regulations governing the particular business over which he has been appointed.

(3)  An administrative receiver is now caught by the statutory provisions giving a summary remedy against those (including officers, liquidators and administrators) who have been guilty of misfeasance or other breach of duty in relation to the company (IA, s. 212).

## ¶508   Rates

As a result of the removal by the Insolvency Act 1986 of local authority rates from the categories of preferential debts (see ¶601–3), the rights of local authorities to seek payment of rates from an administrative receiver and to distrain in respect of pre-receivership arrears and/or post-receivership liabilities arising will be more important than hitherto. As a matter of practice, local authorities have in the past tended not to attempt to distrain after the appointment of an administrative receiver whether for pre- or post-receivership liabilities. They would rely on their preferential claim which might, depending upon the time of appointment, include as preferential a post-receivership period (see CA, Sch. 19, para. 7). The authorities in this area are not clear and not necessarily consistent. The following questions fail to be answered:

(1) After an administrative receiver is appointed, who is primarily responsible for paying rates: has there been a change of occupation such as to make the receiver personally liable?

(2) Can the rating authority distrain against goods caught by the crystallised floating charge after the appointment of the receiver in respect of pre-receivership rates liabilities and/or post-receivership liabilities?

Taking each question in turn:

(1) It now seems clear from *Ratford & Another* v *Northavon District Council* ((1986) 2 BCC 99, 242) that, in the absence of unusual circumstances, an administrative receiver appointed under a floating charge security will not become personally liable for rates, as his appointment will not bring about a change in occupation of the premises. Slade LJ (at p. 99, 255) commented that a letter which the receivers in the case had written gave the rating authority 'reasonable grounds for believing that the receivers might be in rateable occupation of the premises, since they were within the category of those who might prima facie be liable.' He then went on to explain (at pp. 99, 255–256) how this burden of proof shifted:

'. . . the council having shown that the rate in question had been duly made and published, that it has been duly demanded from the receivers and that it had not been paid, the burden fell in the first instance on the receivers to show sufficient cause for not having paid the sum demanded.

. . . In my judgment, however, the receivers prima facie discharged this burden by showing that they had been appointed on terms which, though empowering them to take possession of the company's premises and to carry on and manage its business, did not oblige them to take possession and further provided that in carrying out their activities they should be deemed to be the agents of the company.

. . . This much having been shown, the onus, in my opinion, shifted to the council to show that the receivers had dispossessed the company, or, to put it another way, to show that the quality of any possession of the premises which the receivers might have enjoyed was not that of mere agents. For possession held by a person in his capacity as agent is in law the possession of his principal.'

¶508

(2)   If the rating authority could effectively distrain upon the goods of the company notwithstanding the appointment of an administrative receiver and the consequent crystallisation of a floating charge, it might be asked why the attempt was made in the *Ratford* case to make the receivers personally liable. The Court of Appeal held in *Re Marriage, Neave & Co* ([1896] 2 Ch. 663) that distraint for rates could still be levied notwithstanding the appointment of a receiver. Lindley LJ (at p. 673) said:

> '. . . [The debentures'] only effect is to give the debenture holders an equitable charge upon these goods. That is all the debenture holders want. They do not require to take possession, and they have no right even to take possession. Their only right is to institute an action and get a receiver appointed. The goods are not theirs: they are the goods of the company, subject to the equitable charge created by the debentures.'

The nature of the 'equitable charge' in question is not clear from the report. The crystallisation of a floating charge is now accepted as effecting an assignment of the charged assets in equity to the debenture holder (*N. W. Robbie & Co. Ltd* v *Witney Warehouse Co. Ltd* [1963] 1 WLR 1324). The argument that distraint for rates is not possible against assets caught by a crystallised floating charge is supported by the decision in *Richards* v *Overseers of Kidderminster* ([1896] 2 Ch. 212).

A rating authority cannot enforce payment of rates by an administrative receiver under s. 109(8)(*i*) of the Law of Property Act 1925 (which provides for application of moneys received by a receiver: 'in discharge of all rents taxes rates and outgoings whatever affecting the mortgaged property . . .') as this is merely an obligation of the receiver to his debenture holder and does not give rise to a statutory duty capable of being enforced by the rating authority (*Liverpool Corporation* v *Hope* [1938] 1 KB 751).

## ¶509   Rent

Save where an administrative receiver contracts directly with a landlord to make himself personally liable or where he enters into a new lease without excluding his personal liability, a landlord will not be able to obtain payment of rent under a lease held by a company in receivership from a receiver, personally.

A landlord would seem to be able to distrain for pre- and post-receivership rent against goods over which the receiver has been appointed and hence which are caught by a crystallised floating charge (*Re Roundwood Colliery Co.* [1897] 1 Ch. 373). The debenture holder in most cases will not be able to avail itself of the relief offered to third-party owners by the Law of Distress (Amendment) Act 1908.

Where the company is a lessee and has sub-let, it would appear that the receiver can accept rent from the sub-lessee without having to account to, or pay, the head lessee (*Hand* v *Blow* [1901] 2 Ch. 721).

## ¶510    Concept of the receivership expense

The term 'receivership expense' is widely used in insolvency contexts and, it is submitted, often misused. There are a number of principles which it is worth restating:

(1)    An administrative receiver may be personally liable on contracts which he enters into (in the absence of an express exclusion of personal liability), and on contracts of employment 'adopted' by him, in carrying out his functions (IA, s. 44(1)(*b*)). Thus, an administrative receiver who contracts to buy goods and does not exclude his personal liability under that contract will be liable to pay for the goods personally, as an individual.

(2)    An administrative receiver may choose to make certain payments. For example, in order to preserve a leasehold interest, he may place the company in funds to pay the landlord. Similarly, he may place the company in funds to pay employees in order that his receivership retains a workforce. The receiver has power to make these payments and hence, once they are made, the recipient cannot be made to repay the moneys. In that sense the receiver may be said to have made a payment as a receivership expense.

(3)    The phrase 'receivership expenses' is used in the Insolvency Rules 1986. For example, in r. 3.29(1), the administrative receiver is to defray the reasonable travelling expenses of the creditors' committee 'as an expense of the receivership'. No further explanation is given of this phrase but it would seem to mean that the receiver is obliged to pay the expenses of the member of the committee out of the assets in his hands subject to a floating charge. In the event that there is a creditors' committee and he has no assets to meet such expenses, it would seem necessary for him to seek the directions of the court (provided there are sufficient funds to pay the legal fees!).

(4)    On the basis that he may be liable as a party to fraudulent trading, a receiver will no doubt wish to avoid dishonesty and knowingly incurring credit where there is no reasonable prospect of the debt being paid (see IA, s. 213 and *R* v *Grantham* [1984] QB 675).

(5)   Statute may require an administrative receiver to account for moneys in his hands in a particular way, for example by paying preferential debts (see ¶601 et seq.) or pursuant to specific tax regulations (see reg. 11(1) of the Value Added Tax (General) Regulations 1985, and see also *Re John Willment (Ashford) Limited* [1980] 1 WLR 73 discussed further in Chapter 8 below; but compare *Liverpool Corporation* v *Hope* [1938] 1 KB 751).

(6)   There is no general doctrine of receivership expenses in the same way that certain liabilities have to be paid as an expense of, for example, a liquidation (see *Re ABC Coupler & Engineering Co. Limited (No. 3)* [1970] 1 WLR 702). In respect of a new contract the receiver will only be personally liable if he fails to exclude his personal liability. If he does so exclude, the liability is that of the company. Where he merely enables the company to continue a contract entered into prior to his appointment he cannot be personally liable because the contract is not one that he has entered into (excluding the question of adoption of employment contracts). He will only be liable in respect of a 'continued' contract (other than an employment contract) where he renders himself liable 'as on a novation' (see *Re Botibol* [1947] 1 All ER 26, at p. 28). The position was stated clearly by the Court of Appeal in *Nicoll* v *Cutts* ((1985) 1 BCC 99, 427). The facts of the case and its significance in the field of employment is considered below (¶511). For these purposes the relevant facts are that at the time of an administrative receiver's appointment an employee was in hospital as a result of an accident. The receiver visited him in hospital on a number of occasions but did not actually dismiss him until some two months after the commencement of the receivership. Dillon LJ commented as follows (at pp. 99, 430):

> 'In the case of a weekly paid employee whose services the receiver continued in order to preserve the company's business for sale it would be expected that the receiver would actually pay the employee his wages week by week. In such a case the *actual payments made*, being costs and expenses of the receivership *actually paid*, would have priority to the bank. It seems hard that an employee should lose that priority (except in so far as mitigation is provided by s. 122 of the 1978 Act) if the receiver, in breach of the company's contract, fails to pay the employee's wages or salary during the continuance of his employment after the receiver's appointment. None the less I cannot for my part see how the expression costs and expenses of the receivership (assuming them to have priority) can cover a sum in respect of [the plaintiff's] salary under his previous contract with

¶510

the company which the receiver has not paid and is under no personal liability to [the plaintiff] to pay.' (Emphasis supplied.)

That is, if the receiver does decide to make a payment it may be a valid receivership expense but there is no right for a third party to sue the receiver to require him to make the payment.


# EMPLOYEES

## ¶511   The supposed mischief of Nicoll v Cutts

When the Insolvency Bill (which led to the Insolvency Act 1985) was passing through Parliament, the case of *Nicoll* v *Cutts* ((1985) 1 BCC 99, 427) was decided. The facts of the case are outlined above (¶510). The facts of the case were somewhat unusual and it requires something of a leap to conclude from the decision in *Nicoll* v *Cutts* that it is the norm in administrative receiverships for employees to work for receivers and not be paid. If employees are not paid they will not continue to work and receivers have to put the company in funds to pay the employees as a receivership expense (see ¶510). With the apparent intention of reversing or mitigating the effect of the decision in *Nicoll* v *Cutts*, an amendment to the Insolvency Bill was proposed and the relevant clause is now s. 44(1)(*b*) of the Insolvency Act 1986, which reads as follows:

'[The administrative receiver of a company] . . . is personally liable on any contract entered into by him in the carrying out of his functions (except in so far as the contract otherwise provides) and on any contract of employment adopted by him in the carrying out of those functions. . . '

Section 44(2) provides as follows:

'For the purposes of sub-section (1)(*b*) the administrative receiver is not to be taken to have adopted a contract of employment by reason of anything done or omitted to be done within fourteen days after his appointment.'

To use the one word 'adopted' to attempt to ensure that employees of a receivership are not exploited seemed to those practising in insolvency matters to involve using a blunt instrument to undertake a delicate operation. The meaning of 'adoption' is considered at ¶512.

## ¶512   Meaning of 'adoption'

'Adoption' does not have a universal legal meaning. It is used in a small number of differing legal contexts (consider 'adoption' of children and s. 18, r. 4 of the Sale of Goods Act 1979).

Consideration of the meaning of adoption in s. 44(1)(*b*) came before the court in *Re Specialised Mouldings Limited* (13 February 1987). In this case, administrative receivers found themselves in the position that, on the best estimates available to them, they would be able to pay off their debenture holder pursuant to realizations under fixed charges without the need to rely on realizations under the floating charge. The company had over 100 employees and the potential personal liability of the receivers on contracts of employment should they be held to have adopted them amounted to hundreds of thousands of pounds. Valuations of the floating-charge assets on a break up basis indicated that the amounts realized on such a basis would be less than the amounts necessary to meet the potential liability to employees under adopted contracts.

Faced with this dilemma, the administrative receivers sought the directions of the court under s. 35 of the Insolvency Act 1986. The Department of Employment, the company and an individual employee were joined as respondents to the application and full argument was presented to the court on the meaning of the word 'adoption'. On behalf of the receivers it was argued that whatever may or may not have been the intention of the legislature, the wording in the Insolvency Act 1986 constituted no change in the existing law. Adoption implied evidence of a willingness to assume personal responsibility on the part of an administrative receiver and, where he assumes such personal responsibility, he would be, and always would have been, personally liable, in the words of Evershed J in *Re Botibol* ([1947] 1 All ER 26 at p. 28), 'as on a novation'. And where an administrative receiver made it perfectly clear to employees that he was not and did not intend to adopt a contract of employment he could escape liability under the section provided that he did not in other ways indicate an intention personally to be responsible on the contract.

The contrary argument involved an analysis of the many uses of the word 'adoption' in the various branches of the law, some of which suggested that there could be an adoption by mere continuation. As McPherson J expressed the point (albeit *obiter*) in *Re Diesels and Components Property Limited* (9 ACLR 825 at p. 827):

'What is meant by saying that a receiver has power to "adopt" a pre-receivership contract is that he may refrain from repudiating it.'

Harman J's decision as read out in open court[1] was to the following effect:

(1) It is possible for an administrative receiver to provide specifically that he does not adopt employment contracts and he can, therefore, effectively contract out of any personal liability which might otherwise attach to him under s. 44(1)(*b*) of the 1986 Act.

---

[1] At the time of writing, the full judgment of Harman J was awaited.

(2)     The first limb of s. 44(1)(*b*) contains the words '(except in so far as the contract otherwise provides)'. The presence of these words in the first line does not materially affect the construction of the second limb. Under the second limb, an administrative receiver is able to avoid personal liability by way of adoption provided he makes his intention not to adopt (or not to incur personal liability) sufficiently clear within 14 days of his appointment.

(3)     On the facts of the case before him, Harman J approved a specific form of letter put before the court which, in his judgment, did make it sufficiently clear that the receiver was *not* adopting contracts of employment merely by causing the company to continue them outside the 14 day grace period mentioned in s. 44(2), and hence the receiver would not be personally liable.

The form of letter which the receivers proposed to write and which Harman J ruled indicated sufficiently their intention not to be personally liable by adoption was as follows:

**'Specialised Mouldings Limited**

Dear Sir/Madam,
    I write further to my letter of . . . in which I informed you that my partner, . . . and I were appointed joint administrative receivers of the company by . . . on . . . under the powers contained in their debenture.
    I also informed you that your employment by the company will be continued by it on the same terms as hitherto. I wish to make it clear that this is on the following basis:

(i) we have been acting and will continue to act as the company's agents,

(ii) we are not adopting, and will not at any future date adopt, your contract, and

(iii) we have not assumed, and will not at any future date assume, any personal liability in relation to your employment.

Yours faithfully,

For and on behalf
of Specialised Mouldings
Limited
*Joint Administrative Receiver*'

The worry for the receivers was that if adoption occurred they might be liable for all the incidents of employment (including arrears of pay, redundancy entitlement, minimum notice periods, etc.) and not just wages for the period of employment in the receivership. The decision in the *Specialised Mouldings* case allayed the fears of the receivers in that case in particular, but the judgment of Harman J is of persuasive authority in other receiverships where the facts are not substantially different. Notwithstanding having given a clear disclaimer of liability, a receiver may still be held to have adopted where his subsequent conduct or acts are of such a nature as to show an intention to adopt.

It seems clear that nothing done during the first 14 days from the appointment of an administrative receiver will be taken to mean that they have adopted, and it is for that reason that it is important for a receiver to issue his disclaimer before he enters the 'danger zone' – that is, the period commencing with the expiry of 14 days.

# REALISATION OF ASSETS AND PROPERTY

## ¶513   Sale documentation

When an administrative receiver comes to realise assets and property he will normally instruct his solicitors to draw up suitable contractual documentation to reflect the bargain which, subject to contract, has been struck. The basis of the sale, as an insolvency sale, will be that the assets are sold on an 'as is', 'where is' basis and the contract will state that it is for the purchaser to carry out all such investigations as he deems appropriate in the light of that fact. The contract should also provide that no reliance is to be placed on any statements made by the vendor or the receiver or any of their agents or staff.

All implied warranties as to the state and condition of what is sold will be excluded and, commonly, the receiver will only cause the company to sell such right, title and interest as it may have in the assets sold (see Sale of Goods Act 1979, s. 12).

Most importantly, the receiver will exclude his personal liability on the contract, as permitted by s. 44 of the Insolvency Act 1986. There may be situations in which exclusions of liability by a receiver may be ineffective as a result of the Unfair Contract Terms Act 1977 but it is submitted that the receiver's exclusion of personal liability does not fall within the ambit of the Act.[1]

## ¶514   Negotiating the deal

Although the assumption of control of a business by an administrative receiver may in the short term give a feeling of confidence to the customers and

---

[1] See 'Some Aspects of Receivership Law – 1', [1981] JBL 312 where Professor Goode argues that a receiver's personal liability is imposed by statute and not contract or tort which are the areas covered by the Unfair Contract Terms Act 1977.

suppliers of a business it is likely that, in the longer term, there will be an erosion of goodwill arising from, if nothing else, the uncertainty surrounding the continuation of the business. A receiver will, therefore, seek to sell a business as a going concern sooner rather than later. Once he has found a purchaser at a satisfactory price it is in the interests of both receiver and purchaser to complete the sale as soon as possible. Hence, many receivership sales are conducted under conditions of great pressure over a short period of time and often at anti-social hours.

There is no set format covering all negotiations, and inevitably the atmosphere will be different in a case where there are a number of potential purchasers all making offers at roughly the same level and a case where there is only one purchaser interested. The difference may be between a purchaser who wishes to obtain a business whatever the risks and a purchaser who wishes to obtain the business but only with all the details considered and covered in the documentation, so far as possible.

In the author's experience, negotiations go more smoothly for both sides if the purchaser appreciates that the administrative receiver's position is that of a professional (usually an accountant or lawyer) who, when the receivership in hand is completed, will wish to close it without any subsisting potential liabilities under sale documentation remaining as a source of concern. In the unlikely event that there were special circumstances justifying the giving of some form of warranty or assurance to a purchaser, the well-advised receiver will ensure that its ambit is restricted in both time and amount. Administrative receivers for their part should appreciate a purchaser's legitimate areas of concern. For example, a receiver should be amenable to a purchaser's requests regarding the description of the items sold, particularly where the purchaser is merely trying to spell out in greater detail what he is purchasing and the receiver had always intended that the items of concern were included in the sale. To give a simple example: where a purchaser is buying a piece of equipment, he may be forced to accept that the receiver will not warrant good title nor will he warrant the equipment's state and condition. Where the company had bought the equipment with the benefit of warranties from suppliers and these warranties are still current then it is legitimate for the purchaser to ask the receiver to cause the company to assign the company's rights under these warranties – to the extent that they are capable of assignment.

## ¶515   Common areas of concern

### (1)   Employees
The particular problems for an administrative receiver posed by s. 44 of the

Insolvency Act 1986 are discussed above (¶511). In the context of the realisation of assets and businesses, different difficulties emerge.

## (a)   *Preservation of employment*
The duty of a receiver when realising assets is to get the best price reasonably obtainable (see ¶415(1)). Where no conflict with that duty is involved, a receiver will prefer to realise assets on a basis which preserves employment – preserves a business – than a sale which does not, for obvious reasons. Debenture holders who may fear adverse public criticism of a decision (however justified) to appoint a receiver may feel less vulnerable if it transpires that the business is to be continued by a new company employing some, if not all, of the old workforce.

## (b)   *Liabilities resulting from continuity of employment*
A sale as a going concern may suggest that at least some employees of the business will be re-employed by a purchaser, but a purchaser from a receiver in most such cases will normally not wish to assume any in-built liability to employees who are taken over without any break in continuity of employment. If such employees are later dismissed, (for example by way of redundancy, the purchaser having decided that he needs to thin the workforce) the period of time by reference to which the size of any redundancy payment is computed will include the length of service of the employee with the company in receivership or indeed previous employers where there has been no break in continuity. In general, if a purchaser can buy a business, the workforce having been dismissed shortly before the acquisition, and subsequently engage some or all of the previous workforce without any accrued rights – on the basis that they start with a 'clean sheet' – then a purchaser would, in most cases, prefer to do so. If this is not possible, or if the position is unclear, and if it is also suggested that a purchaser may also be liable for redundancy and unfair dismissal payments to dismissed employees of the business to whom he does *not* offer employment, selling businesses as going concerns becomes ever more difficult.

## (c)   *Employment legislation*
The above factors have to be viewed in the light of the various pieces of legislation in the employment field. Until 1981 the relevant statutory provisions were to be found in the Employment Protection (Consolidation) Act 1978 ('EPCA') and the earlier statute, Employment Protection Act 1975 ('the 1975 Act'). With some repeals, principally of the 1975 Act, these Acts are still in force but later legislation has not been integrated with them.

¶515

The important provisions of the EPCA for these purposes are, in a much simplified form,[1] as follows:

(1)    By s. 84, where an employee's contract is renewed or an employer makes a new offer of employment to an employee prior to dismissing him (or prior to expiry of a fixed term contract – EPCA, s. 83) the ending of the first contract is not to be taken as a dismissal (unless the terms of the new employment differ from the old and the employee terminates his employment during the four-week trial period provided for).

(2)    By s. 94, where a transfer of a business occurs, an employee's contract is terminated by the transferor and the transferee re-engages the employee, s. 84 is to take effect as if the re-engagement by the new owner was a re-engagement by the previous owner – that is, there is no dismissal.

(3)    By para. 17(2) of Sch. 13, for the purposes of calculating an employee's right to redundancy, continuity is not to be broken by the transfer of a business in respect of an employee employed by the transferee who was an employee in the business 'at the time of the transfer'. This latter phrase in this context may not mean at the instant of transfer but may cover a longer period (*Teeside Times Ltd* v *Drury* [1980] ICR 338) although this may need re-examination in the light of the following discussion.

(4)    Section 122 covers the employees' right to payment out of the Redundancy Fund (that is, the right to payment by the State) in the event that the employer who makes him redundant is insolvent (which includes a company which has had a receiver or manager appointed to its undertaking EPCA, s. 127(1)(c)).

(5)    Part IV covers rights to unfair dismissal.

The provisions of ss. 99–101 of the 1975 Act should be noted as they govern 'protective awards' which may be made when an employer fails to fulfil the statutory requirements of consultation prior to redundancy. Although such awards only constitute claims against the company as opposed to the administrative receiver, a receiver will generally try to follow the consultation process (so far as he is able). Insolvency itself is not a special circumstance justifying a failure to comply with the statutory provisions (*Clarks of Hove* v *Bakers' Union* [1978] 1 WLR 1207).

---

[1] For a good summary of the numerous statutory provisions in this area, see Totty and Jordan, *Insolvency*, Chapter 27.

¶515

*(d) EEC Directive and resulting Regulations*

As a result of the entry of the UK into the Common Market, the UK became bound to implement Directives of the Council of the European Communities (Arts. 100 and 117 of the Treaty of Rome and s. 2 of the European Communities Act 1972).

In the employment area, the Council issued Directive No. 77/187. To comply with the Directive the Government, by Order in Council, introduced the Transfer of Undertakings (Protection of Employment) Regulations 1981 (SI 1981 No. 1794). No attempt was made to marry the new provisions with the existing law discussed above (save for a few consequential amendments). The Regulations provide that, on a transfer of an undertaking, contracts of employment which would otherwise have been terminated by the transfer shall take effect after the transfer as though made between the employee and the transferee and not the transferor. The relevant transfer accordingly operates to transfer to the transferee: 'all the transferor's rights, powers, duties and liabilities under or in connection with any such contract . . .' (reg. 5(2)(*a*)). In clarification of what is meant by a person employed by the transferor in an undertaking, the Regulations explain that this is a reference: 'to a person so employed *immediately before* the transfer . . .' (reg. 5(3)) (emphasis supplied).

In a specific provision aimed at avoiding any difficulties for receivers or liquidators when hiving-down, reg. 4 provides that where a receiver or liquidator transfers a company's undertaking or part of a company's undertaking to a wholly-owned subsidiary, the transfer is not to take effect for the purposes of reg. 5 until immediately before the transferee company ceases to be a wholly-owned subsidiary (other than by reason of it being wound up) or the subsidiary itself transfers the undertaking (reg. 4).

If an employee is dismissed before or after a relevant transfer and the transfer or a reason connected with it is the sole or principal reason for the dismissal, then that dismissal is to be treated as an unfair dismissal for the purposes of the ECPA and other related legislation (reg. 8).

However, 'where an economic, technical or organisational reason entailing changes in the workforce of either the transferor or the transferee before or after a relevant transfer is the reason or principal reason for dismissing an employee . . .' (reg. 8(2)), the dismissal is to be regarded as having been for a substantial reason justifying the dismissal. This is subject always to the employer showing that in the circumstances (which include the size and administrative resources of the employer's undertaking), the employer acted reasonably in regarding the reason as an adequate reason for the dismissal (reg. 8(2)(*b*) and see EPCA, s. 57(3)).

¶515

*(e)   Uncertainty arising from the Regulations*
The Regulations introduced a further note of uncertainty into insolvency practitioners' attempts to sell businesses as a going concern. Regulation 5(2)(*b*) provides as follows:

'(*b*) anything done before the transfer is completed by or in relation to the transferor in respect of that contract or a person employed in that undertaking or part shall be deemed to have been done *by or in relation to the transferee.*' (Emphasis supplied.)

An example may illustrate the problems posed. A purchaser wishes to take on 70 per cent of the employees but without being saddled with existing periods of service for continuity purposes. The receiver dismisses the employees around the time he enters into a contract for the sale of the business – say on a Friday evening. An indication is given by the purchaser to the employees that they might like to turn up on Monday morning to see whether there was any possibility of employment with the purchaser. The employees submit claims to the Department for their statutory entitlements, including redundancy pay. Purchasers will have two main fears: first, that in respect of any employees they did not take on, the dismissal would, as a result of reg. 5(3), be deemed to have been effected by them and they would be liable for all the contractual entitlements of an employee, including redundancy, accrued holiday pay, pay in lieu of notice and possibly unfair dismissal (unless reg. 8(2) could be prayed in aid). Secondly, as regards the employees to whom the purchasers offered employment, if the Department of Employment did not agree to meet the redundancy claims, they might find that they had taken those employees on saddled with their accrued rights (EPCA, Sch. 13, para. 17(2)). Cases such as *Apex Leisure Hire* v *Barratt* ([1984] 1 WLR 1062) suggested that these fears were far from groundless. The costs of uncertainty should not be underestimated.[2]

*(f)   The Spence decision*
Fortunately, the Court of Appeal in *Secretary of State for Employment* v *Spence & Others* ([1986] 3 WLR 380), hearing an appeal from the Employment Appeal Tribunal, removed both the uncertainty and the fears. The sequence of events in this case was as follows:

(1)   Dismissal of the employees at 11 a.m. on day 1.
(2)   Sale of the undertaking of the company by the receiver at 2 p.m. on day 1.

---

[2] For a sensible and stimulating discussion of the 'transaction' and other costs involved in this area, see Hugh Collins, 'Dismissals on Transfer of a Business', ILJ Vol. 15 No. 4, December 1986, 244.

¶515

(3) On the morning of day 2 the former workforce of the company in receivership was re-employed by the purchaser.

(4) The employees sought redundancy payments from the Secretary of State and, on the Department refusing to make the payments, the employees took the case to the Industrial Tribunal and the case went to the Court of Appeal via the Employment Appeal Tribunal.

The issues before the Court of Appeal were first, whether there had been a transfer of an undertaking, and secondly whether the employees of the company in receivership had been employed 'immediately before the transfer'.

Balcombe LJ gave a judgment with which Stephen Brown and Mustill L JJ agreed. Balcombe LJ helpfully reviewed the Directive on which the Regulations are based, starting by quoting from Arts. 3 and 4 as follows (at p. 386):

'Article 3(1): "the transferor's rights and obligations arising from the contract of employment or from an employment relationship existing on the date of a transfer . . . shall, by reason of such transfer, be transferred to the transferee." I need read no more of that paragraph or article. Article 4(1): "the transfer of an undertaking, business or part of a business shall not in itself constitute grounds for a dismissal by the transferor or the transferee. This provision shall not stand in the way of dismissals that may take place for economic, technical or organisational reasons entailing changes in the workforce."'

Balcombe LJ considered that reg. 5 was meant to give effect to Art. 3, para. 1 and reg. 8 to give effect to Art. 4. He saw para. 1 of reg. 5 as simply negating the common law rule that on a transfer of a business an employee is not to be required to work for an employer against his wishes and that therefore a transfer of a business should operate to determine a contract of employment. He saw it as having no more significance than that as he commented (at p.388):

'[the] provision can clearly only relate to a contract of employment which is subsisting at the *moment of transfer*; otherwise there is nothing on which the Regulation can operate' (emphasis supplied).

Anticipating the comment that some effect had to be given to reg. 5(3), Balcombe LJ did admit that in the light of his interpretation of para. 1 'the words defining the person employed as meaning a person so employed immediately before the transfer are unnecessary . . .' but he then gave as an example a set of facts which they might have been intended to cover. He referred to the case of *Batchelor* v *Premier Motors (Romford) Ltd* (Case No. 1729/82/LN) where, with a transfer 'in the offing', an employee had indicated that he was not inclined to accept new terms of employment from prospective purchasers although he was never actually dismissed by the transferors. The judge felt that (at p. 389):

' it might have been difficult to see at what precise moment of time in the context of the transfer, he ceased to be employed. There was a situation which the use of the definitive words in [reg. 5] made it clear that the employee, who was employed by the transferor immediately before the relevant transfer, had his contract carried over to the transferee, even though both parties knew that they were not going to implement it; but the definition made it clear who was to be responsible for dismissing him, with all the consequential effects, in those circumstances.'

An interesting feature of the case is that the Court of Appeal clearly considered that reg. 5(2) applied to liabilities in tort and not just in contract although this was not essential for their decision in the case (but note that pension rights are not included – reg. 7).

Having construed the Regulations as he saw them, Balcombe LJ then went on to consider the previous cases and indicated those he thought had been rightly decided and those he thought were incorrect. First he found support from a decision of the European Court on the Directive itself, the case of *Wendelboe & Others* v *L J Music ApS* ([1986] 1 CMLR 476). This supported his view of the interpretation of reg. 5(1). As the Advocate General, Sir Gordon Slynn, in that case expressed it (at p. 480):

'It follows on a literal reading of the text that the rights and obligations of persons who cease to be employed in the undertaking concerned at the time of the transfer are not transferred to the transferee by virtue of the directive.'

Sir Gordon Slynn (at p. 480) then went on to make the helpful comment (one which has been made by lawyers and accountants concerned with insolvency for some time):

'Both the uncertainty and the amount involved could provide a real deterrent to purchasers of the business, and in the result the business might not be sold and a large number of the work force lose their jobs. This is contrary to the principal object of the directive, viz. to protect employees on a transfer'.

A number of cases were disapproved by the Court of Appeal, but *Premier Motors (Medway) Limited* v *Total Oil Great Britain Limited* ([1984] 1 WLR 377) was approved. In that case Browne-Wilkinson J (the President of the Employment Appeal Tribunal) said, *inter alia*:

'a transferee of a business who does not wish to take over the employees of that business would even so be liable to the employees for the redundancy payments. To protect himself the employee must agree with the transferor either that the transferor must dismiss the employee before the transfer or will indemnify the transferee against redundancy payments and other liabilities.'

Although it was not necessary for the purposes of its judgment, the Court of Appeal in *Spence* commented briefly on the question of what is an 'undertaking' for the purposes of the Regulations. Balcombe LJ said (at p. 397) that: 'it cannot be said that the existence of a workforce is vital to the existence of an undertaking' and the Court criticised the finding of the Industrial Tribunal that in this case there was no undertaking to be transferred. The House of Lords case *Melon* v *Hector Powe Limited* ([1981] 1 All ER 313) was cited as authority in this area. In that case a factory in which suits were manufactured for the employer's chain of retail shops was sold, together with work in progress, to a purchaser but without the right to use the employer's well-known name. There was held to be no transfer of an undertaking. The significant factor was held to be that in a mere transfer of assets the purchaser was free to use the assets in whatever business he chose, but could not use them in the business formerly carried on. Balcome LJ considered it significant that the Industrial Tribunal found as a fact in the *Spence* case that the purchaser had the option to 'maintain the business as a going concern.'

*(g)   The use of options*
The *Spence* case is helpful to insolvency practitioners and purchasers alike in the context of business acquisitions. There are, however, grave risks for an administrative receiver who dismisses the workforce at a time when he does not have a binding contract for sale of the business. One possibility is for there to be an exchange of contracts, followed by dismissal of the employees, followed by completion (that is, actual transfer). In *Kestongate* v *Miller* ([1986] ICR 672), however, it was held that in such circumstances employees were employed immediately before the transfer, and, having been dismissed, the transferee was liable for redundancy and other dismissal costs. In the light of the *Spence* case the authority of *Kestongate* was not certain. *Spence* appears not to have been cited (it was only decided some days before) and the Employment Appeal Tribunal may have based their decision on the, now heretical, 'period of time' argument whereas *Spence* makes it clear that 'immediately before' means what it says. The Employment Appeal Tribunal has now said, in *Wheeler* v *Patel and J. Golding Group of Companies* ([1987] IRLR 211), that the decision in *Kestongate* was wrong and incompatible with *Spence*.

To solve the problem of the purchaser wanting the workforce dismissed but the receiver unwilling to do so when he does not have a signed contract, an

¶515

alternative approach has developed. An option is granted by the purchaser to the receiver entitling the receiver to require the purchaser to buy on a notice being served under the option. Properly drafted, this may give a receiver sufficient comfort to enable him to dismiss the employees after its execution, with the sale being agreed and completed after dismissal. This mechanism was recently approved by the Industrial Tribunal in the case of *Permoid Limited* (March 1986, unreported). The facts were that the option was two-way, 'a put and call' option. The Tribunal recognised the problems facing administrative receivers:

> '. . . we accept that receivers at present are entering a minefield when seeking to sell businesses as going concerns. In this case the transferee had made it clear from the very beginning that it did not intend to take over the transferor's workforce and this was agreed. We are well aware that the Secretary of State is concerned that unscrupulous persons may seek to get moneys paid out of the Redundancy Fund when such moneys should come from other pockets. However in this case we are satisfied that if the transferee had been aware that it was to be responsible for the payment of redundancy, etc. it would not have entered into the transfer and then there was every likelihood of the transferor's total workforce being broken up and the assets sold piecemeal. As it happened many jobs were saved.'

This is a refreshingly helpful approach, and in the light of this comment and the comments of the Court of Appeal in *Spence* it may seem reasonable to think that the use of options would be upheld by authority higher than the Industrial Tribunal. The decision in *Wheeler* may make the use of options unnecessary and a sequence of: exchange of contracts – dismissal of workforce – completion may become the norm.

### (2)  Title

As mentioned above, the administrative receiver will simply sell whatever title the company may have to chattels and it will be for the purchaser to make such enquiries as he can to satisfy himself that the company does own them. The position is less acute for a purchaser as regards any real property he is buying. It is easier to investigate title to property and for the purchaser to receive a satisfactory assurance from his solicitors that the vendor is passing a good title. It may also be possible for the purchaser to satisfy himself on other items such as patents and registered trade marks where he can at least carry out a search at the relevant registries by way of investigation of the vendor's title.

### (3)  Hire purchase and leased equipment

Where there is equity in goods held on hire purchase or lease, it may be possible for a receiver to pay a settlement figure to the owners of the goods

¶515

to obtain full title to pass to his purchaser. Where there is no equity or where, as a result of rights of consolidation, the net position over a number of agreements with the same owner is such that there is no worthwhile realisation to be made, it may be possible for the purchaser to make his own approaches to the owners with a view to being given either new hire purchase or lease agreements or a figure at which the goods can be purchased. If the receiver is passing physical possession of these items to the purchaser he will want confirmation from the owners that he may do so.

### (4) Leasehold premises
There can be difficulties where included among the items to be sold are one or more leasehold premises from which parts of the business are run. The landlord's consent to an assignment may be necessary, yet it is usually unsatisfactory to either or both of the receiver and the purchaser for the sale to be conditional upon obtaining the landlord's consent. It is often necessary for the purchaser to buy the business outright and exchange contracts for the purchase of the leasehold, go into occupation on licence (see condition 8 of the National Conditions of Sale), pay any premium due for the lease absolutely on exchange and rely on the strength of its covenant to ensure that consent is obtained from the landlord.

### (5) Contracts
There are many aspects of the contracts of a business which may impact upon a sale. The receiver may be concerned where there are existing book debts under a long-term contract, the collection of which in full might be jeopardized in the event that the contract is not fulfilled. If the business is sold, he will no longer be in a position to complete the contract. It may be important to the receiver, therefore, that the purchaser agrees to fulfil the contract and, where possible, the receiver will wish to obtain the consent of the other contracting party to this assignment or novation as the case may be.

## ¶516 Conveyancing questions
Receivership conveyancing is straightforward. Title to the property remains vested in the company and the principal question is the manner in which the legal estate is going to be transferred to the purchaser. Where the charge is widely drawn there are usually a number of alternatives, as follows:

(1) Where the charge grants a power of attorney to the receiver he may use that power of attorney to convey the company's title to the purchaser. Section 74(3) of the Law of Property Act 1925 provides for a method by which such an attorney can be used and the wording of the section should be followed carefully. The receiver writes the name

of the company beside his own seal and signs his own name as attorney in the presence of a witness. Title may not be effectively transferred where the receiver affixes the company seal and signs his own name as witness (see the discussion at ¶410 and 411).

(2)    The charge may give the chargee a power of attorney on behalf of the company and this can be used effectively to transfer title, whether or not the company is in liquidation (*Sowman and Others* v *David Samuel Trust Limited and another* [1978] 1 WLR 22).

(3)    Transfers in accordance with the above two procedures are not sales by the chargee (*qua* chargee) and subsequent charges are not over-reached. In order to give an unencumbered title to a purchaser a deed of release or a Land Registry Form 53 should be provided by the relevant charge holders. Similarly, these transfers are not transfers free of the charge under which the receiver is appointed and an appropriate release, effective *after* the conveyance or transfer is executed, is necessary.

(4)    The mortgagee may convey or transfer. A well-worded contract signed by the receiver on behalf of the company will give him the right to offer a transfer or conveyance executed by the mortgagee *qua* mortgagee to be accepted as such by the purchaser without complaint. The mort-gagee has power to convey the legal estate where its charge is a mortgage or a charge by way of legal mortgage. Where the charge is a fixed equitable charge different considerations apply. First, there is authority that an equitable chargee with a power of attorney for the chargor may convey a legal estate without going to court (see *Re White Rose Cottage* [1965] Ch. 940, as explained by Fisher and Lightwood's *Law of Mortgage* at p. 380 note (*p*)). It may be simpler, where the chargee has a full covenant for further assurance in the charge coupled with the power of attorney, for it to write itself out a form of legal charge and execute that as attorney on behalf of the chargor. This can be done before or after liquidation, enables the mortgagee to transfer a legal estate, and seems to be acceptable to the Land Registry.

(5)    Is there any way in which a receiver can convey a legal estate not-withstanding liquidation and the consequent termination of his powers of agency and attorney? It would seem that he can. In *Barrows* v *Chief Land Registrar* (*The Times*, 20 October 1977) it was held that as the receiver still retained power to realise assets caught by the security notwithstanding liquidation, he had power to convey a legal estate in the company's property pursuant to that power of sale, in the name of the company. The following wording has been accepted by the Land Registry as suitable for a transfer by a receiver in such circumstances:

SIGNED SEALED and
DELIVERED
by AB Ltd in liquidation by          AB Ltd
CD its receiver pursuant to     by Its receiver (SEAL)
powers granted to him in                  CD
clause . . . of a debenture
dated . . . in favour of EF
Bank plc, in the presence of:

## ¶517   Power to sell charged property

Prior to the Insolvency Act 1986 there could be circumstances in which the existence of a first mortgage, ranking ahead of the charge under which the administrative receiver was appointed, could effectively prevent the receiver from realising the business and property on a sensible basis. Where the amount secured by the prior mortgage was greater than the price that could reasonably be obtained for the property, the receiver would not be able to compel the mortgagee to release his charge nor to pass unencumbered title to a purchaser, and the receiver might find himself faced with a mortgagee who wished to hold on to his charge on the property for the medium-term until, say, the property market showed more buoyancy. An administrative receiver may now apply to the court in such a situation for an order authorising him to sell free of the charge – a form of statutory 'underreaching'! A similar power covering also certain third-party goods is given to an administrator and this power is discussed below at ¶1122.

The administrative receiver must comply with r. 3.31 where he makes an application to court in this respect (and see Form 3.8).

## ¶518   Duties regarding price

The general duty of an administrative receiver in this regard is discussed above at ¶416(1). In the context of a sale including property subject to a prior charge, valuation and apportionments will be of particular importance.

It is usual for there to be some negotiation between vendor and purchaser on the allocation of a global purchase price to the different categories of asset being purchased. An administrative receiver in a receivership where the preferential creditors are so large a group that there will be no return to his appointor as floating chargee, will be conscious that those parts of the price that are paid for fixed-charge assets will maximise the realization for his appointor. He will also be conscious of his need to obtain the best price reasonably obtainable for the floating charge assets pursuant to his duty to the preferential creditors. For tax reasons, a purchaser may wish to pay more for items such as plant and equipment than for goodwill. These conflicting wishes are usually capable of resolution through discussion.

¶518

## ¶519   Considerations for purchasers

There follows a brief (non-exclusive) checklist of the type of points a purchaser and his advisers may wish to consider closely when buying from an administrative receiver:

(1)   A check should be made that the administrative receiver has been validly appointed (but note IA, s. 232).

(2)   In considering the contractual description of the business and property to be purchased, the purchaser must be sure that what he is to be transferred is the entire package he needs to run the business he is buying as a going concern.

(3)   If any item of equipment is subject to hire purchase or lease and it is crucial to the continuation of the business, the purchaser must speak with the owner to ascertain whether he can continue to have the use of the equipment, whether by buying it from the owner or by entering into a fresh hire purchase or lease agreement. Before any agreement is signed, the purchaser should seek the receiver's consent to his making such an approach.

(4)   Are there any contracts of the business which are crucial? If so, the purchaser needs to examine these in detail. Have there been any pre-payments or deposits paid by customers such that it would not be cost-effective for the purchaser to complete the contract? Even if this is the case, is it worthwhile completing the contract to preserve goodwill? Have the contracts been breached or indeed terminated by the third party? Will the third party novate the contract with the purchaser?

(5)   Does the business rely on any licences and, if so, are these licences transferable and to be transferred under the agreement?

(6)   In view of the absence of comfort from the vendor/receiver, the purchaser should consider what surveys/enquiries/investigations he ought to do to be satisfied about the business.

(7)   Where the purchaser is being forced to take leasehold premises with the risk that the landlord may not issue a licence to assign, then it might be prudent to have at least sounded out the landlord prior to completing the acquisition and to have obtained an informal approval or an agreement in principle to the issue a licence to assign. It may be a breach of the lease for the purchaser to be let into occupation and the purchaser should be aware of the risk that the landlord could force him to vacate, which could have serious repercussions on the continued operation of the business. Where there is no shortage of leasehold property in the area, the purchaser may feel more comfortable in that

it would not be commercially sensible for the landlord to refuse to accept him.

(8)  Where it is intended to employ directors or shadow directors of the company in receivership and it is also intended to continue the business in a name similar to that of the company in receivership, thought should be given to the problems posed by s. 216 of the Insolvency Act 1986 (the so-called 'phoenix' section) should the company in receivership later go into insolvent liquidation. Notice should be taken of the limited exceptions offered by the Insolvency Rules, rr. 4.226–230. Further, some thought should be given to the question of whether any of the former directors or shadow directors to be employed are likely to be the subject of applications for disqualification orders as a result of an adverse report of an administrative receiver or liquidator of the vendor company.

(9)  Where the purchaser is not resident in the UK for tax purposes, care should be taken to obtain the appropriate Treasury consent under s. 482 of the Income and Corporation Taxes Act 1970.

¶519

# 6 Payments and Distributions

## PREFERENTIAL CREDITORS

### ¶601 Who are they?

One of the distinctions between a fixed charge and a floating charge is that where a receiver is appointed under a floating charge then before payments may be made to the floating chargee, certain preferential debts must be paid (IA, s. 40). In so far as there are 'free' assets of the company not caught by the charge, such payments 'shall be recouped' out of those free assets (IA, s. 40(3)).

The recent insolvency legislation has significantly reduced the categories of debt afforded preferential status. For example, local authority rates have disappeared from the list. The taxes afforded preferential status have also been reduced and the 'assessed' taxes have been removed, leaving what might be referred to as the 'trust' cases, where the taxpayer has been collecting taxes on behalf of the relevant authorities. Section 386 and Sch. 6 of the Insolvency Act 1986 lay down the various categories of preferential debts and these may be summarised, briefly, as follows:

(1)  Income tax deducted from emoluments for the 12 months prior to the receiver's appointment.

(2)  Value added tax referable to the six months prior to the receivers' appointment and car tax, general betting or bingo duty becoming due within the 12 months before his appointment.

(3)  Certain social security contributions due in the 12 months before the receiver's appointment.

(4)  Certain contributions to occupational pension schemes.

(5)  Sums owing to employees in respect of any or all of the four months prior to the receiver's appointment. The subrogated preferential claims of those who have advanced moneys for payment of wages during the period should be noted (IA, Sch. 6, para. 11). It should also be noted that accrued holiday pay now enjoys preferential status (see IA, Sch. 6, para. 14(2)).

## ¶602 From what assets are they paid?

Prior to the new legislation, the relevant statutory provision (CA, s. 196 prior to its amendment by the Insolvency Acts 1985 and 1986) provided that payment should be made out of assets caught by a floating charge, including a charge that crystallised on the appointment of a receiver. This gave rise to the idea that if it proved possible to crystallise a floating charge prior to the appointment of a receiver such that, when the receiver was appointed, the charge was already effectively a fixed charge (that is, a crystallised floating charge), then the preferential creditors did not need to be paid out of these assets. This 'device' was approved in *Re Brightlife Limited* ([1987] 2 WLR 197; (1986) 2 BCC 99, 359). The new wording refers to payment out of assets caught by a charge which *as created* was a floating charge and closes the loophole. There is in fact an element of 'overkill' in the use of the words 'as created' in s. 40 as 'floating charge' is defined in s. 251 of the Insolvency Act 1986 to mean 'a charge which, as created, was a floating charge . . .' (consider IA, s. 175 for liquidations).[1]

## ¶603 Content of duty to pay

An administrative receiver is under a positive duty to pay preferential creditors under s. 40 of the Insolvency Act 1986 (*Westminster Corporation v Haste* [1950] 1 Ch. 442 and *Inland Revenue Commissioners v Goldblatt* [1972] Ch. 498). In the *Westminster Corporation* case Danckwerts J said (at p. 447):

> 'To my mind [the statutory provision] is not simply a negative provision which means that the receiver is protected if he simply does not pay the debenture holders, it is a provision which requires him to pay the preferential creditors out of any assets coming to the hands of him as receiver. Therefore, it seems to me that, if he has had any assets out of which this payment could have been made, he is under a liability in tort to the plaintiffs.'

This dictum was approved in the *Goldblatt* case. The latter case was one where, in an attempt to avoid payment of the preferential creditors, the receiver was removed from office by his appointer who instructed him to pass the assets back to the company which then assigned them to the debenture holder. An argument was put forward on behalf of the receiver that he was

---

[1] Section 175 provides that in a winding up, the (liquidation) preferential creditors are to be paid out of assets caught by a floating charge (i.e., a charge which, as created, was a floating charge). Although presumably not intended, there may be an argument that where a receiver is appointed and there is, later, a winding up prior to payment of his debenture holder by the receiver under a floating charge, the receiver must now pay the liquidation preferential creditors before paying his debenture holder. Before the new definition of 'floating charge', this would not have had to be contemplated because, at the commencement of winding up, the charge would have been fixed, not 'floating'.

not liable because the duty to pay the preferential creditors was only 'in priority' to payments to his debenture holder and where his debenture holder was not paid the receiver had no duty to pay the preferential creditors. This argument was rejected in favour of a positive duty for the receiver to pay. Goff J recognised the difficulty this might give if one receiver replaces another (at p. 505):

'It would follow that if a receiver be not merely removed but another be appointed, the first cannot safely account to the second nor can the second demand the assets from the first without the preferential debts of which the first receiver has notice being paid or provided for, but I do not shrink from that. In practice, no doubt, the matter will often be dealt with on an indemnity basis, but, in my judgment, once the receiver has collected assets he is liable to the extent of those assets for any preferential debts of which he has notice.'

The debenture holder in this case was also found liable. Section 196 of the Companies Act 1985, as amended by the Insolvency Act 1986 (see IA, Sch. 13, Pt. 1), provides, as did its predecessors, that where chargees take possession of assets subject to a charge which as created was a floating charge, they shall be liable to pay preferential debts in prority to their secured debt. On the facts of the *Goldblatt* case Goff J said (at p. 506):

'. . . it was submitted on behalf of the debenture holder that . . . , because the expression "possession is taken by or on behalf of those debenture holders" refers only to possession taken in exercise of their rights and powers as mortgagees and not to a case where the debenture holder takes, not only possession, but also full ownership in satisfaction of his claim. I can see no justification for so limiting the section. Indeed it would be somewhat extraordinary if the section were to protect the preferential creditors when the debenture holder takes posesssion as mortgagee, leaving the assets available for prior claims, and not if he wholly arrogates them to himself.'

It was also held that a debenture holder may be liable to the preferential creditors where he is guilty of wrongfully procuring and being a party to a breach of statutory duty by the receiver and, further, receipt of moneys by the debenture holder with notice of the receiver's statutory duty meant that the debenture holder held the moneys as constructive trustee for the preferential creditors.

If the administrative receiver dissipates assets which could have been used to pay the preferential creditors, he will be liable personally to them for breach of his statutory duty (*Woods* v *Winskill* [1913] 2 Ch. 303 and see ¶503).

¶603

In the case *Re G. L. Saunders Limited* ([1986] 1 WLR 215) Nourse J expressly approved a passage in Picarda, *The Law Relating to Receivers and Managers*, in which the author states (at p. 193):

'. . . s. 94 (and its predecsssor) [now IA, s. 40] imposes a positive duty upon the receiver. However this positive duty is only a duty to pay the claims of the preferential creditors "out of the assets which would otherwise go to the debenture holders in discharge of their principal and interest". That is why the receiver's costs and expenses and his remuneration have priority to the claims of preferential creditors. But the same reasoning demonstrates that the claims of the preferential creditors to be paid *by the receiver* (as distinct from the company) depend on the continued subsistence of the debt due to the debenture holder. It follows that s. 94 can have no possible application once the claims of the debenture holder have been paid in full, and the contest is between the preferential creditors and the company.' (Emphasis in the original.)

The particular issue being addressed by that passage and by the *G. L. Saunders Ltd* case itself are considered at ¶604, but the width of the above comment has given rise to other doubts. If the debenture holder is paid out by the receiver pursuant to fixed-charge realisations such that it will receive no payment under the floating charge because it has no debt to be repaid, and the effect of payment of the debt by way of fixed-charge realisations is to redeem the floating charge also, does the administrative receiver still have a duty to pay preferential creditors in these circumstances? One argument is that the *Westminster Corporation* and *Goldblatt* cases are clear authorities to the effect that the receiver has a positive duty to pay preferential creditors and that the relevant statutory provision is not merely a provision deciding priorities. The argument continues that the only sensible time at which the rights of the preferential creditors can be ascertained is at the date of the receiver's appointment and at that time the floating charge assets are impressed with a statutory trust in favour of the preferential creditors. If the contrary were to be the case, an administrative receiver would face very difficult problems in practice as the question of whether or not the preferential creditors were paid might depend on the timing of sales of fixed charge assets giving rise to conflicts of interest. The *G. L. Saunders Ltd* case was dealing merely with the question of fixed charge surpluses and Nourse J commented specifically that on the facts of the case before him there were floating-charge realisations which were 'clearly payable' to the preferential creditors. The decision in *G. L. Saunders Ltd* and the comment from *The Law Relating to Receivers and Managers* cited above, can be seen as being addressed to the particular question of the destination of surplus fixed-charge realisations.

¶603

The alternative argument is that the intention of the statutory provision is to put preferential creditors in the same preferred position whether there is a receivership or a liquidation, i.e., to ensure that in either case they are paid before the holder of a floating charge. Where such a charge is not being paid, the preferential creditors do not need to be 'protected' in the manner envisaged by the section and hence should not be paid. The objection that a later liquidation may materially alter the make-up of the preferential creditors is met by saying that the (preferential) creditors are able to present a winding-up petition to protect their status, at any time. This 'alternative' argument has a pleasing logic about it but most insolvency practitioners would hope that, on the question ever coming before the court, the great practical difficulties which would be caused if the argument were upheld would weigh heavily in the balance and encourage the court to hold that a receiver should remain in office to pay preferential creditors.

## ¶604    Surplus of fixed-charge realisations

In *Re G. L. Saunders Limited* ([1986] 1 WLR 215), receivers applied to the court for directions (see now IA, s. 35) as to the manner in which they should treat certain realisations of their receivership. They had realised sums in respect of assets caught by their debenture holder's fixed charge sufficient to pay the secured debt and leave a significant surplus. Realisations had been made of floating-charge assets but these were not sufficient to pay preferential creditors in full. There appeared to be two alternative destinations for the surplus moneys. If the equity of redemption in the fixed charge was caught by the floating charge and on the fixed charge being redeemed the floating charge caught the surplus, the money should go to the preferential creditors. The alternative argument was that by definition when the debenture holder was repaid out of fixed-charge moneys this not only redeemed the fixed charge but simultaneously redeemed the floating charge and the floating charge could never attach to the equity of redemption in the fixed charge, certainly where both securities secured the same debt. This latter view was preferred by Nourse J and surplus fixed-charge realisations in these circumstances must be paid to the company or, as is more likely to be the case, to the liquidator.

## ¶605    Crown set-off

What if the Crown has a part preferential and part non-preferential claim? Can the Crown set-off against the non-preferential claim leaving its full preferential claim intact? The argument that it can would be based on an analogy with the position of a secured creditor who in a liquidation may apply the proceeds of the sale of security against the non-preferential debt to preserve, as far as possible, its preferential claim (*Re William Hall (Contractors) Limited (In Liquidation)* [1967] 1 WLR 948). However, in liquidations, the recent case of *Re Unit 2 Windows Limited (In Liquidation)* ([1985] 1 WLR 1383; (1985) 1 BCC 99, 489) decided (criticizing *obiter dicta* in *Re E. J. Morel (1934) Limited* [1962] Ch. 21) that set-off should be pro rata against preferential and non preferential claims. Although such a ruling in the case of a liquidation is not necessarily authority in the case of a receivership, there is an element of fairness and common sense about this approach which might prove attractive to the court should the point ever be tested.

## ORDER OF PAYMENTS

### ¶606    General principles

Most well-drafted charges will stipulate precisely the method of distribution of the proceeds of realisations, although it is submitted that, in view of *Woods v Winskill* ([1913] 2 Ch. 303), a contractual provision entitling a receiver to pay unsecured creditors in priority to preferential creditors could not safely be followed by a receiver. It would not be correct to say that a receiver can in no circumstances pay an unsecured creditor. Where, for example, he needs supplies from a person who is an unsecured creditor and he is unable to obtain supplies without making a form of 'ransom' payment to that creditor, he is entitled to do so provided that there is a net benefit to the receivership or, perhaps, that he has reasonable grounds for believing there will be a net benefit to the receivership.

In the absence of any provisions in the debenture itself (see *Yourell* v *Hibernian Bank Ltd* [1918] AC 372), s. 109(8) of the Law of Property Act 1925 steps into the vacuum and gives the following order:

' (i)    In discharge of all rents, taxes, rates, and outgoings whatever affecting the mortgaged property; and

(ii)    In keeping down all annual sums or other payments, and the interest .on all principal sums, having priority to the mortgage in right whereof he is receiver; and

(iii)    In payment of his commission, and of the premiums on fire, life or other insurances, if any, properly payable under the mortgage deed or under this Act, and the cost of executing necessary or proper repairs directed in writing by the mortgagee; and

(iv)    In payment of the interest accruing due in respect of any principal money due under the mortgage; and

(v)    In or towards discharge of the principal money if so directed in writing by the mortgagee;

and shall pay the residue, if any, of the money received by him to the person who, but for the possession of the receiver, would have been entitled to receive the income of which he is appointed receiver, or who is otherwise entitled to the mortgaged property.[1]

As regards the phrase 'who is otherwise entitled to the mortgaged property', where an administrative receiver has been appointed under a subsequent charge the accounting will normallly be to that subsequent receiver in the event of there being a surplus. In this regard note should be made of *Re Quest Cae Limited* ([1985] BCLC 266). In that case the debenture holder whose charge contained a convenant by the mortgagor to pay 'all moneys and/or discharge all liabilities whether certain or contingent now or hereafter owing by or incurred by the company to the lender on any account whatever . . .' took assignments of unsecured stock at a percentage of its face value and sought to argue that the full amount of the face value was caught by the security. The argument failed as a matter of construction of the convenant to pay but arguments were addressed to the court to the effect that even were the wording sufficiently wide, it would be against the policy of the insolvency scheme of English law for such tactics to be permitted. Nourse J noted the arguments but in view of his decision on the construction point he did not feel that it was appropriate to take the questions of public policy further.

# CONTRIBUTION BETWEEN CO-GUARANTORS

## ¶607    Introduction

Often, where a bank is lending to a group of companies it will take security from all the companies within the group. In addition to such security the bank will commonly require cross guarantees between the companies comprised in the group. The parent company will guarantee the indebtedness of its sub-sidiaries to the bank. The subsidiaries will give upstream guarantees of the parent's liability to the bank and each subsidary will guarantee the indebt-edness of its sister subsidiaries (for a consideration of the questions of legal validity raised by these arrangements see ¶1016(2)).

If the bank enforces its security and makes demand under any of the guarantees which have been given, any administrative receiver appointed under the security held by the bank must bear in mind the possibility that certain companies within the group may obtain rights of contribution as against other members of the group if they pay off (whether in whole or in part) the indebtedness of any other members of the group to the bank.

¶607

It is important that any administrative receiver in such a situation is aware of the possible need to allocate the proceeds of realisation of the assets of the group members in a manner which takes into account any rights of contribution that may have been acquired. Where one or more members of the group is able to meet its own indebtedness as principal out of its own assets and would, other than for its liability under any guarantee it has given, have a surplus, the problem becomes more acute, particularly if there is more than one secured lender in respect of that company's assets. The holder of a second debenture over the assets of a guarantor company will be anxious to ensure that any surplus assets are avaiable to reduce his indebtedness if possible.

A brief summary of the relevant legal principles and some of the problems which may occur is given below.

## ¶608   Co-guarantors' rights

### (1)   Indemnity from principal debtor

Where a surety ('S') makes a payment to reduce or extinguish the indebtedness of a principal debtor ('D') to his creditor ('C'), S will generally be entitled to call upon D to reimburse him in respect of any amount which he has paid to C.

An indemnity from D to S may be an express indemnity contained in a written instrument (*Bradford* v *Gammon* [1925] Ch. 132; *Craven-Ellis* v *Canons Ltd* [1936] 2 KB 403 where, in an analogous situation, a director whose service contract was void recovered remuneration on a quantum meruit). Alternatively, it may be an implied indemnity, as where S guarantees the indebtedness of D to C at D's request (*Anson* v *Anson* [1953] 1 QB 636). If there is no written indemnity and S did not give the guarantee at D's request, it is possible that S will not have any right to be indemnified by D. In some circumstances, where no request has been made, it will be possible for S to bring a restitutionary claim in quasi contract against D. However, as Goff and Jones point out in *The Law of Restitution* (3rd edn) at p. 324:

'Typical examples of a contractual right of indemnity are the right of a surety who has given a guarantee at the request of the principal debtor. . . . [S's] right of recovery is not limited to the benefit, if any, conferred on [D] by [S's] payment. [S] will be entitled to be indemnified against his expenditure, even though his payment may have conferred no benefit on the defendant, by discharging a liability or otherwise. Where, however, [S's] claim is quasi-contractual, his right is not to indemnity but to reimbursement to the extent that his payment has conferred a benefit on [D].'

So, where there is an express or implied right of indemnity from D, S can recover under it even though the payment he makes to C confers no benefit

¶608

on D – for example, where D had a full defence to C's claim and need not have paid any sum to him (*Brittain* v *Lloyd* [1845] 14 M & W 762; *Warlow* v *Harrison* [1858] 1 El & El 295). However, if S has no express or implied indemnity and is relying upon a claim in quasi contract he must show that his payment to C conferred a benefit on D. If D has a full defence to C's claim, no benefit at all is conferred upon D by S's payment and S may be unable to recover from D any payments he has made to C (*Brook's Wharf and Bull Wharf Limited* v *Goodman Bros* [1937] 1 KB 534; *Re Cleadon Trust Limited* [1939] Ch. 286).

In cases where security and guarantees are taken by a bank which is lending to a group of companies, it should almost always be possible to imply a request by each of the principal debtors to its guarantors to enter into a bank guarantee. However, to put the matter beyond doubt, it may be appropriate for the companies to record in the board minutes relating to the creation of such security that the guarantees were entered into at the specific request of the other members of the group. Having established a request, those guarantors paying off the indebtedness of other members of the group will be entitled to an indemnity from the assets of the principal debtor. In practice, the problem will be that the principal debtor will usually be insolvent and any indemnity worthless.

The right to an indemnity arises as soon as S makes a payment to C which reduces the indebtedness of D to C (*Re Fenton* [1931] 1 Ch. 85; *Re A Debtor* [1937] Ch. 156; *Re Mitchell, Freelove* v *Mitchell* [1913] 1 Ch. 201; but see *Spark* v *Heslop* (1859) IE & E 563 where the court found an express agreement to the effect that the right of indemnity accrued prior to the surety paying out sums).

A surety's indemnity will only extend to the amount of any payments he has made in reduction of his principal's indebtedness. If, for example, D owes C £600 but S pays C £450 in full and final settlement of that debt, S can only claim an indemnity in respect of £450 from D.

**(2)   Contribution between co-sureties**
Where more than one guarantor is liable for the same debt of a principal debtor it has long been established that equity requires each solvent co-guarantor to share the burden of that debt equally (*Deering* v *The Earl of Winchelsea* (1787) 1 Cox Exch Cas 318; *Ellesmere Brewery Co.* v *Cooper* [1896] QB 75).

For example, D owes C £3,000 and S1, S2 and S3 have given C an unlimited guarantee in respect of this debt. If D defaulted and S1 paid the debt in full to C and was unable to recover under his indemnity from D (see above) he would acquire rights of contribution against S2 and S3. If both S2 and S3 were solvent S1 could call upon each of them to pay him £1,000. If S3 was insolvent he would only be entitled to look to S2 for a contribution towards the payments he had made to C. S2 would be required to pay S1 £1,500 (*Lowe* v *Dixon* (1885) 16 QBD 455).

The right of a guarantor who has paid more than his fair proportion of a principal's indebtedness to call upon his solvent co-guarantors for a contribution does not arise out of any express or implied contract. The right of contribution is founded on more general equitable principles that the common burden should be shared equally (*Craythorne* v *Swinburne* (1807) 14 Ves Jun 160; *Deering* v *The Earl of Winchelsea* (1787) 1 Cox Exch Cas 318). It is not necessary for the co-guarantors to be aware of one another or for their guarantees to be contained in the same written instrument.

There can be no claim for contribution unless the co-guarantors are all subject to a common demand (*Coope* v *Twynam* (1823) Turn & R 426; *Reynolds* v *Wheeler* (1861) 10 CBNS 561). So, where S has given an unlimited guarantee of the indebtedness of D to C and X gives a further unlimited guarantee of the indebtedness of S to C, there can be no claim for contribution by S against X even if S pays all of the indebtedness of D. This is so even if the only liability of S to C arises under the guarantee that S gave to C of D's indebtedness (*Craythorne* v *Swinburne* (1807) 14 Ves Jun 160; *Re Denton's Estate* [1904] 2 Ch. 178). Similarly, where S1 and S2 have guaranteed different debts of D to C (for example specific debts arising under different contracts), S1 could not call upon S2 to contribute if it were called on its guarantee. There is no common burden and so the equitable principles would not apply.

Although it is uncommon, it is possible for co-guarantors to agree that their rights of contribution will be circumscribed, e.g., limited to a specific amount or excluded altogether. If this is the case, a readjustment of the proportions in which the co-guarantors must bear the loss occasioned by D's default will be necessary.

A co-guarantor has the right to claim contribution from his solvent co-guarantors as soon as (*a*) he has paid more than his fair proportion of the principal's indebtedness (*Davies* v *Humphreys* (1840) 6 M & W 153; cf. *Stirling* v *Burdett* [1911] 2 Ch. 418 where the principal's indebtedness was payable in instalments and the co-sureties' rights to contribution were held not to arise until such time as they had paid more than their proportion of the whole of the principal debt) and (*b*) he has failed to recover pursuant to the right of indemnity which he has against the principal debtor.

## (3) Subrogation to creditor's security

If S pays off C he is entitled to the benefit of any security which C may have had as against D (*Craythorne* v *Swinburne* (1807) 14 Ves Jun 160; *Duncan, Fox & Co.* v *North and South Wales Bank* [1880] 6 App Cas 1). For example, C advances £100,000 to D and as security for this advance takes a debenture

¶608

over the whole of the assets and undertaking of D. C demands repayment from D of the advance. D defaults and S pays C in full having received a demand under a guarantee given by him to C for D's indebtedness. S is subrogated to C's rights under its security (*Re M'Myn* (1886) 33 ChD 575; *Re Lamplugh Iron Ore Co. Ltd* [1927] 1 Ch. 308).

The right to be subrogated to a creditor's security taken from the principal debtor does not arise until such time as the debt of D to C has been repaid in full (*Re Howe* [1871] 6 Ch. App 838). In order to be subrogated to a creditor's rights a surety need not pay the whole of the debt himself. His rights of subrogation will, however, only extend to any payment he has made in reduction of the principal's debt. The surety is thus able to enforce its right of indemnity against the principal debtor with the benefit of the creditor's security. This may be of particular benefit to a surety where the principal debtor has granted several tiers of security as it would allow the surety to gain priority over subsequent charges.

In addition to having the benefit of any security granted by the principal debtor to the creditor, a guarantor who has paid more than his fair proportion of the debt is entitled to the benefit of any security given by a co-guarantor to the creditor to enforce his rights of contribution against those co-guarantors (*Steel* v *Dixon* (1881) 17 ChD 825). On the other hand a surety who is seeking a contribution from a co-surety must take into account securities he has the benefit of from the principal debtor (*Berridge* v *Berridge* (1890) 44 ChD 168; *Re Arcedeckne* (1883) 24 ChD 709). In each case the subrogated guarantor enjoys the priority which the creditor enjoyed over the general body of creditors. The fact that the creditor's debt has been repaid does not affect the position of the co-guarantor who succeeds to the creditor's rights (s. 5 of the Mercantile Law Amendment Act 1956).

It is possible, though unusual, for a co-guarantor to agree to forego its rights of subrogation by express agreement. A co-guarantor may also by his conduct waive his right to be subrogated to the creditor's security.

## ¶609    Receiver's power and duty to allocate funds

Section 109(8) of the Law of Property Act 1925 states *inter alia* that a receiver shall apply 'the residue' of any moneys received by him 'to the person who, but for the possession of the receiver, would have been entitled to receive the income of which he is appointed receiver, or who is otherwise entitled to the mortgaged property'.

A receiver will not obtain a good discharge unless he acts in accordance with s. 109(8) (as amended by the security). Where rights of contribution have arisen between members of the group, two questions arise:

(1)　How can a receiver be sure of obtaining a good discharge when he has surplus funds in his hands at the end of his receivership?

(2)　What power does a receiver have to move funds around the group to give effect to the rights of contribution which have arisen?

The practical answer to the first question is to obtain the consent of all the parties concerned to a distribution of any surplus held by a receiver at the end of his administration on an agreed basis. Where a liquidator has been appointed, his consent to the distribution of funds in a receiver's hands will need to be obtained. Where no liquidator has been appointed, any consent required will need to be obtained from the company itself acting through its directors. If any relevant consent cannot be obtained, a receiver can apply to the court for directions, under s. 35 of the Insolvency Act 1986, as to the way in which funds should be distributed. In straightforward cases it may not be necessary or cost-effective for a receiver to make an application for directions and he will simply pay over funds to the liquidator or company concerned.

A receiver will commonly obtain an indemnity from a liquidator when handing over assets to him (see ¶709). In some cases, it will be necessary to provide in such indemnity for the possibility of a claim being made against a receiver by a co-surety for wrongfully disposing of funds in which that co-surety had some proprietry right.

It is not part of the functions of a receiver (once his appointer has been redeemed and any preferential creditors paid) to distribute funds within a group so as to give effect to any rights of contribution which may have arisen. This task would normally be left to a liquidator. However, it is submitted that it is good practice for a receiver to move funds around to give effect to such rights where this can be done without exposing him to any risk of a third-party claim.

Further, there are suggestions in the judgment of Blackett-Ord J in *Brown v Cork and Another* ((1984) at first instance, unreported) to the effect that a receiver may have a duty in such situations to make distributions giving effect to rights of contribution.

# REMUNERATION

## ¶610　Generally

The administrative receiver appointed under a security out of court with powers of management, to all intents and purposes as wide as those of the directors and the company itself, is a comparatively recent phenomenon.

Many of the early cases concern receivers appointed by the court. Further, the main function of a receiver appointed out of court at one time was to receive the income of property over which he was appointed, say collecting the income from tenants of a block of flats. This old fashioned view of receivers appointed out of court is reflected in the provisions of the Law of Property Act 1925. In the absence of any provisions in the security document, the remuneration of a receiver will be governed by s. 109(6) of the 1925 Act which reads as follows:

> 'The receiver shall be entitled to retain out of any money received by him, for his remuneration, and in satisfaction of all costs, charges and expenses incurred by him as receiver, a commission at such rate, not exceeding 5 per centum on the gross amount of all money received, as is specified in his appointment, and if no rate is so specified, then at the rate of 5 per centum on that gross amount, or at such other rate as the Court thinks fit to allow, on application made by him for that purpose.'

Accountants and solicitors in common with many other professionals now operate on the basis of hourly charge-out rates. A flat rate commission of five per cent is rather a crude measure of the worth of a receiver in any particular case. In some cases five per cent may be far less than is appropriate, yet in others it may be somewhat excessive.

Charges should contain a clear right for a chargee to agree the quantum of an administrative receiver's remuneration with him and to agree that the remuneration should be charged on the assets. The provision should go on to provide that the remuneration may be settled by reference to the receiver's or his firm's usual charging rates for such work.

In the event that there is no express power in the charge and the Law of Property Act formula must be used, the following points should be noted:

(1)  Although a receiver appointed under s. 101 of the Law of Property Act 1925 is expressed to be 'a receiver of . . . income' (see s. 101(1)(iii)) it would seem that where he has wider powers including, for example, power to sell property (which power is not included in the Law of Property Act), then five per cent means five per cent of sums such as proceeds of sale (*Marshall* v *Cottingham* [1981] 3 WLR 235).

(2)  Where a security document provides, by way of variation of s. 109(8) of the Law of Property Act 1925, for payment of the receiver's 'remuneration and the costs of realisation', then such costs of realisation as estate agents' fees, legal costs and costs of a caretaker are not to be included in computing the five per cent gross which is available to pay the receiver's remuneration. The receiver can therefore take five per cent for his remuneration and pay the costs of realisation out

of the proceeds of sale as a separate matter (*Marshall* v *Cottingham*, as cited above).

(3)   If the receiver is satisfied with five per cent he does not need to go to court (*Marshall* v *Cottingham* as cited above). If, however, five per cent is clearly inadequate, he may apply to the court for a more realistic rate of remuneration and the court would recognise that a professional should be paid an appropriate amount for his remuneration.

It is always open to a liquidator to make an application to the court to fix the amount of a receiver's remuneration (IA, s. 36). The court's power extends to covering a period prior to the making of the order, whether or not the receiver has died or ceased to act and, where there are special circumstances making it proper for the court to do so, extends to making a receiver's personal representative account for any excess (IA, s. 36(2)). The section does not permit the court to interfere with the receiver's right of indemnity in respect of disbursements (*Re Potters Oils Limited (No. 2)* (1985) 1 BCC 99, 593; [1986] 1 All ER 890). In the *Potters Oils* case (99, 593 at p. 99, 599; 890 at pp. 895–6) Hoffmann J explained how he thought the court should deal with its power under the section:

'The section confers two separate discretions. The first is a discretion as to whether to interfere at all. The second, once the decision has been made to fix the remuneration, is a discretion as to the amount. Both appear to be entirely unfettered.

In exercising these discretions I bear in mind the following considerations. Firstly, the exercise of the power involves interference with contractual rights in the interests of the unsecured creditors. As Sir Andrew Clark KC said in argument in *Re Greycaine Limited* [1946] Ch. 269 at p. 274, the mischief at which the section is aimed is that –

"Unsecured creditors may find themselves bound by an improvident bargain entered into by the directors and see the assets frittered away on the agent of the secured creditors."

I respectfully adopt this description which suggests to me that interference should be confined to cases in which the remuneration can clearly be seen as excessive rather than take the form of a routine taxation by the court of receivers' remuneration.

Secondly, the Court is ill-equipped to conduct a detailed investigation of receivers' charges on an itemised basis. . . .

Thirdly, clause 8 of the debenture contemplates remuneration calculated as a percentage of the sum realised by the receiver. . . . This is of course not of itself a reason for not interfering. . . . In this case, however, there is nothing to show that either a percentage calculation or the five per cent maximum is unreasonable.

Guidance may be obtained from the fact that the fees of liquidators and trustees in bankruptcy are ordinarily calculated as a percentage of the moneys which pass through their hands. . . .'

# 7 Termination

## METHODS OF TERMINATION

### ¶701 Repayment of secured debt: duty to cease to act

Although there appear to be no authorities precisely on the point, it seems settled as a matter of general principle that an administrative receiver is under a duty to close his receivership and hand any surplus assets or moneys over to the company or the liquidator, as the case may be, when he is in a position to repay the secured debt of his debenture holder (and, in priority thereto, the proper costs, charges, expenses and liabilities of the receivership, his remuneration, and in respect of floating charge realisations, the preferential creditors). The danger in not ceasing to act is that of being held to be a trespasser and being unable to claim remuneration for work done from the time when he ought to have ceased to act.

Where an administrative receiver vacates the office on completing his receivership, he must give notice forthwith to the liquidator (if the company is in liquidation) and in any event to the members of any creditors' committee which may have been formed in the receivership (IR, r. 3.35(1)). An administrative receiver has a duty under s. 405(2) of the Companies Act 1985 to give notice to the Registrar of Companies that he is ceasing to act, and that fact is noted in the charges register. He also has to give notice to the Registrar within 14 days of vacation of office (otherwise than by death) under s. 45(4) of the Insolvency Act 1986. The two duties are tied together by the Insolvency Rules, r. 3.35(2), which provides that the notice to the Registrar under s. 45(4) may be an endorsement on the notice required under s. 405(2) of the Companies Act.

### ¶702 Dismissal

Prior to the recent insolvency legislation, an administrative receiver was in the invidious position that, while his appointer could dismiss him without cause, he had no right to resign his office without first obtaining the agreement of the chargee. It now requires an order of the court for an administrative receiver to be removed (IA, s. 45(1)).

¶702

It would appear that the receiver needs to comply with the notice requirements under s. 405(2) of the Companies Act 1985 and s. 45(4) of the Insolvency Act 1986 when he is removed from office by the court.

## ¶703   Resignation

An administrative receiver may now resign his office (IA, s. 45(1)). Before he may resign, the receiver must give at least seven days' notice to his appointor and the company or, where the company is in liquidation, the liquidator (IR, r. 3.33(1) and note IR, rr. 12.4 and 13.3). The notice must specify the date on which the resignation is to take effect. Again, the receiver will have to give notice to the Registrar of Companies in the manner described above (¶701).

## ¶704   Death

While a deceased administrative receiver does not have to give notice to the Registrar of Companies under s. 45(4) of the Insolvency Act 1986 (although he would appear to be required to do so under s. 405(2) of the Companies Act 1985!), his appointor must, forthwith on becoming aware of his death, give notice to the Registrar of Companies and the company itself or, if the company is in liquidation, to the liquidator (IR, r. 3.34 and Form 3.7).

## ¶705   Vacation of office

An administrative receiver is required to vacate office in two circumstances. First, if he ceases to be qualified to act as an insolvency practitioner in relation to the copany (IA, s.45(2)). Secondly, he must vacate office where an administration order is made in respect of the company (IA, s. 11(2)).

It might have been thought that vacation of office in these circumstances would be automatic, first in view of the criminal liability attaching to someone who acts as an insolvency practitioner when not qualified to do so (IA, s. 389(1)) and, secondly, in view of the need for an administrator to take over immediately an administration order is made. The Insolvency Rules, r. 3.33(3), in making it clear that where a receiver vacates office because an administration order is made he does not need to give the notices referred to in the rule, uses the phrase, 'If the receiver *resigns*' (emphasis supplied). This suggests that some formal resignation is required. Although a receiver who vacates office because he is not qualified to act as an insolvency practitioner is not specifically exempted from the ambit of r. 3.33 in the same way as a receiver vacating office when an administration order is made, the fact that r. 3.35 specifically covers the notices to be given in that situation suggests that, even if some formal act of resignation is required, he may cease to act immediately. This would seem appropriate in view of the danger of criminal liability. Rule

3.35 obliges an administrative receiver vacating office on ceasing to be qualified to give the same notices as a receiver vacating office on completing his receivership, that is, to the company or to the liquidator of the company if it is in liquidation, and, in any case, to the members of any creditors' committee.

In either of the above cases of vacation of office, the provisions of s. 405(2) of the Companies Act 1985 and s. 45(4) of the Insolvency Act 1986 must be complied with. As in all cases involving these sections, it is a criminal offence for the receiver not to comply (CA, s. 405(4) and IA, s. 45(5)).

Where a receiver is required to vacate office as a result of an administration order being made, he is relieved from any duty that he may have to pay preferential creditors (IA, s. 11(5) and see ¶601–3).

## INDEMNITIES

### ¶706   Statutory provisions

There are two distinct statutory indemnities given to an administrative receiver when he vacates office. Section 11(4) of the Insolvency Act 1986 provides that:

> 'Where at any time an administrative receiver of the company has vacated office [on the making of an administration order] . . . –
>
> (*a*) his remuneration and any expenses properly incurred by him, and
>
> (*b*) any indemnity to which he is entitled out of the assets of the company,
>
> shall be charged on and (*subject to subsection (3) above*) paid out of any property of the company which was in his custody or under his control at that time in priority to any security held by the person by or on whose behalf he was appointed' (emphasis supplied).

Section 11(3) referred to in s. 11(4) lists the prohibitions resulting from an administration order, included in which is the prohibition on enforcing any security over the company's property. This would seem to suggest that an administrative receiver's indemnity is charged on the relevant property, but he is not entitled to enforce that security without the leave of the court.

Section 45(3) of the Insolvency Act 1986 is in similar terms to s. 11(4), save that the indemnity applies 'at any time an administrative receiver vacates office' and the payment out of the charged property is not limited. It would seem that s. 45(3) must be read as applying to any time an administrative receiver vacates office *except* where that occurs as a result of the making of an administration order.

¶706

As regards the administrative receiver's statutory charge under s. 11(4) or s. 45(3), whoever is in control of these assets after the receiver will need to clear the charge in order to give unencumbered title to any purchaser. Although the position is not clear, it would seem that an administrator may need an order of the court under s. 15 to dispose of the property if the statutory charge can be described as 'security'. Section 248(*b*) of the Insolvency Act 1986 gives this definition of 'security': 'any mortgage, charge, lien or other security . . .' which appears on the face of it to be a wide enough definition to cover the statutory charge. By s. 15(3) it would appear that the security, not being a floating charge, falls under the category of 'any other security', which means that the administration requires a court order and the administrative receiver is entitled to the proceeds of sale or market value.

Both indemnities are to be charged out of 'any property' which is in the administrative receiver's custody or control in priority to 'any security' of his appointor. This would seem to suggest that the receiver might have a statutory charge for his remuneration and expenses from not just floating-charge assets, but also fixed. It would be a surprising result if remuneration and expenses relating to floating-charge matters could be charged out of fixed assets. It seems unlikely that the court would reach such a result, and the solution may be that the charge relates to floating-charge assets and fixed-charge assets respectively to the extent that the remuneration and expenses relate to matters falling under each particular head.

## ¶707    Relationship with appointor

An administrative receiver will wish to make distributions to his appointor as soon as is reasonably practicable. Interest will be accruing on the secured debt while it is still outstanding.

A receiver may wish to make an interim distribution to his appointor where he has contingent liabilities still outstanding, to meet which he might require to use the moneys distributed. For example, an administrative receiver may think he has a reasonable estimate of the quantum of the preferential creditors but these turn out to be larger than anticipated. There may be circumstances which give rise to doubts as to the validity of the security under which he has been appointed which, if well founded, might render the receiver personally liable to the company or a liquidator. In these types of circumstance (and notwithstanding the receiver's statutory right to apply to the court for an indemnity in respect of an invalid appointment (see IA, s. 34)) an administrative receiver may come to an indemnity arrangement with his debenture holder when passing over funds, whereby the debenture holder acknowledges the receiver's right to recall the funds in certain eventualities.

## ¶708    Relationship with administrator

There may be difficulties facing an administrative receiver who is required to vacate office on the appointment of an administrator. Where the security has been shown to be vulnerable the argument may run that the receiver was never validly in office and is not entitled to any remuneration or indemnity. Even where the administrator takes over with the consent of the administrative receiver's appointor, it would seem that the receiver has no right to have any liabilities settled by the administrator, but merely has a statutory charge on the assets. What if the receiver has ordered goods which have been delivered but not yet paid for? It would appear that, if he has personally assured a supplier that these goods will be paid for, he will be personally liable to settle the outstanding invoice yet will be unable to enforce his statutory charge against the assets in the administration. This appears to give the receiver cash-flow problems. It is to be hoped that, in practice, administrators as insolvency practitioners will ensure that any problems are minimised. There are at least two steps that an administrative receiver could take. First, he could try to ensure that he settles all his outstanding liabilities from company assets prior to the relevant hearing. Secondly, he might fall into the category of a creditor of the company and apply to the court for relief on the grounds that the administrator's conduct is unfairly prejudicial to him (IA, s. 27(1)).

## ¶709    Relationship with a liquidator

As a matter of convention, when an administrative receiver passes assets or moneys to a liquidator, he seeks a form of indemnity from the liquidator. There is no legal requirement that the liquidator give an indemnity but a receiver is entitled to hold on to assets and moneys where there is still a potential liability which he might have to meet out of the assets (and consider also *Re Fosters and Rudd, The Times*, (1986) 2 BCC 98, 955, which decided that a mortgagee may hold on to security which secures a contingent liability where the contingency has not yet occurred). The format of such indemnities is for the liquidator to indemnify the receiver, to the extent of the moneys passed over, against any liability arising in the receivership and, in particular, such matters as the liability to pay preferential creditors and suppliers claiming reservation of title. The liquidator's liability will reduce to the extent that he distributes funds properly to creditors in his liquidation or in paying his remuneration, but he will undertake to give a period of notice to the receiver before making any such payment, which enables the receiver to call on the indemnity in time to prevent a dissipation of the assets. These arrangements seem to work satisfactorily in practice.

Where an administrative receiver is appointed after the company has gone into liquidation, all the expenses of the winding-up rank in priority to the preferential creditors and the debt of the charge holder (*Re Barleycorn Enterprise Limited* [1970] 1 Ch. 465). In the case of a compulsory winding-up, a company is not deemed to be 'in the course of being wound up' for the purposes of this rule until after the winding-up order is made (*Re Christonette International Limited* [1982] 1 WLR 1245). These legal rules seem unaffected by the new formulation of liquidation expenses in the Insolvency Act 1986 and the Insolvency Rules 1986 (see IA, ss. 115 and 156 and IR, r. 4.218 – although it is not immediately clear what is the significance of the removal of the words 'costs charges and' from s. 115's predecessor CA, s. 604: it is believed that the change may have been made to bring the wording into line with the wording that was used in Scotland).

# ACCOUNTS

## ¶710   Abstract of receipts and payments

The provisions formerly contained in s. 497 of the Companies Act 1985 are now to be found in r. 3.32. Within two months of the end of each year of his receivership and within two months of ceasing to act, an administrative receiver has to send to the Registrar of Companies, to the company, to his appointor, and to any member of the creditors' committee, a receipts and payments account (IR, r. 3.32(1) and Form 3.6). Where a receiver makes an application, the court can extend the period for filing the accounts (IR, r. 3.32(2)).

The accounts are to be in abstract form showing receipts and payments for the relevant 12 months and, where the receiver is ceasing to act, for the relevant part of the year since his appointment or since the last return (IR, r. 3.32(3)). The receiver is liable to a fine if the fails to comply with these rules (IR, r. 3.32(5)).

As already discussed, (¶415(2)) an administrative receiver may have wider duties to account to the company, and the Rules provide that the abstracted accounts which are required to be filed are without prejudice to any other requirement of the receiver to produce proper accounts (IR, r. 3.32(4)), and see *Smiths Ltd* v *Middleton* [1979] 3 All ER 842, as explained in *Gomba Holdings UK Limited and Others* v *Homan and Another* (1986) 2 BCC 99, 102; [1986] 3 All ER 94).

Where a receiver has failed to make a return or to file accounts or documents as required by law after 14 days have elapsed since a notice requiring him to make good the default, a member or creditor or the Registrar of Companies may apply to the court for an order requiring him to remedy the position (IA,

s. 41 and see *Re Arctic Engineering* [1986] 1 WLR 686; (1985) 1 BCC 99, 563). Similarly, a liquidator may apply to the court where a receiver has not rendered proper receipts and payments accounts nor handed over to the liquidator sums properly due (IA, s. 41). In both these cases the receiver has to bear all costs of, and incidental to, the application (IA, s. 41(2)). These remedies are quite apart from any default fines to which the receiver may otherwise be liable (IA, s. 41(3)).

# 8 Tax

This chapter deals with the circumstances in which receivers may become liable for tax liabilities incurred by the company before and during the receivership. The chapter does not deal with particular computational points nor with tax law in general: for a discussion of these problems reference should be made to the appropriate standard textbooks.

## EXISTING LIABILITIES

### ¶801 General rule

'Existing liabilities' means liabilities for income tax, corporation tax or value added tax (VAT) which have accrued due at the date on which the administrative receiver is appointed. The general rule is that a receiver will not incur any personal liability for accrued taxation. Subject to what is said in the rest of this chaper, existing liabilities for tax are ordinary debts having preference or not depending on the application of the rules relating to preferential debts.

Although s. 108 of the Taxes Management Act 1970 provides that 'everything to be done by a company under the Taxes Acts shall be done by the company acting through the proper officer of the company . . .', any fears that a receiver could be considered to be the 'proper officer', and as such be personally liable for the company's liabilities, have been dismissed by the Privy Council decision in *Income Tax Commissioner* v *Chatani* ([1983] STC 477). That case was an appeal from the Court of Appeal in Jamaica and dealt with a provision of the Jamaican Income Tax Act which was similar to the provisions of s. 108. The effect of that decision is that, although the proper office is liable to take all administrative steps in connection with tax, that does not mean he is personally answerable for payment (unless, possibly, the way in which he performs his duties lays him open to a claim by the Revenue or Customs & Excise in tort).

### ¶802 Preferential payments

The general rule is modified for receivers by the rules relating to preferential payments. Debts which are to be treated as preferential in insolvencies are dealt with in s. 386 of, and Sch. 6 to, the Insolvency Act 1986. Schedule 6 categorises preferential debts, and categories 1 and 2 of the Schedule deal respectively with debts due to the Inland Revenue and debts due to the Customs & Excise. Both categories of debts are defined by reference to the 'relevant date' which, for the purposes of a receivership, is in England and Wales the date of the appointment of the receiver by the debenture holders.

A comparison between categories 1 and 2 of the Insolvency Act and Sch. 19 to the Companies Act 1985 will show that for receiverships commencing on or after 29 December 1986, the Crown's preference for tax has been substantially restricted. Before that date the preference was for all taxes included in an assessment on the company up to the 5th April next before the relevant date, not exceeding in the whole one year's assessment, together with any sums due on account of PAYE deductions and certain deductions required to be made from payments to subcontractors in the construction industry. The preference for VAT was for any tax due at the relevant date which had become due within the period of 12 months next before that date.

The preferential debts of the Inland Revenue are now categorised as (IA, Sch. 6):

'**1.** Sums due at the relevant date from the debtor on account of deductions of income tax from emoluments paid during the period of twelve months next before that date.

Deductions here referred to are those which the debtor was liable to make under section 204 of the Income and Corporation Taxes Act 1970 (Pay As You Earn), less the amount of the repayments of income tax which the debtor was liable to make during that period.

**2.** Sums due at the relevant date from the debtor in respect of such deductions as are required to be made by the debtor for that period under section 69 of the Finance (No. 2) Act 1975 (Sub-Contractors in the Construction Industry).'

The regulations dealing with payments both of PAYE and tax deducted under the nominated subcontractor scheme are similar (see Income Tax (Sub-Contractors in the Construction Industry) Regulations 1975, SI 1975 No. 1960, as amended). In each case deductions required to be made during an income tax month must be paid to the collector within 14 days of its end (in some instances PAYE may be paid quarterly). For this purpose 'income tax month' means '. . . the period beginning on the 6th day of any calendar month and ending on the 5th day of the following calandar month.' It seems therefore that tax for an 'income tax month' is not 'due' until the fifteenth day of the next month.

Identifying the preferential liability for PAYE should not be too difficult but, since failure to pay preferential payments can result in personal liability

¶802

for a receiver (see ¶804–5), it is prudent to investigate the affairs of a company to see whether it is a company to which s. 69 of F (No. 2) A 1975 applies. In most cases the section would probably not apply but it would be unsafe to assume that, merely because the company is not engaged in the building trade, the section can have no application. This is because of an amendment to the section introduced by s. 43 of FA 1980. As amended, the section applies (as might be supposed) to any person carrying on a business which includes construction operations, but it also applies:

'to a person carrying on a business at any time if:

(*a*) his average annual expenditure on construction operations in the period of three years ending with the end of the last period of account before that time exceeds £250,000, or

(*b*) where he was not carrying on the business at the beginning of that period of three years one third of his total expenditure on construction operations for the part of that period during which he has been carrying on the business exceeds £250,000;

and in this section "period of account" means a period for which an account is made up in relation to the business in question.'

It follows that even companies which have no obvious connection with the building trade may nevertheless be included within the scheme. Indeed it is unsafe to assume that merely because the company is not currently engaged in construction operations on the scale necessary it will be outside the scheme. This is because, having once qualified under that provision, a person continues to be within the scheme of the section until he is able to satisfy the Board of Inland Revenue '. . . that his expenditure on construction operations has been less than £250,000 in each of three successive years beginning in or after that period of account'. A prudent receiver should therefore make enquiry of the Inland Revenue if he is uncertain whether or not the section applies to his company.

If the section applies, the company should, on paying anything to any subcontractor, have deducted tax at the basic rate from such part of the payment as cannot be shown to represent the direct cost of materials used or to be used in the construction operations.

The preference accorded to VAT is for:

'3. Any value added tax which is referable to the period of six months next before the relevant date (which period is referred to below as "the six-month period").

For the purpose of this paragraph:

¶802

(*a*) where the whole of the prescribed accounting period to which any value added tax is attributable falls within the six-month period, the whole amount of that tax is referable to that period; and

(*b*) in any other case the amount of any value added tax which is referable to the six-month period is the proportion of the tax which is equal to such proportion (if any) of the accounting reference period in question as falls within the six-month period;

and in sub paragraph (*a*) "prescribed" means prescribed by regulations under the Value Added Tax Act 1983.'

Since an accounting period for value added tax purposes will normally come to an end on the appointment of a receiver or administrator (see reg. 58(3) of the Value Added Tax (General) Regulations 1985 (SI 1985 No. 886)) there will always be at least two prescribed accounting periods falling wholly within the six month period. That is because a prescribed accounting period is normally a period of three months ending on dates notified to the taxpayer either in his certificate of registration or by some other method (see reg. 58(1)). It is interesting to note the differing terminology: for VAT the word 'referable' is used whereas 'due' is used for the other taxes. Clearly, VAT need not be 'due' at the date of the appointment, as might be supposed: other taxes must be.

# ACCRUING LIABILITIES

## ¶803   Value added tax accruing

Accruing liabilities for VAT are crystallised by the appointment of a receiver (or by the making of an administration order). This is made clear by reg. 58(3) of the Value Added Tax (General Regulations) 1985 (SI 1985 No. 886) which provides that:

'. . . where under any of the enactments mentioned in paragraph 12(1) of Schedule 7 to the Act, control of the assets of any registered person passes to another person, being a trustee in bankruptcy, receiver, liquidator or person otherwise acting in a representative capacity, the period in respect of which the registered person is currently making supplies shall end on the day previous to the relevant date. . . .'

The accruing liability therefore ceases immediately before the appointment. (Note: para. 12(1) of Sch. 7 was repealed with effect from 27 December 1986 but the effect of the reference is preserved by IA, Sch. 11, para. 27.)

## ¶804   Tax liabilities incurred during the receivership

### (1)   A receiver's responsibility for tax

The question whether a receiver is liable for tax liabilities incurred by the company is relevant for both accruing liabilities and liabilities to be incurred. The short answer might be that since all taxes are creatures of statute a receiver can have no liability for tax in the absence of an express statutory provision. This simplistic view is complicated by the only two cases where a receiver's liability for tax was in point. Those cases are *IRC* v *Thompson (Receiver for John A. Wood Limited)* ((1936) 20 TC 422) and *Re John Willment (Ashford) Limited* ([1980] 1 WLR 73).

The *Thompson* decision is now of limited interest since it was decided on the interpretation of statutory rules which, at any rate since 1965, have ceased to apply to companies. The decision in the case was that a receiver was a person receiving the income of a company within the meaning of what has now become s. 114(1) of the Taxes Act 1970. Section 114(4) of the Taxes Act 1970 in turn says that that subsection is not to apply to companies and that 'for the purpose of corporation tax the provisions of Chapter 1 of Part IX of this Act have effect to the exclusion of subsections (1) to (3) above'.

The *Willment* decision is a more recent decision and the reasoning employed by the judge, Brightman J, is instructive because from it can be derived the way in which a receiver should approach the question of his responsibility (if any) for taxes. The case concerned the liability of a receiver for VAT. The receiver as agent for the company had caused the company to continue to trade and the receiver had made taxable supplies and had charged VAT on those supplies. He issued a summons to determine whether he should account to his debenture holder or to the Commissioners of Customs & Excise for the net amount of VAT which was, admittedly, a liability of the company as a result of its continuing to trade during the receivership.

The reasoning process adopted by the judge was:

(1)   The receiver's appointment had not brought about any change of taxpayer. The person primarily liable for the tax remained the company (and the receiver, as its agent). In the absence of any statutory provision fixing him with liability, the tax could not be recovered from the receiver as a debt due to the Crown.

(2)   The position was not affected by what is now s. 44(1)(*b*) of the Insolvency Act which provides that a receiver incurs personal liability on any contract entered into by him in discharging his functions unless he takes steps to ensure that the contract contains a provision excluding personal liability (see ¶401 and ¶510). Since tax debts do not arise as a result of any contract with the Crown, that section has no application.

(3)   Moneys collected in by a receiver were not impressed with any trust to pay tax. That proposition is illustrated by the case of *Attorney General* v *Antoine* ((1949) 31 TC 213). In that case an employer who was responsible for the operation of the PAYE system had deducted sums for PAYE from wages paid to employees. Apparently the sums so deducted had been put into a bag and placed in a locked safe. The bag of money was stolen and, in an action to recover the tax, the employer claimed that having so set aside and segregated the money, the risk of loss fell on the Crown. It was held that even though it had been segregated the money remained the employer's money and the risk of loss therefore fell on her.

(4)   Section 109(8) of the Law of Property Act 1925 sets out the order in which moneys received by a receiver should be applied, and indicates that the receiver may discharge '. . . all rents, taxes, rates, and out-goings whatever affecting the mortgaged property . . .' in priority to the sums secured by the mortgage or debenture pursuant to which he is appointed. *Liverpool Corporation* v *Hope* ([1938] 1 KB 751) indicates that the provisions of s. 109 of the Law of Property Act 1925 are permissive only and afford no independent right of action against the receiver to the taxing or (as in the case) rating authorities. The section merely permits a receiver to use moneys collected pursuant to the mortgage in discharge of rates and taxes in priority to claims of the mortgagee or debenture holder, thus affording the receiver a defence against any claim by a mortgagee or debenture holder that he has improperly paid away moneys but not affording any independent right of action to the authorities (see ¶508).

## (2)   A receiver's discretion

As a result of the line of reasoning outlined above, Brightman J reached the conclusion that a receiver has a discretion whether or not to pay taxes. He held that, in the particular circumstances, the discretion was one which the receiver could only exercise in one way and that he was bound to pay over the VAT. He based his decision on the point that if the receiver paid the tax over to the debenture holder he would, by so doing, cause the company to commit a criminal offence (because non-payment of VAT is an offence). He said (at pp. 77–8):

'. . . in the instant case there is only one way in which that discretion can properly be exercised in relation to value added tax, so perhaps it is not correct to describe it as a discretion at all. The reason for this conclusion is that if the receiver does not pay the tax he will cause the company to commit a criminal offence. In the present circumstances, and I would think in most if not all circumstances, it cannot possibly be right for the holder of a discretion to exercise it in such a way as to bring about a criminal result.'

He then explained why non-payment of VAT is a criminal offence and went on to say (at p. 78):

'Accordingly, if the receiver does not make value added tax returns and pay the tax, he will be causing the company to commit a criminal offence. In the result the receiver, who is entitled as between himself and the debenture holder to pay taxes, has no option but to make value added tax returns and to pay the tax due.'

Although the conclusion that, on the facts, a receiver should account for VAT seems undoubtedly correct, the reason given by the learned judge seems somewhat hard to justify. Simple failure to make returns and pay income tax or corporation tax is not a criminal offence in the same way that the same conduct is an offence for VAT purposes. That the liability of a receiver to account for VAT but not for income tax or corporation tax should rest on such a slender distinction seems wrong. But the learned judge obviously felt that it would be unconscionable to permit a receiver to collect money as VAT from customers and fail to account for that tax to the Customs & Excise and, indeed, when opening his judgment he described (at p. 75):

'. . . the apparently absurd alternative that [the receiver] is entitled to collect the tax and apply the money in discharge of the principal, interest and other moneys due under the debenture.'

### (3)   Exercise of the discretion

There seem to be three possible sets of circumstances that a receiver might face. There will certainly be cases where the receiver has no discretion at all but is bound to pay tax. Thus, the Commissioners of Customs & Excise may treat the receiver as a taxable person carrying on the business and if they do so the provisions of the Value Added Tax Act and Regulations will apply to him (see Value Added Tax (General) Regulations 1985, reg. 11(1)). Alternatively, on making a payment of interest, e.g. to a debenture holder, the receiver may be obliged to deduct and account for income tax under the procedure set out in s. 54 of the Taxes Act 1970. Those cases are clear cases where the receiver is personally answerable for seeing that the tax is paid and are properly analysed as cases where the receiver has a duty imposed on him personally to see to the payment of tax. He has the funds in hand to pay.

The remaining cases are cases of discretion and divide into cases where there is a one-way discretion and cases where there is a complete discretion. One-way discretion cases will be those like the *Willment* case where the receiver must exercise his discretion so as to avoid the company committing a criminal offence. Again, he has the funds to make the payment.

The cases where the receiver has a genuine discretion appear to be those where the tax liability is a by-product of his realisation of assets of the company. Thus corporation tax on profits or gains made by the company during the course of a receivership may be a natural result of sales made by the receiver, but is not the prime result. It is (see ¶1301) merely a possible consequence of the sale and the funds may not be in hand to pay the tax. In those circumstances a receiver can fairly be said to have a discretion and it is also fair to note that, invariably, receivers exercise their discretion in favour of the debenture holders rather than in favour of the Revenue. This is reinforced to some extent by s. 23(2) of the Capital Gains Tax Act 1979 which makes it clear that a receiver incurs no capital gains tax liability personally as a result of sales by him of chargeable assets. It is also reinforced by an examination of the *Mesco Properties* case (see ¶1301): that case arose for decision because receivership sales had produced an unsatisfied corporation tax liability which the liquidator had insufficient assets in hand to meet.

## ¶805   Obligations to deduct

Sundry provisions of the Taxes Acts impose an obligation on a receiver to deduct income tax on making certain payments. The principal sections which impose obligations are:

| | |
|---|---|
| Taxes Act 1970 | Section 53 (annual payments) |
| | Section 54 (interest) |
| | Section 89 (rents paid to non-resident landlord) |
| | Section 94 (Schedule C) |
| | Section 156 (rents from mines and quarries) |
| | Section 157 (wayleave rents) |
| | Section 159 (foreign dividends) |
| | Section 204 (PAYE) |
| | Section 380 (patent royalties) |
| | Section 391 (copyright royalties) |
| Social Security Act 1975 | Schedule 1 paragraphs 4 & 5 – National insurance contributions |
| Finance (No. 2) Act 1975 | Section 69 (construction industry) |
| Finance Act 1983 | Section 27 (public lending rights income) |
| Finance Act 1986 | Section 44 (foreign entertainers/sportsmen) |

A receiver will be responsible for making those deductions.

## ¶806   Value added tax

Provisions relating to VAT pursue a steadily independent line from those
relating to other taxes. Both a receiver and an administrator will have responsibility (to uoe a noutral word) in aooordanoo with tho dooioion of Brightman J
in *Re John Willment (Ashford) Limited* explained at ¶804. They each may
incur direct personal responsibility by statute and regulation. There seems to
be a difference in the extent of the liability under case law and statute.

The limits of the *Willment* decision were explored and explained in the later
case of *Re Liverpool Commercial Vehicles Limited* ([1984] BCLC 587). That
was a case where goods had been supplied to a company on the usual
reservation of title terms (see ¶506) that the property would remain with the
supplier until payment in full had been received or until the company sold the
goods to a customer, in which event the proceeds of sale would be held upon
trust for the supplier. A tax invoice had been issued to the company when it
took possession of the goods and it had duly claimed the VAT shown in those
invoices as input tax, thus reducing the amount of output tax for which it
was liable. A receiver of the company was appointed and the goods were
repossessed by the original supplier who issued a credit note. The Commissioners of Customs & Excise claimed to be entitled to increase the amount
of their preferential debt by the amount of the VAT shown in the credit notes,
arguing that the original supply was in some sense a provisional supply and
that if it transpired subsequently that property in the goods never passed to
the company they were entitled to revise the claims for credit previously made
by the company and hence increase their preferential claim. Vinelott J rejected
that argument and held that when the goods had been delivered to the
company, even though title had been retained, there was a supply within the
VAT legislation and he rejected the argument that that supply was contingent
only. He went on to say (at pp. 591–2):

'. . . I can see no ground on which a delivery of goods pursuant to a contract
which contains a title retention clause and which constitutes a supply in
respect of which VAT has become due within the clear terms of the
legislation can later be said not to constitute a supply because the goods
are repossessed by the vendor. Whether the repossession of the goods
constitutes a further supply is a question which does not arise for decision
in this case. It is conceded by counsel for the Commissioners (Mr
Mummery), and I think rightly conceded, that if in the instant case there
was a supply of the vehicles by [Liverpool Commercial Vehicles Limited]
when they were returned to Iveco, the joint receivers cannot be required
and indeed have no power to pay the VAT included in the credit notes in
priority to the principal and interest payable under the bank's charge. The
joint receivers have not received moneys representing VAT payable on a

supply by them, and the principle explained by Brightman J in *Re John Willment (Ashford) Limited* . . . can have no application. If output tax did become so payable it would be payable by the liquidator out of moneys, if any, coming into his hands, and the liquidator is not a party to this application.'

That the judge felt able to say that '. . . the joint receivers cannot be required . . . to pay the VAT included in the credit notes . . .' seems puzzling, because at the time the judge was speaking of (1979–81) the position was covered by a statutory instrument: reg. 56 of the Value Added Tax (General) Regulations 1977 (SI 1977 No. 1759) reconsolidated as reg. 63 of the Value Added Tax (General) Regulations 1985 (SI 1985 No. 886), which provides:

'Where any person subject to any requirements under this Part of these Regulations dies or becomes incapacitated and control of his assets passes to another person, being a personal representative, trustee in bankruptcy, receiver, liquidator, or person otherwise acting in a representative capacity, that other person shall, if the Commissioners so require and so long as he has such control comply with those requirements:
Provided that any requirement to pay tax shall only apply to that other person to the extent of the assets of the deceased or incapacitated person over which he has control; and save to the extent aforesaid this Part of these Regulations shall apply to such person, so acting, as if he were the deceased or incapacitated person.'

The solution to the puzzle may be that these regulations (in an even earlier incarnation) were dealt with by Brightman J in the *Willment* case. He said that it had been common ground between the receiver and the Commissioners of Customs & Excise that the regulation did not apply because the receiver had not been 'required' to comply by the Commissioners. He went on to say (at p. 76) 'Furthermore, it is open to argument whether a receiver appointed by a debenture holder is within that regulation'. Presumably the argument which the judge thought was open was caused by the curious terminology of reg. 63. It is not a very apt description to say that an insolvent company has become 'incapacitated' when a receiver, or for that matter an administrator, is appointed. The obscurity has now been cured and cured in favour of the Customs & Excise. Section 31 of FA 1985 amended s. 31 of the Value Added Tax Act 1983. The latter section empowers the Commissioners of Customs & Excise to make Regulations providing that persons who '. . . carry on a business of a taxable person who has died or become bankrupt or incapacitated . . .' are to be treated as taxable persons and FA 1985 added a new subsection which reads:

¶806

'In relation to a company which is a taxable person the reference . . . to the taxable person having become bankrupt or incapacitated shall be construed as a reference to its being in liquidation or receivership or to an administration order being in force in relation to it.'

As a result of those changes the rules about VAT applying to receivers and administrators can be summarised as follows:

(1) On the appointment of a receiver or administrator the current VAT accounting period comes to an end (Value Added Tax (General) Regulations 1985 reg. 58(3)).

(2) Either a receiver or an administrator who makes taxable supplies and collects consideration in cash or kind will, consistently with the *Willment* decision, have to account to the Commissioners of Customs & Excise for the net VAT due during a prescribed accounting period. Conversely, following the *Liverpool Commercial Vehicles Limited* decision, any event giving rise to a notional VAT liability with no corresponding collection will result in an unsecured liability which the receiver cannot be compelled to meet.

(3) The Customs & Excise may treat the receiver or administrator as continuing the taxable business and in consequence may treat him as a separate taxable person and, if they do so, the Act and Regulations apply as if he were a taxable person (reg. 11).

(4) Regulation 63 (quoted above), which appears to be to similar effect, may also apply although if it does the company remains the taxable person but the receiver or administrator is responsible for compliance with the Act and the Regulations.

(5) Failure by a receiver or administrator to make a return will be treated as a failure by the company (see Value Added Tax Act 1983, Sch. 7, para. 4(4)).

(6) Notification to a receiver or administrator is treated as notification to the company (Value Added Tax Act 1983, Sch. 7, para. 4(10)).

## ¶807  Value added tax: bad debt relief

The Value Added Tax Act 1983 and Regulations made pursuant to it, afford important relief to creditors of insolvent companies. The essence of the relief is that by limiting their claim in the insolvency to the VAT-exclusive consideration they can recover the VAT element from the Commissioners of Customs & Excise.

In order to make a claim a creditor must have made a taxable supply of goods or services for a consideration equal to or less than the market value of that supply and, if the supply was the supply of goods, property in the goods must have passed. He must have accounted for and paid tax on the supply and the debtor must have become insolvent without having paid the consideration. So far as relevant to receivers and administrators a company becomes insolvent if:

'A person who has been appointed in Great Britain to act as its administrator or administrative receiver issues a certificate of his opinion that, if it went into liquidation, the assets of the company would be insufficient to cover the payment of any dividend in respect of debts which are neither secured nor preferential' (Value Added Tax Act 1983, s. 22(3)(*b*)).

In order to claim VAT bad debt relief in a receivership or administration the test, therefore, is fairly stiff. The company on any view must be hopelessly insolvent and unable to provide even the smallest dividend to unsecured creditors. An administrative receiver (like an administrator) is obliged to issue the certificate referred to '. . . forthwith upon his forming the opinion' described in the section (see IR, rr. 2.56 and 3.37). On giving a certificate the administrator or receiver must specify in it the name of the company and its registered number, the name of the administrator or receiver, the date of his appointment and the date on which the certificate is issued. Unsecured creditors must be notified that the certificate has been issued on the later of three months from the date of appointment of the administrator or the receiver or within two months of the issuing of the certificate.

The claimant makes his claim for the relief on the prescribed return which he must deliver to the Commissioners at the end of his normal VAT accounting period. At the time he makes the claim the claimant must have the notice he has been given by the receiver or administrator, a copy of every invoice issued for each taxable supply for which the claim is made or, if he was not required to issue an invoice, some document indicating the time, nature of, and consideration for the supply on which the claim is based, plus some evidence showing that he has accounted for and paid the tax claimed to be refunded.

Regulations made pursuant to s. 22 of the Value Added Tax Act 1983 (see the Value Added Tax (Bad Debt Relief) Regulations 1986 SI 1986 No. 335) make provision for restricting the amount of relief that can be claimed where amounts can be set off between the claimant and the debtor under the insolvency rules or otherwise (see reg. 8). Furthermore, where a series of supplies have been made at differing rates of tax (including supplies at a zero rate), there are provisions for attributing the debt owed to supplies made. Broadly speaking, the debt owed is attributed to the supplies which are most recent in time before the debtor became insolvent, unless the debtor had made a specific appropriation of the consideration paid at the time of payment (see reg. 9).

¶807

The relief afforded is clawed back if the claimant subsequently claims for an amount including the amount of any tax refunded in the insolvency of the debtor (see reg. 10).

## ¶808   Hive-downs

### (1)   Purpose and practice

For some considerable time receivers have found it convenient to realise assets of a company by selling or hiving-down the business to a subsidiary specially formed for that purpose, and the practice has received statutory recognition in the first Schedule to the Insolvency Act 1986 which makes it plain that an administrative receiver has:

'**15.** Power to establish subsidiaries of the company.

**16.** Power to transfer to subsidiaries of the company the whole or any part of the business and property of the company.'

This is discussed further at ¶504.

There are tax-driven motives for hive-downs which were given impetus by s. 252 of the Taxes Act 1970. This section, in certain circumstances, would treat losses sustained by the parent as being available for set-off against profits subsequently made by the subsidiary. The scope of the relief was originally cut down in 1969 by the enactment of what is now s. 483 of the Taxes Act 1970 (although it was claimed at the time that the measure was merely a modification of existing law and practice) and has recently been more seriously restricted in FA 1986.

### (2)   Impact of Furniss v Dawson

Some concern was felt about the possible impact of *Furniss* v *Dawson* ([1984] AC 474) on hive-downs. *Furniss* v *Dawson* marks a considerable change in the approach to tax-avoidance schemes: as a result, substance may now prevail over form. In order to dispel some of the uncertainty caused by the case, the Institute of Chartered Accountants in England and Wales wrote a letter to the Inland Revenue on 8 July 1985 which, among other things, dealt with hive-downs as follows:

'**7.** One of the first priorities of a receiver appointed under a floating charge is to establish whether part or the whole of the business can be disposed of as a going concern. If this is viable it will invariably produce a greater return (and incidentally, preserve jobs) than a piecemeal sale of the assets. It will also, subject to the provisions of sections 252 and 483 [of the Taxes Act 1970], enable the tax losses of the business to be preserved and made available to the purchaser, the value of which will be taken into account in arriving at the sale price.

**8.** For this purpose it is the normal practice, having established the position, to hive-down part or all of the business and relevant assets into a newly-formed subsidiary the shares in which are disposed of. There are sound commercial reasons for disposing of the business in this way, and it is of course important to effect the hive down as soon as possible and certainly before a liquidator is appointed; once that happens the company is no longer the beneficial owner of its assets and section 252 will not apply.

**9.** The reasons for the hive-down are therefore founded on sound insolvency practice so that the benefit of the tax losses, representing additional funds, is available to creditors. We have encountered cases where inspectors have stated that they will seek to apply section 483 but if this fails invoke the doctrine in *Furniss* v *Dawson*. Since the disposal of a business by the receiver is governed by commercial considerations it would be helpful if an assurance could be given that the *Furniss* v *Dawson* principle will not be applied and that the transaction only requires consideration under existing law and practice as outlined above.'

The reply of the Inland Revenue was:

'This is one of the topics on which it is particularly difficult to see at present where exactly the new approach might apply, if at all. On the face of it, the new approach might have some relevance in cases where little more than the tax losses are being hived-down, though even then it would be necessary to demonstrate that there was a composite transaction and the insertion of a "non-commercial" step in that transaction. However, we would not normally expect the new approach to be relevant in cases where an entire trade, or part trade, together with its related assets and liabilities, are hived-down with a view to its being carried on in other hands – although of course in those circumstances section 483 might apply.'

### (3)  Specific tax considerations
Against the background outlined above, particular taxation points to bear in mind are:

(1)  If the whole of the trading activities of the vendor are transferred to a subsidiary this may cause an accounting period of the vendor to come to an end (s. 247 of the Taxes Act 1970).

(2)  The rules governing the valuation of trading stock and work in progress on the discontinuance of a trade may apply (see s. 137 of the Taxes Act 1970). Provided, as will invariably be the case, the successor continues the trade transferred to it, the transaction should be tax neutral.

¶808

(3)   Parent and subsidiary will in normal cases form a group for tax purposes (s. 272 of the Taxes Act 1970). A group consists of the principal company and its '75 per cent subsidiaries'. A company is:

'a "75 per cent subsidiary" of another body corporate if and so long as not less than 75 per cent of its ordinary share capital is owned directly or indirectly by that other body corporate.' (s. 532(1)(*b*) of the Taxes Act 1970.)

'Ordinary share capital' means:

'. . . all the issued share capital (by whatever name called) of the company, other than capital the holders whereof have a right to a dividend at a fixed rate, but have no other right to share in the profit of the company' (s. 526(5) of the Taxes Act 1970 as amended).

Given the parent/subsidiary relationship, capital assets could be sold by the receiver on a hive-down of a trade to a subsidiary because by s. 273 of the Taxes Act 1970 the effect of a sale of a capital asset by one group company to another is to treat the sale as having taken place at such a price as would result in no gain and no loss to the vendor, regardless of any actual consideration paid. Since, however, the main aim of a receiver in hiving-down to the subsidiary is to facilitate a sale of the subsidiary with its new trade as a going concern, this apparently beneficial treatment of sales of capital assets between group companies would be withdrawn. That is because, by s. 278 of the Taxes Act 1970, if the subsidiary ceases to be a member of the same group as the parent within six years of the date of the acquisition of the capital asset, the subsidiary is treated as having disposed of the asset immediately after acquiring it for a consideration equal to its then market value. The result is that a receiver normally retains capital assets within the company in receivership, granting a licence to use or occupy the capital assets pending a sale, hiving-down the other assets to the subsidiary. Once the shares in the subsidiary have been sold to a purchaser and the company has left the group, the receiver will also sell the capital assets to the purchaser sustaining a gain (or loss) in the company in receivership.

If, on the other hand, the base value of a capital asset is more than its market value there is no reason not to transfer the asset to a subsidiary on a hive-down. In the days before *Furniss* v *Dawson*, receivers were accustomed to using s. 278 to secure benefits for the insolvent company and there was at one time an active trade in 'capital loss' companies.

The scheme normally applied to a group of companies that went into receivership as a whole. In the ordinary course of events a parent company would have invested capital in a subsidiary and as a result of the insolvency that investment would have been reduced to nil. Shares would be sold to a newly formed subsidiary and the shares in the subsidiary then sold by the receiver to an outside purchaser who had a use for capital losses.

The question of capital-loss schemes was also raised with the Inland Revenue in the exchange of correspondence referred to above. The Revenue had this to say about capital losses:

'I agree that this is an important area where, in our view, the *Ramsay* principles are likely to have considerable application. Let me say at once that the Board stands by the assurance given on 6 January 1982, about straighforward transfers of assets between members of the same group. By contrast, as you are no doubt aware, inspectors have advanced *Ramsay* contentions in a number of cases where the effect of a series of transactions has been to transfer the benefit of capital losses from one group to another. Whether the "new approach" is thought to be applicable will depend on the facts of particular cases bearing in mind, for example, the relationship between the amounts of the loss involved, the period for which the company with the loss has been within the group and on the circumstances in which the losses have arisen. On this approach it would seem unlikely that the judgment would be involved where the losses were a relatively insubstantial element in the acquisition, as evidenced by the circumstances in which they were utilised and the commerciality of the circumstances surrounding the acquisition.'

In those circumstances it seems likely that a bare sale of shares in a company which possesses little more than a realised capital loss will henceforth be unlikely to succeed.

(4)    The new subsidiary ('the successor') may be entitled to relief under s. 177(1) of the Taxes Act 1970 for losses sustained by the parent ('the predecessor') in carrying on the trade (s. 252 of the Taxes Act 1970). Briefly the rules for entitlement to relief are:

(*a*)    Within the period of two years from the transfer an interest amounting to not less than 75 per cent in it must belong to the same persons as the trade belonged to at some time during the year before the transfer (s. 252(1)(*a*) of the Taxes Act 1970). The rules about what amounts to a 75 per cent interest are complex (s. 253 of the Taxes Act 1970), probably because the section started life in the 1950's as an anti-avoidance measure. Provided the assets are sold by a parent company to a '75 per

¶808

cent subsidiary' the test will be satisfied. Note also that the 75 per cent interest rules need only to be satisfied for a very short period after the transfer (a legal *scintilla temporis* would theoretically suffice).

(*b*)   During the relevant three-year period (one year before sale, two years after) the trade must have been carried on '. . . by a company which is within the charge to tax in respect of it'. (s. 252(1)(*b*) of the Taxes Act 1970).

(*c*)   If assets retained and not transferred by the predecessor plus the consideration given by the successor for the purchase are less than the amount of liabilities of the predecessor outstanding at the date of transfer and not transferred to the successor, the relief is restricted. Relief is only afforded if and to the extent that the excess of liabilities over assets is less than the amount of loss available for carry-forward (s. 252(3A) of the Taxes Act 1970). This provision, introduced by FA 1986 has severely limited the benefits obtainable.

(*d*)   The transaction is likely to be treated as a sale of a going concern for VAT purposes (see The Value Added Tax (Special Provisions) Order 1981 SI 1981 No. 1741, reg. 12). This will mean that a supply of business assets will be treated as neither a supply of goods nor as a supply of services provided that:

   (i) the assets are sold as a going concern;

   (ii) if the transferor is a taxable person, either the transferee is also a taxable person or immediately becomes one;

   (iii) the assets are to be used by the transferee in carrying on 'the same kind of business'; and

   (iv) Where the assets consist of part only of a business, that part must be capable of separate operation.

(*e*)   The agreement for sale may be stampable (see s. 59(1) of the Stamp Act 1891).

## REVENUE POWERS

The remedies that the Inland Revenue and Customs & Excise may pursue against an administrative receiver are dealt with at ¶809 and 810.

### ¶809   Distress

Both the Inland Revenue (see s. 61 of the Taxes Management Act 1970) and the Customs & Excise (see reg. 65 of the Value Added Tax (General)

Regulations 1985) have a statutory right to levy distress against a taxpayer who has neglected or refused to pay tax which is due. Although this remedy would not seem to be available against a receiver once the floating charge has been crystallised (but see ¶810 dealing with s. 62 of the Taxes Management Act 1970) it seems that a distress levied before the appointment of a receiver will be upheld (see *Re Roundwood Colliery Company* [1897] 1 Ch. 373 and see also *Herbert Berry* v *Inland Revenue Commissioners* [1977] 1 WLR 1437 and ¶508).

## ¶810   Section 62 of the Taxes Management Act 1970

A puzzling question is whether the restrictions on the Inland Revenue's preference for unpaid taxes effected by the Insolvency Act 1986 have given new life to a little-noticed section contained in the Taxes Management Act 1970. Section 62 of that Act provides:

'(1)   No goods or chattels whatever, belonging to any person at the time any tax becomes in arrear, shall be liable to be taken by virtue of any execution or other process, warrant, or authority whatever, or by virtue of any assignment, or any account or pretence whatever, except at the suit of the landlord for rent, unless the person at whose suit the execution or seizure is made, or to whom the assignment was made, pays or causes to be paid to the collector, before the sale or removal of the goods or chattels, all arrears of tax which are due at the time of the seizure, or which are payable for the year in which the seizure is made:
Provided that, where tax is claimed for more than one year, the person at whose instance the seizure has been made may, on paying to the collector of the tax which is due for one whole year, proceed in his seizure in like manner as if no tax had been claimed.

(2)   In case of neglect or refusal to pay the tax so claimed or the tax for one whole year, as the case may be, the collector shall distrain the goods and chattels notwithstanding the seizure or assignment, and shall proceed to the sale thereof, as prescribed by this Act, for the purpose of obtaining payment of the whole of the tax charged and claimed, and the reasonable costs and charges attending such distress and sale and every collector so doing shall be indemnified by virtue of this Act.'

The section has led a relatively obscure existence, tucked away in the tax legislation since the nineteenth century. Certainly there is no case in which its interpretation has been in issue and even the Inland Revenue (see p. 38 of the Consultative Document issued in response to the proposals of the Keith Committee) admit that it has been criticised for its obscurity. The reason it has caused so little practical difficulty possibly rests in the proviso, which allows seizure to continue provided one year's taxes are paid. This coincides with the Crown's preference for unpaid taxes as it existed before the Insolvency Act 1986 (see Companies Act 1985, Sch. 19, para. 2), and it also corresponds with amendments proposed by the Inland Revenue (see the Consultative Document referred to above) which would restrict the taxes recoverable as a result of s. 62 to those which the Insolvency Act 1986 makes preferential. Thus a receiver who pays preferential debts in full can claim to have satisfied any liability incurred as a result of the section.

The section does still pose difficulties: first it is not clear whether a receiver (or administrator) really is affected by it; secondly, until (if ever) the Revenue's proposed amending legislation is enacted the preferential payments do not correspond with the provisio; and, thirdly, it is not clear what is to happen should the receiver not have sufficient moneys in his hands from a realization of floating-charge assets to pay preferential creditors in full.

The language of the section, on one view, is wide enough to catch a receiver's realization of floating-charge assets: a receiver who takes possession of floating-charge assets would seem to have taken them by virtue of an 'authority'. The best argument that the section does not apply to realizations by a receiver is that, since the section is inconsistent with s. 386 of and Sch. 6 to the Insolvency Act 1986 (as applied by s. 40), the particular code contained in the Insolvency Act should prevail over the general code in the Taxes Management Act. That argument, if correct, would also resolve the difficulty caused by the change in the category of preferential tax debts and potentially caused where realizations of floating-charge assets produce insufficient to pay off all preferential creditors.

Whether the section (even as intended to be amended) applies to an administrator is difficult. What the section prohibits is a taking of possession of goods unless the specified tax debts are paid. This may conflict with the positive duty which an administrator has to '. . . take into his possession or under his control all the property to which the company is or appears to be entitled' (IA, s. 17(1)).

# PART III
# ADMINISTRATORS

# 9 Appointment of an Administrator

## INTRODUCTION

### ¶901 Rationale of the administration process

The value of the floating charge and an appointment of a receiver thereunder as a means of preserving businesses of insolvent companies as going concerns has been mentioned above (¶303). Not every company, however, grants a floating charge over its business to those financing it. The classic exception is what is often referred to as the 'fading blue chip', that is, the large famous concern (often a household name) which suddenly runs into financial difficulty. Its bankers may find themselves with no security in place. In certain cases it is possible for a form of 'rescue' operation to be mounted by the bank or consortium of banks financing the company pursuant to which a new repayment programme is agreed with the lenders who take full security at that stage.

There may not always be time to implement a rescue. The company's financial position may be too grave. In a large case it is not uncommon for months to be consumed in the negotiation of non-binding heads of agreement between the parties, pursuant to which the legally binding documents will be prepared. Further, the introduction of the concept of 'wrongful trading' (IA, s. 214) exposes directors (and shadow directors) to greater risks of personal liability for the debts of their companies.

Directors are likely as a result to be much less willing to risk trading on during the lengthy interim period while the rescue package is put together and fresh finance, sufficient for the company's short-to medium-term needs (and sufficient to ensure a reasonable prospect of ultimate survival), is forthcoming.

The Cork Committee justified their suggestion for the introduction of a form of administration procedure in the following way (paras. 496–7):

'. . . Where there is no [floating] charge, the choice lies between an informal moratorium or a scheme of arrangement under the [Companies Acts]. Neither is wholly satisfactory. . . . We are satisfied that in a significant number of cases, companies have been forced into liquidation, and potentially viable business capable of being rescued have been closed down, for want of a floating charge under which a receiver and manager could have been appointed.

Accordingly, we propose that in all cases, and whether or not there is a floating charge in existence, provision should be made to enable a person (whom we shall call an administrator) to be appointed . . . with all the powers normally conferred upon a receiver and manager appointed under a floating charge, including power to carry on the business of the company . . .'.

It is worth noting that directors are being encouraged to take action earlier in their companies' difficulties. The administration procedure may be used where the company is not yet insolvent, just 'likely to become' so (IA, s. 8(1)(*a*)). And the most radical departure is that creditors may present a petition on the same basis and thus, if an order is made, effectively strip the directors of a company of control at a time when the company may still be solvent.

Technically, an administration order is:

'. . . an order directing that, during the period for which the order is in force, the affairs, business and property of the Company shall be managed by a person ("the administrator") appointed for the purpose by the court . . .' (IA, s. 8(2)).

Both Australia and South Africa have analogous rehabilitation procedures. In Australia it is termed 'official management' and in South Africa 'judicial management' (for further reference see Ford, *Principles of company law*, 4th edn (1986) Chapter 21 'Official management' and Cilliers and Benade, *Company law*, 4th edn (1982) Chapter 39, 'Judicial management').

## ¶902   Outline of the procedure

### (1)   The administration procedure generally

The idea of the administration procedure is to offer the possibility of the preservation of an insolvent business along the lines of a floating-charge receivership, but not pursuant to such a charge. The statutory list of powers granted to the administrator is identical to the list of those deemed to be included in any floating charge under which an administrative receiver is appointed (see ¶411 and ¶1009, and Appendix 5 below, although the list is not exhaustive of an administrator's powers). The procedure is court-based and involves a petition and a subsequent order, in similar manner to the mechanism for a compulsory winding-up.

An important aspect of the administration procedure is that on presentation of a petition for an administration order, there is an effective 'freezing' of the company's position in that no distress may be levied or execution commenced or continued on the company's goods and, further, owners of goods supplied to the company on hire purchase or lease terms or on terms providing for retention of title are not permitted to repossess (IA, s. 10(1)). In short, the company is given a breathing space by being protected from immediate action by its creditors.

The petition must be for one of a number of 'purposes' being either the preservation of all or part of the business of the company as a going concern, or the implementation of a form of scheme of arrangement with its creditors, or, finally, that a more advantageous realisation of the company's assets can be effected than in a winding-up (IA, s. 8(3)).

Evidence is adduced to the court in support of the petition and if an administration order is made the insolvency practitioner named in the petition is appointed administrator (IA, s. 8(1) and (2)). Pursuant to the order, the company is afforded continued protection from action by its creditors (IA, s. 11(3)). The administrator has up to three months to produce 'proposals' for the implementation of the purpose for which he was appointed and these proposals are put to a meeting of the company's creditors (IA, s. 23(1)). For the proposals to be passed, a majority in value of those present and voting at the creditors' meeting is necessary (IR, r. 2.28(1)).

Where the purpose is the implementation of a form of scheme with the company's creditors then the administrator will need to follow the relevant statutory procedure, whether it be a scheme of arrangement under s. 425 of the Companies Act 1985 or a voluntary arrangement under ss. 1–7 of the Insolvency Act 1986.

The administrator will either follow his 'purpose' through to its implementation and seek the termination of his administration and his discharge or else he will seek to terminate where either the creditors reject his proposals or he considers that they are incapable of implementation (IA, s. 18(1) and (2)).

Before considering the detail of the various stages mentioned above there follows an example of how a typical administration might appear in theory.

## (2)   An example of a 'typical' administration

Company X invents a design for an everlasting lightbulb. In order to produce this lightbulb it requires a licence to use certain patented rights of company Y. Company X is granted a 15-year licence to use the patented rights but the licence is personal to the company. The company estimates the amount of capital expenditure necessary to advance the project to a stage where the lightbulb can be mass-produced. In fact the technical problems are much greater than anticipated and the capital expenditure required is twice as much as the company had thought. Unfortunately, the company reaches a situation where it has huge loans with crippling interest payments on them and hence has difficulty in meeting its debts as they fall due. It does, however, have a good and potentially successful product if only its accumulated debt liability did not hang like a millstone round its neck. Liquidation and a subsequent sale of the company's business would not seem a good idea as it is only possible to make the lightbulb using the personal licence from company Y which would not be capable of transfer on a sale, thus reducing the value of the business to a purchaser to greatly below its value as a going concern.

Company X petitions the court for an administration order, the purpose of which is a scheme of voluntary arrangement. The administration creditors, accepting that the best prospect of payment of their debts is the continuation of the company by one means or another, vote in favour of the proposal. The administrator will then prepare (or, possibly, have prepared) proposals for the voluntary arrangement. The basis of the scheme will be to tidy up the company's balance sheet. All the creditors are asked to convert 50 per cent of their debts into equity – shares in the company. The interest bill of the company will be greatly reduced, the company balance sheet in an insolvent liquidation would no longer show a deficit and hence the directors would feel safe in continuing to trade without fear of a subsequent liability for wrongful trading.

The requisite meetings of the members and creditors of company X will then be called by the administrator. The creditors accept the 'cramming-down' of part of their debts into equity and pass the proposals by the required majority. The members for their part agree to the issue of the necessary shares.

The supervisor of the voluntary arrangement will see that the reconstruction is implemented. The administration can then effectively terminate. The administrator would be paid his remuneration and be discharged. The company would then be placed back in the hands of its directors to continue trading in the normal way.

This is, to assist illustration, necessarily a simple example. There is no mention of whether the bank has security and in particular whether it has a fixed charge on book debts. Further, the whole question of cashflow in the period between presentation of petition and implementation of the proposals is a vexed one and the lack of any easy solutions may be the downfall of the administration procedure. This and the other aspects of the procedure are discussed in more detail below.

## APPLICATION FOR AN ADMINISTRATION ORDER

### ¶903   Details of the application

#### (1)   Meaning of 'company'

The provisions of the Insolvency Act 1986 dealing with administrations refer simply to 'companies'. By s. 251 of the Act, terms not specifically defined in that section are to be construed in accordance with any definition contained in Pt. XXVI of the Companies Act 1985. By s. 735(1) of that Act, 'company' means: '. . . a company formed and registered under this Act, or an existing company', where 'existing company' means:

'a company formed and registered under the former Companies Acts, but does not include a company registered under the Joint Stock Companies Acts, the Companies Act 1862 or the Companies (Consolidation) Act 1908 in what was then Ireland',

and here 'the former Companies Acts' means:

'the Joint Stock Companies Acts, the Companies Act 1862, the Companies (Consolidation) Act 1908, the Companies Act 1929 and the Companies Acts 1948 to 1983'.

In general terms, therefore, an administrator cannot be appointed to an overseas or otherwise unregistered company or to a partnership. In the event of the insolvency of such a company or other association it may still be possible to wind them up compulsorily under Pt. V of the Insolvency Act 1986 where there are assets within the Court's jurisdiction (see, for example, *Re Compania Merabello San Nicholas SA* [1973] 1 Ch. 75).

### (2)   Inability to pay debts

The court may make an administration order only where it is satisfied that the company is, or is likely to become, unable to pay its debts as that phrase is defined by s. 123 of the Insolvency Act 1986. This provides as follows:

'(1)   A company is deemed unable to pay its debts –
   (*a*)   if a creditor (by assignment or otherwise) to whom the company is indebted in a sum exceeding £750 then due has served on the company, by leaving it at the company's registered office, a written demand (in the prescribed form) requiring the company to pay the sum so due and the company has for 3 weeks thereafter neglected to pay the same or to secure or compound for it to the reasonable satisfaction of the creditor, or
   (*b*)   if, in England and Wales, execution or other process issued on a judgment, decree or order of any court in favour of a creditor of the company is returned unsatisfied in whole or in part, or
   (*c*)   if, in Scotland, the induciae of a charge for payment on an extract decree, or an extract registered bond, or an extract registered protest, have expired without payment being made, or

¶903

(d)   if, in Northern Ireland, a certificate of unenforceability has been granted in respect of a judgment against the company, or

(e)   if it is proved to the satisfaction of the court that the company is unable to pay its debts as they fall due.

(2)   A company is also deemed unable to pay its debts if it is proved to the satisfaction of the court that the value of the company's assets is less than the amount of its liabilities, taking into account its contingent and prospective liabilities.'

Section 123 constitutes the test of insolvency for the purposes of presenting a petition for the winding-up of a company. Section 123(2) embodies a 'balance sheet' test of insolvency which is a stiff test to pass as it includes contingent and prospective, as well as present, liabilities and the test applies whether or not the company may be able to pay its debts as they fall due in the ordinary course. No guidance is given as to the basis of valuation of assets for the purpose of the test. It is submitted that the only fair test is the usual accountancy test of 'going concern' value and not, for example, a 'break-up' valuation.

### (3)   Statutory purposes

Besides being satisfied as to the company's insolvency, the court must also be satisfied that the making of an order would be likely to achieve at least one of the following purposes:

(1)   The survival of the company, and the whole or any part of its undertaking, as a going concern. (It is to be noted that the survival of part of the undertaking is *in addition* to the survival of the company itself).

(2)   The approval of a voluntary arrangement under the Insolvency Act 1986.

(3)   The sanctioning of a scheme of arrangement under s. 425 of the Companies Act 1985.

(4)   A more advantageous realisation of the company's assets would be effected on the winding-up of the company.

If an administration order is made, the order itself will specify the purpose or purposes for which it is made.

### (4)   The petition

The application to the court for an administration order is made by way of petition which may be presented by any or all of the following:

(1)   the company itself (IA, s. 9(1));

(2)   the directors of the company (IA, s. 9(1));

¶903

(3)    a creditor or creditors of the company including contingent or pro-spective creditors (IA, s. 9(1));

(4)    the supervisor of a voluntary arrangement (IA, s. 7(4)(*b*)); and

(5)    a 'recognised self-regulating organisation', a 'recognised professional body' or the Secretary of State for Trade and Industry in certain circumstances under the Financial Services Act 1986.[1]

It is not clear why the distinction is made between an application by the company and an application by its directors. Where a petition is presented by the directors it is in any event to be treated for all purposes as the petition of the company (IR, r. 2.4(3)).

In the event of the supervisor of a voluntary arrangement presenting the petition, the petition is to be treated as that of the company (IR, r. 2.1(4)).

**(5)    Contents of the petition**

The petition itself is to be a brief document. It must, however, contain the following details (IR, r. 2.4):

(1)    Where the petition is presented by the company, its directors, or the supervisor of a voluntary arrangement, it has to give the name of the company and its address for service, which will, in the absence of special circumstances, be its registered office.

(2)    Where a single creditor presents a petition, his name and address for service must be given.

(3)    Where two or more creditors present a petition, they should be named and described as presenting it, but thenceforth the petition is to be treated as that of only one of them and he is to be treated as if petitioning on behalf of the other creditors. This one creditor's address is to be given for service purposes.

(4)    The name and address of the proposed administrator is to be set out, coupled with a statement that to the best of the petitioner's knowledge and belief that person is qualified to act as an insolvency practitioner in relation to the company.

The Rules contain a prescribed form (Form 2.1). Where the proposal nominates more than one administrator to hold office, space should be found

---

[1] The relevant provisions are to be found in s. 74 of the Financial Services Act 1986. They apply to: (*a*) authorised persons under the Act, (*b*) authorised persons whose authorisation has been suspended, (*c*) persons under a direction from the Secretary of State pursuant to s. 33 of the Act, and (*d*) appointed representatives under the Act. Generally speaking, the organisation or body may make the application for the administration order where its rules apply to the relevant company and, where they do not, the Secretary of State may apply. At the time of writing s. 74 is not yet in force.

¶903

on the form for the required declaration as to whether acts are to be done by any or all of the administrators (IA, s. 231).

### (6)   The affidavit

Much of the information in any application for an administration order will be contained in the affidavit which must be sworn in support (IR, r. 2.1(1)). In the case of a petition presented by the company, its directors, or the supervisor of a voluntary arrangement, the affidavit has to be made by one of the directors or the secretary of the company and in so doing that person must state that he is making it on behalf of the company or, as appropriate, on behalf of the directors (IR, r. 2.1(2) and (4)). Where the petition is being presented by creditors generally the affidavit must be made by a person 'acting under the authority of them all', although the person making the affidavit need not be a creditor himself (IR, r. 2.1(3)). It seems that it would be possible for solicitors or accountants acting for one of the creditors to swear the affidavit. In any event, the affidavit must recite the authority of the person making the affidavit and the means of his knowledge.

The affidavit has to cover the following ground (IR, r. 2.3):

(1)   The deponent has to state that he believes that the company is or is likely to become unable to pay its debts (as that phrase is explained above) and give grounds for that belief.

(2)   The purpose or purposes for which the administration order is sought must be stated.

(3)   A statement of the company's financial position has to be included, giving details, to the best of the deponent's knowledge and belief, of the company's assets and liabilities (including contingent and prospective liabilities).

(4)   Details of security held over the company's property, including details of security entitling a mortgagee to appoint an administrative receiver and, indeed, details of any appointment of such a receiver which has been made.

(5)   Where there is a petition pending for the winding-up of the company, the details known to the deponent.

(6)   Any other information known to the deponent which the persons presenting the petition believe may assist the court in deciding whether to make an order.

The Rules provide that there may be exhibited to the affidavit an independent report on the company's affairs (IR, rr. 2.2(1) and 2.4(6)(c)). The report is to be by an 'independent person' and is to be to the effect that the appointment of the administrator would be 'expedient' (IR, r. 2.2(1)). The report must also identify the purposes which may be achieved by the making of an administration order. 'Independent' for these purposes means someone other than a director, secretary, manager, member or employee of the company, being someone with an adequate knowledge of the company's affairs (IR, r. 2.2(2)). It may be made, as one would expect it most commonly to be made, by the person being proposed as administrator (IR, r. 2.2(2)).

It is likely that in a well-planned application there will be a thorough and detailed independent report. It is likely to be normal for a report to be prepared. If a report is not to be prepared, the affidavit must state this fact and explain why (see IR, r. 2.3(6)). Where the application is necessarily being made in a hurried fashion (for example, one creditor may be about to take action against the company's property), then there may not be time for an independent report to be prepared and the need for a swift application may constitute the required explanation. Also, where the purpose is merely a more advantageous realisation of assets than in a winding-up, there may be little need for a lengthy report.

A likely scenario is that the directors (or a creditor) of a company in financial difficulties will seek the advice and assistance of an insolvency practitioner (either an accountant or a solicitor) and the practitioner and his team will be able to assist with the preparation of the affidavit and the report on the basis of the information supplied by the client.

In addition to the report, other exhibits to the affidavit must be a copy of the petition and a written consent to act signed by the person nominated as administrator (IR, r. 2.4(6) and see Form 2.2).

### (7)  Filing of the petition
When the petition has been settled and the affidavit prepared and sworn they have to be filed in court together with a sufficient number of copies to serve all those required to be served (IR, r. 2.5(1)). Those required to be given notice are considered below.

The court will affix its seal to each of the copies and issue them to the petitioner, and the date and time of filing is to be endorsed on each copy (IR, r. 2.5(2)). The precise time may be important in the light of the consequences of the presentation of a petition.

The Rules provide that the court will fix a 'venue' for the hearing of the petition with the details to be endorsed on each copy of the petition (IR, r. 2.5(3)). 'Venue' is given an artificially extended definition by the Rules and means the time, date and place of the hearing (IR, r. 13.6).

### (8)  Notice of the petition
It is crucial to the administration scheme that notice of a petition be given forthwith to the holder of a charge entitling that person to appoint an

administrative receiver whether or not he has appointed such a receiver (IA, s. 9(2)(*a*)). The Act uses the words '. . . any person who has appointed, or is or may be entitled to appoint an administrative receiver of the company . . .' (IA, s. 9(2)(*a*)) while the Rules use the words: ' any person who has appointed an administrative receiver for the company, or has the power to do so . . .' (IR, r. 2.6(2)(*a*)). It could be said to be rare for the holder of a charge to be entitled on the terms of his security to appoint a receiver without any further action such as, for example, making demand for repayment of the secured debt or declaring an event of default followed by demand. It might be thought, therefore, that the wording of the Act and the Rules is not particularly apt if it is intended to provide that notice is to be given to any person who 'is entitled' or 'has power' to appoint an administrative receiver provided that person takes some action to trigger the entitlement of power. It is submitted that it would not be safe for a petitioner not to give notice to such a mortgagee as the court would strive to find that notice should be given in these circumstances. Further, the following transitional provision, albeit itself somewhat inaptly expressed, may be of assistance in the case of security granted before 29 December 1986:

> '. . . Where any right to appoint an administrative receiver of a company is conferred by any debentures or floating charge created before the appointed day, the conditions precedent to the exercise of that right are deemed to include the presentation of a petition applying for an administration order to be made in relation to the company . . .' (IA, Sch. 11, Pt. 1, para. 1(1)).

It is important that those taking security after 29 December 1986 provide for the right to appoint an administrative receiver on presentation of a petition for an administrator.

The other persons to be given notice of the presentation of a petition are the following (IR, r. 2.6(2) and (3)):

(1) any administrative receiver of the company already in office;

(2) where there is a winding-up petition pending, the petitioning creditor (and any provisional liquidator);

(3) the person proposed as administrator; and

(4) where creditors have presented the petition, the company.

'Service' means providing a copy of the petition, the affidavit and documents (other than the petition) exhibited to the affidavit (IR, r. 2.6(1)). There are technical rules governing the manner and proof of service and the filing of documents for the hearing (see IR, rr. 2.7 and 2.8 and Form 2.3).

¶903

**(9)   Time of service**

The service must have been effected no less than five days before any hearing of the petition (IR, r. 2.7(1)). It is submitted that this provision in the Rule does not necessarily vary the duty to give notice 'forthwith' after presentation of the petition in accordance with the Act (s. 9(2)(*a*)). In the case of *Re a Company No. 00175 of 1987* (2 February 1987, unreported) Vinelott J abridged the five-day notice period. He said:

> '[Counsel for the secured creditor] submitted that the [secured creditor] was entitled to five clear days' notice of the hearing. I do not think that there is anything in Part 2 of the 1986 Act which can be read as impliedly restricting the power of the court to abridge the time for service of a petition for an administration order in an appropriate case.'

**(10)   Practical aspects of petitions**

As mentioned above (see ¶902(6)), an application for an administrator should be as well planned as possible and therefore the ideal petition will contain a full report by an independent person in support of the application. This is important, first because it is clearly better that such an important (even drastic) step should be well planned, and secondly because, in view of the critical hiatus periods (see ¶904), there is a greater chance of continued support for the company from its bankers, suppliers and customers if the scheme gives confidence by being carefully thought out. It must be remembered, also, that, once presented, a petition cannot be withdrawn without the leave of the court (IA, s. 9(2)(*b*)).

The need to seek shelter from action by a company's creditors should not necessarily prompt the directors of a company to apply for an administration order. It must appear to them that one or more of the four statutory purposes could be achieved even if only that the assets of the company could be realised on a more orderly basis than in a liquidation. The need for a full affidavit and, in most cases, an independent report, both of which will, more often than not, require professional assistance to prepare or settle, means that an administration is likely to prove more expensive than, say, a voluntary winding-up of the company. Further, the need to produce written proposals for approval by the creditors and the fact that the procedure is court-based, thus requiring the involvement of lawyers at most stages, builds in further costs.

Where a creditor is about to enforce a judgment by levying execution or a landlord or HM Customs & Excise is about to distrain, the position of creditors generally may be protected by placing the company in voluntary liquidation. As a result of the Insolvency Act 1986, it is no longer any breach of the Companies Act to place a company into voluntary liquidation by a special or extraordinary resolution of the members passed at a meeting called at short notice. The old rules (Companies Act 1948, s. 293, Companies Act 1981, s. 106 and CA, s. 588) variously provided (on pain of a fine) that a statutory meeting of creditors had to be held on the same day or that following the members' meeting and that at least seven days' notice of the members' meeting had to be given (see *Re Centrebind Ltd* [1967] 1 WLR 377 and *E. V. Saxton & Sons Ltd* v *R Miles (Confectioners) Ltd* [1983] 1WLR 952; (1983) 1 BCC 98, 914). Now the practice of 'centrebinding' has been legitimised and any abuses of the procedure are covered by limiting the powers of the liquidator in the interim period between the members' and creditors' meetings (IA, s. 166), the latter having to be called within 14 days of the members' meeting, and at least seven days' notice having been given to the creditors (IA, s. 98).

It may become standard insolvency practice where at least 95 per cent of the members of a company are prepared to consent to short notice of an extraordinary general meeting (CA, s. 369), to place a company into voluntary liquidation immediately. This would give execution and other creditors the minimum notice possible and would guard against any of them taking action which might give them an advantage on a winding-up. And if the members will not cooperate, the directors can petition the court for a winding-up order (IA, s. 124(1)).

The significance of these facts for the purposes of a consideration of the administration procedure is that there are alternative, and cheaper, methods of seeking speedy protection from creditors and there must therefore be a good reason why an administration should be pursued. Insolvency practitioners should be able to assist directors of companies in difficulties who wish to make the right decisions and who no doubt wish to be seen to have taken (at least from that point on) 'every step with a view to minimising the potential loss to the company's creditors . . .' (IA, s. 214 and see ¶901).

There is likely to be a marked difference in the detail of petitions presented by directors of the company itself and those presented by a creditor or creditors. It is comparatively rare for a creditor to have a detailed knowledge of the financial affairs of debtor companies and that lack of information will be reflected in any petitions which they may present. Further, the lack of information is likely to mean that creditors will often not be able to identify a situation where one of the purposes for an administration order could be achieved.

There is provision in the Rules for the costs of the petitioner to be paid as an expense of the administration (IR, r. 2.9(2) and see Form 2.4)). It would seem unlikely, however, that an insolvency practitioner or other 'independent person' will be prepared at the outset to incur expense and run up fees merely in the hope that the application will be successful and the costs will ultimately be borne in the administration. It seems highly likely (and only prudent) that practitioners will require that their costs up to and including the hearing of the petition are paid in advance by the petitioner.

## ¶904 Consequences of application

### (1) Legal consequences

*(a)  Generally*

As with compulsory winding up, an administration order is made at a hearing which is held pursuant to a petition issued previously. Neither the Insolvency Act 1986 nor the Rules lay down the precise period which is to elapse between the presentation of a petition and its hearing, a fact which depends to a great extent on court administration. The provision that service of the petition must take place not less than five days before the date fixed for the hearing indicates that the gap will normally be at least five days (IR, r. 2.7(1) but see *Re a Company No. 00175 of 1987* ((1987) 3 BCC 124) where the company's position was 'parlous' and the period was abridged to a period sufficient to give the secured creditor 'an adequate opportunity' of considering whether or not to appoint an administrative receiver). There may be a significant period during which the fate of the company will be to some extent uncertain and the Act provides a measure of protection to the company against hostile action by its creditors.

During the period between presentation of the petition and a hearing at which an administration order is made or the petition is dismissed, the following rules apply:

(1)   The company may not be put into liquidation – whether by way of a winding-up order made by the court or by a resolution of the members of the company (IA, s. 10(1)(*a*)). It is the duty of anyone petitioning for an administration order to inform the court in writing of any winding-up petition presented against the company of which he is or becomes aware (IR, r. 2.5(4)).

(2)   Without leave of the court (and subject to any terms it may impose) 'holders of security' (see ¶908) may not enforce that security over the company's property (IA, s. 10(1)(*b*)), save that a mortgagee who is entitled to appoint an administrative receiver may do so (IA, s. 10(2)(*b*). Such a receiver does not require the leave of the court to carry out his functions (IA, s. 10(2)(*c*)).

(3)   Without leave of the court (and, again, subject to any terms imposed) creditors who have supplied goods to the company under hire-purchase, conditional sale, chattel leasing or retention of title agreements are not permitted to repossess goods in the company's possession (IA, s. 10(1)(*b*) and (4)).

(4)   Without leave, and subject to the terms of the court, no proceedings other than the administration petition and no execution or other legal process are to be started or progressed, and similarly no distress may be levied, against the company or its property (IA, s. 10(1)(c)) As regards proceedings, the presentation of a petition for the winding-up of the company is permitted without leave (IA, s. 10(2)(a)).

The precise wording of the Act on this last point ('No other proceedings and no execution or other legal process may be commenced or continued . . .') seems to suggest that it may not be possible, without leave, to present a second administration petition. What if, for example, the directors have presented a petition for an administration with the expressed purpose of seeking a voluntary arrangement but creditors would rather see an administration to pursue a realisation programme (more advantageously than in a winding-up)? They could wait and seek modifications to the company's proposals after the order is made (see ¶1105) but could they present their own petition for an administration for a different purpose without specific leave?[1]

The argument that there is a right to present further petitions rests on the wording of s. 9(1) of the Insolvency Act 1986:

'An application to the court for an administration order shall be by petition presented either by the company or the directors, or by a creditor or creditors (including any contingent or prospective creditor or creditors), *or by all or any of those parties, together or separately*' (emphasis supplied).

The words emphasised either provide for multiple applications or they provide that a single petition may be made on a joint basis by, for example, the company *and* its creditors. If multiple applications without leave were envisaged, then it is perhaps surprising that there are no provisions governing this in the way that there are provisions governing subsequent winding-up petitions (consider, for example, IA, ss. 10(2)(a), 11(1)(a) and IR, r. 2.5(4)).

It is submitted that if leave is required for a second petition to be presented then the court should grant leave and arrange for the petitions to be heard together. It would seem sensible, in any event, for pending administration and winding-up petitions to be heard by the court at the one joint hearing in order that the competing arguments may be heard together (and consider *Re Knit 'n Wool Centre Pty Ltd* [1969] VR 244 and *Re Palmer Marine Surveys Ltd* [1986] 1 WLR 573; (1985) 1 BCC 99, 557).

As regards the prohibition on distress being 'levied' consider *Herbert Berry Associates Ltd* v *Inland Revenue Commissioners* ([1977] 1 WLR 1437) and *Re Memco Engineering Ltd* ([1985] 3 WLR 875; (1985) 1 BCC 99, 460).

---

[1] That they could is the view taken in Lingard, *Corporate rescues and insolvencies*, para. 916.

¶904

These 'protective' provisions do not apply where there is an administrative receiver in office unless and until such time as the appointor of the administrative receiver indicates his consent to the making of an order (IA, s. 10(3)). There is no requirement that this consent be given in writing (compare 'Notices' under the Rules – IR, r. 12.4). It would seem that consent can be oral or indicated by conduct, and mortgagees will need to be careful at any meetings with petitioners not to appear to consent. The petitioner will, however, wish to have some note to enable him to satisfy the court at the hearing (IA, s. 9(3)).

### (b)   An example
An administrative receiver is appointed to company X by a bank.

The directors of the company, in consultation with their advisers, consider that one of the four purposes of an administration order could be achieved and they present a petition to the court for an administrator. They meet with the bank and pursuade them that an administration would be a good idea but the bank indicates that its formal response, if it is to constitute a consent, will be made in writing. The bank writes formally to the petitioner or his advisers indicating that the bank consents to the making of an administration order. From that moment the statutory prohibitions apply and, for example, any creditors claiming reservation of title to goods must cease any attempts to repossess as against the receiver. The receiver remains in office. At the hearing the administration order is made. The receiver vacates office (IA, s. 11(1)(*a*)) but is relieved of any duty to pay preferential creditors (IA, s. 11(5)).

### (c)   Appointment of administrative receiver after presentation of petition
It is interesting to note that where an administrative receiver is appointed after the presentation of a petition for an administration, it would appear that the statutory prohibitions will apply (even where the receiver's appointor objects, and will object, to the making of the administration order) until such time as the petition may be dismissed. In such circumstances the court may be inclined to grant leave to creditors such as hire purchase or leasing companies who wish to enforce their rights.

### (2)   Practical consequences

### (a)   Scope of the protection offered
The Act can and does give a company a measure of protection from hostile acts by its creditors. What the Act does not, and could not, do is legislate for the type of positive co-operation and assistance necessary for the continued operation of the company's business and affairs. There may be a situation where a widget vital for the manufacture of the company's product is and can

¶904

only be supplied by one 'monopoly' supplier. The Act prevents such a supplier, where he has supplied goods on retention of title terms (and has not been paid), from retaking possession of those goods without leave of the court. What is not prohibited is the withdrawal of future supplies by that supplier. Similarly, the position might be that the company's bank which operates the company's overdraft (repayable on demand) has a legal charge on the company's freehold property. The presentation of a petition prevents the bank from appointing a receiver or in any other way enforcing its security (for example by taking possession and attempting to sell it). It does not prevent the bank from terminating the overdraft facilities and making demand for the sums owing. Such a severing of the company's main financial artery is likely to lead to the instant death of the business leaving the desired preservation of a company's undertaking as a going concern (if that was the purpose for which the administration petition was presented) looking like wishful thinking. The legislation makes no attempt to prevent third parties from providing, as a matter of contract, that the presentation of a petition or the making of an administration order is an event giving them rights such as the right to terminate contractual relations and seek damages.

On one reading of the administration provisions, it might be thought that the Act envisaged a short, simple petition, with the details of how a company is to be reconstructed being presented in due course (and after some thought) by the administrator when appointed, and that these detailed provisions would be embodied in his proposals to the company's creditors. This first 'hiatus' period may, however, give rise to substantial and indeed insuperable problems for a company which has simply stumbled into the presentation of a petition for an administrator without having made adequate arrangements to cope with these immediate problems. This problem appears to have been recognised by Vinelott J in *Re a Company No. 00175 of 1987* ((1987) 3 BCC 124) when he was prepared to abridge the notice provisions to ensure the gap between petition and order was as short as reasonably practicable.

Wherever, for example, the banking facilities afforded to the company are not terminable on demand or indeed on presentation of a petition for an administrator or on one of the variety of 'general jeopardy' grounds normally included as 'events of default' by banks in their loan documentation, it might be possible for a company to continue to operate during the hiatus period provided it keeps within its facilities. This type of lending is not typical in the UK although it is more commonly found in the US. But, again, taking the situation of the bank in the example above, with the difference that the bank has a full debenture on the assets of the company including a fixed charge on book debts – as is perhaps likely to be the case – then the bank will be entitled to the proceeds of the book debts pursuant to its security and, again, the company's vital cash-flow will have been cut off.

¶904

Even if the first hiatus period can be abridged (*Re a Company No. 00175 of 1987*, cited above) these problems will have to be faced by the company, in the same way, after the administration order has been made, and further consideration is given to this matter below (¶1104). Where possible, administration petitions for the purpose of preserving the company or the undertaking as a going concern should be adequately prepared and thought out and may involve discussions and possibly agreements with the company's bankers and suppliers prior to the presentation of the petition itself. It is unlikely to be advisable for a company in severe difficulties to present a petition simply to obtain relief from the attacks of its creditors, save perhaps for the limited purpose of achieving a more advantageous realization than in a winding-up. And as a general rule, 'going-concern' administration petitions ought to be presented much earlier in the company's financial crisis if they are to have a realistic chance of success.

*(b)   Running the company between petition and order*
From the time of presentation of the petition until such time as an administration order is made (placing an administrator in charge of the company), the directors of the company will continue to be in day-to-day control. The legislation gives little guidance on how they are to run the company during this time. It is submitted that they should simply take such steps as are necessary to preserve the company's business and property and should not take any major steps or alter the company's business in any significant way prior to the hearing of the petition. It will be for the administrator to make the important decisions on the future of the company and its business. The directors must consider carefully their potential liabilities for wrongful and/ or fraudulent trading (IA, ss. 214 and 213 respectively). As discussed above (¶901), the intention of the Cork Committee was that the seeking of an administration order in an appropriate case at an early stage should prevent directors from attracting personal liability. For the purposes of wrongful trading, where directors are advised professionally and before their company's financial position has become grave, they may be able to show either that they had never reached a point at which they knew or ought to have concluded that there was no reasonable prospect of the company avoiding insolvent liquidation or, alternatively, if that point had been reached, that taking professional advice and seeking an administration order was taking every step a reasonably diligent person would take with a view to minimising the potential loss to the company's creditors. As regards fraudulent trading there is still the possibility that in the hiatus period between petition and administration order the directors will be a party to the incurring of credit at a time when they know there is no reasonable prospect of the debt being paid (for example, because the purpose of the administration is to seek a voluntary arrangement

¶904

converting, say, 50 per cent of the unsecured debt at the date of administration into equity). It may be possible, in such circumstances, for the directors to argue that they were not acting 'dishonestly' and hence are not liable (see, generally, *R* v *Grantham* [1984] QB 675)

*(c) Interim orders*

The proposed administrator appears to have no particular role between petition and the making of any administration order. The Insolvency Act 1986, s. 9 does, however, provide as follows:

'(4) . . . on hearing a petition the court may dismiss it, or adjourn the hearing conditionally or unconditionally, or make an interim order or any other order that it thinks fit.

(5) Without prejudice to the generality of subsection (4), an interim order under that subsection may restrict the exercise of any powers of the directors or of the company (whether by reference to the consent of the court or of a person qualified to act as an insolvency practitioner in relation to the company, or otherwise).'

Although the terminology is not free from obscurity, s. 9(4) appears to suggest that interim orders may be sought between petition and winding-up order if it can be said that the hearing of an application for an interim order is in any sense a hearing of 'a petition'. The reference in s. 9(5) to restrictions on the powers of the directors in the company is unnecessary where an administration order has been made as one of the effects of the making of an administration order is to prevent the company or its officers from exercising powers so as to interfere with the functions of the administrator (IA, s. 14(4)). In the case of *Re a Company No. 00175 of 1987* ((1987) 3 BCC 124), Vinelott J analysed this type of position as follows:

'. . . the court has no power to appoint an interim administrator . . . The court has power under section 9(4) on the hearing of a petition to adjourn it, or to "make an interim order, or any other order it thinks fit". I can see no reason why, if satisfied that the assets or business of a company are in jeopardy, and that there exists a prima facie case for the making of an administration order, the court should not abridge the time for service of the petition, and if at the hearing a person with power to appoint a receiver seeks further time in which to consider whether to exercise that power, should not adjourn the hearing and appoint the proposed administrator or some other suitable person to take control of the property of the company and manage its affairs pending the hearing. Such an appointment would be analogous to the appointment of a receiver of a disputed property which is in jeopardy'.

¶904

He feared that if the court did not have such a power the 'destruction' of the company could result.

## ¶905   Attitudes of secured creditors

### (1)   Generally
The court may not make an administration order where an administrative receiver has been appointed unless the appointor of the administrative receiver consents to the appointment being made (IA, s. 9(3)(*a*)). This provision is important. On its face, it is designed to assist and protect the position and security of secured creditors who might be less inclined to lend to companies and businesses or perhaps would lend on a different basis if a petition for an administrator presented by a company or its creditors could effectively deprive it of the opportunity to appoint its own administrative receiver under its security to manage the business and realise the assets. There will also be the inevitable effect that more and more creditors will seek to take floating charges (perhaps fully postponed) simply to be able as a last resort to block an administration. Mortgagees are given notice of the presentation of a petition (see ¶903(8)) and will have to decide whether or not to appoint their own administrative receiver. In general terms, this may well force lenders to appoint administrative receivers rather earlier than they would otherwise wish to do. What are the advantages and disadvantages of an administration from the point of view of such a secured creditor?

### (2)   Advantages
The advantages of an administration in such circumstances are as follows:

(1)   It may be that the rescue plan prepared and embodied in the administration scheme, in simple terms, provides the best chance of the secured creditor being repaid the money it has lent where, for example, the assets secured are insufficient to pay the secured debt.

(2)   Supporting a petition of, for example, the company or its directors (who may be guarantors of the secured creditor) may be seen as a more positive and helpful attitude from the mortgagee and may, in certain cases, be preferable to an opposed receivership.

(3)   There are no preferential creditors in an administration. Where the secured lender merely has a floating charge and the preferential creditors are likely to be high in value there may be little likelihood of a return in a receivership and, therefore, little could be lost in giving the administration a chance.

(4)   There could conceivably be cases where an administrative receivership would encounter insuperable problems in the face of hostile action by retention of title suppliers (see ¶407(3)) and/or suppliers of goods on lease or hire purchase, and hence it would be better to have an administration as the administrator would be protected from hostile action by these creditors (see ¶908).

(5)   Transactions at an undervalue and preferences (IA, ss. 238–40) may be attacked in an administration but not in a receivership. Where for example the directors are thought to have been guilty of misfeasance in this way, secured creditors might see advantages in permitting an administration.

(6)   Occasionally secured creditors may fear bad publicity if they appoint their own receiver because of the nature of the company's business and an administration might, in those circumstances, be considered preferable.

## (3)   Disadvantages

The disadvantages of an administration for such a secured creditor are as follows:

(1)   An administration may be costly to set up, both in terms of time and expense, while a receivership is a tried and tested mechanism which can be put into operation quickly and cheaply.

(2)   There is inevitably an attraction to the secured creditor in having, in the form of an administrative receiver, an insolvency practitioner in control of the company who is, subject always to the duties previously discussed (see ¶415 et seq.), essentially appointed to attempt to obtain repayment of the secured debt. The administrator (even someone whom the secured creditor may, in other cases, have appointed as administrative receiver) will be seen as someone charged with the task of furthering the aims of all the creditors (and the company).

(3)   The administrator's right to deal with property caught by the security (IA, s. 15) is unfettered in the case of floating-charge assets and constitutes a right to 'dispose' with the leave of the court where there is a fixed charge in place. These rights are a fundamental abrogation of the secured creditor's rights as mortgagee and are unattractive, notwithstanding the statutory safeguards (in the case of fixed-charge property) as to price and as to receipt of the proceeds of sale (see ¶1008 and ¶1122).

(4)   The difficulties over financing administrations may involve close scrutiny of fixed charges on future book debts and secured creditors may

¶905

wish to sidestep the issue by appointing their own administrative receiver.

(5) If the secured creditor is a bank with a finance house subsidiary which carries on a leasing or hire-purchase business, the appointment of an administrative receiver would help that subsidiary to avoid the restrictions on its rights which would be imposed by an administration order (IA s. 11(3)(*b*) – discussed at ¶908).

**(4) Summary**

In summary, for secured creditors the appointment of their own administrative receiver will, in the majority of cases, be the preferred option. It constitutes a tried and tested remedy and there will have to be particular circumstances applicable before they are likely to consent to an administration order being made.

## ¶906 The hearing of the application

**(1) General**

On the hearing of the petition the court must decide whether or not to make the order. As we have seen, the court is empowered to make an administration order on the hearing of a petition if two conditions are satisfied. First, the court must believe that the company is, or is likely to become, unable to pay its debts and secondly, the court must consider that the making of an administration order would be likely to achieve one or more of the various purposes for an administration order. It is open to the court not to make the order even if both conditions are satisfied. For example, if there was evidence before the court that a majority in value of the company's creditors opposed the petition (and perhaps supported instead a winding-up petition) then there would seem little point in the court making the order only for the administration to fail at the hurdle of the creditors' meeting.

In exercising its discretion whether or not to make the order, the court will assess the evidence before it and is required in effect to form its own view. It is unlikely, however, to wish to become involved in commercial evaluations. The following may appear or be represented at the hearing of a petition (IR, r. 2.9(1)):

(1) the petitioner;

(2) the company itself;

(3) any person who has appointed or has power to appoint an administrative receiver;

(4) where an administrative receiver has been appointed, he is entitled to appear;

(5)　anyone who has presented a petition for the winding-up of the company;

(6)　the proposed administrator; and

(7)　any other person with an interest justifying his appearance may be heard, with the leave of the court.

## (2) 'Trial within a trial'

There are circumstances in which an administrator can be appointed notwithstanding the fact that there is an administrative receiver in office and his debenture holder has not consented to the making of the administration order. Such circumstances are where the security under which the receiver has been appointed would on the order being made be vulnerable to challenge on any of the following grounds (IA, s. 9(3)(*b*)):

(1)　as being (*a*) a transaction at an undervalue and/or (*b*) a preference (IA, ss. 238–40);

(2)　(in the case of the floating charge) as a security invalid under s. 245 of the Insolvency Act 1986.

Where the petitioner is able to show that the security is open to attack under any of these heads, the court can make the order and on the order being made the administrative receiver has to vacate office. It will thus be necessary to conduct a form of 'trial within a trial' where the debenture holder's right to have appointed an administrative receiver is disputed. Disputes of this kind may make the administration procedure difficult to work in practice as the legal and factual complexities surrounding transactions at an undervalue, preferences and the invalidity of floating charges are likely to lead to hearings of some length and the administrator procedure is ill-designed to accommodate this. The petitioner, whether that is the company or the directors, may have difficulty financing a protracted legal argument. A petitioning creditor may have difficulty in obtaining the necessary evidence to establish a preference or a transaction at an undervalue.

It remains to be seen whether any petitioners will try to widen the argument even further by arguing that if the security is void (see the discussion at ¶313) the 'administrative receiver' is no more than a purported administrative receiver, a trespasser and, hence, that there is no bar to the appointment of an administrator. It should be remembered that the original trial of the action which led finally to the judgment of the Court of Appeal in the case *Rolled Steel Products (Holdings) Ltd* v *British Steel Corp* ([1985] 2 WLR 908 at p. 913) was 19 days! It also remains to be seen whether a finding by the court at such a 'trial within a trial' means that the matter is *res judicata* between the parties or whether the same issues could be considered afresh at a later trial.

¶906

The court need not make the order or dismiss the petition and it is open to it to adjourn the hearing conditionally or unconditionally or to make interim or other orders as it thinks fit (IA, s. 9(4)).

If an administrative order is made (Form 2.4) the petitioner's costs are to be payable as an expense of the administration (IR, r. 2.9(2)). Similarly the court is given power to make the costs of any other party appearing at the hearing an expense of the administration (IR, r. 2.9(2)). The well-organised practitioner will not wish to have his fee depend on success at the hearing and will have been paid in advance for his work.

## ¶907  Notice of the order

There are a number of actions that have to be taken immediately upon an administration order being made, as follows:

(1)   The court must forthwith give notice of the making of the order to the person appointed as the administrator (IR, r. 2.10(1)).

(2)   The administrator must, forthwith after the order is made, advertise his appointment in the *London Gazette* (see IR, r. 13.13(4)) and in such other newspaper as he thinks most appropriate to give notice to the company's creditors (IR, r. 2.10(2) and Form 2.5).

(3)   The administrator must also give notice of the making of the order to any administrative receiver or any mortgagee entitled to appoint one, to any petitioner for winding-up (and any provisional liquidator appointed) and finally to the Registrar of Companies (IR, r. 2.10(3) and Form 2.6).

(4)   The administrator must send a notice of the order to the company itself (IA, s. 21(1)(*a*)).

(5)   Within 28 days of the making of the order and unless the court directs otherwise, the administrator must send a notice of his appointment to all the creditors of the company to the extent that he is aware of their addresses (IA, s. 21(1)(*b*)).

(6)   The court will send two sealed copies of the administration order to the administrator and he has to forward one of these to the Registrar of Companies within 14 days of the making of the order (IA, s. 21(2), IR, r. 2.10(4) and Form 2.7).

(7)   The court may provide for further notices to be given where it makes an order other than an administration order (for example an interim order) on the hearing of the petition (IR, r. 2.10(5)).

The administrator must fulfil his obligations described above on pain of a fine for failure without reasonable excuse (IA, s. 21(3)).

While the administration order is in force every invoice, order for goods or business letter which is issued by or on behalf of the company or the administrator and on which the company's name appears is also to contain the administrator's name and state that the affairs, business and property of the company are being managed by the administrator (IA, s. 12(1)). Failure to comply means that the company is liable to a fine, as is the administrator and any officers of the company who authorised or permitted the default, without reasonable excuse (IA, s. 12(2)). This follows a similar form to that for liquidations (see IA, s. 188 – formerly CA, s. 637).

## ¶908   Consequences of order

Where an order is made the two immediate effects are that any petition for the winding-up of the company must be dismissed by the court and any administrative receiver must vacate office (IA, s. 11(1)). A receiver of part only of the company's property may be required to vacate office by the administrator (IA, s. 11(2)).

The protection afforded to the company on presentation of the petition is continued, to the following effect (IA, s. 11(3)):

(1)   no resolution may be passed or order made for the winding-up of the company;

(2)   no administrative receiver may be appointed;

(3)   no steps can be taken to enforce any security over the company's property;

(4)   goods in the company's possession under hire-purchase, conditional sale, chattel leasing or retention of title agreements cannot be repossessed by their owners (note the cross-reference to IA, s. 10(4) for the full list of third parties); and

(5)   no proceedings, execution or other legal process can be commenced or continued and distress cannot be levied against the company or its property.

For these purposes 'security' has a wide meaning, being any mortgage, charge, lien or other security (IA, s. 248(*b*)).

In the case of points (3), (4) and (5) above, the prohibitions apply unless the administrator consents or the court gives leave, in which event the third party must abide by any terms imposed by the court (IA, s. 11(3)(*c*) and (*d*)).

## ¶909   Invalid appointments

As an administrator is appointed by the court there are fewer traps which might lead to invalidity than exist for appointments of administrative receivers.

There would no doubt be problems of invalidity if the administrator was not qualified to act as an insolvency practitioner in relation to the company, for example because he is not authorised, or because his security is not properly in place (contrary to IA, s. 390).

Where there are defects in the appointment, nomination or qualifications of an administrator which can be regarded as 'slips', the acts of an administrator are valid notwithstanding these defects (IA, s. 232 and see the discussion of this section at ¶313(2)).

# 10  Nature, Capacity, Powers and Duties of an Administrator

## INTRODUCTION

### ¶1001  Comparison with other office-holders

The administrator was conceived as being an administrative receiver without the floating charge (see ¶901). He is, however, a court appointee and, as such, he will bear some similarity to a liquidator in a compulsory liquidation and to a court-appointed receiver. As a result, some authorities in these areas may be of assistance in interpreting the legislation covering the administration procedure.

### ¶1002  Purpose of appointment

Administrations are by their very nature likely to be more varied and offer more challenges to office-holders than administrative receiverships and liquidations. With a few notable exceptions, most receiverships and liquidations lead inexorably to a realisation of assets and a distribution of the proceeds according to an established system of priority. The administration procedure, if it works, offers great scope to the ingenuity and the inventiveness of insolvency practitioners.

In one case an administrator may find himself running a major public company, organising a rationalisation programme of its activities, sacking the existing board and replacing them with directors who have the confidence of the company's customers and suppliers and, if successful, eventually returning control of the company to the new board to continue the slimmed-down operation. In another case, however, he may simply be realising assets of a small private company in a more advantageous fashion than he would otherwise be able to do in a liquidation.

The methods employed and the skills required of the administrator will depend on the purpose for which he is appointed and the nature of the proposals he puts forward.

¶1001

## AGENCY AND POSITION

### ¶1003   Nature and extent

The administrator is deemed to be the agent of the company in exercising his powers (IA, s. 14(5)). The effect of the agency is to make the company the principal in all the administrator's dealings with third parties and the administrator will not be personally liable in contract (compare, tort). It is theoretically possible for the administrator to be personally liable in contract where express provision is made in the relevant contract. For example, where the administrator requires a supply of gas, electricity, water or telephone services he must be prepared to give a personal guarantee of payment for the supplies (IA, s. 233 and see ¶1011(2)). It seems likely that the administrator will include in his contractual documentation a clause to the effect that he is acting only as agent and is not personally liable. The same practice is followed in liquidations (where it is arguably not strictly necessary in the light of *Re Anglo-Moravian Hungarian Junction Railway Company ex p Watkins* [1875] 1 Ch. 130 but note *Plant Engineers (Sales) Ltd* v *Davis* (1969) 113 SJ 484).

The statutory agency provides no greater protection from tortious liability than the contractual agency of the administrative receiver (see ¶406).

### ¶1004   Officer of the court

As a court appointee, the administrator is an officer of the court. He must be impartial as between the various competing interests in his administration and he must, under a duty owed to the creditors and shareholders, make himself fully conversant with the company's business and affairs and he must not suppress relevant information (*Gooch's case* (1871) 7 Ch. App 207).

He must not take unfair advantage of third parties who act in good faith even if, legally, he is strictly entitled to do so – the principle known as 'the rule in *ex parte James*' (*Re Condon ex p James* (1874) 9 Ch. App 609). As it was put by Kekewich J at first instance in *Re Opera, Limited* ([1891] 2 Ch. 154 at p. 161):

'. . . it is not a question of equity, it is not a question of law, but it is a question of honesty; . . . when the court comes to deal with an officer of its own, it will do that which it cannot make an ordinary litigant do – that is to say, avoid doing the shabby thing, and do what is really honest'.

The concept was restated recently by Lawton LJ in *Re Multi Guarantee Co Ltd* (17 June 1986, Lexis):

'Various words have been used in the cases to indicate the kind of conduct to which the principle of *Ex parte James* may apply, such as "a point of

¶1004

moral justice", "dishonest", "dishonourable", "unworthy", "unfair" and "shabby". Those words are not words of art at all. They are words of ordinary English usage and the concept behind them is, as I understand the cases, that an officer of the court, such as a trustee in bankruptcy or a liquidator, should not behave in a way which a reasonable member of the public, knowing all the facts, would regard as either dishonest, unfair or dishonourable.'

## ¶1005    Officer of the company

The definition of 'officer' in the Companies Act 1985 (applicable to the Insolvency Act 1986 by virtue of s. 251 of that Act) reads as follows:

'An "officer" in relation to a body corporate, includes a director, manager or secretary'.

An administration order is one which directs that a company's affairs be 'managed' by an administrator (IA, s. 8(2)) and it follows that an administrator will be an officer of the company. In this he will be like a liquidator (*Hillman* v *Crystal Bowl Amusements Ltd* [1973] 1 WLR 162) but unlike an administrative receiver (*Re B Johnson & Co (Builders) Ltd* [1955] Ch. 634). A number of consequences flow from the conclusion that he is an officer:

(1)    He is liable to a fine for failing to cause the company to fulfil various duties under the Companies Act 1985 (see, for example, CA, ss. 380 and 382).

(2)    There are other statutory regulations which may result in liabilities for 'officers' of companies and which may therefore affect an administrator.

(3)    As officer, the administrator owes fiduciary duties to the company in much the same way as a director. He has a duty not to make a secret profit out of his office even where no loss results to the company (*Re Gertzenstein Ltd* [1937] Ch. 115 and *Boardman* v *Phipps* [1967] 2 AC 46) and he should not allow a conflict of interest to arise in carrying out his duties (*Gooch's case* (1871) 7 Ch. App 207). This latter area may also be covered by the internal rules of the recognised professional body which grants the insolvency practitioner his licence.

(4)    He must show due care and skill in carrying out his functions and the level of skill and competence required will be higher than that of an ordinary director.

(5)    It may be open to the court to grant relief to the administrator qua officer for negligence, defaults, breach of duty or breach of trust where the administrator acted honestly and reasonably in all the

circumstances and ought fairly to be excused either in whole or in part (CA, s. 727).

In common with officers of the company, liquidators and administrative receivers, administrators may be liable to summary action in a winding-up for misapplication of funds, misfeasance or breach of duty (IA, s. 212). The proceedings may be brought by the official receiver, the liquidator, a creditor or contributory and, although in the case of the latter the leave of the court is necessary, it is no bar to action that the contributory will not benefit (IA, s. 212(5)). The court may order repayment plus interest or such other monetary compensation as it thinks fit (IA, s. 212(3)). Where the administrator has had his statutory release (see ¶1211) the leave of the court is required before an application may be made (IA, s. 212(4)).

## PROPERTY COVERED BY THE APPOINTMENT

### ¶1006   Apparent entitlement

The administrator's duty, on his appointment, is to take possession or gain control not just of property of the company but property to which the company 'appears to be entitled' (IA, s. 17(1)). This notion has similarities to the old bankruptcy doctrine of 'reputed ownership'. The statutory duty would not appear to go so far as to give the administrator or the company any title to the assets seized but would seem designed to give the administrator a measure of protection from suit if it later turns out that the company is not entitled to an item despite having appeared to be so (and see also IA, s. 234(3) and (4)). In practice, this 'right to possession' will constitute a significant tactical weapon in the administrator's armoury when dealing with third-party claims to title to assets in the custody of the administrator. The administrator may also make a summary application to court to enforce this right (IA, s. 234(2) and see ¶1011(2)).

### ¶1007   Third-party property

As mentioned above (see ¶908), owners of equipment and assets supplied to the company on hire purchase, chattel leasing (see IA, s. 251), conditional sale or retention of title agreements (see IA, s. 251) may not seek to recover their goods against the administrator without his consent or the leave of the court. This restriction on the remedies of the creditor does not of itself give any substantive rights to the company or the administrator. Leasing and hire-purchase companies may insert clauses in their agreements purporting to prevent administrators from using their equipment. The administrator has a right of disposal of the goods with the leave of the court and subject to his accounting for the proceeds or market value, if greater (IA, s. 15 and see ¶1122), but that seems different to 'use' for the purposes of the business, for example. Save as specifically provided by statute, he can be in no better position than the company itself.

The serious effects on their rights which result from the appointment of an administrator may encourage leasing and hire-purchase companies to produce schemes to avoid being caught by the statutory provisions. Contractual restrictions, as mentioned above, are one possibility. Another scheme which has been suggested is for the leasing or hire-purchase company to enter into the relevant agreement with an otherwise dormant subsidiary of the company ('company X') which wishes to use the equipment. The subsidiary then loans the equipment to company X. If an administration order is subsequently made in respect of company X the argument would run that the owner could repossess as against the subsidiary and the administrator (although he might be able initially to take the equipment into his custody on the grounds that company X appeared to be entitled to it) would not be able to resist the claim of the owner as company X did not hold the equipment 'under' a leasing or hire-purchase agreement, merely pursuant to a bailment by the subsidiary. With the court's increasing tendency to focus on substance rather than form such artificial schemes may be vulnerable to attack. There may also be arguments that some schemes constitute an attempt to contract out of the statutory scheme (see *British Eagle International Airlines Ltd* v *Compagnie Nationale Air France* [1975] 1 WLR 758).

Subject to his initial duty to take possession of all property apparently belonging to the company, the administrator will need to consider the same questions relating to reservation of title and trust as were considered above (¶407(3) and (4)) in connection with administrative receivers.

## ¶1008   Charged property

The rights of an administrator in respect of property subject to a security vary depending on whether the security is subject to a floating charge or, alternatively, some other form of security.

In the case of security other than a floating charge, the administrator may only 'dispose' of the property with the leave of the court (IA, s. 15 and see ¶1122).

In the case of property subject to a floating charge the administrator may 'dispose or otherwise exercise his powers in relation to [it] . . . as if the property were not subject to the security' (IA, s. 15(1)). The administrator could, for example, charge a piece of equipment and the charge created would appear to rank in priority to the earlier floating charge.

¶1008

It is more likely that the main item caught by a floating charge will be stock which the administrator will sell. On such a disposal it appears that the interest of the floating chargee transfers to the proceeds of sale and any property subsequently purchased with the proceeds, and so on (IA, s. 15(4)). On this analysis, the chargee retains the same priority in respect of the revolving fund that he enjoyed in respect of the stock originally caught (in this example). The wording of s. 15(4) is, however, far from a model of clarity and may be open to interpretation.

## POWERS OF AN ADMINISTRATOR

### ¶1009   Statutory list of powers

The administrator is granted very extensive powers to enable him to fulfil his functions. He is given, first, the general power to do all such things as may be necessary for the management of the affairs, business and property of the company (IA, s. 14(1)(*a*)). In addition and without prejudice to these powers he is given a specific list of powers (IA, s. 14(1)(*b*) and Sch. 1). This list is the same as for an administrative receiver (see ¶411) and is set out in Appendix 5 below. As these powers are granted with statutory force there can be little argument about the ability of the administrator to use them. For example, just as a liquidator is authorised by ss. 165 and 167 and Sch. 4, Pt. III, para 7 of the Insolvency Act 1986 to use the company seal, so the administrator is empowered so to do by virtue of para. 8 of Sch. 1 to the Act. This should be accepted by, for example, the Land Registry.

### ¶1010   Directors of the company

The administrator is, in addition, given power to dismiss and appoint directors to the company (IA, s. 14(2)). This is a power somewhat different to those normally exercised by insolvency practitioners.[1]

Where the purpose for which the administrator is appointed is to pursue the continued survival of the company as a going concern there could be circumstances in which the continued presence on the board of a particular director may hinder the successful implementation of the administrator's plan, whether because he has lost the confidence of the company's customers or creditors, or its employees, or his fellow directors. Insolvency practitioners

---

[1] One well-known insolvency practitioner has a rule not to insist that the managing director of a company in receivership should give up his office notwithstanding an administrative receiver's power to require this.

will have to identify such 'problem cases' and use their powers to dismiss them and, if necessary, replace them. The nearest insolvency practitioners came to such considerations prior to the Insolvency Act 1986 is when they were instructed to carry out an investigation, as investigating accountants, into a company about which a lender is concerned and they would occasionally comment on the abilities and performance of the board.

Besides being liable to dismissal, directors are not to be allowed to continue to exercise their powers in the face of the appointment of an administrator. Any powers which the company or its officers possess, either under the Companies Acts or the company's memorandum and articles of association, which could be exercised so as to 'interfere' with the exercise of the administrator's own powers are not to be capable of exercise except with the administrator's consent (IA, s. 14(4)). This consent can be specific or general. There will be cases where a director can greatly assist an administration simply by being left to get on with a particular task – running one division of a large operation for instance – particularly where this is popular with customers and employees. Administrators will be slow to grant consent to directors to exercise their former powers and are more likely to utilise the skills of directors as employees answerable to the administrator as such.

## ¶1011   Information and powers as 'office-holder'

### (1)   Statement of affairs

To enable the administrator to have in his possession all relevant information relating to the company and its affairs, there is provision in the Insolvency Act 1986 for the preparation of a statment of affairs for the administrator (IA, s. 22 and IR, rr. 2.11–15). He is required to initiate the process in that he has a duty forthwith on his appointment to require the statement to be prepared. He may require any or all of the following to prepare the statement (IA, s. 22(1) and (3)):

(1)   anyone who is or has been an officer of the company;

(2)   those who have taken part in the company's affairs at any time within a year before the date of the administration order. This will cover a situation where the administration order is made within 12 months of the company's incorporation;

(3)   employees of the company or those who have been employees during the year prior to the administration order and, in either case, whom the administrator considers can give the required information; and

(4)   where an officer of the company is itself a company, any officers or employees of that company or anyone who had been an officer or employee during the year prior to the administration order.

For the purposes of (1)–(4) above, 'employees' include those who were self-employed but under a contract for services with the company (IA, s. 22(3)), which seems to catch the company's accountants and solicitors.

Where the administrator requires a person to submit a statement of affairs he must send him a notice in prescribed form (Form 2.8). The notice is to tell the deponent (as he is called) of the names and addresses of the others to whom the notice has been sent, tell him the time within which the statment must be delivered to the administrator, explain to him the penalty for non-compliance with his duty to submit the statement, and contain a reminder of the provisions of s. 235 of the Insolvency Act 1986 which sets out the general duty of the deponents to provide information to the administrator, and to meet him to provide the information, if required (IR, r. 2.11(3)).

On request, the administrator is to provide each deponent with instructions on how to prepare the statement and also with the necessary forms to be completed (IR, r. 2.11(4)).

The statement is to be completed on Form 2.9 and hence is to include a summary of assets and liabilities and a list of creditors.

The deponents are required to complete the statement and submit it to the administrator within a period of 21 days starting with the day after the notice is served on them (IA, s. 22(4)). The administrator has the power to extend the time period either when giving the notice or subsequently, and indeed the administrator has power to release someone from his obligations in an appropriate case (IA, s. 22(5)). In the event that the administrator refuses either to extend or to release, the deponent can apply to the court for relief (IA, s. 22(5)).

A deponent who fails to carry out any of his obligations when required so to do is liable to a fine (IA, s. 22(6)).

The deponents have to verify the statements by affidavit and they all have to use the 'same form' (Form 2.9) implying that they will all agree on the details to go in the form (IR, r. 2.12(1)). The administrator has the power to require anyone who could have been asked to submit a statement of affairs to submit an affidavit concurring with that prepared by the deponents (IR, r. 2.12(2)). The person making this affidavit of concurrence is not required to agree with the deponents and he may qualify his affidavit where he does not agree or where he considers the statement to be wrong or misleading (IR, r. 2.12(3)). Similarly, he may qualify his affidavit where he does not have the direct knowledge necessary to say that he concurs (IR, r. 2.12(3)).

The deponent who swears the affidavit, or one of them if more than one person swears the affidavit, is required to deliver the statement to the administrator along with a copy of the verified statement (IR, r. 2.12(4)). Similarly, anyone making an affidavit of concurrence has to deliver it to the administrator together with a copy (IR, r. 2.12(5)).

¶1011

The administrator is required to file the verified copy of the statement and any affidavits of concurrence with the court (IR, r. 2.12(6)).

Where a deponent applies to the court for a release from his obligation or an extension of time the court may dismiss the application if it thinks that no sufficient cause has been shown, but in any event it must allow the applicant an opportunity to attend an *ex parte* hearing of which at least seven days' notice must be given (IR, r. 2.14(3)). Where the court does not immediately dismiss the application it shall decide the time, date and place for a hearing of the application and give notice to the deponent (IR, r. 2.14(3)). The deponent is required at least 14 days before the hearing to give the administrator notice of the venue together with a copy of the application and the evidence that the deponent intends to produce in support (IR, r. 2.14(4)).

The administrator has the right to appear and be heard on the application and in any event he may submit a written report of matters which he thinks ought to be brought to the court's attention (IR, r. 2.14(5)). Where he files such a report, the administrator must send it to the deponent not less than five days before the hearing of the application (IR, r. 2.14(5)).

Copies of any order made at the hearing, to which the court seal must be affixed, are to be sent by the court to the deponent and the administrator (IR, r. 2.14(6)).

The general rule is that the applicant's costs of the application are to be paid by him, although the court may order that an allowance towards them shall be made out of the assets of the company (IR, r. 2.14(7)).

Deponents are to be paid as an administration expense ('paid by the administrator out of his receipts' IR, r. 2.15(1) – and see generally ¶1115). The expenses paid are any which were incurred by the deponent in making the statement of affairs and affidavit and which the administrator considers reasonable. It is not immediately clear whether the deponent would be entitled to ask, for example, the company's auditors to assist with the statement of affairs and charge the cost of the auditors' work to the administration, on this ground. The Rules expressly provide that any decision made by the administrator in this respect is subject to appeal to the court (IR, r. 2.15(2)). Lest a dispute over expenses were to be thought by a deponent to give him an excuse for not completing the statement of affairs, the Rules expressly provide that nothing in this respect is to relieve the deponent of his obligations, whether in respect of the statement of affairs or generally, as regards providing information to the administrator (IR, r. 2.15(3)).

There is an interesting and imaginative provision in the Rules that the administrator may apply to the court for an order that restrictions be placed upon disclosure of the statement of affairs – for example, that it should not have to be filed in court or only in part or that it should not be inspected without the leave of the court (IR, r. 2.13). The administrator may make this

¶1011

application where he considers that disclosure may prejudice the conduct of his administration. Perhaps the statement might reveal the existence of assets of the company in the possession of third parties. The administrator might wish to investigate further without revealing the knowledge he had gained. He might fear that the assets would be transferred out of the jurisdiction and hence would want to be in a position to issue 'Mareva' injunctions without any warning. There will be other sets of circumstances where these 'limited disclosure' powers will be helpful.

### (2) Powers as 'office-holder'

There are a number of powers in the Insolvency Act 1986 given to an administrator as 'office-holder'. These are as follows:

(1) power to require supplies of services (IA, s. 233, and for this paragraph and paras. (2), (3) and (4) below see ¶414 discussing the same powers of an administrative receiver);

(2) power to ask the court to require delivery of property (IA, s. 234(1) and (2));

(3) power to require cooperation (IA, s. 235); and

(4) power to question relevant persons (IA, ss. 236–7).

A lien (save where it gives title to property) on books, papers or other records of the company is unenforceable against an administrator to the extent it would deny him possession of such items (IA, s. 246).

The power of the office-holder to investigate antecedent transactions might equally be seen as a duty and is considered under that head below (¶1016).

### (3) Other powers

The administrator has power to call meetings of the members or creditors of the company should the need arise (IA, s. 14(2)(*b*)). This is a general power distinct from the various meetings he may or must call in connection with his proposals (see ¶1103 et seq.).

As is the case with an administrative receiver and a liquidator, an administrator is able to apply to court for directions on any particular question arising in the administration (IA, s. 14(3)). With an entirely new insolvency procedure administrators should feel free to avail themselves of this facility in an appropriate case. It should be noted, however, that the provision for an administrator to apply to the court does not appear to give the court the power to give declaratory judgment affecting persons' rights in the way that it can on an application by a receiver and manager (compare IA, ss. 14(3) and 35(2)).

¶1011

## ¶1012   Limitations on powers and their exercise

An administrator is restricted in the exercise of his powers in a number of ways:

(1)   First, his appointment and his powers do not sweep away the fundamental rules of company law. He should not cause the company to continue manufacturing widgets (even if that is part of the purpose for which he has been appointed) if the principal object of the company is pig-breeding (see *Re Introductions Ltd* [1970] Ch. 199). In short the administrator must ensure that the company is not acting ultra vires. Further, it would be an abuse of power by the administrator to use an express power for an ultra vires purpose (*Rolled Steel Products (Holdings) Ltd* v *British Steel Corp* [1985] 2 WLR 908).

(2)   It may not be open to the administrator to exercise a power, say, to cause the company to give a guarantee where the Memorandum does not provide for the giving of guarantees by the company.

(3)   He must exercise the powers bona fide for the purpose of the administration (see ¶1014), and any other exercise is an abuse.

Third parties are given a measure of protection in their dealings with administrators – provided they are acting in good faith and for value they are not to be concerned to inquire whether the administrator is acting within his powers (IA, s. 14(6)). Note, however, the danger that knowledge or wilful blindness may destroy 'good faith' (see Lingard, *Bank security documents*, para. 2.5).

## ¶1013   Exercise of powers in joint appointments

Depending on the terms of the appointment, joint administrators either must exercise their powers together, in the sense of jointly, or may exercise them individually or severally (IA, s. 231).

# DUTIES OF AN ADMINISTRATOR

## ¶1014   Purposes of the appointment

The principal duty of the administrator is to carry out the purpose or purposes of his administration. He should exercise his powers towards that end. There are two distinct phases in an administration – before and after the proposals of the administrator are considered by the creditors.

In his management of the company's affairs, business and property the administrator has to act as follows (IA, s. 17(2)):

(1)     Before the creditors have approved his proposals, he has to follow any directions which may have been given by the court. The general brief given by the order itself – that the administrator manage the affairs, business and property (IA, s. 8(2)) – may be thought sufficient by the court. In some cases it will be appropriate to request that, on making the order, the court also makes ancillary orders directing the administrator's management of company affairs pending consideration of his proposals by the creditors.

(2)     Once the proposals have been approved by the creditors, the administrator's duty is to act in accordance with those proposals, as revised from time to time, and the fulfillment of the purposes of the administration is considered below (Chapter 11).

## ¶1015     Reporting on unfit directors

Like administrative receivers and liquidators, administrators have to report to the Secretary of State on directors and shadow directors who are unfit to be concerned in the management of a company. Similar considerations, therefore, to those discussed above (at ¶415) in connection with administrative receivers, apply. The relevant forms for administrators are Forms D6 and D7.

## ¶1016     Investigating antecedent transactions

### (1)     Introduction

The Insolvency Act 1986 introduced a number of new concepts whereby antecedent transactions affecting the company's property to the detriment of its creditors may be re-opened. The administrator, like the liquidator but not the administrative receiver, is an office-holder for the purposes of attacking 'preferences' and 'transactions at an undervalue'. He does so by making an application to the court for an order to restore the position to what it would have been if the transaction had not been entered into (IA, s. 238(2)). While the specific provisions are new, the concepts are not unknown to company law. First, preferences replace what were formerly known as 'fraudulent preferences' under s. 615 of the Companies Act 1985. And, secondly, it is arguable that as a matter of company it has never been open to an insolvent company to enter into a transaction at an undervalue. The new provisions provide a statutory code for considering this question but the doctrine of abuse of director's powers where such transactions are entered into, so lucidly explained by the Court of Appeal in *Rolled Steel Products (Holdings) Limited v British Steel Corp* ([1985] 2 WLR 908), is to a similar effect. In general terms, it was never open to a company to alienate its assets and property to the detriment of its unsecured creditors where an insolvency was in prospect (the new remedies are cumulative with existing remedies in this area – see IA, s. 241(4)). One effect of the new provisions may be to have shifted the burden of proof from the liquidator (and now the administrator) to the person endeavouring to uphold the transaction.

**(2)  Transactions at an undervalue**
A company may be held to have entered into transaction at an undervalue in one of two ways, as follows (IA, s. 238(4)):

(1)   where the company makes a gift to another person or, in some other way, enters into a transaction the terms of which provide for the company to receive no consideration; or

(2)   where the transaction is for a consideration the value of which is 'significantly less' than the consideration provided by the company (and both 'value' and 'consideration' are to be measured in money or money's worth).

The first limb is intended simply to cover gifts or like transactions: it is unlikely for a commercial transaction to 'provide' that the contracting party shall receive no consideration.

The second limb seems inevitably to take the court into the difficult area of assessment of value and consideration and then to require it to decide what is meant by 'significantly less'.

Even if a particular arrangement falls to be described as a transaction at an undervalue pursuant to the above test, the court may not make an order if it is satisfied on two counts (IA, s. 238(5)):

(1)   that the company was acting in good faith in entering into the transaction and that it did so for the purpose of carrying on its business; and

(2)   that at the time of the transaction being entered into there were reasonable grounds for believing that the transaction would benefit the company.

The burden of proving the two limbs of the 'defence' is placed upon the person seeking to uphold the transaction, whereas in the area of abuse of directors' powers it is for the liquidator to prove that there was no 'commercial benefit' to the company in any particular arrangement.

In the second limb, the test of 'reasonable grounds' is objective in nature. The question is whether there were reasonable grounds for the directors of the company to believe that the transaction would benefit the company.

¶1016

The administrator may only apply to the court for an order where the transaction was entered into at a relevant time (IA, ss. 238(2) and 240). In deciding what is a relevant time, the following rules apply:

(1)  it is any time during the period of two years prior to the 'onset of insolvency', and also the period between the presentation of a petition for an administrator and the making of an order pursuant to that petition (IA, s. 240(1)(*a*) and (*c*));

(2)  'onset of insolvency' for these purposes means the date of presentation of the petition for the administration (and this date applies where on the discharge of the administration order a winding-up order is made and a liquidator is making the application) (IA, s. 240(3)(*a*));

(3)  at the time of entering into the transaction or as a result of so doing, the company was unable to pay its debts for the purposes of s. 123 of the Insolvency Act 1986 (IA, s. 240(2) and see ¶903(2)); and

(4)  for the purposes of (3) above, there is a presumption of inability to pay debts where the other party is 'connected' with the company (IA, s. 240(2) and see Appendix 3 below): this means that normally the administrator must prove insolvency but the burden of proof shifts if the other party is connected.

An example of a typical transaction at an undervalue would be a transfer of a valuable asset from a company in financial difficulties to a company controlled by one of the directors at a knockdown price, and shortly thereafter (that is, within two years) the transferor company has an administration order made against it. It should not be difficult for the administrator to show that the consideration received was 'significantly less', at which point the 'connected' transferee would have to show an ability of the transferor to pay its debts or that the reasonable director would have considered that the transaction would benefit the company. This would seem to be an onerous task.

### (3)  Preferences

*(a)  Generally*
The old concept of fraudulent preference concerned dispositions of a company's property where the dominant intention of the directors in causing the company so to act was to prefer one creditor of the company over the others (see for example *Re M Kushler Ltd* [1943] Ch. 248). The task of proving a dominant intention to prefer was often difficult for liquidators, as was recognised by the Cork Committee (see the Cork Report, para. 12.57), and the intention of the new formulation is to catch more unfair dispositions. The

tone is set by the dropping of the word 'fraudulent' (a misnomer, in any event) from the description.

The new doctrine of preference is not limited to transfers of property. The critical wording for preferences is as follows (IA, s. 239):

'(4) For the purposes of this section . . . a company gives a preference to a person if –
(*a*) that person is one of the company's creditors or a surety or guarantor for any of the company's debts or other liabilities, and
(*b*) the company does anything or suffers anything to be done which (in either case) has the effect of putting that person into a position which, in the event of the company going into insolvent liquidation, will be better than the position he would have been in if that thing had not been done.

(5) The court shall not make an order under this section in respect of a preference given to any person unless the company which gave the preference was influenced in deciding to give it by desire to produce in relation to that person the effect mentioned in subsection (4)(*b*).'

There are a number of points to note:

(1)    In the case of a connected person (other than merely an employee) the desire to produce the effect is to be presumed unless the contrary is shown (IA, s. 239(6)). That is, the onus is on the connected person wishing to justify the transaction to prove that the company was not influenced by the desire to produce the more advantageous effect in an insolvent liquidation.

(2)    It would seem in keeping with the purpose of the legislation that a creditor for this purpose to be held to include a contingent creditor.

(3)    There is, strangely, no definition of 'insolvent liquidation'. As the section is aimed at benefit to creditors, the most appropriate definition would seem to be a liquidation where the assets are insufficient to meet the debts and liabilities (including contingent liabilities) and the expenses of the winding-up (see IA, s. 214(6)).

(4)    The width of the wording 'does anything or suffers anything' has two effects. First it may cover the incurring of contractual obligations – such as the giving of a guarantee for the debts of a third party – as the right to prove means that the third party is in a better position in an (insolvent) liquidation. Secondly, a passive acceptance of action by creditors – say, suffering a judgment to be entered and enforced against the company's property – is to be conduct amounting to a preference (whether or not pursuant to a court order – IA, s. 239(7)).

¶1016

(5)  The intention of the new provisions is that it should be easier for an administrator (or a liquidator) to show (or correspondingly more difficult for a connected person to rebut the presumption) that the directors of a company were 'influenced by a desire to produce' a particular effect than it was for a liquidator to show a dominant intention to prefer. Save where the influence is minimal, most cases where the directors are so influenced will be caught. There may still be scope for those allegedly preferred to argue that the only influence on the directors was the pressure they put on them, for example by threatening legal action (see *Sharp* v *Jackson* [1899] AC 419 and *Re Cutts* [1956] 1 WLR 728) or that the real reason was to fulfil an existing obligation (*Re F & E Stanton, Ltd* [1929] 1 Ch. 180), but more transactions should be caught.

As with transactions at an undervalue, the administrator (or the liquidator) makes an application to the court for an order restoring the position to what it would have been without the preference having been given (IA, s. 239(3)).

Again, the application may only be made where the preference occurred at a 'relevant time' (IA, s. 239(2)) but the rules differ slightly from transactions at an undervalue:

(1)  A relevant time is any time during the period of six months prior to the 'onset of insolvency', except in the case of persons connected (other than a connection solely as a result of being a company employee) with the company, in which case the period is two years; and

(2)  'onset of insolvency' bears the same meaning as regards inability to pay debts and, again, this is presumed as against a connected person.

Set out below is a difficult example on a particular set of facts.

*(b)   An example*
Company X is in financial difficulty. Its major creditor is also its monopoly supplier of specially made widgets required to make the company's products and there is no feasible alternative source.

The supplier demands payment of the sum of the existing indebtedness before further supplies are forthcoming. This threatens to bring production to a halt. The board of company X assign to the supplier debts due under company X's contract for the sale of the finished products to its major customer. At the board meeting of company X at which the decision to assign the debt was taken, the main consideration of the directors was to keep the company trading and hence to ensure continued supplies of widgets and this is reflected in the minutes. Their minds did not advert to insolvent liquidation. Under the old fraudulent preference test, the benefit to the supplier would

¶1016

not have been the dominant factor behind the directors' action. The true intention of the directors was to ensure a perceived benefit to company X (a continued supply of widgets) and there would have been no fraudulent preference (consider *Re FLE Holdings Ltd* [1967] 1 WLR 1409). Under the new test, there may be an argument that if the thought of the insolvent liquidation of company X did not cross their minds, the directors could not be said to have been influenced by a desire to produce an effect relating to that concept. If, in this example, the directors had previously personally guaranteed company X's debts to the supplier then the task of upholding the transaction would be more difficult. There is the further question of whether the time period is either six months or two years (or both) as there are two parties preferred, but only one is connected.

**(4)   Court orders**
Section 241 of the Insolvency Act 1986 sets out particular orders the court might make without prejudice to its general brief to make orders with a view to 'restoring the position to what it would have been if the company had not entered into [the transaction at an undervalue or preference]'. The court can require property transferred to be vested back in the company, the release or discharge of security, sums to be paid to the office-holder, provide for suretyships to be revived, and decide the extent to which people should be allowed to prove in the winding-up of the company (IA, s. 241(1)). There are provisions protecting certain third parties dealing in good faith, for value and without notice and those interested through such persons (IA, s. 241(2) and (3)).

**(5)   Transactions at an undervalue and preferences: an overview**
There follow a number of much simplified diagramatic explanations of the scheme of the new provisions governing transactions at an undervalue and preferences, which may be helpful by way of overviews:

¶1016

*Fig. 1*

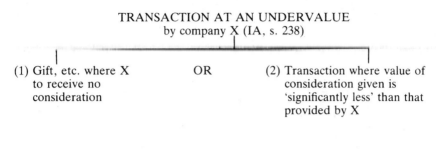

TRANSACTION AT AN UNDERVALUE
by company X (IA, s. 238)

(1) Gift, etc. where X          OR          (2) Transaction where value of
to receive no                               consideration given is
consideration                               'significantly less' than that
                                            provided by X

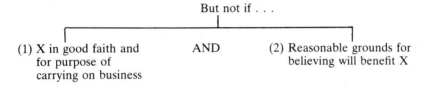

But not if . . .

(1) X in good faith and          AND          (2) Reasonable grounds for
for purpose of                                 believing will benefit X
carrying on business

*Fig. 2*

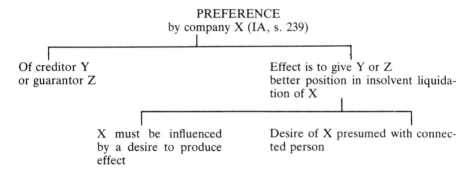

PREFERENCE
by company X (IA, s. 239)

Of creditor Y                    Effect is to give Y or Z
or guarantor Z                   better position in insolvent liquida-
                                 tion of X

X must be influenced             Desire of X presumed with connec-
by a desire to produce           ted person
effect

*Fig. 3*

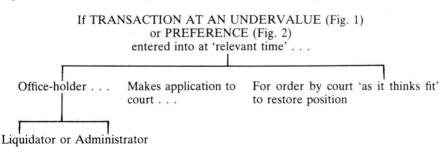

If TRANSACTION AT AN UNDERVALUE (Fig. 1)
or PREFERENCE (Fig. 2)
entered into at 'relevant time' . . .

Office-holder . . .    Makes application to      For order by court 'as it thinks fit'
                       court . . .               to restore position

Liquidator or Administrator

¶1016

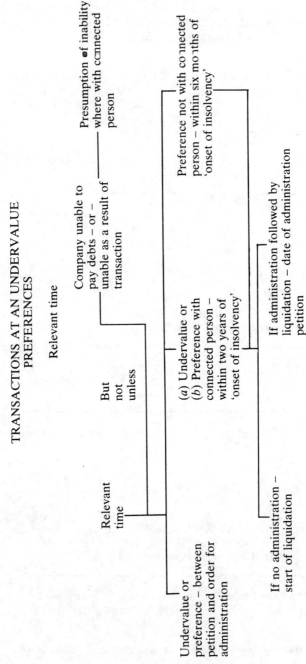

Fig. 4

TRANSACTIONS AT AN UNDERVALUE PREFERENCES

¶1016

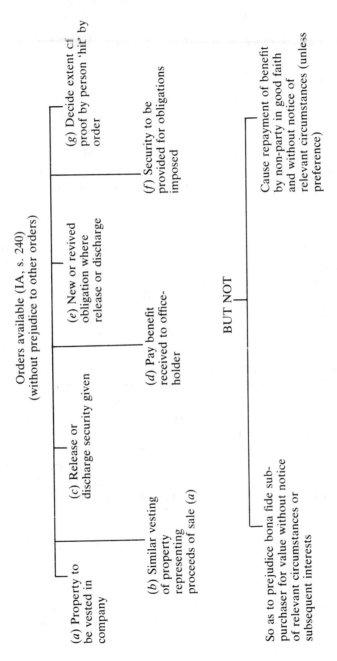

Fig. 5

TRANSACTIONS AT UNDERVALUE
PREFERENCES

Orders available (IA, s. 240)
(without prejudice to other orders)

(*a*) Property to
be vested in
company

(*b*) Similar vesting
of property
representing
proceeds of sale (*a*)

(*c*) Release or
discharge security given

(*d*) Pay benefit
received to office-
holder

(*e*) New or revived
obligation where
release or discharge

(*f*) Security to be
provided for obligations
imposed

(*g*) Decide extent of
proof by person 'hit' by
order

BUT NOT

So as to prejudice bona fide sub-
purchaser for value without notice
of relevant circumstances or
subsequent interests

Cause repayment of benefit
by non-party in good faith
and without notice of
relevant circumstances (unless
preference)

**(6)   Extortionate credit transactions**

The administrator may apply to the court for an order in respect of an extortionate credit transaction which was entered into within three years of the date of the administration order (IA, s. 244(1) and (2)). A transaction is extortionate if (IA, s. 244(3)):

'. . . having regard to the risk accepted by the person providing the credit –

> (*a*)   the terms of it are or were such as to require grossly exhorbitant payments to be made (whether unconditionally or in certain contingencies) in respect of the provision of the credit, or

> (*b*)   it otherwise grossly contravened ordinary principles of fair dealing;

and it shall be presumed, unless the contrary is proved, that a transaction with respect to which an application is made under this section is or, as the case may be, was extortionate.'

What is or is not extortionate may depend on prevailing market conditions and the court will admit evidence as to what is current business practice in similar circumstances (*Woodstead Finance Ltd* v *Petrou, The Times*, 23 January 1986 and *Davies and Hedley-Cheney* v *Directloans Ltd* [1986] 2 All ER 783).

The court has wide powers including powers to set aside the transaction, vary its terms, provide for release of security or provide for payments to be made to the office-holder (IA, s. 244(4)).

**(7)   Avoidance of floating charges**

Section 245 of the Insolvency Act 1986 replaces s. 617 of the Companies Act 1985 and its predecessor, s. 322 of the Companies Act 1948. The intention of the new section, as with its predecessors, is to render invalid in a liquidation (and now also in an administration) floating charges created by a company within a specific period prior to the commencement of the insolvency and at a time when it was unable to pay its debts. There is no need for the office-holder to apply for a court order as such. If the conditions are satisfied the charge is simply invalid against him. The debt remains valid although unsecured or only partially secured.

The charge is, however, validated to the extent of cash (and now goods or services supplied) to the company in consideration of, and at the time or subsequent to the creation of, the charge. The new provisions (IA, s. 245(2)) specify the aggregate of:

'(*a*)   the value of so much of the consideration for the creation of the charge as consists of money paid, or goods or services supplied, to the company at the same time as, or after, the creation of the charge,

¶1016

(*b*)   the value of so much of that consideration as consists of the discharge or reduction, at the same time as, or after, the creation of the charge, of any debt of the company, and

(*c*)   the amount of such interest (if any) as is payable on the amount falling within paragraph (*a*) or (*b*) in pursuance of any agreement under which the money was so paid, the goods or services were so supplied or the debt was so discharged or reduced.'

The following points should be noted about the new formulation in s. 245:

(1)   interest now accrues at the contractual rate and is not limited to five per cent as hitherto;

(2)   goods and services supplied may now help validation whereas previously it was only cash and there is a mechanism for valuation – a form of reasonable market value (see IA, s. 245(6));

(3)   as previously, debits to a bank account may constitute cash advanced subsequently to the creation of the charge (*Clayton's case* (1816) 1 Mer 572 and *Re Yeovil Glove Co. Ltd* [1965] Ch. 148);

(4)   the effect of s. 245(2) (*b*) set out above may be to reverse the decision in *Re G. T. Whyte & Co. Ltd* ([1983] BCLC 311) where the provision of 'fresh' cash by an existing creditor simply to repay an existing loan from the creditor was held not to be provision of 'new money';

(5)   save where the mortgagee is a connected person, there is no invalidity unless the company was, or became as a result of the arrangements pursuant to which the charge was created, unable to pay its debts tested in accordance with s. 123 of the Insolvency Act 1986 (IA, s. 245(4) and see ¶903(2));

(6)   the period for which a charge is vulnerable after its creation remains 12 months, save where the chargee is a connected person in which case the period is two years (IA, s. 245(3)). The commencement of insolvency is the date of presentation of the petition for an administration order (IA, s. 245(5)(*a*)). The charge is vulnerable, also, if created in the period between the presentation of a petition for an administrator and the making of an order on that petition (IA, s. 245(3)(*a*)). Curiously, in contrast with the position for transactions at an undervalue and preferences (see IA, s. 240(3)), if a liquidator appointed pursuant to a winding-up order made on discharge of an administration order seeks to invoke these provisions he can only go back 12 months or two years (as the case may be) from the company 'going into liquidation', not from the date of presentation of the petition for an administration order (IA, s. 245(5)(*b*) – for the meaning of 'going into liquidation' see IA, s. 247(2)).

¶1016

**(8)   Transactions defrauding creditors**

Section 423 of the Insolvency Act 1986 applies both to companies and individuals, is applicable outside the insolvency context and effectively replaces what was s. 172 of the Law and Property Act 1925. It covers transactions at an undervalue (in very similar terms to IA, s. 238) entered into for the purpose (IA, s. 423(3)):

'(*a*) of putting assets beyond the reach of a person who is making, or may at some time make, a claim against him, or

(*b*) of otherwise prejudicing the interests of such a person in relation to the claim which he is making or may make'.

An administrator may apply for an order under the section (IA, s. 424(1)(*a*)) but the added purpose given above will make it less attractive than s. 238 as a remedy. Its advantage is that there is no time limit and the administrator could go back as long as he wished prior to the administration. He is limited to two years under s. 238. On the other hand the further back he goes, the more difficult it will be to show that the purpose was to put assets beyond the reach of creditors. The court is given a wide range of orders which it may make (IA, s. 425) to restore the position and protect those prejudiced by the transaction (IA, s. 423(2) and (5)).

## ¶1017   Miscellaneous requirements

There are numerous other duties imposed on administrators by the Insolvency Act 1986 and the Insolvency Rules 1986 and these have already been considered above or are considered below in connection with fulfilling the purpose of the administration (Chapter 11) and termination (Chapter 12).

## ¶1018   Duties owed to the company

The duties of the administrator as an officer of the company have already been discussed (¶1005). His duties are owed primarily to the company and his position is similar to that of a liquidator.

The role of the administrator is potentially more varied and extensive than that of a liquidator. There are more areas in which he is required to exercise care and skill. He must prepare his proposals promptly and to a proper professional standard. If his proposals are prepared negligently or implemented in a careless fashion such that the company suffers loss it is submitted that he would be liable to the company. There is a summary remedy set out in s. 212 of the Insolvency Act 1986 (although there may be the possibility of relief from the court under CA, s. 727).

When realising assets the administrator will have duties regarding the price obtained (compare *Standard Chartered Bank Ltd* v *Walker* [1982] 1 WLR

1410 and *Harold M Pitman & Co. v Top Business Systems (Nottingham) Ltd* (1985) 1 BCC 99, 345).

## ¶1019   Duties owed to the creditors and members?

It is submitted that, like a liquidator, an administrator does not owe duties to creditors or members of the company, as such. He is not a trustee for the creditors (*Knowles* v *Scott* [1891] 1 Ch. 717), he is an agent of the company (*Re Anglo-Moravian Ry Co.* (1875) 1 ChD 130) to which alone he is accountable.

He owes a duty of care to the company in his management of its business affairs and property. He will be expected to carry out a proper professional job in all that he does. He will be liable for any loss suffered by the company in the event that he breaches his duty. For example, if the administrator failed to insure the company's business and property and it was destroyed by fire, he would be liable to the company for the loss.

# 11 Fulfilling the Purpose of the Administration

## THE EARLY DAYS

### ¶1101 Preliminary steps

An administrator will follow the same initial steps after appointment as an administrative receiver (see ¶501). He will want to ensure that the company's property and assets are in his possession or under his control as soon as possible. He will wish to be present personally at the company's main place of business as soon as possible after his appointment and his staff will attend at all the company's locations. He will arrange insurance cover effective immediately on his appointment.

The administrator must take control of assets and property to which the company appears entitled, not just those items which the company owns (IA, s. 17(1)). In practical terms this is unlikely to make his approach much different to that of an administrative receiver, as the latter will, in the case of doubt, normally take into his possession assets which might be caught by the security under which he is appointed on the basis that they are better safe and under his control than not. He can always return them if a third party proves good title.

In view of the comparatively greater importance to him of unsecured claims, the administrator will want to acquaint himself particularly closely with all contracts of the company, as there are likely to be more complications for an administrator in causing a company to repudiate unprofitable contracts than for an administrative receiver (compare ¶406 with ¶1118).

An administrator will want to make his mind up quickly about employees and how he wishes to deal with them, and certainly within the first 14 days (see IA, s. 19(5)). If the directions he received from the court on the making of the order[1] prevent the administrator from taking any particular action, for example slimming the workforce to reduce overmanning, he will need specific sanction from the court (IA, s. 17(2)).

---

[1] The early administration cases do not seem to have involved specific directions from the court and the trend has been for administrators to feel free to act, for example by selling the business of the company where the purpose of the administration is a better realisation of assets than on a winding-up, without sanction of the court and prior to any consideration of proposals by the creditors (see Tony Richmond, 'Acting under orders' [1987] SJ 427).

## ¶1102 Establishing procedures

The insolvency practitioner will ensure that his firm's standard systems and procedures for running an administration operate from the outset and the chain of command among his staff will be established and checklists followed.

## ADMINISTRATOR'S PROPOSALS

### ¶1103 Formal requirements

The provisions of the Insolvency Act 1986 and the Insolvency Rules 1986 give what is essentially a skeletal outline of the administration procedure and it is for companies, creditors, insolvency practitioners and their legal advisers to put flesh on the bones.

The administrator is required to produce a 'Statement of Proposals' within three months of his appointment or longer if the court permits an extension (IA, s. 23(1)). This statement has to be sent to the Registrar of Companies and to all creditors, so far as the administrator is aware of their addresses, within the three-month period (IA, s. 23(1)(*a*)). The statement has to be presented to a meeting of the creditors of the company of which at least 14 days' notice has been given (in fact, by virtue of the Rules 21 days notice must be given – compare IA, s. 23(1)(*b*) and IR, r. 2.19(4)). The meeting itself has to be held within three months of his appointment (unless the court orders otherwise) (IA, s. 23(1)(*b*)). It would seem preferable for the creditors to have the statement sent together with notice of the meeting in order that they have time to reflect on the proposals but it would seem to be possible for the administrator simply to present the statement at the meeting and send the copies later provided this all occurs within the three-month period.

The Rules distinguish between the administrator's 'Statement of Proposals' which they simply term 'his proposals' and a statement which must be annexed to his proposals when they are sent to the Registrar and laid before the meeting. It would not seem necessary to send this to creditors (IR, r. 2.16). The statement envisaged by the Rules in fact will contain the substance of the proposals of the administrator and r. 2.16 provides that it is to contain:

'(*a*)  details relating to his appointment as administrator, the purposes for which an administration order was applied for and made, and any subsequent variation of those purposes;

(*b*)  the names of the directors and secretary of the company;

(*c*)  an account of the circumstances giving rise to the application for an administration order;

(d)    if a statement of affairs has been submitted, a copy or summary of it, with the administrator's comments, if any;

(e)    if no statement of affairs has been submitted, details of the financial position of the company at the latest practicable date (which must, unless the court otherwise orders, be a date not earlier than that of the administration order);

(f)    the manner in which the affairs of the company will be managed and its business financed, if the administrator's proposals are approved; and

(g)    such other information (if any) as the administrator thinks necessary to enable creditors to decide whether or not to vote for the adoption of the proposals.'

Paragraphs (f) and (g) will require the most thought on the part of the administrator.

The members of the company have also to be informed of the administrator's proposals within three months of the making of the order or longer if the court allows (IA, s. 23(2)). They are either to be sent a copy of the statement of proposals (so far as the administrator is aware of their addresses) or else the administrator may publish a notice giving an address to which members can write for a copy of the statement to be sent free of charge. Where the administrator elects to publish a notice, it is to be published in the *London Gazette* and also advertised once in the newspaper in which the administration order was advertised (IR, r. 2.17).

Failure by the administrator to comply with the obligations in respect of preparing his proposals leaves him open to a fine (IA, s. 23(3)).

## ¶1104    Examples of possible proposals

### (1)    The content of the proposals

The Insolvency Act 1986 devotes merely one section to the administrator's proposals for achieving the purpose or purposes for which he was appointed. The detail will depend upon the facts of each case.

The administrator has three months in which to produce his proposals. A number of the comments made above (¶904) in connection with what might be termed the first hiatus period between petition and order, apply with even greater force to this second hiatus period running from the administration order until the proposals of the administrator are accepted or rejected by the creditors. In many businesses a substantial measure of agreement will have to have been reached with a number of key creditors including the company's bankers if the business and the administration is to survive that far. For such a consensus to have been achieved with the company's creditors, those creditors must have had a fairly detailed idea of the plans for the company which the administrator has had in mind and thus the proposals in many cases may simply be formal confirmation of a generally understood basic plan but now complete with detail.

One of the important aspects of administration trading will be cash-flow. Where the company has given no security to its bankers, then in theory at least there should be trading receipts which may enable the administration to function.

The proposals put forward by the administrator are going to be different depending upon the purpose or purposes for which he has been appointed. In the case of an appointment to achieve a better realisation of the company's assets than on a winding-up, the proposals may cover a short period of continued trading simply with a view to selling the business as a going concern and not having to cease trading immediately and sell on break-up.

More often than not, the survival of the company and at least part of the undertaking will be coupled with a voluntary arrangement or a scheme of arrangement. That is, the administrator would be appointed for more than one purpose. It may be that one purpose will be the survival of the company and its undertaking as a going concern, with a fall-back purpose of a better realisation of assets than on a winding-up which could be pursued if survival seems impossible (which is allowed, see *Re Vosper Shiprepairers Ltd*, 17 February 1987, unreported).

There follow a number of examples of possible administrations. They are not intended as a prescription for action in any particular case but are merely intended to highlight areas which will have to be considered by insolvency practitioners in practice.

**(2)  Example 1**

X Ltd is considering administration. It has given no security to its bankers. Its start-up costs and initial investment have in fact proved crippling burdens to the company. It is insolvent on a balance sheet test and, indeed, is struggling to pay its debts as they fall due. The business of the company, however, is fundamentally sound and, freed from part of its interest payments and if part of its debt could be converted into equity, it would be a viable proposition and could look to expand and be profitable. In such a case, an administration petition and order would effectively prevent creditors from taking action against the company. If the bank could be persuaded that on a sale of the business in a liquidation the amount realised would leave it with a significant shortfall on its debt whereas, if the company were to be restructured along the lines mentioned, the bank would on any analysis almost certainly stand a better chance of getting more of its money back and might at some point in the future see some return on the new equity aspect of its 'investment', it

¶1104

might be prepared to allow the company to continue to operate a bank account after the date of the petition and to allow the administrator facilities.

Where X's principal suppliers and creditors are vital to the company's continued trading (for example because they are single-source suppliers) then they will also have to be persuaded both that the proposed rescue of the company is a worthwhile idea to be supported at creditors' meetings and that they ought to continue supplies post-petition and post-order.

The purposes of an administration in these circumstances would be the survival of the company and its undertaking as a going concern and the approval of a voluntary arrangement, and a persuasive case could no doubt be put to the creditors in favour of approval of the scheme.

### (3)   Example 1A

In this example, the facts in example 1 in respect of company X remain the same, save that the bank concerned has a fixed charge on future book debts and a separate floating charge on the undertaking and all the other assets of company Y. The bank does not wish to appoint an administrative receiver under its security because of fears of bad publicity in the local community.

The main problem for anyone contemplating an administration is the fact that the existing book debts and those generated in the future will be claimed by the bank under the fixed-charge security.

There may be an argument that assets (such as stock and work in progress and finished goods) caught by the floating charge at the date of the administrator's appointment are available to the administration even when converted into debts and proceeds. There are two lines of thought. First, by analogy with administrative receiverships, where debts created by receivership trading are still part of the floating charge fund for the purposes of paying preferential creditors (and this applies even where the debenture holder has a fixed charge on future book debts). Secondly, the holder of security in the form of a floating charge has the same 'priority' to property (which includes debts and money – IA, s. 436) representing the sold goods as he had to the goods prior to that disposal (IA, s. 15(4)). The counter-arguments are that administration is different to receivership – there are no preferential creditors in an administration – and, secondly, that the 'priority' laid down by the Act simply covers the floating charge and has no reference to the 'new' fixed charge which attaches to the debt on its coming into existence.

A further complication for the bank is that it might not be entitled to collect book debts after the presentation of the petition or after the order as this might amount to enforcing its security (IA, ss. 10(1)(b) and 11(3)(c)).

But, on the other hand, the administrator is not able to use proceeds of book-debt realizations to finance trading.

¶1104

One compromise may be for the administrator to permit the bank to collect book debts generated up to the date of the order and for the bank to consent to the administrator having the benefit of debts generated thereafter. There may be scope for the use of factoring by the administrator, to which the bank might consent. This solution has the merits of being cheap (avoiding expensive court battles), and fair, in that, if an administrative receiver had turned work-in-progress and finished goods into debts, the preferential creditors would in any event have had first claim on the proceeds as the bank would not have had a fixed charge. The compromise may be much more attractive than simply to continue lending to the administrator with no certainty that the latest tranche of lending will be repaid.

### (4) Example 2

Company Z has four trades. Three trades are successful and profitable but the fourth is highly unsuccessful. The fourth trade is, however, a personal whim of the managing director and principal shareholder. If the court can be satisfied that with the millstone of the fourth trade round its neck Z is likely to become insolvent then the creditors could petition for an administration, the purpose of which would be the survival of the company and (most of) its undertaking as a going concern. The administrator's proposals might be the cessation of trade in the loss-making division, the redundancy of the employees of that section and the sale of the premises from which it operated. It is worth noting that the Redundancy Fund would pay the cost of these redundancies just as if the company were in liquidation (see s. 218(6) of the Insolvency Act 1985 which is still in force).

Where a voluntary arrangement is the ultimate purpose of the administration then the administrator's proposals are likely to be rather more complex and will need in general terms to be thought out in more detail. If the balance sheet is to be tidied up and certain debts converted into share capital, some thought will have to be given to the type of shares to be created – perhaps some form of preference share – and the skills of company lawyers will need to be tapped in the preparation of appropriate rights to attach to the shares. If the shares are intended to give the shareholders a real preferential right to a dividend then control of the award of remuneration to directors may be necessary – problems of negotiation familiar to those involved in the provision of equity finance to businesses, which is, in effect, what is under discussion.

## ¶1105 Revision of proposals

There is provision for the administrator to change course where he considers that 'substantial' changes should be made to the original proposals which have already been approved and to which he is working (IA, s. 25).

Where the administrator wants to make such changes he requires the approval of a meeting of the creditors in the same way as for the approval of the proposals themselves, and the procedure and rules operate in a broadly similar fashion. He cannot act on the revised proposals until such time as they may have been approved, with or without modifications, by the creditors (IA, s. 25(2)).

# MEETINGS

## ¶1106   Creditors' meetings

### (1) General rules

Where the administrator calls a meeting to consider his proposals, he must give notice to all the creditors of the company identified in the Statement of Affairs submitted to him or who are known to the administrator and had claims against the company at the date of the administration order (IR, r. 2.18(1)). The notice must be in writing (IR, r.12.4(1) and Form 2.11). Those who have become creditors of the company after the administration order are not creditors for the purposes of the creditors' meeting in the administration and so will not be given notice. The administrator must also give notice of the meeting by advertising in the same newspaper as he advertised the administration order (IR, r. 2.18(1)).

When sending out notices to the creditors, the administrator is also to send out notices to present or past directors or officers of the company whose presence at the meeting is 'required' (IR, r. 2.18(3) and Form 2.10). As to whether or not a director or officer is required, it is the administrator's opinion which is important. Notwithstanding the use of the word 'required' there is no specific provision making it incumbent upon such an officer to attend. There is, however, a general duty upon past and present officers of the company to cooperate with an administrator (IA, s. 235 – see ¶1011(2)), and it is submitted that it would be a breach of that duty to cooperate to fail to attend such a meeting without reasonable excuse if the administrator has indicated that their presence is required. Such a breach is evidence of unfitness to be a director or be otherwise concerned in the management of a company (CDDA, s. 9 and Sch. 1, para. 10).

There are four main heads under which creditors' meetings in an administration will be called. First, there is the general power of the administrator to call a meeting as he thinks fit (IA, s. 14(2)(*b*)). Secondly, the administrator may be required to summon a meeting, either by (at least ten per cent in value of) the creditors, or by the court (IA, s. 18(3)). Thirdly, the administrator must call a meeting to consider his proposals (IA, s. 23 (1)). Finally he must call a meeting to consider any substantial revisions to the proposals he wishes to put forward (IA, s. 25(2)).

One of the practices of 'rogue' liquidators whose activities were criticised by the Cork Report was to hold creditors' meetings at venues quite inconvenient for the bulk of the company's creditors. An administrator is required when fixing the place of his meetings to have regard to the convenience of the creditors (IR, r. 2.19(2)). Further, the meeting must be arranged to start between 10 a.m. and 4 p.m. on a business day unless the administrator obtains the court's sanction to arrange otherwise (IR, r. 2.19(3)).

The Rules require that at least 21 days' notice of creditors' meetings must be given to the creditors (IR, r. 2.19(4)). This effectively extends the minimum 14 days' notice laid down in the Act (IA, s. 23(1)(*b*)) as regards the meeting to consider the administrator's proposals. Thus, even if an administrator had his proposals largely in shape prior to the administration order being made, it would seem that he would need to wait at least 21 days before he could have his proposals considered by the creditors. In the event that he felt he needed to take urgent action before that date, he would be able to ask the court to sanction any steps he wished to take (IA, s. 14(3) and consider IR, r. 12.9). Where the purpose of the administration is the better realization of the company's assets than in a liquidation, the administrator might want to be able to accept an offer to buy the business if it was an extremely good price and the offeror was not prepared to wait at least three weeks before doing the deal. There may, also, be other cases where the good will and connections of the business are in danger of disappearing over a three-week period.

Notices of meetings have to give the reason why the meeting has been called and state the entitlement of a creditor to vote in an administration (IR, r. 2.19(4)). The notice must be accompanied by forms of proxy (IR, r. 2.19(5) and Form 8.2).

### (2) Chairman

The administrator has a right to be chairman of the creditors' meetings he calls but he may if he wishes nominate someone else to take his place (IR, r. 2.20(1)). He has to make this nomination in writing. The person nominated must be a person qualified to act as an insolvency practitioner in relation to that company or simply an employee of the administrator or his firm who is 'experienced in insolvency matters' (IR, r. 2.20(2)). In simple terms this would seem to mean that the administrator, or either joint administrator, can chair a meeting or else an administrator can ask one of his more senior insolvency managers to take the meeting. The reference to another insolvency practitioner who is qualified to act in relation to the company appears to mean that the practitioner must have security in place (see ¶206), which will be unlikely as regards the specific penalty as opposed to general bonding. This may mean that an administrator cannot ask one of his insolvency partners to take the meeting but can ask one of his managers, a slightly strange result (but compare IA, s. 2(4)). It is interesting to note the reference in the rules to the 'firm' of the administrator as the law can sometimes read as though it thinks that administrators (and administrative receivers and liquidators) are generally sole practitioners.

In the unlikely event that within 30 minutes of the time appointed for the meeting there is no one present to act as chairman, the meeting is automatically adjourned to the same day seven days hence or, if that is not a business day, the business day following that (IR, r. 2.19(6)). The chairman has a general discretion to adjourn meetings from time to time for anything up to 14 days from the date on which the meeting was scheduled to start (IR, r. 2.19(7)). This provision is in addition to a chairman's specific right to adjourn where there is not a required majority for his proposals (IR, r. 2.18(4)). In the latter case he must adjourn the meeting if the creditors pass a resolution to that effect.

### (3)  Requisitioning of meetings by creditors
The creditors of the company have a general right, if at least 10 per cent of them in value so wish, to require the administrator to call a meeting of all the company's creditors (IA, s. 19(3)(*a*)).

The rules governing this right show the balance which it was felt the law had to strike. On the one hand, it is recognised that a system designed to assist creditors should enable a significant minority of them to call a general meeting to discuss matters they consider of importance. An untrammelled right to call meetings would, however, constitute an inconvenience to the administration were it to be abused. The law accordingly provides that if creditors wish to call a meeting, they have to be prepared to pay for the privilege if their fellow creditors feel there was no good reason for calling the meeting. The creditors calling the meeting are to be responsible for the expenses of summoning and holding the meeting (IR, r. 2.21(3) and (5)). Pursuant to that obligation they must deposit with the administrator security for payment of those expenses (IR, r. 2.21(3)). The administrator is allowed to determine the sum to be deposited and the Rules state that 'he shall not act without the deposit having been made' (IR, r.2.21(4)).

The likely quantum of the deposit that the administrator may require should not be underestimated. There will be the administrative time of the staff of the administrator in drawing up the requisite notices and issuing them, and the time required to be spent by the administrator and his staff (and possibly also his legal advisers) in attending the meeting and preparing appropriate notes and minutes of the proceedings. In some cases there may even be the

¶1106

experse of hiring a suitable venue to hold the meeting. By way of security an administrator will want cash or 'nearly cash' – for example a demand guarantee or bond from a clearing bank.

The creditors' meeting, once convened, may resolve that the expenses of the meeting shall be payable out of the assets of the company as an administration expense (IR, r. 2.21(5)) but for those requisitioning the meeting there must always be the risk that such a resolution will not be passed. When indicating the purposes for calling the meeting those requisitioning should state that a resolution will be proposed to the effect that the expenses be paid out of the administration assets (IR, r. 2.21(1)(*c*)). Where the money deposited with the administrator is not required for paying the expenses of the meeting it is to be repaid to the depositors (IR, r. 2.21(6)).

The Rule setting out the manner in which a request for a meeting should be made (r. 2.21) reads as follows:

'(1) Any request by creditors to the administrator for a meeting of creditors to be summoned shall be accompanied by –

(*a*) a list of the creditors concurring with the request, showing the amount of their respective claims in the administration;

(*b*) from each creditor concurring, written confirmation of his concurrence; and

(*c*) a statement of the purpose of the proposed meeting.

This paragraph does not apply if the requisitioning creditor's debt is alone sufficient, without the concurrence of other creditors.'

The final sentence would seem to indicate that where a single creditor comprises at least 10 per cent in value of the total creditors he need not give to the administrator a statement of the purpose of the proposed meeting.

On receipt of a request which appears to the administrator to be properly made, he must call a meeting of the creditors within 35 days of receipt of the request, giving at least 21 days notice of the meeting to the creditors (IR, r. 2.21(2)). In effect, therefore, he has a maximum of 14 days within which to arrange to call the meeting.

**(4)  Voting entitlement**

To be entitled to vote at a creditors' meeting, a creditor has to lodge with the administrator not later than 12 noon on the business day before the relevant meeting a detailed written note of the debt claimed as due from the company (IR, r. 2.22(1)(*a*)). The administrator then has to consider whether or not to admit the claim for voting purposes. Further, if the creditor intends to vote by proxy then the proxy must have been duly lodged (IR, r. 2.22(1)(*b*)). The chairman of the meeting has the power to relax the rule regarding submission of written details of the claim of the creditor where he is satisfied that failure

¶1106

to supply the details was due to circumstances beyond the control of the creditor (IR, r. 2.22(2)).

In respect of any claim, the administrator or the chairman of the meeting may call for supporting evidence to prove that the claim is in fact due (IR, r. 2.22(3)).

Where a creditor is owed £x at the date of the administration order but part of the debt, £y, is paid prior to the meeting of the creditors, that creditor may only vote the net amount, that is $£(x - y)$ (IR, r. 2.22(4)). For example, in order to obtain supplies from an important supplier, the administrator might have had to make some payment towards the debt of the company to that supplier incurred prior to the date of the administration order.

All debts would seem to give rise to an entitlement to vote save where the debt is for an unliquidated amount or where for some other reason the value is not ascertained (IR, r. 2.22(5)). In such circumstances, the chairman of the meeting has a discretion to agree to an estimated minimum value of the debt for voting purposes (IR, r. 2.22(5)).

In general, the chairman of the meeting has power to admit or reject a creditor's claim, either in whole or in part. If the chairman is in doubt about whether to admit or reject a claim, his duty is to mark it as 'objected to' and allow the creditors to vote, subject to that vote subsequently being declared invalid (IR, r. 2.22(3)). In other words, the chairman is to err in favour, at least initially, of allowing purported creditors to vote. In this and other areas where the chairman rules on the question of entitlement to vote a creditor may appeal to the court (IR, r. 2.23(2)). Where the court makes an order varying or reversing the chairman's decision or declaring that a creditor's vote is invalid it may order that another meeting be called or make such other order as it thinks just (IR, r. 2.23(4)). There are unlikely to be appeals to court unless the decision of the chairman has had a material effect on the result (note, generally, IR, r. 7.55). Similarly, the court will be unlikely to call a new meeting unless its decision means that the creditors' meeting might have had a different result. There is a time limit for appeal to the court against the decision of the chairman in the case of a meeting held to consider the administrator's proposals. The application to court must be made not later than 28 days after delivery of the administrator's report on the meeting. The administrator or chairman of the meeting is not to be personally liable for any costs of any person in connection with an application to the court unless the court orders otherwise (IR, r. 2.23(6)). It would seem likely that where the administrator or the chairman has acted in good faith he will not be punished by being made to pay the costs.

**(5)    Evaluation of secured and other debts**
Where a secured creditor wishes to vote at an administration creditors'

meeting, he must deduct from his debt the estimated value of such security as he may have and is entitled to vote only for the balance, if any (IR, r. 2.24).

Where a creditor's debt is on, or secured by, a current bill of exchange or promissory note he cannot vote unless he treats as security the liability to him on the bill of all persons liable on the bill prior to the company (save where such persons are bankrupt or, in the case of a company, in liquidation). The holder of the negotiable instrument estimates the value of his 'security' and is entitled to vote for the balance, if any (IR, r. 2.25).

Suppliers whose terms included the retention of title must deduct from their claim the value of their rights under the agreement that provided for the retention of title (IR, r. 2.26).

Owners of goods under hire-purchase or chattel-leasing agreements or vendors of goods under a conditional-sale agreement are entitled to vote in respect of the debt due to them at the date of the administration order. However, in calculating that sum they are not entitled to take into account any termination sum payable as a result of the company going into adminis-tration and the effect is that they may only vote in respect of periodic payments outstanding at the date of the administration order (IR, r. 2.27).

## (6) Proxies

There is a prescribed form of proxy for use in connection with administration creditors' meetings (IR, r. 8.1 and Form 8.2). There are a number of points to note about proxies under the new procedures:

(1) A proxy may give the holder particular instructions on how to vote or give a discretion; it may authorise or direct the holder to propose a resolution (IR, r. 8.1(5)), and, generally the holder may vote and speak (IR, r. 8.1(1)).

(2) The holder is to be one individual, over 18, although alternatives may be listed in order (IR, r. 8.3).

(3) The proxy may be for the chairman (IR, r. 8.1(4)); where the admin-istrator receives a proxy for himself as chairman he can use the proxies (IR, r. 8.3(3)); where, however, a resolution means that the administrator would directly or indirectly receive remuneration if it were passed, the chairman (whether or not the administrator) may not use the proxy to vote in favour (IR, r. 8.6).

(4) In the interests of fairness proxy forms when sent out are not to be completed with the name of a supported proxy-holder (IR, r. 8.2(1)).

(5) Proxies are to be retained after a meeting by the administrator (IR, r. 8.4) and rights of inspection of proxies are granted to creditors and directors before, during and after creditors' meetings (IR, r. 8.5).

¶1106

(6) It would seem that proxies may be lodged with the administrator at any time up to the moment of voting. However, there is one peculiarity. The proxy has to be lodged with *the administrator* (IR, r. 2.22(1)(*b*)) and he might not be chairing, and hence present at, the meeting. The intention of the Rules would seem to be that there is no fixed time by which proxies are to be lodged (contrast with details of debts under (IR, r. 2.22(1)(*a*)) and para. 154 of the Winding-up Rules 1949) and the chairman ought to accept, on the administrator's behalf, proxies lodged with him prior to, and at, the meeting.

(7) As regards execution of proxies, the rule is (IR, r. 8.2(3)):

'A form of proxy shall be signed by the principal, or some person authorised by him (either generally or with reference to a particular meeting). If the form is signed by a person other than the principal, the nature of the person's authority shall be stated.'

The proper approach is for a company creditor to pass a board resolution authorising (say) a credit controller to sign forms of proxy for creditors' meetings. A certified minute of the board resolution could be issued every time the credit controller signed a proxy, and after his signature the credit controller could state that he is authorised to sign pursuant to the particular board resolution. The Rules do not require this evidential support as such and there may be an argument that proxies duly signed and reciting authorisation on their face are to be accepted without anything further. Where a representative of a corporation (under CA, s. 375) appears at a meeting he requires a copy of the relevant resolution giving him authority and this must either have been sealed by the company or certified as a true copy by a director or secretary (IR, r. 8.7). There would appear to be no requirement to show evidence that the director or secretary was duly appointed.

### (7) Conduct of meetings

No precise guidance is given either by the Act or the Rules on how creditors' meetings are to be conducted. To an extent it will depend on their purpose. The most important meeting is always likely to be the meeting at which the administrator's proposals are considered. The administrator, or the chairman of the meeting if that is not the administrator, should give the creditors an opportunity to discuss adequately the proposals made and vote to accept or reject them. In view of the references in the Act and the Rules to 'modifications' it seems that a creditor is entitled to suggest modifications to the administrator's proposals although it is up to the administrator whether he consents to any suggested modifications (IA, s. 24(2)).

¶1106

The chairman has wide powers of adjournment of the meeting (for example, IR, rr. 2.18(4) and 2.19(7)) and he may use these if he judges that the creditors need more time to reflect on what is being suggested (or perhaps to gather more information to clear up some point of doubt). The administrator seems entitled actively to seek a majority for his proposals (see IR. r. 2.18(4)) and, therefore, if there is a major creditor who is not present but with whose support a majority could be obtained, the chairman may wish to adjourn and seek to ensure that the creditor is present at the adjourned meetings.

For a resolution to be passed at a creditors' meeting in an administration, a majority in value of those present and voting must have voted in favour (IR, r. 2.28(1)). It is not necessary to exclude the votes of connected persons in any way (contrast voluntary arrangements ¶1111(6)).

No quorum is laid down for a creditors' meeting in an administration. This might suggest that the presence of one creditor would suffice, or that, even where no creditors turned up, the meeting could proceed. However, the very concept of a 'meeting' suggests that at least two persons must be present for it to take place (*Re Sanitary Carbon Co.* [1877] WN 223; *Sharp v Dawes* (1876) 2 QBD 26).

### (8)  Minutes

Minutes of creditors' meetings have to be kept and it is the duty of the chairman of the meeting to arrange for this to be done and for them to be entered in the company's minute book (IR, r. 2.28(2)). The minutes have to include a list of the creditors who attended, whether in person or by proxy, and details of any creditors elected to the creditors' committee, if one is set up (IR, r. 2.28(3)).

### (9)  Notice of results

Notice of the result of the creditor's meeting has to be given to the Registrar of Companies (IA, s. 24(4)). Within 14 days of the conclusion of a meeting (whether to consider proposals or to revise proposals) a notice of the result and, where proposals were approved, details of the proposals, has to be sent to every creditor who was given notice of the meeting and any other creditors the administrator has since discovered (IR, r. 2.30 and Form 2.12).

## ¶1107   Creditors' committee

### (1)  Functions

Once the creditors' meeting has approved the administrator's proposals it can establish a creditors' committee for various purposes (IA, s. 26(1)). The main function of the committee is to 'assist the administrator in discharging his functions, and act in relation to him in such manner as may be agreed from time to time' (IR, r. 2.34(1)). A creditors' committee can be of assistance to an insolvency practitioner. It can be a sounding board for any ideas the administrator may have or difficult decisions he has to take and it is less unwieldy than a meeting of the creditors in general. The committee must also review the adequacy of the administrator's security from time to time (IR, r. 12.8(2)).

### (2)  Membership

The committee must be made up of at least three but not more than five creditors (IR, r. 2.32(1)). They are to be elected at the meeting at which the administrator's proposals are approved (IR, r. 2.32(1)). Any creditor whose claim has not been rejected for the purposes of entitlement to vote may be a member (IR, r. 2.32(2)). Where a company or other body corporate is a member it acts through its duly appointed representative (IR, r. 2.32(3)). Indeed any member of the committee may be represented by someone else provided that he holds a letter of authority from the member which may be in general or specific terms (IR, r. 2.37(1) and (2)). It must be signed by the committee member (IR, r. 2.37(2)). The chairman at any meeting of the committee may at any time call for proof of due authorisation in the form of the letter of authority and exclude anyone where the authority is lacking (IR, r. 2.37(3)).

A company cannot act as a representative nor can an undischarged bankrupt or someone who has made a composition or arrangement with his creditors (IR, r. 2.37(4)). Further, one person cannot be on the committee acting on behalf of more than one committte member nor as a member of the committee in his own right and the representative of another member (IR, r. 2.37(5)). It is provided that any document signed by a representative should state the fact that the signatory is the representative of a true member (IR, r. 2.37(6)).

### (3)  Certificate

Before the committee is formally in being the administrator has to issue a certificate of 'due constitution' (IR, r. 2.33(1) and Form 2.13). Once there are three persons who have agreed to be members the administrator can issue a certificate and may do so at the meeting of creditors at which the committee is formed (IR, r. 2.33(2)). Where further members are proposed but they are not at that stage able to agree to act (for example, because they are not present) the administrator must issue an amended certificate as and when others do agree to act (IR, r. 2.33(3)). The certificates and amended certificates are to be filed in court by the administrator and any later changes in the membership of the committee are to be reported to the court (IR, r. 2.33(4) and (5) and Form 2.14).

¶1107

## (4) Meetings

It is for the administrator to call meetings of the committee when he thinks appropriate (IR, r. 2.34(2)). He must, however, call a first meeting of the committee not more than three months after it is set up (IR, r. 2.34(3)). After the first meeting any member of the committee or his representative may request a meeting and it has to be held within 21 days of receipt of the request by the administrator (IR, r. 2.34(3)(*a*)). A meeting also has to be called where the committee has resolved that a meeting be held on a specific date (IR, r. 2.34(3)(*b*)).

The administrator has to give the committee members or their representatives seven days' writen notice of the venue (that is, time, date and place – see IR, r. 13.6) unless they choose to waive that requirement, either before or at the meeting (IR, r. 2.34(4)).

With one exception (mentioned below), at meetings of the committee (as with meetings of the creditors) the administrator is to be the chairman or else he is to nominate another insolvency practitioner qualified to act in relation to the company or an experienced employee (IR, r. 2.35 and see the discussion at ¶1106(2)). A creditors' committee meeting is quorate if due notice has been given to all the members and two members are present or represented (IR, r. 2.36).

Although it has few specific powers, those the committee has are quite significant. The committee has the extraordinary power to require the administrator to appear before it on giving him at least seven days' notice (IA, s. 26(2)). The notice must be in writing and signed by a majority of the members of the committee or their representatives (IR, r. 2.44(1)). The committee may stipulate the business day on which the meeting is to be held but the administrator has the right to decide the time and place (IR, r. 2.44(2)). The idea is to enable the committee to seek information from the administrator. There appears to be no specific relief for an administrator who finds himself being hounded by an unreasonable committee save that the committee may not recover their expenses (see below). It would seem that the administrator's only remedy is to go to the court and seek an order that the creditors' committee desists from making unreasonable demands (on the grounds that it would not be fulfilling its duty to assist him in his functions).

## (5) Resignation and vacancies

Resignation of a committee member may be affected by notice in writing to the administrator (IR, r. 2.38). Membership automatically comes to an end in the event of a member becoming bankrupt or making a composition or arrangement with his creditors. It also ends if a member neither turns up nor is represented at three successive committee meetings unless, at the third meeting, there is a specific resolution to waive the rule in his case. Finally, membership ends automatically if the person ceases to be, or never was, a creditor (IR, r. 2.39(1)). In the event of termination owing to bankruptcy, the member's trustee in bankruptcy takes his place on the committee (IR, r. 2.39(2)). In addition, the creditors' committee itself may remove a member of the committee by a resolution passed at a meeting of which at least 14 days' notice of intention to propose such a resolution has been given (IR, r. 2.40).

A vacancy on the committee need not be filled if both the administrator and the majority of the rest of the committee agree, provided the remaining members number at least three (IR, r. 2.41(2)). The administrator may fill a vacancy with the agreement of the majority of the committee provided the person concerned fulfils the requirements for a committee member and he is agreeable to acting (IR, r. 2.41(3)).

**(6)   Proceedings**
At creditors' committee meetings each member of the committee has a vote irrespective of the value of the debt for which he is a creditor, and resolutions are passed by simple majority (IR, r. 2.42(1)). Resolutions passed are to be recorded in writing although they may be part of the minutes of the meeting, and the chairman has to sign a record to be placed in the company's minute book (IR, r. 2.42(2) and (3)).

**(7)   Written resolutions**
To save the time and expense of meetings of the committee, the administrator can send to members or their representatives copies of a resolution to which he seeks their agreement (IR, r. 2.43(1)). He has to send a statement containing the resolution to each person and if there is more than one resolution then each resolution has to be in a separate document (IR, r. 2.43(2)). Where the administrator is notified in writing by a majority of the members that they agree with the resolution, then it is deemed passed, save where a member of the committee within seven days of the resolution being sent out requires the administrator to summon a meeting of the committee to discuss the issues covered by the resolution or resolutions (IR, r. 2.43(3) and (4)). Thus, a resolution can never be passed until at least seven business days after the administrator has sent out the statement containing the proposed resolution. The administrator must ensure that any resolutions passed in this manner are duly entered in the company's minute book along with details of the concurrence of the committee (IR, r. 2.43(5)).

**(8)   Expenses**
The administrator is to pay, as an expense of the administration, the reasonable travelling expenses directly incurred by committee members or of their representatives in attending committee members or 'otherwise on the committee's

business' (IR, r. 2.45(1)). There is a limit on recovery of expenses. Where a meeting of the committee is held within three months of a previous meeting (unless at the administrator's instigation), travelling expenses are not recoverable (IR, r. 2.45(2)).

### (9) Conflict of interest
In liquidations, the rule was (and still is: IR, r. 4.170) that members of the committee of inspection could not profit out of dealings in the winding-up (see Companies (Winding-up) Rules 1949, para. 163). Membership of an administration creditors' committee does not prevent dealings with the company provided such dealings are in good faith and for value (IR, r. 2.46(1)). Any person interested may apply to the court to set aside a transaction which breaches this rule and the court is given a wide discretion to make consequential orders to compensate the company for any loss incurred (IR, r. 2.46(2)).

### (10) Remuneration of administrator
One of the main 'powers' or functions of the creditors' committee is in agreeing the remuneration of the administrator. This is considered below (¶1202).

## ¶1108 Members' meetings

The administrator has power to call meetings of the members of the company (IA, s. 14(2)(*b*)). He may, for example, want to call a meeting of the company to implement a change in the company's share structure pursuant to a voluntary arrangement, or perhaps to change its objects clause, or for some other reason to obtain the sanction of the members of the company. When setting the time, date and place of the meeting, he is to have regard to the convenience of the members (IR, r. 2.3(1)).

In general terms the method of calling and conducting the meeting is to be the same as that laid down in the company's Articles of Association and the Companies Act (IR, r. 2.31(5)). However, the following specific rules apply:

(1)  The chairman of the meeting is to be the administrator or his nominee who, as with creditors' meetings, must be nominated in writing and either qualified to act as an insolvency practitioner in relation to the company or an employee of the administrator or his firm and experienced in insolvency matters (IR, r. 2.31(2)).

(2)  If 30 minutes after the time for commencement of the meeting there is nobody present to act as chairman the meeting is automatically adjourned to the same time and place one week hence or, where that is not a business day, to the business day next following (IR, r. 2.31(4)).

(3)   The chairman of the meeting is to cause minutes of proceedings to be entered in the company's minute book (IR, r. 2.31(6)).

# PROTECTION OF CREDITORS AND MEMBERS

## ¶1109   Unfairly prejudicial management and acts

### (1)   The relief generally

The Insolvency Act 1986 provides that during an administration an aggrieved member or creditor of the company may apply to the court on the grounds of 'unfair prejudice'.

There is also provision for such relief from unfair prejudice in connection with voluntary arrangements (IA, s. 6 and see ¶1111(11)). The concept of 'unfair prejudice' is not a new concept in company law. Where there is a variation of class rights of shareholders, 15 per cent in value of the shareholders of an affected class may apply to the court which may (CA, s. 127(4)):

'. . . if satisfied having regard to all the circumstances of the case, that the variation would unfairly prejudice the shareholders of the class represented by the applicant, disallow the variation and shall, if not satisfied, confirm it.'

Similarly, there is specific provision for protection of members of a company, generally (CA, s. 459(1)):

'A member of a company may apply to the court by petition for an order under this Part on the ground that the company's affairs are being or have been conducted in a manner which is unfairly prejudicial to the interests of some part of the members (including at least himself) or that any actual or proposed act or omission of the company (including an act or omission on its behalf) is or would be so prejudicial'.

Finally, there are cases on schemes proposed under s. 425 of the Companies Act 1985 which show that the court will reject schemes which are unfair or unreasonable.

The law in these analogous areas will be of assistance to the court in hearing claims of unfair prejudice in administrations. There is an important rider which must be added to that general statement. In the other statutory examples given above, the oppressive conduct likely to be complained of is conduct of those likely to stand to gain as a result of their actions – other directors or shareholders. The administrator acting in good faith should be impartial and, by definition, should be seeking what is best for the company and its creditors.

¶1109

Further, as a licensed insolvency practitioner there may be a presumption that he is acting in good faith. This is not to suggest that the court will not use its powers in an appropriate case, but the context of such applications is subtly different to those where directors/shareholders are oppressing a minority. The argument that the majority are acting to pursue their own interests and not for the benefit of the creditors as a whole (see, for example, *Re Holders Investment Trust Ltd* [1971] 1 WLR 583) may be harder to sustain where the administrator drew up the proposals.

## (2) The legislation and points arising

The relevant provisions offering relief in this area are as follows (IA, s. 27(1)):

'At any time when an administration order is in force, a creditor or member of the company may apply to the court by petition for an order under this section on the ground –
   (*a*) that the company's affairs, business and property are being or have been managed by the administrator in a manner which is unfairly prejudicial to the interests of its creditors or members generally, or some part of its creditors or members (including at least himself), or
   (*b*) that any actual or proposed act or omission of the administrator is or would be so prejudicial.'

The following points might be noted about these provisions:

(1)   The ambit of the section is wide. The application may be made by any creditor or member and not by a minimum percentage of their number and 'creditor' would seem to include creditors who become creditors after the date of the administration order. An application may be about the conduct of the administration prior to the administrator's proposals being considered, or it may be about the proposals themselves (subject to certain time-limits for objection discussed below), or about an act (or failure to act) which has not yet occurred.

(2)   The unfairly prejudicial management or act must affect the member or creditor in that capacity, that is, qua member or qua creditor, as the case may be. For example, it is submitted that a creditor who also formerly supplied goods to the company could not complain under this head if the administrator chose to buy similar goods from another supplier. The creditor suffers qua supplier of goods not qua creditor. The position might be different if the administrator bought from another supplier at grossly inflated prices as this might be prejudicial to the creditor, as a creditor.

(3)   The general principle stated above was recently affirmed by Hoffmann J in *Re a Company (No. 00477 of 1986)* (1986) 2 BCC 99, 171) in a

¶1109

case brought under s. 459 of the Companies Act 1985. He added a gloss to the proposition when he said (at p. 376): 'The use of the word "unfairly" . . . enables the court to have regard to wider equitable considerations'. On the facts before him Hoffmann J felt that the law would not draw a firm distinction in the case of a small private company between a person's interest qua member and his interest qua managing director/employee. What if an administrator dismissed a director who was a principal shareholder? Could he complain qua member?

(4)   It would seem likely that, in the absence of bad faith, the court will be reluctant to question the commercial judgement of the administrator. The court felt that in theory it could examine business decisions of directors under this heading in *Re a Company (No. 004475 of 1982)* ([1983] Ch. 178). Where the administrator's proposals have been approved by a majority of the creditors then, in the absence of evidence that the majority are furthering sectional interests or obtaining a collateral advantage, or evidence that the complaints are being singled out for worse treatment, the court may take the view that ( per Lindley LJ in *Re English, Scottish, and Australian Chartered Bank* [1893] 3 Ch. 385 at p. 409):

'If the creditors are acting on sufficient information and with time to consider what they are about, and are acting honestly, they are, I apprehend, much better judges of what is to their commercial advantage than the court can be'.

(5)   Proposals which further the interests of the majority of creditors, to the disadvantage of a few, may be open to criticism. For example, if the proposals for trading attempted to utilise the inability of landlords and leasing companies to distrain and repossess respectively by suggesting that they be singled out and are not paid their contractual entitlements notwithstanding use of premises and equipment by the administration, the court might consider that 'unfair' (and note IA, s. 27(5)).

(6)   The reference to 'creditors or members generally' meets a criticism of s. 459 of the Companies Act 1985 to the effect that conduct prejudicial to the entire membership is not caught by s. 459 (see, for example, *Re Carrington Viyella plc* [1983] 1 BCC 98, 951).

(7)   Members are perhaps unlikely to bring applications under this head where the purpose of the administration is the realisation of assets unless, in a subsequent winding-up, there is likely to be a distribution to shareholders – as otherwise they are not financially affected.

¶1109

(8)   There are other ways for creditors to air grievances. The restrictions on taking proceedings and repossessing equipment that is subject to a hire-purchase agreement and leased equipment, etc. (IA, s. 11(3)) may be lifted by the court, and a creditor could apply accordingly. It has also been suggested[1] that the court could be petitioned for the removal of the administrator (IA, s. 19(1)).

## ¶1110   Court orders and time limits

On hearing an application of this type, the court has the wide discretion seen elsewhere in the administration procedure (see for example IA, s. 9(4)): it may make such orders as it thinks fit to give relief, adjourn the hearing conditionally or unconditionally, make an interim order or make any other order as it decides (IA, s. 27(2)). The Act gives four particular examples of matters which may be covered by an order (IA, s. 27(4)).

(1)   The order may be to regulate the future management of the company's affairs, business and property by the administrator.

(2)   It may effectively injunct the administrator from carrying out a proposed act or require him to take some action.

(3)   It may require that a creditors' meeting be called to consider the matters laid down by the court.

(4)   It may discharge the administration order itself and make an order consequential upon that.

Where the administrator's proposals have been approved by the creditors of the company or a revised set of proposals have been approved by the creditors then the implementation of those proposals is not to be prejudiced or stopped by any orders of the court on 'unfair prejudice' grounds where the application to the court was made more than 28 days after the approval of the proposals or revised proposals (IA, s. 27(3)(*b*)). Thus, a typical sequence may be that a creditor at the creditors' meeting argues against specific proposals and votes against them but is out-voted by a majority in value. If he considers that the proposals are unfairly prejudicial to him or to him and others, he has the comparatively short period of 28 days within which to organise his complaints and make his application to the court for relief or he is forever barred (but see IR, r. 12.9 for a glimmer of hope).

There is a further restriction on the effect of any order. Where the administration proposals are approved by the creditors and include a voluntary arrangement scheme or a scheme of arrangement under s. 425 of the Companies Act 1985, either of which is approved or sanctioned as required, then

---

[1] Lightman and Moss, *Law of Receivers of Companies*, para. 23–28.

the court cannot prejudice or prevent the implementation of such a scheme. The voluntary arrangement system itself provides for petitioning of the court by a member or creditor who considers himself unfairly prejudiced by that scheme (see ¶1111(11)).

# SCHEMES

## ¶1111    Voluntary arrangement scheme

In many cases where a company or its creditors see a voluntary arrangement as holding the key to a company's survival, the administration procedure will be invoked first, with the preparation of a scheme of voluntary arrangement as one of the purposes of the administration. The reason for this is that the presentation of a petition for an administrator affords a company immediate protection from action by its creditors while a voluntary arrangement on its own does not. While a voluntary arrangement scheme may be instituted without an administration, it would seem unlikely that the company will be able to survive action in the interim by its creditors, as the time necessary to put a scheme into place will not be available. It may be that creditors will know that should they try to take action to achieve an advantage over other creditors it will be open to the supervisor of the scheme to petition for an administrator (IA, s. 7(4)(*b*)) – the effect of which will be to increase costs – and thus the very threat of an administration may serve to protect voluntary arrangements. The treatment below is of a voluntary arrangement as a purpose of an administration.

### (1)    General outline
A voluntary arrangement involves a proposal to the company and its creditors 'for a composition in satisfaction of its debts or a scheme of arrangement of its affairs' (IA, s. 1(1)). The wording is deliberately wide with a view to affording as much scope as possible to the company and its creditors and advisers to find an imaginative solution to the company's difficulties. The essence of an approved voluntary arrangement is that it is a contract between a company and its creditors on the terms set out in the scheme.

The proposal has to provide for a person, to be known as a nominee (acting 'as trustee or otherwise'), to supervise the implementation of the voluntary arrangement (IA, s. 1(2)). The nominee becomes the 'supervisor' in the event that the proposals are accepted by the relevant meetings of the company and its creditors (IA, s. 7(2)). The nominee and the supervisor must be insolvency practitioners qualified to act as such in relation to the company in question (IA, ss. 1(2) and 388(1)(*b*)).

Where an administration order is in force, the proposal may be made by the administrator (IA, s. 1(3)(*a*)) (and it would be his duty to make the proposal in the event that this is the approved purpose of the administration) and he may propose himself as nominee (IA, s. 3(2)). The administrator need not put himself forward as nominee (IA, s. 2(1)) although it will be rare for him not to do so, convenience and expense militating against it. The administrator (or anyone else preparing proposals for a voluntary arrangement) will wish to take great care in preparing the proposals in an effort to avoid any danger of allegations later of negligent misstatement.

The detailed proposals for the voluntary arrangement are to be prepared and placed before meetings of the company's members and creditors specially convened for the purpose of considering them (IA, s. 3(2)). The meetings may modify the proposed scheme (IA, s. 4(1)). One modification upon which they may insist is that an insolvency practitioner other than the person proposed as nominee be charged with the task of implementing the proposals (IA, s. 4(2)). In short, therefore, while the creditors' meeting in an administration cannot resolve to replace an administrator, the creditors agreeing to a voluntary arrangement may refuse to permit him to act as supervisor of the voluntary arrangement.

Where the proposals are approved by the requisite majorities, the company and all creditors are bound (even although they may have voted against the scheme in their meeting) (IA, s. 5(2)). They do, however, have a statutory right of objection to the court, such objection to be made within a comparatively short time after the relevant meetings (IA, s. 6). Thereafter they have a right to apply to the court by way of objection to particular decisions of the supervisor (IA, s. 7(3)).

The supervisor proceeds to implement the proposals. The administration may continue in parallel, subject to any particular guidance given by the court from time to time (IA, s. 5(3)).

When the voluntary arrangement has been fully implemented the supervisor serves notice of this fact and his role comes to an end (IR, r. 1.29), and where the company is also in administration and the purpose of the administration was to implement a voluntary arrangement, it will be appropriate for the administration to come to an end also.

Consideration in more detail is given below to the various aspects of a voluntary arrangement.

### (2)  Types of scheme
It was (and is) possible, under s. 425 of the Companies Act 1985 (and its predecessors), for a company to agree a compromise or arrangement with its

¶1111

creditors provided the sanction of the court was obtained and the various statutory requirements were complied with. The procedure was considered somewhat unwieldy, however, and never enjoyed much popularity (see the brief discussion at ¶1112)

A voluntary arrangement in an administration does not require court sanction as such, although the results of the various meetings do have to be reported to the court (IA, s. 4(6)). There is provision for dissenters to apply to the court to strike down a particular scheme on the grounds of 'unfair prejudice' (IA, s. 6). As with s. 425, the idea behind voluntary arrangements is to bind the dissenters to the scheme, in the absence of unfair prejudice brought to the court's attention in the manner laid down in the statute. But a voluntary arrangement itself is still in essence an agreement between company and creditors and the authorities on s. 425 make it clear that all other legal rules apply to such an agreement and will be in point. For example, all the elements of a scheme must be intra vires (*Re Oceanic Steam Navigation Co Ltd* [1939] Ch. 41). The wording describing what may be classified as a voluntary arrangement (' . . . a proposal . . . to the company and to its creditors for a composition in satisfaction of its debts or a scheme of arrangement of its affairs . . .' IA, s. 1(1)) is slightly different to that in s. 425 ('. . . a compromise or arrangement . . . proposed between a company and its creditors, or any class of them, or between the company and its members, or any class of them . . .'). It would still seem necessary, however, for *the company* to agree (see *Re Savoy Hotel Ltd* [1981] Ch. 351).

In the majority of cases it seems likely that the balance sheet of the company will have to be made solvent, perhaps to a greater or lesser extent by the cancellation or deferral of a company's indebtedness or its conversion into share capital. The rest is left to the ingenuity of company lawyers and accountants. Those designing schemes should remember the concepts of 'composition' and 'scheme of arrangement'. 'Composition', according to the Concise Oxford Dictionary (7th edn), means 'compromise; agreement for payment of sum in lieu of larger sum or other obligation'. Considering the words 'compromise' and 'arrangement' (in the predecessor of s. 425) Brightman J in *Re NFU Development Trust Ltd* ([1972] 1 WLR 1548) said (at p. 1555):

'The word "compromise" implies some element of accommodation on each side. It is not apt to describe total surrender. A claimant who abandons his claim is not compromising it. Similarly, I think that the word "arrangement" in this section implies some element of give and take. Confiscation is not my idea of an arrangement'.

There are two statutory riders. First, schemes may not affect the rights of a secured creditor to enforce his security, save where the secured creditor consents (IA, s. 4(3)). Secondly, preferential debts (IA, s. 386) are to be afforded priority of payment ahead of unsecured debts and similarly within the class of preferential creditors no one creditor is to be paid a greater proportion of his debt than any other preferential creditor (IA, s. 4(4)). Again, it is possible for the preferential creditor or creditors to consent to any particular proposal (IA, s. 4(4)).

### (3) Preparation of proposals by the administrator

There are different procedures to be followed when the administrator makes proposals depending on whether he is, or is not, the nominee under the scheme.

Where the administrator is the nominee, he simply calls the relevant meetings of the company and the creditors to consider his proposals (IA, s. 3(2)). Where the nominee is not the administrator, the administrator gives notice in writing to the intended nominee accompanied by a copy of the proposals (IA, s. 2 and IR, rr. 1.12(2) and 1.4). He must also send him a copy of the company's 'Statement of Affairs' (IR, r. 1.12(5)). It is not clear whether this statement is the same statement submitted to him in the administration by the directors (IA, s. 22) or the statement amplifying the proposals as necessary under r. 1.5 as a result of r. 1.12(1).

The administrator in this situation may already have discussed the matter with the nominee, and obtained his informal agreement to act. Where a nominee does agree to accept appointment, he has to endorse a copy of the notice stating that he has received it and giving the date, and return that to the administrator, and he has 28 days (unless the court orders a longer period) within which to submit a report to the court (IA, s. 2(2) and IR, r. 1.4). This report is to say whether he thinks meetings of the company and creditors should be summoned and when and where the meeting should be held (IA, s. 2(2)). In short, he must say whether he thinks that the scheme is a good idea and worth putting to the members and creditors.

Where the nominee fails to submit the report to the court within the 28 days or any extension, the administrator may apply to the court for the nominee to be replaced by another insolvency practitioner qualified to act in relation to the company (IA, s. 2(4)).

### (4) Content of proposals

The proposals of the administrator must have a short recital giving the reasons why a voluntary arrangement is thought desirable and must further indicate why the company's creditors might be expected to approve the scheme (IR, r. 1.3(1)). The areas to be covered by the document setting out the proposals are explained in some detail by the Rules and the relevant provisions are worth stating in full (IR, r. 1.3(2)):

¶1111

'The following matters shall be stated, or otherwise dealt with, in the directors' proposal –

(*a*) the following matters, so far as within the directors' immediate knowledge –
    (i) the company's assets, with an estimate of their respective values,
    (ii) the extent (if any) to which the assets are charged in favour of creditors,
    (iii) the extent (if any) to which particular assets are to be excluded from the voluntary arrangement;

(*b*) particulars of any property, other than assets of the company itself, which is proposed to be included in the arrangement, the source of such property and the terms on which it is to be made available for inclusion;

(*c*) the nature and amount of the company's liabilities (so far as within the directors' immediate knowledge), the manner in which they are proposed to be met, modified, postponed or otherwise dealt with by means of the arrangement, and (in particular) –
    (i) how it is proposed to deal with preferential creditors (defined in section 4(7)) and creditors who are, or claim to be secured,
    (ii) how persons connected with the company (being creditors) are proposed to be treated under the arrangement, and
    (iii) whether there are, to the directors' knowledge, any circumstances giving rise to the possibility, in the event that the company should go into liquidation, of claims under –
    section 238 (transactions at an undervalue),
    section 239 (preferences),
    section 244 (extortionate credit transactions), or
    section 245 (floating charges invalid);
    and where any such circumstances are present, whether, and if so how, it is proposed under the voluntary arrangement to make provision for wholly or partly indemnifying the company in respect of such claims;

(*d*) whether any, and if so what, guarantees have been given of the company's debts by other persons, specifying which (if any) of the guarantors are persons connected with the company;

(*e*) the proposed duration of the voluntary arrangement;

(*f*) the proposed dates of distributions to creditors, with estimates of their amounts;

(*g*) the amount proposed to be paid to the nominee (as such) by way of remuneration and expenses;

¶1111

(*h*) the manner in which it is proposed that the supervisor of the arrangement should be remunerated, and his expenses defrayed;

(*j*) whether, for the purposes of the arrangement, any guarantees are to be offered by directors, or other persons, and whether (if so) any security is to be given or sought;

(*k*) the manner in which funds held for the purposes of the arrangement are to be banked, invested or otherwise dealt with pending distribution to creditors;

(*l*) the manner in which funds held for the purpose of payment to creditors, and not so paid on the termination of the arrangement, are to be dealt with;

(*m*) the manner in which the business of the company is proposed to be conducted during the course of the arrangement;

(*n*) details of any further credit facilities which it is intended to arrange for the company, and how the debts so arising are to be paid;

(*o*) the functions which are to be undertaken by the supervisor of the arrangement; and

(*p*) the name, address and qualification of the person proposed as supervisor of the voluntary arrangement, and confirmation that he is (so far as the directors are aware) qualified to act as an insolvency practitioner in relation to the company.'

In addition to the specific items which must be contained in the proposal, as listed above, the administrator must also include; 'such other matters (if any) as [he] considers appropriate for ensuring that members and creditors of the company are enabled to reach an informed decision on the proposal' (IR, r. 1.10(1)(*b*)).

Where the administrator is not the nominee, there is provision for the proposals to be amended up to the date of delivery of the nominee's report to the court with the consent of the nominee (IR, r. 1.3(3)). This is intended to facilitate the incorporation of improvements to the scheme suggested by the nominee – again statute proceeds on the assumption that the nominee has not in fact himself drafted the proposals. A more likely sequence of events is that a company in difficulty has been directed towards an insolvency practitioner and he has prepared the scheme's details.

All those who receive notice of the meetings are sent, either by the nominee or the administrator (as the case may be), a copy of the proposals, a copy or summary of the Statement of Affairs, including (at least) details of creditors and the size of their debts and, in the case of the proposal of a nominee other than the administrator, any comments the nominee made on the proposals in his report to the court (IR r. 1.9(3)). The notice must also explain the effect of the rules governing the passing of resolutions – for example what majorities

¶1111

are required and how they are arrived at (see ¶1111(5) and (6)) – to assist the creditors and members in consideration of the proposals (IR, r. 1.9(3)).

The nominee or the administrator, as the case may be, must give at least 14 days' notice of the meetings of the members and creditors, and the creditors who have to receive notice are all those named in the statement of affairs or any others of whom the nominee or administrator is aware for any other reason (IR, rr.1.9 and 1.11). The members who are to receive notice are those who are members, to the best of the insolvency practitioner's belief (IR, rr. 1.9(2)(*b*) and 1.11(1)(*b*)).

### (5)   Meetings
The rules for calling meetings in a voluntary arrangement are not dissimilar to those for an administration. First, the practitioner must 'have regard primarily to the convenience of the creditors' in calling both members' and creditors' meetings (IR r. 1.13(1)). The meetings are to start between 10 a.m. and 4. p.m. on a business day and they are to be held on the same day and in the same place but with the creditors' meeting scheduled to start before the company meeting (IR, r. 1.13). The notices of the meeting (for which there is no prescribed form) have to be sent together with forms of proxy (Form 8.1). The provisions governing use of the proxies are not dissimilar to the rules in an administration (see IR, rr. 1.15, 1.19(*b*), 1.20(3) and 8.1–8.7).

The convener of the meetings will be chairman in each case, although there is provision that he may instead nominate someone else to be chairman, being someone qualified to act as an insolvency practitioner in relation to that company, or an employee of the convener's firm who is experienced in insolvency matters (IR, r. 1.14).

It may be of assistance to the meetings to have the directors present. Thus, whoever is convening the meetings must give at least 14 days' notice to attend to all directors and to any persons the convener thinks should be present as officers of the company or who had been officers or directors within two years of the notice being sent out (IR, r. 1.16(2)). It is equally possible that free discussion at the meetings may be hindered by the presence of the directors and accordingly the chairman of the meeting has the right to exclude any present or former director or officer of the company from attending the meeting (IR, r. 1.16(2)). This may be a complete bar or he may simply be asked to leave the meeting for part (IR, r. 1.16(2)).

Where there is any degree of complexity in the form of the scheme under consideration at the creditors' and members' meetings, it may be difficult logistically for the convener to obtain the necessary consents where the meetings follow one after the other in conventional fashion. Thus the chairman of the meeting is given licence to adjourn either or both meetings from time to time and, where he wishes to obtain simultaneous agreement at both meetings (as is likely to be the case), he may hold the meetings together (IR, r. 1.21).

Where the chairman cannot obtain the requisite majorities for the scheme with or without modifications, he can adjourn the meetings (and must do so if the meetings resolve to that effect) for a period up to 14 days (IR, r. 1.21). Within that 14-day period there may be any number of adjournments, although there is a qualification that adjourned meetings may only be held on a business day and there can be no adjournment of one meeting without the other meeting being adjourned to the same business day (IR, r. 1.21).

Ultimately, failure to obtain the agreement of both meetings to proposals, amended as necessary, constitutes a deemed rejection of them (IR, r. 1.21(6)).

There will be ample scope at these meetings for insolvency practitioners to show their skills – both of persuasion and of commercial ingenuity – in attempting to keep everyone satisfied to the extent necessary to achieve the requisite majorities.

### (6) Voting

*(a) The rules*
The right of creditors to vote is, in general terms, similar to that in an administration (see ¶1106(4)). The date for calculation of the creditor's debt is, however, the date of the administration order and there is no specific provision for deducting amounts paid in respect of the debt since the date of the administration order (IR, r. 1.17(2)). Perhaps a vital supplier might have been able to hold the administrator to ransom in respect of future supplies and have had part or all of his debt paid. On the face of the Rules he would appear to be entitled to vote his entire debt at the date of the administration order although common sense would suggest that he should not be entitled to vote that part of his debt which has been paid prior to the meeting.

In the case of the members' meeting, members may vote according to the rights their shares enjoy under the company's Articles of Association (IR, r. 1.18).

Where a member's shares give no entitlement to vote, the rules provide that the member shall nevertheless be entitled to vote with the caveat that the votes are not to be included in deciding whether the requisite majorities have been obtained (IR, rr. 1.18(2) and 1.20(2)). The effect of this is to give the member concerned the right to object to the court on the grounds of unfair prejudice (IA s. 6(2) and see ¶1111(11)).

As in the administration procedure, certain creditors are not allowed to be included in the vote calculation. First, creditors may only be included where written notice of their claim was given at the meeting or before it to the chairman or convener as the case may be (IR, r. 1.19(3)(a)).

¶1111

There are rules similar to those in an administration for reducing the voting entitlement of those with security to the extent of the security (see IA, s. 248(*b*)), and similarly as regards debts 'secured' on bills of exchange or promissory notes (IR, r. 1.19(3)(*b*) and (*c*)). There are no restrictions on the voting entitlements of creditors who have rights in respect of retention of title or who own goods under hire-purchase or leasing agreements with the company (compare IR, rr. 2.26 and 2.27).

It would appear that a secured creditor may vote only in respect of the unsecured part of his claim although the wording in the rules is not as clear for voluntary arrangements as it is for administrations (IR, r. 1.19(3)(*b*) providing that '. . . there is to be left out of account a creditor's vote in respect of any claim or part of a claim . . . where the claim or part is secured . . .'). In the case of debt 'secured' by a bill of exchange, a calculation of the unsecured value of the debt must be made by the creditor. The majority required to approve the proposals at a creditors' meeting is a majority greater than 75 per cent in value of the creditors present at the meeting, whether in person or by proxy, and voting on the resolution. Thus, those who abstain will be left out of account in calculating the 75 per cent. Other resolutions at creditors' meetings require a majority in excess of 50 per cent (IR, r. 1.19(2)).

There is the further limitation on the voting rights of a creditor, seen also in connection with administrations, that there is no right to vote in respect of a debt which is unliquidated or whose value is otherwise not ascertained save that the chairman of the meeting may agree to an estimated minimum value for the purpose of an entitlement to vote (IR, r. 1.17(3)). Similar rules relating to appeals from the decision of a chairman in connection with voting apply for voluntary arrangements as they do for administrations (IR, r. 1.17(4)–(9), and compare IR, r. 2.23). In particular, the 28-day time limit from submission of the first report on the meetings should be noted (IR, r. 1.17(8)).

There is a second majority test which also has to be passed, otherwise any resolution is 'invalid'. There has to be a majority in excess of 50 per cent of those who are entitled to vote and who have been sent notice of the meeting other than those who are connected with the company (IR, r. 1.19(4)). In short, it is a test of independent majority opinion. As to whether someone is connected, the chairman must rule on this to the best of his belief (IR, r. 1.19(4)(*c*)).

The effect of these rules regarding majorities may be illustrated by examples. For convenience, it is assumed in these examples, that all the connected creditors who vote, vote in favour of the scheme.

¶1111

*(b) Example 1*

|  | | £ (millions) | £ (millions) |
|---|---|---|---|
| Value of creditors to whom notices sent | = | | 1.30 |
| Of those (a) the value of secured creditors | = | 0.10 | |
| (b) the value of creditors who do not give written notice of claim | = | 0.10 | 0.20 |
| ∴ Value of creditors eligible to vote | = | | 1.10 |
| Of those (a) connected creditors | = | 0.65 | |
| (b) unconnected creditors | = | 0.45 | 1.10 |
| At the creditors meeting the voting is | | | |
| (a) in favour of scheme | = | 0.78 | |
| (b) not in favour | = | 0.22 | |
| (c) abstained or did not attend meeting | = | 0.10 | |
| | | | 1.10 |

*Test 1*

% of creditors entitled to vote and in favour $\dfrac{0.78}{1.10}\%$ = 71%

BUT % of creditors present and voting in favour $\dfrac{0.78}{1.00}\%$ = 78%

Test 1 has been passed

*Test 2*

| Creditors for the purposes of the second test (those to whom notices sent) | = | 1.30 |
|---|---|---|
| *Less* creditors (a) secured, or (b) not giving notice of claim } | = | 0.20 |
| | | 1.10 |
| *Less* connected creditors | | 0.65 |
| Total of 'creditors' | = | 0.45 |
| Value of creditors not in favour | = | 0.22 |
| ∴ % of unconnected creditors voting against | = | $\dfrac{0.22}{0.45}\%$ |
| | = | 49% |

∴ The creditors have approved the scheme.

¶1111

*(c)   Example 2*

Take the facts of example 1, but with the difference that the £0.1m in value of creditors who gave written notice but did not vote or did not attend the meeting, do not in this example give written notice.

| | | |
|---|---|---:|
| *Test 1* is unaffected, but | | |
| *Test 2* | | |
| Creditors for the purposes of the second test (those to whom notices sent) | = | 1.30 |
| *Less* creditors (*a*) secured, or | | |
| (*b*) not giving notice | = | 0.30 |
| | | ──── |
| | | 1.00 |
| *Less* connected creditors | | 0.65 |
| | | ──── |
| Total of 'creditors' | = | 0.35 |
| | | ════ |
| Value of creditors not in favour | = | 0.22 |
| ∴ % of unconnected creditors voting against | = | $\dfrac{0.22}{0.35}\%$ |
| | = | 63% |
| | | ════ |

∴ The creditors have not approved the scheme.

Once notice of a claim is given (IR, r. 1.19(3)(*a*)), a failure to attend the meeting or an abstention may operate in favour of the scheme being approved by enlarging the pool of unconnected creditors among whom there must not be more than 50 per cent against the scheme for it to be approved.

**(7)   Meaning of 'creditor'**

Neither the Insolvency Act 1986 nor the Insolvency Rules 1986 contains a definition of 'creditor' for these purposes. In dealing with compromises with creditors and members under s. 425 of the Companies Act 1985 the courts have tended to take a wide definition of creditor. It has been said that a creditor is someone who has or may have any pecuniary claim against the company.[1]

The significance of having a wide definition of creditor is twofold. First, a major alteration in the company's status is clearly something which is of concern to a contingent creditor almost as much as to an existing creditor

---

[1] *Pennington's Company Law* (5th edn) at p. 588 and the authorities cited therein.

and therefore it is right that they should be involved in consideration of a voluntary arrangement. Secondly, having been given notice of the meeting, and whether or not they take any action on the notice, the contingent creditor or a creditor for an unliquidated sum will be bound by the terms of the voluntary arrangement 'as if he were a party' (IA, s. 5(2)(b)). Thus, in many cases it may be important that all possible creditors are bound by the scheme. Nominees will, therefore, wish to check carefully whether the company was ever, for example, the original tenant under a lease which it has since assigned and in respect of which it may still be liable contractually to the landlord in the event that the assignee and any subsequent assignees fail to pay rent and comply with the other obligations under the lease. A creditor not bound by a scheme retains his claim against the company (*Sovereign Life Assurance Company* v *Dodd* [1892] 2 QB 573).

### (8) Implementation of a voluntary arrangement

If the company and creditors' meetings finally agree to proposals (and if modifications have been put forward, with the same modifications) then the voluntary arrangement takes effect 'as if made by the company at the creditors' meeting' (IA, s. 5(2)(a)). The arrangement binds all creditors who had notice of the meeting in accordance with the rules and who were entitled to vote at it (IA, s. 5(2)(b)). In short, creditors' rights may have been reduced or otherwise varied without their consent.

Where someone other than the nominee is put forward at the meetings to be the supervisor of the voluntary arrangement, then either that person must be at the meeting and signify his consent to act or he must have provided a written consent to act which must be presented to the chairman at the meeting. In either case, the meeting has to have before it his written confirmation that he is qualified to act as an insolvency practitioner in relation to the company (IR, r. 1.22(3)).

It may be the case that joint supervisors are appointed. The meeting appointing the practitioners may resolve whether they are to act together in all things or whether they may act individually (IR, r. 1.22(1) and compare IA, s.231). In almost all cases it will be advantageous for the appointees to be able to act separately (in many cases they will be members of the same firm). It is unlikely in practice that there will ever be a situation where two appointees have diametrically opposed views on what actions to take.

### (9) Position of supervisor

Neither the Act nor the Rules give detailed guidance on the role and powers of the supervisor. As the voluntary arrangement essentially constitutes a contract, the terms of the scheme should lay down the powers of

¶1111

the supervisor and the manner in which he is to exercise them. Where the administrator is the supervisor there should be little practical difficulty. Where, however, the supervisor is someone other than the administrator, the administrator must do all that is required to put the supervisor into possession of the assets which are the subject of the voluntary arrangement (IR, r. 1.23(1)). The court will make any necessary orders as to the future conduct of the administration to facilitate implementation of the scheme of voluntary arrangement (IA, s. 5(3)). An order cannot be made before creditors' appeals to the court (whether under IR, r. 1.17(5) or IA, s. 6) are settled or time-barred (IA, s. 5(4)). In a case where the idea of the scheme is to write off indebtedness in order to produce balance sheet solvency, the taking effect of the voluntary arrangement may largely have completed the task of the administrator, and it will simply remain for him to achieve a smooth transfer of control of the company back to the directors and to seek his release and discharge.

The administrator may still have remuneration payable to him and other costs and expenses outstanding. A supervisor taking charge of assets from an administrator must discharge such liabilities and also any advances made in respect of the company, together with statutory interest on them (IR, r. 1.23(2)). Alternatively, the supervisor may provide a written undertaking to pay these sums out of his first realisation of assets (IR, r. 1.23(3)). The administrator is stated to have a charge on the assets in the voluntary arrangement in respect of any of these sums until they have been discharged, provided that the supervisor can deduct the proper costs and expenses of realisation of the assets (IR, r. 1.23(4)). The supervisor has further to discharge from time to time out of the proceeds of the realization of assets all guarantees given by the administrator for the benefit of the company and is to pay the administrator's 'expenses' (IR, r. 1.23(5)).

**(10)  Reports**
The chairman of the meetings has to prepare a report to the court on the outcome of the meetings, giving full details of the resolutions and modifications considered, how the creditors and members voted, and any further information that he considers the court ought to know (IR, r. 1.24). This report has to be prepared quickly – it has to be filed in court within four days of the meetings (IR, r. 1.24(3)). Notice of the result of each meeting is to be sent to all those who received notice of the calling of the relevant meeting (IR, r. 1.24(4)), and where the voluntary arrangement is approved (whether or not amended) the supervisor must file with the Registrar of Companies a copy of the chairman's report on the meetings (IR, r. 1.24(5) and Form 1.1).

There are provisions in the Rules governing the supervisor's duty to

¶1111

keep accounts and make periodic reports to the creditors and others (IR, r. 1.26 and Form 1.3). The Secretary of State may require the supervisor to produce his accounts and reports for inspection, and the Secretary of State may require them to be audited (IR, r. 1.27).

### (11) Protection of creditors

Creditors who are aggrieved by the outcome of meetings to consider proposals for a voluntary arrangement have a number of protections and remedies.

First, there is a right of appeal to the court (IA, s. 6). The right to complain is open not just to creditors but also to anyone entitled to vote at one of the meetings, the nominee or his replacement, or the administrator (IA, s. 6(2)). The appeal can be on either or both of two grounds. The complaint may be that the voluntary arrangement unfairly prejudices the interests of a creditor, member or contributory, or it may be that there was a 'material irregularity' at one of the meetings (IA, s. 6(1) but note IR, r. 7.55). The complainant must react quickly. He has 28 days to make his application from the time when the reports of the chairman have been filed with the court (IA, s. 6(3)). It is clearly preferable that such matters are dealt with swiftly and, in the interests of certainty, a short period for dissent has been laid down (and note particularly the validating effect of IA, s. 6(7)). The discussion of the concept of 'unfair prejudice' in administrations (at ¶1109) is equally in point in connection with voluntary arrangements.

It is likely that the court will ignore irregularities at meetings which are *de minimis*. It remains to be seen whether 'material' means that the result of the meeting might have been different if the irregularity had not occurred.

Where the court is persuaded that there is unfair prejudice or that a material irregularity has occurred, it has a wide discretion to remedy matters by either revoking or suspending approvals and it may direct that fresh meetings be called and give supplemental directions (IA, s. 6(4)-(6) and note IR, r. 1.25 and Form 1.2 governing procedure on a revocation or suspension).

To deter deception of creditors and members, it is a criminal offence for a past or present officer (including a shadow director) of a company to make a 'false representation' or to commit 'any other fraud' to obtain approval of a voluntary arrangement (IR, r. 1.30).

### (12) Remuneration and termination

The scheme may provide for payment of the nominee's disbursements in the period leading up to approval of the voluntary arrangement and whatever remuneration may be agreed for his work on the voluntary arrangement (IR, r. 1.28(*a*)). Any nominee when first approached would be well advised to seek payment in advance for his work on a scheme which may never be approved. The same fees, costs, charges and expenses which may be incurred in an administration may be incurred for the purposes of the voluntary arrangement, in addition to any specifically covered by the terms of the arrangement (see IR, r. 1.28(*a*) and (*b*) and ¶1115).

There are certain termination procedures which a supervisor must follow when the voluntary arrangement has been 'fully implemented' (IR, r. 1.29 and Form 1.4).

## ¶1112   Section 425 schemes

It is not proposed to give extended treatment to schemes under s. 425 of the Companies Act 1985 (for which reference should be made to the standard textbooks). The introduction of the concept of the voluntary arrangement was in response to criticisms of the time-consuming, expensive and complex nature of the s. 425 procedure (see paras. 400–430 of the Cork Report). Although an administration order will buy the company time to construct a scheme under s. 425 by giving the company a measure of protection from action by individual creditors, the defects of excessive formality and complexity remain. It seems likely that voluntary arrangements will be the more popular route for compositions between a company and its creditors.

## TRADING

## ¶1113   Considerations for administrators

An administrator must always bear in mind the purpose or purposes for which he has been appointed. He may trade as part of the process of preserving a going concern or he may trade briefly prior to a realisation of assets, but any trading undertaken must have the purposes of the administration in view. This general principle is subject to one caveat. Until such time as the creditors' meeting may approve his proposals, an administrator must run the company in accordance with any specific directions of the court (IA, s. 17(2)(*a*)). It is always open to him to go to the court for guidance if there is something that he wishes to do but he is unsure about whether it is covered by his existing remit from the court (IA, s. 14(3)). At all times the administrator should bear in mind his general duty to seek the discharge (or variation of the aims) of the administration when it appears to him that the existing purposes of the administration cannot be achieved (IA, s. 18(2)(*a*)). Where his trading in the administration (say for the purpose of preserving a going concern) is incurring losses (perhaps as a result of a loss of business confidence in the company as a result of the administration), there will come a point when the administrator is satisfied that this is not a temporary setback and that the interests of the creditors would be better served by an immediate winding-up or perhaps a switch of purpose in the administration to that of realising assets more advantageously than in a winding-up (IA, s. 8(3)(*d*)).

The administrator will wish his trading, in general terms, to be conducted to the usual professional standards of care and skill to be expected of an insolvency practitioner. His firm's procedures for insolvencies should ensure that he has full financial and management information and figures on a regular basis to enable him to take trading decisions. Where necessary, he will enlist the aid of those with technical ability in a specialist area.

Where the administration trades with third parties who are creditors of the company the administrator will seek, out of an abundance of caution, to exclude any rights of such third parties to set-off debts owed to them by the company against any sums they may owe the administration (see *Hanak v Green* [1958] 2 QB 9, but consider *Ince Hall Rolling Mills Co. Ltd v Douglas Forge Co.* (1882) 8 QBD 179).

## ¶1114   Hiving-down

Hiving-down is discussed above in the context of receiverships (¶504).

In the right case, hiving-down may be an attractive option to an administrator which he might pursue. Where only one division of a company is profitable it might be an appropriate sale technique to hive this 'jewel in the crown' down into a subsidiary with a view to selling it off. The administrator is given express power to hive-down (IA, Sch. 1, paras. 15 and 16).

As a result of the Transfer of Undertakings (Protection of Employment) (Amendment) Regulations 1987 (SI 1987 No. 442) which came into force on 24 April 1987, hiving-down by administrators has the same consequences as for receivers (see ¶515(1)). The effect is that employees do not follow the undertaking immediately on a hive-down but only when the subsidiary or the undertaking is further on-sold by the subsidiary.

## TRADING AND OTHER LIABILITIES

## ¶1115   Concept of the administration expense

What happens to liabilities incurred and created as a result of trading by the administrator? There is little direct guidance in the legislation. The following are the most relevant provisions (IA, s. 19):

'(3) Where at any time a person ceases to be an administrator, the next two subsections apply

(4) His remuneration and any expenses properly incurred by him shall be charged on and paid out of any property of the company which is in his custody or under his control at that time in priority to any security [which, as created, was a floating charge].

(5) Any sums payable in respect of debts or liabilities incurred, while he was administrator, under contracts entered into or contracts of employment adopted by him or a predecessor of his in the carrying out of his or the predecessor's functions shall be charged on and paid out of any such property as is mentioned in subsection (4) in priority to any charge arising under that subsection . . .'

The provisions of s. 19(4) and (5) are complex in themselves, but the first point to note is that they apply on the administrator ceasing to act as such. It would seem strange that the right of a supplier to be paid for goods supplied arises only at the close of the administration which may be long after the supply of the goods. There may be an implication that the administrator ought to run the administration in such a way as not to disturb the priorities set out in these subsections.

The Insolvency Rules 1986 refer to payments being made by the administrator in a number of places, for example:

'. . . the costs of the petitioner . . . are payable as an expense of the administration' (IR, r. 2.9(2));

'A deponent . . . shall be . . . paid by the administrator out of his receipts . . .' (IR, r. 2.15(1));

'. . . the administrator shall out of the assets of the company defray . . . travelling expenses . . . as an expense of the administration' (IR, r. 2.45(1)); and

'In any insolvency proceedings the cost of the responsible insolvency practitioner's security shall be defrayed as an expense of the proceedings' (IR, r. 12.8(3)).

The concept of the administration expense as covering payments made during the course of the administration, in the ordinary course of business, is attractive. The intention is perhaps that the administrator's proposals should cover the various expenses of his trading (see IR, r. 2.16(f) and note IA, s. 17(2)(a)). The concept of 'expense' echoes the position in liquidations. For example, the position in a voluntary winding-up is as follows (IA, s. 115):

¶1115

'All expenses properly incurred in the winding-up, including the remuneration of the liquidator, are payable out of the company's assets in priority to all other claims'.

This is a somewhat clearer statement than the provisions for administration. A liquidator has been held liable for rent accrued due after the date of liquidation (as a liquidation expense) where he retained possession of leasehold premises 'for the convenience of the winding-up' (*Re A.B.C. Coupler & Engineering Co. Ltd (No. 3)* [1970] 1 WLR 702, decided on the provisions of the Companies Acts prior (and similar) to IA, s. 115). It is theoretically possible for a liability in a liquidation to constitute neither a pre-liquidation provable debt nor an expense of the liquidation (see *Re Denton Sub-Divisions Pty Ltd (In Liquidation) and the Companies Act* (1968) 89 WN (Pt. 1) (NSW) 231, where it was held that a liability to the Crown became a form of deferred debt).

Where an administrator does not make payments as an expense of the administration to post-order creditors, this might be a case where the court would grant leave if the creditor sought to bring an action on, for example, a debt, or perhaps a landlord would be given leave to distrain (IA, s. 11(3)(*d*)). Where the administrator's proposals include provision for payment of such a sum and it is not paid this might persuade the court to give leave or it could require the administrator to make the payment on the creditor bringing an 'unfair prejudice' action. The administrator has a duty to manage the company in accordance with his proposals (IA, s. 17(2)(*b*)).

As a matter of practice, to preserve goodwill for example, or to ensure future supplies, an administrator may make the usual business payments. A massive product liability claim, perhaps not fully covered by insurance, might constitute a more difficult example.

The liability of an administrative receiver for rates has already been considered (see ¶508). The decision of the Court of Appeal in *Ratford* v *Northavon District Council* ((1986) 2 BCC 99, 242) is to the effect that the receivers in that case were not liable personally for rates on two grounds. First, although pursuant to the debenture under which they were appointed the receivers had *power* to take possession of the relevant premises, in fact they had not done so and in an ordinary receivership would seem unlikely to do so. An administrator has a specific duty, however, to take into his custody or under his control all the company's property (or property to which it appears to be entitled – IA, s. 17(1)) and it might be argued that this constitutes the taking of possession, rendering the *Ratford* case distinguishable. However, the second or additional ground for the decision in the *Ratford* case was that the receivers were agents for the company and that the 'quality of the receivers' possession' was merely as agent. The quality of an administrator's possession will (in the

¶1115

ordinary course) be merely as agent for the company (IA, s. 14(5)). It seems likely, therefore, that an administrator will not be held personally liable for rates. A failure by the administrator to make provision for, and pay, rates accruing during the administration might result in an application by the rating authority for leave to distrain on the company's goods (IA, s. 11(3)(d)) and the court might look sympathetically on such an application.

In Australian law there is a system not dissimilar to administrations called 'official management'. Under s.349(5) of the Australian Companies Act 1981 the application of funds by the official manager is stated to be:

'(a) first, in the payment of the costs of the official management, including the remuneration of the official manager . . .;
(b) second, in discharge of the liabilities of the company incurred in the course of the official management; and
(c) third, in discharge of any other liabilities of the company . . .'.

These provisions seem a model of simplicity and clarity.

With reference to the specific provisions of s. 19 of the Insolvency Act 1986 the following points might be noted:

(1)   The reference to 'remuneration and any expenses' in s. 19(4) seems in contradistinction to 'debts or liabilities incurred' in s. 19(5) and 'expenses' might be thought to mean, say, solicitors' and agents' fees and the miscellaneous expenses set out in the Rules, but not to bear the wide meaning it has had in the context of liquidation (as regards tax, see Chapter 13).

(2)   Section 19(5) creates a form of statutory charge. It is not clear whether it is intended to be directly enforceable by creditors. Section 19(4) grants a similar charge for the administrator's remuneration.

(3)   The benefit of the statutory charges seems to be limited to the value of the unencumbered assets of the company and to assets subject to a floating charge. This is a point for administrators and creditors to note.

(4)   The statutory charge in s. 19(5) ranks in priority to the charge under s. 19(4) (which supports the administrator's remuneration) and this will be of significance in the event that the assets are insufficient to meet all the liabilities.

(5)   The subordination of the holder of the floating charge to these statutory charges is a factor which will bear on any decision that the mortgagee has to make on whether or not to appoint an administrative receiver.

(6)   The wording of s. 19(5) does not appear to cover the case where the administrator takes delivery of goods pursuant to a contract entered

¶1115

into by the company prior to the administration. That is not a contract 'entered into' by the administrator nor is it a contract of employment 'adopted' by him.

The question of administration expenses with particular reference to tax in an administration is considered below (Chapter 13).

## ¶1116 Liability in tort

Although the administrator's agency for the company means that he is not personally liable in contract he is potentially liable, in the same way as an administrative receiver, for his tortious acts (see ¶507).

An administrator is within the definition of 'office-holder' for the purposes of the relief from liability in the case of a non-negligent wrongful seizure or disposal of goods (IA, s. 234(3) and (4) and see ¶414).

There may be a number of statutory regulations where as the responsible officer of a company, the administrator may be personally at risk in the event of breach (consider *Meigh* v *Wickenden* [1942] 2 KB 160).

## ¶1117 Suppliers of utilities

An administrator has the same right to demand supplies of gas, electricity, water and telecommunications as does an administrative receiver (see ¶414). The supplier may require a personal guarantee as a condition of supply (IA, s. 233).

## ¶1118 Existing contracts

What can and should an administrator do about subsisting contracts of the company which he thinks are not profitable (for example long-term contracts for the purchase of raw materials at prices which are (now) above current market levels)? The following are possible courses of action:

(1) He can seek to renegotiate the contracts to provide for a more realistic price.

(2) He can cause the company to fulfil the contract and the 'loss' will have to be built into his projections.

(3) He can refuse to allow the company to fulfil the contract, that is, he can repudiate it. The other party would then have a claim for damages (unless it was such an extreme case that the contract constituted a transaction at an undervalue – see ¶1016(2)). If the other party wished to pursue the damages claim, he would need the leave of the court (IA, s. 11(3)(*d*)). He would seem to be a creditor for the purposes of alleging unfair prejudice in the conduct of the administration (IA,

s. 27(1)). There is the further possibility that if, as a post-administration order creditor, he cannot be bound by any scheme in the administration or voluntary arrangement, he could simply await any composition of the company's other debts and sue the company (once it has been restored to solvency) with a better chance of having his entire claim settled. In these circumstances it might be preferable for a company to have such contracts repudiated prior to the making of the administration order, so that such creditors can be brought into, and bound by, any scheme.

## ¶1119   Employees

The liability to pay employees as an expense of the administration only arises in respect of contracts of employment 'adopted' by the administrator (IA, s. 19(5)). This adoption does not involve the administrator in personal liability. The problem of the true construction of the word 'adoption' is considered in connection with the parallel provision for administrative receivers (IA, s. 44(1)(b), and see ¶512). As with receivers, the administrator is not to be taken to have 'adopted' by reason of anything done within the first 14 days of his appointment (IA, s. 19(5)). It may be a prudent move to issue a letter to employees in the form considered by the court in the case of *Re Specialised Mouldings Ltd* (13 February 1987, unreported), although the significance of non-adoption by someone not open to personal liability is not clear.

## REALISATION OF ASSETS AND PROPERTY

## ¶1120   Considerations for administrators

The terms and conditions of sale used by administrators and their advisers will be similar to those utilised by administrative receivers and liquidators, that is, on an 'as is', 'where is' basis excluding, so far as possible, all warranties (see ¶513). It will be for a purchaser to satisfy himself on all relevant matters and to make such enquiries as he deems necessary.

Administrators, like other insolvency practitioners, may consider it prudent to seek advice from specialist valuers to ensure that any price they obtain is a proper market price (*American Express International Banking Corp* v *Hurley* (1986) 2 BCC 98, 993; [1985] 3 All ER 564, and see ¶1018).

## ¶1121   Conveyancing questions

Title to property will not be vested in the administrator, and the vendor in any sale will be the company.

It is submitted that the following wordings will suffice for execution of agreements and conveyances by administrators:

CONTRACT
SIGNED for and on behalf of X
LIMITED by AB Administrator as     }     [Usual signature of
its agent and without personal                  Administrator]
liability

................................................

DEED
THE COMMON SEAL of X
LIMITED was hereunto affixed in     }     L.S.
the presence of AB, its
Administrator:

[Usual signature of Administrator]

................................................
                    Administrator

## ¶1122   Power to deal with charged and third-party property

The administrator is free to deal with property which is subject to a floating charge (that is, a charge which, as created, was a floating charge) as if the property were not subject to the charge (IA, s. 15(1) and (3)). He does not need to go to court.

The rights of the chargee are preserved to an extent in that, on a disposal, the interest of the chargee (presumably under his original security) is automatically transferred to any property 'directly or indirectly representing' the property sold but with the same priority (that is, ranking after the administrator's rights) as he enjoyed in respect of the original property (IA, s. 15(4)). In short, the floating charge is forced to float (even if it has crystallised at an earlier stage).

The administrator also has the right, this time with the leave of the court, to dispose of property subject to a fixed charge or held by the company pursuant to a hire-purchase, conditional sale, chattel-leasing or retention of title agreement (IA, s. 15(2), (3) and (9)). The disposition may be with or without other assets (IA, s. 15(2)). The court will make the order if it is persuaded that the purposes of the administration order will be promoted. The mortgagee or the owner, as the case may be, will be given notice of the application and details of where and when the hearing is taking place (IR, r. 2.51). It would seem to be open to the party served to appear and argue (and note IA, s. 27(5)).

Where the court gives leave it must make it a condition of the order that the net proceeds of disposal are used to reduce the secured debt or the sum outstanding under the relevant agreement as the case may be (IA, s. 15(5)). Where the court is persuaded that if the relevant item had been sold on the open market by a willing vendor a higher price would have been obtained then the deficiency has to be made good (IA, s. 15(5)). The use of the passive means that it is not entirely clear who is to 'make good the deficiency' – presumably the administrator as an expense of the administration. The provisions are aimed at situations where the administrator is, say, obtaining a good global price for all the assets and business of the company but on a strict apportionment of price, each item is allocated slightly less than might have been paid for it if sold individually. In effect, there is a discount reflecting the advantage of being able to sell everything together. The administrator would therefore use some of the other proceeds of sale (presumably of free assets or assets caught by a floating charge) to make up the shortfall. It is important to an administrator to have detailed apportionments of any price obtained and proper valuations both of all the assets and business and also any item to which a third party has a claim under this head.

The margin note to s. 15 of the Insolvency Act 1986 reads 'Power to *deal with* charged property etc.' (emphasis added). In the case of property which is caught by a fixed charge or which is the subject of an agreement whereby title is vested in a third party, the only right is to 'dispose' (with the leave of the court). Further, the attachment of an original floating charge to the property directly or indirectly representing floating-charge assets only arises when there is a disposal (IA, s. 15(4)). In *Rhyl Urban District Council* v *Rhyl Amusements Ltd* ([1959] 1 WLR 465) Harman J had to consider the word 'dispose' as it was used in the Rhyl Improvement Act of 1893 and he held that it meant an absolute or out-and-out disposition (and hence did not include a letting), although he noted that in a different statutory context it had been held (in *Carter* v *Carter* [1896] 1 Ch. 62 at p. 67) 'to extend to all acts by which a new interest (legal or equitable) in the property is effectually created'. As the consent of the court is necessary to 'dispose' of fixed-charge and third-party items, the administrator may seek the guidance of the court on the use of the term in this statutory context.

¶1122

# 12 Remuneration and Termination

## REMUNERATION

### ¶1201 Pre-order

There are two distinct stages in the work of a person who is appointed administrator. First, there is the period from the moment he is approached and instructed by a company or its directors or its creditors until such time as an administration order may be made. Secondly, there is the period of the administration.

Where an administration order is made the petitioner's 'costs' are payable as an expense of the administration, as are the costs of any person appearing at the hearing whose costs the court chooses to allow (IR, r. 2.9(2)).

It is envisaged that a person proposed as an administrator may have a great deal of work to do in preparation for the presentation of a petition for an administration order and in assisting the company in ensuring the survival of its business in the pre-order hiatus period. It would seem prudent for an insolvency practitioner to seek payment in advance for work he and his firm are to do in connection with the petition, because otherwise he will simply be an unsecured creditor in the administration.

Payment of the administrator's remuneration should be made a part of the proposals to be put to creditors, and these should provide for periodic payments on account.

On the administrator vacating office any unpaid remuneration is charged on the assets of the company in priority to the claims of holders of floating charges (see ¶1115).

### ¶1202 Creditors' committee

The right to fix the basis and quantum of the administrator's remuneration is given principally to the creditors' committee in the administration and, if none has been formed, the creditors in general meeting (IR, r. 2.47(3) and (5)). In the absence of a determination by either of these bodies the administrator may apply to the court to fix the remuneration (IR, r. 2.47(6)).

The creditors' committee may settle the remuneration on one of two bases. Either it is on the basis of a percentage of the value of the property 'with which the administrator has to deal' or on a 'time-spent' basis (IR, r. 2.47(2)(b)). The creditors' committee decides what percentage is appropriate (IR, r. 2.47(3)) but in the latter case the practitioner will expect to charge the rates per hour spent which his firm normally charges when dealing with insolvencies.

The committee is required to take into account a number of factors in reaching their determination of remuneration. These are (IR, r. 2.47(4)):

(1)   the degree of complexity or simplicity of the case;

(2)   any exceptional responsibility which the administrator is requested to bear in conducting the administration;

(3)   the effectiveness of the administrator's performance in carrying out his duties; and

(4)   the value of the assets and property with which he has to deal, and their nature.

These factors are not unknown in the preparation of bills by professional people. The concept of an evaluation of the administrator's performance is novel and one which, in a few cases, may lead to difficulties.

## ¶1203   Applications to court

If the administrator is dissatisfied with the determination of the creditors' committee he may seek a resolution of the body of creditors to increase his remuneration (IR, r. 2.48).

If he is dissatisfied with either a determination of the committee or the creditors generally, the administrator may apply to the court for an increase (IR, r. 2.48). The following rules govern such an application (IR, r. 2.49):

(1)   at least 14 days' notice must be given to the members of the creditors' committee, if there is one. They may nominate one or more of their number to appear or be represented at the hearing of the application;

(2)   where there is no creditors' committee the court will direct which creditors should be given notice and they have a right to be heard or represented; and

(3)   the court has power to order that the costs of the application, including the costs of any committee member or creditor appearing, be paid as an administration expense in a 'proper case'. This latter phrase suggests that the payment of the administrator's costs will not be automatic: the question of who gets the costs may depend to an extent on how the court decides on the merits of the dispute between the administrator and the committee/creditors.

¶1203

There is a general right of complaint available to creditors where they consider that the determined remuneration of the administrator is excessive (IR, r. 2.50). A creditor might wish to object, for example, where he disagrees with a decision of the creditors' committee or the general body of creditors. The following provisions govern this right to object (IR, r. 2.50):

(1)  the creditor must himself, or together with others of like mind who will join in the application, constitute 25 per cent in value of the company's creditors;

(2)  the court may dismiss the application if it considers that 'no sufficient cause' has been shown for a reduction but before this can be done the applicant must have been afforded the opportunity of an *ex parte* hearing of which he has had at least seven days' notice;

(3)  where the court does not summarily dismiss the application in this manner, a time, date and place is to be set for a hearing, and notice is to be given to the applicant;

(4)  the applicant must give at least 14 days' notice of the hearing to the administrator together with a copy of the application and any evidence to be adduced by the applicant in support;

(5)  the court is to order that the remuneration be reduced if it considers the application 'well-founded'; and

(6)  the normal rule is that the applicant will have to bear the costs of the application unless the court makes an order that he be paid as an expense of the administration.

# TERMINATION

## ¶1204  Discharge of administration order

There are a number of ways of which an administrator may vacate office.

The administrator has the right at any time to apply to the court for the administration order to be discharged (or to be varied or to have an additional purpose specified – IA, s. 18(1)).

The administrator has a duty to make such an application in two circumstances (IA, s. 18(2)):

(1)  where the purpose or all of the purposes for which he has been appointed either have been achieved or are in his opinion incapable of achievement; or

¶1204

(2)   if a meeting of the company's creditors called for the purpose under the rules requires him so to do.

On hearing the administrator's application the court has the wide discretion seen elsewhere in the legislation. It can 'discharge or vary the administration order, make such consequential provision as it thinks fit, or adjourn the hearing conditionally or unconditionally, or make an interim order or any other order it thinks fit' (IA, s. 18(3)). An interesting question arises as to whether the court may simply make an order placing the company in compulsory liquidation. Section 122 of the Insolvency Act 1986 provides what appears to be an exhaustive list of the circumstances in which a company may be wound up by the court. These include:

'. . .

(*f*)  the company is unable to pay its debts;
(*g*)  the court is of the opinion that it is just and equitable that the company should be wound up.'

It might not be too dificult in many cases for the court to hang a decision to make a winding-up order on one of those two pegs. The compulsory winding-up scheme, however, presupposes that a petition has been presented for a winding-up order. For example, consider s. 124 of the Act:

'(1) . . . an application to the court for the winding-up of a company shall be by petition presented . . .'

and s. 129:

'(2) . . . the winding-up of a company by the court is deemed to commence at the time of the presentation of the petition for winding-up.'

Various other sections of the Act envisage a winding-up order being made immediately on discharge of an administration order. Consider s. 140:

(1) 'When a winding-up order is made immediately upon the discharge of an administration order, the court may appoint as liquidator of the company the person who has ceased on the discharge of the administration order to be the administrator of the company.'

and also s. 240(3):

'(*a*) . . . by reason of a company going into liquidation immediately upon the discharge of an administration order . . .'

A petition for the winding-up of a company cannot rest on the file during an administration as any petitions on the file are dismissed on the making of the order (IA, s. 11(1)(*a*)) and there is a bar on further proceedings being brought against the company without the leave of the court (IA, s. 11(3)(*d*)).

¶1204

It is submitted that the intention of the legislature is sufficiently clear to enable the court to decide that it may make a winding-up order on discharging an administration order without needing a petition as such. The winding-up commences as from the order (as IA, s. 129(2) only *deems* commencement as at the date of the petition and by implication this is not so where there is no petition – see IA, s. 247(2)). Until this point is settled, the prudent course for someone seeking a winding-up order is to obtain the court's leave to present a petition for winding-up returnable on the date set to hear the administrator's application for discharge (see, further, ¶1302).

Any discharge or variation must be reported by the administrator to the Registrar of Companies by means of an office copy of the order within 14 days on pain of a fine (IA, s. 18(4) and (5) and Form 2.19).

## ¶1205   Vacation of office

The court may, by order, remove an administrator from office at any time (IA, s. 19(1)). This power of the court appears unfettered but it is likely that the court will only exercise this power where there is a good reason for so doing. The comparable provision in the case of liquidation is found in s. 108(2) of the Insolvency Act 1986:

'(2) The court may, *on cause shown*, remove a liquidator and appoint another' (emphasis supplied).

The administrator is under a duty to vacate office where:

(1)   the administration is terminated by the discharge of the administration order (IA, s. 19(2)(*b*)); or

(2)   the administrator ceases to be qualified to act as an insolvency practitioner in relation to the company (IA, s. 19(2)(*a*)).

## ¶1206   Resignation

An administration may, in certain circumstances, resign (IA, s. 19(1), IR, r. 2.53 and Form 2.16). He has the right to resign on any of the following grounds:

(1)   for reasons of health;

(2)   he intends to stop practising as an insolvency practitioner; and

(3)   because of a conflict of interest or a change in his personal circumstances that 'precludes or makes impracticable the further discharge by him of the duties of administrator'.

With the leave of the court the administrator may resign for any other reason (IR, r. 2.53(2) and Form 2.17).

The administrator is required to give at least seven days' notice of his intention to resign, or to apply to the court for leave to do so, to the following (IR, r. 2.53(3)):

(1) any joint administrator;

(2) where there is no joint appointee, to the creditors' committee; and

(3) where there is neither a joint appointee nor a creditors' committee, to the creditors generally and the company itself.

The responsible administrator will in any event give as much notice as is reasonably practicable of his intention to resign to ensure a smooth transfer of control.

## ¶1207　Death

The Insolvency Rules 1986 impose certain duties to report the death of an administrator in office. The primary duty falls on the personal representatives of the deceased who must give notice to the court indicating the date of death (IR, r. 2.54(1)). Notice can be by production of the original death certificate or a copy (IR, r. 2.54(3)).

The personal representatives are relieved of their duty to give notice where the deceased is a partner in a firm and notice is duly given by another partner who is either licensed to act as an insolvency practitioner or is a member of a recognised body (IR, r. 2.54(2)). Notice being given by one of a practitioner's partners will be the most common form of notice given.

## ¶1208　General considerations on termination

The aim of the administrator on any termination of his office will be for as smooth a transfer as possible to either the continuing and/or new administrators, a liquidator or the directors of the company, depending on the outcome of the administration.

Where survival of the company's business has been incapable of achievement or where the administrator's proposals have been rejected by the creditors or where a realisation of the assets has been achieved, it will normally be appropriate for the company to be placed in liquidation on discharge of the administration order. To preserve the liquidator's rights to attack transactions occurring prior to the presentation of the petition for an administrator it will be advisable for the creditors to seek to have a winding-up order made on discharge of the administration order (see IA, s. 240(3)(*a*)).

An insolvency practitioner who acts as an administrator in relation to a company may also act as its liquidator (IA, s. 140(1)). This is subject to any rules about conflict of interest that have been laid down by his professional body.

## ¶1209 Expenses and floating charges

This subject is discussed at ¶1115.

It is worth noting that where the company is placed in liquidation on termination of an administration, the order of payment of expenses etc out of assets subject to a floating charge would seem to be:

(1) debts and liabilities as described in IA, s. 19(5);

(2) remuneration and expenses of the administrator as described in IA, s. 19(4);

(3) expenses of the liquidation (IA, s. 115);

(4) preferential creditors in the liquidation pursuant to IA, s. 175;

(5) existing floating chargees; and

(6) unsecured creditors.

By s. 175, the preferential creditors only have priority over mortgages secured by a floating charge (as created).

## ¶1210 Accounts

An administrator is required to file accounts of his receipts and payments from time to time in abstracted form (IR, r. 2.52 and Form 2.15). The relevant time limits for filing are within two months (unless that time is extended by the court) of (1) the end of the first six months of the administration, (2) every subsequent six months, and (3) his ceasing to act as administrator (IR, r. 2.52(1)). The accounts are to be sent to the court, the Registrar of Companies, and each member of the creditors' committee. The period covered will be the relevant six-month period from the end of the last such period to the date of the administrator ceasing to act, or, where there have been no previous accounts filed, covering the period from appointment to the date of ceasing to act (IR, r. 2.52(3)). Note the requirement for an administrator to give progress reports and a vacation report to creditors under r. 2.30.

## ¶1211 Release

There is provision for an administrator, like a liquidator, to be released or discharged from liability for his acts and omissions in the administration and his conduct as administrator (IA, s. 20(2), and see also ss. 173–4).

Where an administrator dies in office, the release takes effect when notice of the death is given in accordance with the Rules (IA, s. 20(1)(*a*), and see ¶1207). Otherwise, the court decides when the release shall take effect and presumably will not give the release until satisfied as to the conduct of the administration (IA, s. 20(1)(*b*)).

There are two points to note:

(1)  The release will operate to prevent a summary misfeasance action under s. 212 of the Insolvency Act 1986, save where the court gives leave to bring an action (IA, ss. 20(3) and 212(4)).

(2)  It would still seem possible, notwithstanding release, for the Official Receiver to ask the court for a public examination of an administrator under s. 133 of the Act.

# 13  Tax

As with the corresponding chapter for administrative receivers, no attempt is made in this chapter to deal with general points of tax law: for a discussion of the principles involved reference should be made to the standard text books on the subject.

## BEFORE THE ORDER

### ¶1301  Corporation tax

Corporation tax for accounting periods ending before the making of the administration order will be a debt of the company, and will be an actual or a contingent debt depending on whether the due date for payment of the tax has passed at the time the order is made (Taxes Act 1970, ss. 243(3) and 244).

The Inland Revenue may therefore be 'creditors' and able, should occasion arise, to make an application under s. 27 of the Insolvency Act 1986 for an order that the administration is being conducted in a manner which is in some way prejudicial to their interests (see ¶1109).

Corporation tax for companies is assessed and charged by reference to accounting periods, and the times at which accounting periods for companies begin and end are governed by s. 247 of the Taxes Act 1970. An accounting period begins when a company comes within the charge to corporation tax for the first time or when a previous accounting period of the company ends without the company creasing to be within the charge to corporation tax. Section 247(3) sets out the circumstances in which an accounting period ends and provides:

'An accounting period of a company shall end for purposes of corporation tax on the first occurrence of any of the following:

(*a*) the expiration of twelve months from the beginning of the accounting period;

(*b*) an accounting date of the company or, if there is a period for which the company does not make up accounts, the end of that period;

(c) the company beginning or ceasing to carry on any trade, or to be, in respect of a trade, within the charge to corporation tax;

(d) the company beginning or ceasing to be resident in the United Kingdom;

(e) the company ceasing to be within the charge to corporation tax.'

Additionally, s. 247(7) makes it clear that when a company begins to be wound up, an accounting period ends and a new one begins, and that an accounting period always ends on the finalisation of a winding-up.

If corporation tax is likely to be treated as an expense of the administration (see ¶1304), the question of whether or not the administration order does cause an accounting period to end may assume crucial significance. That is because transactions undertaken during an accounting period may or may not result in a tax liability. Whether they do or not will not be known until the accounting period has ended and an account has been drawn up. This was expressly recognised by the Court of Appeal in *Re Mesco Properties Limited* (54 TC 238), a case deciding that corporation tax on chargeable gains was a necessary disbursement of the liquidator in a winding-up. In that case Buckley LJ said (at p. 245):

'Brightman J expressed the opinion that corporation tax on a capital gain, made when a liquidator sells an asset, is not an "expense incurred in realizing that asset". I agree with this. The liability to tax is a consequence of, amongst other things, the realization, but it is not a direct consequence of the realization. It depends upon the amount of the company's "profits" as defined in section 238 of the Income and Corporation Taxes Act 1970 (if any) for the entire relevant accounting period. It is, as the learned Judge said, merely a possible consequence of a sale at a profit.'

For most companies whose affairs are made subject to an administration order, corporation tax will not be a problem. In the ordinary course of events they will have sustained trading losses of sufficient magnitude to eliminate any corporation tax, so that whether the making of an administration order causes an accounting period to end will be of little practical significance. There may equally, however, be cases (for example where capital assets have been disposed of) when it will be extremely significant. If an administration order was made early in a company's 'normal' accounting period and during that period, but just before the administration order, the company (in an attempt to stave off insolvency) disposed of a capital asset making a large capital profit, trading losses in that accounting period might not be sufficient to eliminate that capital profit. At the time of the appointment corporation tax on the chargeable gain will still be '. . . merely a possible consequence . . .' but the likelihood of a large tax bill may be one of the risks that the administrator runs. Fortunately s. 247 of the Taxes Act 1970 contains the remedy. It seems that in an appropriate case it would be prudent for the administrator to change the accounting date of the company and make up accounts to the date of his appointment.

It seems desirable that an administrator should retain some flexibility in choosing whether or not to cause an accounting period of the company to end. The reason for saying that is to be found in the rules governing the use to which trading losses sustained by a company may be put. Briefly, trading losses of an accounting period may be set against profits of whatever description of that period or, provided the company was then carrying on the trade, of preceding accounting periods ending within a time equal in length to the accounting period in which the loss is incurred. Prematurely ending an accounting period, therefore, may limit the amount of loss that may be carried back to an earlier accounting period and also may limit the amount of losses available to reduce capital gains made by the administrator.

## ¶1302 Preferential debts in an administration

The Act contains no obligation for an administrator to pay or satisfy preferential debts (see ¶802). There are two ways in which preferential debts may have relevance in an administration: first, where the purpose of the order is the sanctioning of a voluntary arrangement and, secondly, where the administration is immediately followed by a compulsory winding-up.

Where the purpose for which the administration order was made is the approval of a voluntary arrangement under Pt. 1 of the Act (see IA s. 8(3)(*b*)), no voluntary arrangement can take effect if it means that a preferential creditor is to lose his priority or be paid proportionately less for his preferential debt than other preferential creditors (unless the creditor consents) (see IA, s. 4(4)).

Creditors who have debts that would have been preferential debts if the date on which the administration order was made had instead marked the start of a receivership or liquidation may need to take careful note of any proposals to bring an administration to an end. That is because the manner in which it is terminated may materially affect their right to preference. The 'relevant date' which determines both existence and extent of preference will only be the date of the administration order where discharge of the administration order is followed 'immediately' by a winding-up by the court (IA, s. 387(3)). In any other case some other date is taken which will usually be later than the date of the administration order. If there is doubt about whether preferential debts will be paid, therefore, such a creditor will normally try to ensure that a compulsory winding-up follows immediately upon administration.

## ¶1303   Value added tax accruing

As has already been noticed in the section dealing with administrative receivers (¶803) the making of an administration order causes the company's then current VAT accounting period to come to an end (see Value Added Tax (General) Regulations 1985, reg. 58(3)). All accruing VAT liabilities will therefore crystallise.

## AFTER THE ORDER

## ¶1304   Corporation tax as an administration expense

To ask whether an administrator has any liability to pay tax incurred by a company during the course of an administration is really to ask the wrong question. Administrators are not personally liable for tax in the absence of some specific charging provision in the Taxes Acts. The company in administration remains the person liable. A more relevant question is the extent to which the courts will enforce against a company in administration a tax liability incurred during that administration.

Companies subject to an administration order lead a charmed existence, protected by a statute from some of the harsher realities of life (see, for example, ¶908). It is unlikely, however, that the courts will permit an administrator to conduct the affairs of a company in blithe disregard of all obligations incurred during the administration. The court exercises a threefold control over the administrator. First, as already noted, it may give leave for proceedings to be brought against the company, secondly, it will exercise a general control over the way in which the administrator carries out his duties and, thirdly, it may grant relief against the company in administration at the suit of any creditor claiming to be unfairly prejudiced by the way in which the company is being administered.

How the courts should exercise this threefold control is a question left unanswered by the Insolvency Act 1986. The only section dealing with the expenses and liabilities of administrators is s. 19 which deals with what happens when a person ceases to be an administrator. Whether the section gives any guidance on how the courts will approach the question of administration expenses has been discussed (¶1115).

It is quite possible that the section was intended more as a protection for an outgoing administrator than as a guide to what the expenses and liabilities of the administration are and how they are to be discharged. It was probably inserted to protect the claim that an administrator may have to an indemnity for any liability he has incurred personally on contracts, together with his own claim to be reimbursed for remuneration and out-of-pocket expenses.

The court is unlikely to be prepared to see persons who have voluntarily dealt with a company in administration go unpaid. Thus, the supplier of goods and services can make his supplies in the knowledge that although he might not have an action against the administrator personally (because the administrator is acting as agent for a disclosed principal) he would nevertheless be granted leave to sue if the administrator in the exercise of his powers chooses to cause the company to withhold payment. If that is so, it seems even more likely that the court will wish to aid involuntary creditors of the administration, since by definition they had no choice but to deal with the company (see the comments of Vinelott J in *Re Stanford Services Ltd and Others* (1987) 3 BCC 326).

The way in which a similar question was approached by Buckley LJ in *Re Mesco Properties Limited* ((1979) 54 TC 238) may be instructive. In that case he was dealing with a company in liquidation which faced a bill for corporation tax on chargeable gains exceeding the amount of the available assets once the secured creditors had been satisfied. The question to be decided was whether corporation tax was a necessary disbursement of the liquidator within the meaning of r. 195(1) of the Companies (Winding-Up) Rules 1949. Buckley LJ said:

'The company is liable for the tax which is due. The tax ought to be paid. The liquidator is the proper officer to pay it. When he pays it he will clearly make a disbursement. In my judgment it will be a necessary disbursement within the meaning of the rule. Moreover, commonsense and justice seem to me to require that it should be discharged in full in priority to the unsecured creditors, and to any expenses which rank lower in priority under rule 195. The tax is a consequence of the realization of the assets in the course of the winding-up of the company. That realization was a necessary step in the liquidation; that is to say, in the administration of the insolvent estate. The fact that in the event there may be nothing available for the unsecured creditors does not, in my view, mean that the realization was not a step taken in the interests of all who have claims against the Company. Those claims must necessarily be met out of the available assets in due order of priority. Superior claims may baulk inferior ones, but the liquidator's duty is to realize the assets for the benefit of all in accordance with their rights. If in consequence of the realization, the Company incurs a liability, the discharge of such liability must, in my judgment, constitute a charge or expense incurred in the winding-up within the Companies Act 1948, section 267, and must also, in my view, fall within rule 195.'

¶1304

Another liquidation case which might have a bearing on this point is *Re Beni-Felkai Mining Co.* ([1934] 1 Ch. 406) where Maugham J held that income tax had to be paid as an expense of a liquidation. He commented (at p. 418 and 422):

'I have a difficulty in seeing how a liquidator who, in the course of his liquidation carries on the business of the company at a profit, the consequence being the assessment of the company to income tax, can avoid the conclusion that this is one of the expenses in the winding-up . . . In my opinion rates and taxes – and for this purpose I can group them together, although there is for some purposes a distinction between them – falling due subsequently to the winding-up are part of the expenses of the winding-up . . . It seems to me, in the normal case, expenses which he has incurred, whether by the employment of agents or, for example, in respect of gas and electric light or for rents, or any other of the numerous expenses which he may incur in the winding-up of a company, are things which he is bound to provide out of the assets of the company as far as he is enabled to recover them. If his position is that, having provided for them, there will be no remuneration left for him, then he is entitled to say: "I cannot go on unless the creditors or shareholders or others will put up a fund for my benefit." He is the person who can see what the position is . . .'

The alternative argument to this is that administration is not like liquidation, but is more like receivership in that there is no procedure subsequent to liquidation and, if tax were not paid as an expense of liquidation, it would be quite significantly deferred in the order of priorities. It could be argued that administration is like receivership in that there is still liquidation – and hence the proper treatment of unsecured claims according to law – to come. This practical approach which would certainly assist and simplify administrations and may find favour with the courts.

The tentative conclusion to be reached in the absence of decisive authority is that there is a danger of which administrators (and those considering accepting appointments as administrators) should be aware, that a court would hold that the expenses of an administration such as a liability to tax ought to be paid out of the company's assets in priority to the claims of those creditors who were unsecured at the time the administration commenced.

## ¶1305   Value added tax

The provisions dealing with the liability of an administrator to account for VAT are, it is submitted, virtually identical to those for a receiver: reference should be made to the section dealing with VAT and receivers (¶804, 806 and ¶807).

¶1305

## ¶1306   Hive-downs

The consequences of a hive-down are dealt with above (¶808). The only point of distinction between a receiver's or an administrator's hive-down concerns corporation tax on chargeable gains. If, as suggested above (¶1304) corporation tax will be treated as an administration expense, there may be some point in hiving-down capital assets. Although tax will be triggered on a disposal of shares in the relevant subsidiary (Taxes Act 1970, s. 278) the tax will be chargeable by reference to the value of the asset at the date of hive-down, and not necessarily by reference to the price paid by a subsequent purchaser (although the price or agreed price would be a strong indication of prior value).

## ¶1307   Revenue powers

The provisions dealing with Revenue powers are dealt with above (see ¶809 and ¶810) in the case of an administrative receiver. Administration will fetter both the Inland Revenue and Customs & Excise. The reason is that from the time a petition for an administration order is presented until an administration order (if made) is discharged '. . . no distress may be levied against the company or its property' unless either the court grants leave or the administrator (once appointed) consents (IA, ss. 10(1)(*c*) and 11(3)(*d*)).

# Appendix 1

## Transitional Provisions

The transitional provisions governing the new insolvency legislation are set out in Sch. 11 to the Insolvency Act 1986 which, so far as relevant, is reproduced below:

### PART I

### COMPANY INSOLVENCY AND WINDING-UP

#### Administration orders

**1.** (1) Where any right to appoint an administrative receiver of a company is conferred by any debentures or floating charge created before the appointed day, the conditions precedent to the exercise of that right are deemed to include the presentation of a petition applying for an administration order to be made in relation to the company.
(2) 'Administrative receiver' here has the meaning assigned by section 251.

#### Receivers and managers (England and Wales)

**2.** (1) In relation to any receiver or manager of a company's property who was appointed before the appointed day, the new law does not apply; and the relevant provisions of the former law continue to have effect.
(2) 'The new law' here means Chapter I of Part III, and Part VI, of this Act; and 'the former law' means the Companies Act and so much of this Act as replaces provisions of that Act (without the amendments in paragraphs 15 to 17 of Schedule 6 to the Insolvency Act 1985, or the associated repeals made by that Act), and any provision of the Insolvency Act 1985 which was in force before the appointed day.
(3) This paragraph is without prejudice to the power conferred by this Act under which rules under section 411 may make transitional provision in connection with the coming into force of those rules; and such provision may apply those rules in relation to the receiver or manager of a company's property notwithstanding that he was appointed before the coming into force of the rules or section 411. . . .

#### Winding up already in progress

**4.** (1) In relation to any winding up which has commenced, or is treated as having commenced, before the appointed day, the new law does not apply, and the former law continues to have effect, subject to the following paragraphs.
(2) 'The new law' here means any provisions in the first Group of Parts of this Act which replace sections 66 to 87 and 89 to 105 of the Insolvency Act 1985; and 'the

former law' means Parts XX and XXI of the Companies Act without the amendments in paragraphs 23 to 52 of Schedule 6 to the Insolvency Act 1985, or the associated repeals made by that Act).

### Statement of affairs

**5.** (1) Where a winding-up by the court in England and Wales has commenced, or is treated as having commenced, before the appointed day, the official receiver or (on appeal from a refusal by him) the court may, at any time on or after that day:

(a) release a person from an obligation imposed on him by or under section 528 of the Companies Act (statement of affairs), or

(b) extend the period specified in subsection (6) of that section.

(2) Accordingly, on and after the appointed day, section 528(6) has effect in relation to a winding-up to which this paragraph applies with the omission of the words from 'or within' onwards.

### Provisions relating to liquidator

**6.** (1) This paragraph applies as regards the liquidator in the case of a winding-up by the court in England and Wales commenced, or treated as having commenced, before the appointed day.

(2) The official receiver may, at any time when he is liquidator of the company, apply to the Secretary of State for the appointment of a liquidator in his (the official receiver's) place; and on any such application the Secretary of State shall either make an appointment or decline to make one.

(3) Where immediately before the appointed day the liquidator of the company has not made an application under section 545 of the Companies Act (release of liquidators), then:

(a) except where the Secretary of State, otherwise directs, sections 146(1) and (2) and 172(8) of this Act apply, and section 545 does not apply, in relation to any liquidator of that company who holds office on or at any time after the appointed day and is not the official receiver;

(b) section 146(3) applies in relation to the carrying out at any time after that day by any liquidator of the company of any of his functions; and

(c) a liquidator in relation to whom section 172(8) has effect by virtue of this paragraph has his release with effect from the time specified in section 174(4)(d) of this Act.

(4) Subsection (6) of section 174 of this Act has effect for the purposes of sub-paragraph (3)(c) above as it has for the purposes of that section, but as if the reference to section 212 were to section 631 of the Companies Act.

(5) The liquidator may employ a solicitor to assist him in the carrying out of his functions without the permission of the committee of inspection; but if he does so employ a solicitor he shall inform the committee of inspection that he has done so.

### Winding-up under supervision of the court

**7.** The repeals in Part II of Schedule 10 to the Insolvency Act 1985 of references (in the Companies Act and elsewhere) to a winding-up under the supervision of the court do not affect the operation of the enactments in which the references are contained in relation to any case in which an order under section 606 of the Companies Act (power to order winding-up under supervision) was made before the appointed day.

## Saving for power to make rules

**8.** (1) Paragraphs 4 to 7 are without prejudice to the power conferred by this Act under which rules made under section 411 may make transitional provision in connection with the coming into force of those rules.

(2) Such provision may apply those rules in relation to a winding-up notwithstanding that the winding-up commenced, or is treated as having commenced, before the coming into force of the rules or section 411.

## Setting aside of preferences and other transactions

**9.** (1) Where a provision in Part VI of this Act applies in relation to a winding-up or in relation to a case in which an administration order has been made, a preference given, floating charge created or other transaction entered into before the appointed day shall not be set aside under that provision except to the extent that it could have been set aside under the law in force immediately before that day, assuming for this purpose that any relevant administration order had been a winding-up order.

(2) The references above to setting aside a preference, floating charge or other transaction include the making of an order which varies or reverses any effect on a preference, floating charge or other transaction.

## PART III

## TRANSITIONAL EFFECT OF PART XVI

**20.** (1) A transaction entered into before the appointed day shall not be set aside under Part XVI of this Act except to the extent that it could have been set aside under the law in force immediately before that day.

(2) References above to setting aside a transaction include the making of an order which varies or reverses any effect of a transaction.

## PART IV

## INSOLVENCY PRACTITIONERS

**21.** Where an individual began to act as an insolvency practitioner in relation to any person before the appointed day, nothing in section 390(2) or (3) prevents that individual from being qualified to act as an insolvency practitioner in relation to that person.

## PART V

## GENERAL TRANSITIONAL PROVISIONS AND SAVINGS

### Interpretation for this Part

**22.** In this Part of this Schedule, 'the former enactments' means so much of the Companies Act as is repealed and replaced by this Act, the Insolvency Act 1985 and the other enactments repealed by this Act.

### General saving for past acts and events

**23.** So far as anything done or treated as done under or for the purposes of any provision of the former enactments could have been done under or for the purposes of the corresponding provision of this Act, it is not invalidated by the repeal of that provision but has effect as if done under or for the purposes of the corresponding provision; and any order, regulation, rule or other instrument made or having effect under any provision of the former enactments shall, insofar as its effect is preserved by this paragraph, be treated for all purposes as made and having effect under the corresponding provision.

### Periods of time

**24.** Where any period of time specified in a provision of the former enactments is current immediately before the appointed day, this Act has effect as if the corresponding provision had been in force when the period began to run; and (without prejudice to the foregoing) any period of time so specified and current is deemed for the purposes of this Act:

(*a*) to run from the date or event from which it was running immediately before the appointed day, and

(*b*) to expire (subject to any provision of this Act for its extension) whenever it would have expired if this Act had not been passed;

and any rights, priorities, liabilities, reliefs, obligations, requirements, powers, duties or exemptions dependent on the beginning, duration or end of such a period as above mentioned shall be under this Act as they were or would have been under the former enactments.

### Internal cross-references in this Act

**25.** Where in any provision of this Act there is a reference to another such provision, and the first-mentioned provision operates, or is capable of operating, in relation to things done or omitted, or events occurring or not occurring, in the past (including in particular past acts of compliance with any enactment, failures of compliance, contraventions, offences and convictions of offences), the reference to the other provision is to be read as including a reference to the corresponding provision of the former enactments.

### Punishment of offences

**26.** (1) Offences committed before the appointed day under any provision of the former enactments may, notwithstanding any repeal by this Act, be prosecuted and punished after that day as if this Act had not passed.

(2) A contravention of any provision of the former enactments committed before the appointed day shall not be visited with any severer punishment under or by virtue of this Act than would have been applicable under that provision at the time of the contravention; but where an offence for the continuance of which a penalty was provided has been committed under any provision of the former enactments, proceedings may be taken under this Act in respect of the continuance of the offence on and after the appointed day in the like manner as if the offence had been committed under the corresponding provision of this Act.

### *References elsewhere to the former enactments*

**27.** (1) A reference in any enactment, instrument or document (whether express or implied, and in whatever phraseology) to a provision of the former enactments (including the corresponding provision of any yet earlier enactment) is to be read, where necessary to retain for the enactment, instrument or document the same force and effect as it would have had but for the passing of this Act, as, or as including, a reference to the corresponding provision by which it is replaced in this Act.

(2) The generality of the preceding sub-paragraph is not affected by any specific conversion of references made by this Act, nor by the inclusion in any provision of this Act of a reference (whether express or implied, and in whatever phraseology) to the provision of the former enactments corresponding to that provision, or to a provision of the former enactments which is replaced by a corresponding provision of this Act.

### *Saving for power to repeal provisions in section 51*

**28.** The Secretary of State may by order in a statutory instrument repeal subsections (3) to (5) of section 51 of this Act and the entries in Schedule 10 relating to subsections (4) and (5) of that section.

### *Saving for Interpretation Act 1978, ss. 16, 17*

**29.** Nothing in this Schedule is to be taken as prejudicing sections 16 and 17 of the Interpretation Act 1978 (savings from, and effect of, repeals); and for the purposes of section 17(2) of that Act (construction of references to enactments repealed and replaced, etc.), so much of section 18 of the Insolvency Act 1985 as is replaced by a provision of this Act is deemed to have been repealed by this Act and not by the Company Directors Disqualification Act 1986.

# Appendix 2

## Insolvency Act 1986

### Section 72

(1) A receiver appointed under the law of either part of Great Britain in respect of the whole or any part of any property or undertaking of a company and in consequence of the company having created a charge which, as created, was a floating charge may exercise his powers in the other part of Great Britain so far as their exercise is not inconsistent with the law applicable there.

(2) In subsection (1) 'receiver' includes a manager and a person who is appointed both receiver and manager.

### Section 426

(1) An order made by a court in any part of the United Kingdom in the exercise of jurisdiction in relation to insolvency law shall be enforced in any other part of the United Kingdom as if it were made by a court exercising the corresponding jurisdiction in that other part.

(2) However, without prejudice to the following provisions of this section, nothing in subsection (1) requires a court in any part of the United Kingdom to enforce, in relation to property situated in that part, any order made by a court in any other part of the United Kingdom.

(3) The Secretary of State, with the concurrence in relation to property situated in England and Wales of the Lord Chancellor, may by order make provision for securing that a trustee or assignee under the insolvency law of any part of the United Kingdom has, with such modifications as may be specified in the order, the same rights in relation to any property situated in another part of the United Kingdom as he would have in the corresponding circumstances if he were a trustee or assignee under the insolvency law of that other part.

(4) The courts having jurisdiction in relation to insolvency law in any part of the United Kingdom shall assist the courts having the corresponding jurisdiction in any other part of the United Kingdom or any relevant country or territory.

(5) For the purposes of subsection (4) a request made to a court in any part of the United Kingdom by a court in any other part of the United Kingdom or in a relevant country or territory is authority for the court to which the request is made to apply, in relation to any matters specified in the request, the insolvency law which is applicable by either court in relation to comparable matters falling within its jurisdiction.

In exercising its discretion under this subsection, a court shall have regard in particular to the rules of private international law.

(6) Where a person who is a trustee or assignee under the insolvency law of any part of the United Kingdom claims property situated in any other part of the United Kingdom (whether by virtue of any order under subsection (3) or otherwise), the submission of that claim to the court exercising jurisdiction in relation to insolvency

law in that other part shall be treated in the same manner as a request made by a court for the purpose of subsection (4).

(7) Section 38 of the Criminal Law Act 1977 (execution of warrant of arrest throughout the United Kingdom) applies to a warrant which, in exercise of any jurisdiction in relation to insolvency law, is issued in any part of the United Kingdom for the arrest of a person as it applies to a warrant issued in that part of the United Kingdom for the arrest of a person charged with an offence.

(8) Without prejudice to any power to make rules of court, any power to make provision by subordinate legislation for the purpose of giving effect in relation to companies or individuals to the insolvency law of any part of the United Kingdom includes power to make provision for the purpose of giving effect in that part to any part provision made by or under the preceding provisions of this section.

(9) An order under subsection (3) shall be made by statutory instrument subject to annulment in pursuance of a resolution of either House of Parliament.

(10) In this section 'insolvency law' means:

(*a*) in relation to England and Wales, provision made by or under this Act or sections 6 to 10, 12, 15, 19(c) and 20 (with Schedule 1) of the Company Directors Disqualification Act 1986 and extending to England and Wales;

(*b*) in relation to Scotland, provision extending to Scotland and made by or under this Act, sections 6 to 10, 12, 15, 19(*c*) and 20 (with Schedule 1) of the Company Directors Disqualification Act 1986, Part XVIII of the Companies Act or the Bankruptcy (Scotland) Act 1985;

(*c*) in relation to Northern Ireland, provision made by or under the Bankruptcy Acts (Northern Ireland) 1857 to 1980, Part V, VI or IX of the Companies Act (Northern Ireland) 1960 or Part IV of the Companies (Northern Ireland) Order 1978;

(*d*) in relation to any relevant country or. territory, so much of the law of that country or territory as corresponds to provisions falling within any of the foregoing paragraphs;

and references in this subsection to any enactment include, in relation to any time before the coming into force of that enactment the corresponding enactment in force at that time.

(11) In this section 'relevant country or territory' means:

(*a*) any of the Channel Islands or the Isle of Man, or

(*b*) any country or territory designated for the purposes of this section by the Secretary of State by order made by statutory instrument.

# Appendix 3

## Connected Persons

Section 249 of the Insolvency Act 1986 sets out the test of whether a person is 'connected' with a company:

### Section 249

For the purposes of any provision in this Group of Parts a person is connected with a company if –

  (*a*) he is a director or shadow director of the company or an associate of such a director or shadow director, or

  (*b*) he is an associate of the company;

and 'associate' has the meaning given by section 435 in Part XVIII of this Act.

By s. 251 of the Act:

'"shadow director", in relation to a company, means a person in accordance with whose direction or instructions the directors of the company are accustomed to act (but so that a person is not deemed a shadow director by reason only that the directors act on advice given by him in a professional capacity). . . .'

Section 435 of the Act covers the meaning of 'associate':

### Section 435

(1) For the purposes of this Act any question whether a person is an associate of another person is to be determined in accordance with the following provisions of this section (any provision that a person is an associate of another person being taken to mean that they are associates of each other).

(2) A person is an associate of an individual if that person is the individual's husband or wife, or is a relative, or the husband or wife of a relative, of the individual or of the individual's husband or wife.

(3) A person is an associate of any person with whom he is in partnership, and of the husband or wife or a relative of any individual with whom he is in partnership; and a Scottish firm is an associate of any person who is a member of the firm.

(4) A person is an associate of any person whom he employs or by whom he is employed.

(5) A person in his capacity as trustee of a trust other than:

  (*a*) a trust arising under any of the second Group of Parts or the Bankruptcy (Scotland) Act 1985, or

  (*b*) a pension scheme or an employees' share scheme (within the meaning of the Companies Act),

is an associate of another person if the beneficiaries of the trust include, or the terms of the trust confer a power that may be exercised for the benefit of, that other person or an associate of that other person.

(6) A company is an associate of another company:

(*a*) if the same person has control of both, or a person has control of one and persons who are his associates, or he and persons who are his associates, have control of the other, or

(*b*) if a group of two or more persons has control of each company, and the groups either consist of the same persons or could be regarded as consisting of the same persons by treating (in one or more cases) a member of either group as replaced by a person of whom he is an associate.

(7) A company is an associate of another person if that person has control of it or that person and persons who are his associates together have control of it.

(8) For the purposes of this section a person is a relative of an individual if he is that individual's brother, sister, uncle, aunt, nephew, niece, lineal ancestor or lineal descendant, treating:

(*a*) any relationship of the half blood as a relationship of the whole blood and the stepchild or adopted child of any person as his child, and

(*b*) an illegitimate child as the legitimate child of his mother and reputed father;

and references in this section to a husband or wife include a former husband or wife and a reputed husband or wife.

(9) For the purposes of this section any director or other officer of a company is to be treated as employed by that company.

(10) For the purposes of this section a person is to be taken as having control of a company if:

(*a*) the directors of the company or of another company which has control of it (or any of them) are accustomed to act in accordance with his directions or instructions, or

(*b*) he is entitled to exercise, or control the exercise of, one third or more of the voting power at any general meeting of the company or of another company which has control of it; and where two or more persons together satisfy either of the above conditions, they are to be taken as having control of the company.

(11) In this section 'company' includes any body corporate (whether incorporated in Great Britain or elsewhere); and references to directors and other officers of a company and to voting power at any general meeting of a company have effect with any necessary modifications.'

# Appendix 4

## Relevant Forms

(Note that the Government intends to introduce a statutory instrument in the autumn of 1987 which will amend certain practical and technical errors in the Insolvency Rules 1986. As a result, certain of the forms prescribed in Sch. 4 to the Rules will be amended and certain new forms introduced. Contact the Department of Trade and Industry, Insolvency Service – Policy Branch for further details.)

This Appendix sets out the following forms from The Insolvency Rules 1986, Sch. 4:

### Sch. 4, Pt. 1: Company Voluntary Arrangements

*Form No.*
1.1 Report of a meeting approving voluntary arrangement
1.2 Order of revocation or suspension of voluntary arrangement
1.3 Voluntary arrangement's supervisor's abstract of receipts and payments
1.4 Notice of completion of voluntary arrangement

### Sch. 4, Pt. 2: Administration Procedure

2.1 Petition for administration order
2.2 Consent of administrator(s) to act
2.3 Affidavit of service of petition for administration order
2.4 Administration order
2.5 Notice of administration order (for newspapers)
2.6 Notice of administration order
2.7 Copy of administration order to registrar of companies
2.8 Notice requiring submission of administration statement of affairs
2.9 Statement of affairs
2.10 Notice to directors and others to attend meeting of creditors
2.11 Notice of meetings in administration proceedings
2.12 Report of meeting of creditors
2.13 Certificate of constitution [amended certificate] of creditors' committee
2.14 Notice by administrator of a change in committee membership
2.15 Administrator's abstract of receipts and payments
2.16 Notice to court of resignation of administrator under Rule 2.53 of the Insolvency Rules 1986
2.17 Notice of resignation by administrator pursuant to Rule 2.53(2) of the Insolvency Rules 1986
2.18 Notice of order to deal with charged property
2.19 Notice of discharge of administration order
2.20 Notice of variation of administration order

*Form No.*
2.21 Statement of administrator's proposals
2.22 Statement of revised proposals and notice of meeting to consider them
2.23 Notice of result of meeting of creditors

## Sch. 4, Pt. 3: Administrative Receivership

3.1  Notice requiring submission of administrative receivership statement of affairs
3.2  Statement of affairs
3.3  Statement of affairs in administrative receivership following report to creditors
3.4  Certificate of constitution [amended certificate] of creditors' committee
3.5  Administrative receiver's report as to change in membership of creditors' committee
3.6  Receiver or manager or administrative receiver's abstract of receipts and payments
3.7  Notice of administrative receiver's death
3.8  Notice of order to dispose of charged property
3.9  Notice of resignation of administrative receiver pursuant to section 45(1) of the Insolvency Act 1986
3.10 Administrative receiver's report

## Sch. 4, Pt. 8: Proxies and Company Representation

8.1  Proxy – company or individual voluntary arrangements
8.2  Proxy – administration
8.3  Proxy – administrative receivership

**Form 1.1**

**Rule 1.24**

The Insolvency Act 1986
## Report of a Meeting
## Approving Voluntary Arrangement
**Pursuant to Section 4 of the
Insolvency Act 1986**

To the Registrar of Companies

# S.4

**For official use**

Company Number

Name of Company

(a) Insert full name of company

(a)

Limited

(b) Insert full name and address

I (b)

(c) Insert date

the chairman of a meeting held in pursuance of section 4
of the Insolvency Act 1986 on (c)
enclose a copy of my report of the said meeting.

Signed                                    Date

Presenter's name, address and reference (if any):

**For Official Use**

Liquidation Section          Post Room

**Form 1.2**

**Rule 1.25** The Insolvency Act 1986
Order of Revocation or
Suspension of Voluntary
Arrangement
**Pursuant to Section 6 of the
Insolvency Act 1986**

# S.6

**For official use**

To the Registrar of Companies

Company Number

Name of Company

(a) Insert full name of
company

(a)

Limited

(b) Insert full name(s)
and address(es)

I/We (b)

enclose a copy of the order of the court dated
(c) Delete as applicable    (c) [revoking] [suspending] the voluntary arrangement approved
(d) Insert date    on (d)

Signed

Date

Presenter's name,
address and reference
(if any):

**For Official Use**
Liquidation Section         Post Room

Form 1.3

**Rule 1.26** The Insolvency Act 1986

Voluntary Arrangement's Supervisor's Abstract of Receipts and Payments

# R.1.26(2)(b)

**Pursuant to Rule 1.26 (2)(b) of the Insolvency Rules 1986**

**For official use**

To the Registrar of Companies

Company Number

Name of Company

(a) Insert full name of company

(a)

Limited

(b) Insert full name(s) and address(es)

I/We (b)

(c) Insert date

supervisor(s) of a voluntary arrangement approved on (c)

present overleaf my/our abstract of receipts and payments for the period

from

to

Number of continuation sheets (if any) attached

Signed                                          Date

Presenter's name, address and reference (if any):

**For Official Use**

Liquidation Section                    Post Room

**Rule 1.29** The Insolvency Act 1986

Notice of Completion of
Voluntary Arrangement

**Pursuant to Rule 1.29 of the
Insolvency Rules 1986**

# R.1.29

To the Registrar of Companies

For official use

Company Number

Name of Company

(a) Insert full name of company

(a)

Limited

(b) Insert full name and address

I (b)

(c) Insert date the supervisor of a voluntary arrangement approved on (c)
enclose a copy of my notice to the creditors and members of the above-named
company that the voluntary arrangement has been completed, together with a
report of my receipts and payments.

Signed

Date

Presenter's name,
address and reference
(if any):

**For Official Use**

Liquidation Section     Post Room

## Rule 2.1 Petition for Administration Order

(TITLE)

(a) Insert title of court    To (a) _____

_____

(b) Insert full name(s) and address(es) of petitioner(s)    The petition of (b) _____

_____

_____

_____

(c) Insert full name of company subject to petition    1. (c) _____

(d) Insert date of incorporation    (hereinafter called "the company") was incorporated on (d) _____ under the Companies Act 19____

(e) Insert address of registered office    2. The registered office of the company is at (e) _____

_____

_____

(f) Insert amount of nominal capital and how it is divided    3. The nominal capital of the company is (f) £ _____ divided into _____ shares of £ _____ each  The amount of the capital paid or credited as paid up is (g) £ _____

(g) Insert amount of capital paid up or credited as paid up    4. The principal objects for which the company was established are as follows

_____

_____

and other objects set forth in the memorandum of association thereof.

5. The petitioner(s) believe(s) that the company is or is likely to become unable to pay its debts and that an administration order would be likely to achieve

(h) Delete such as are inapplicable    (h)    (i) the survival of the company and the whole or some part of its undertaking as a going concern

(ii) the approval of a voluntary arrangement with its creditors under Part 1 of the Insolvency Act 1986

(iii) the sanctioning of a compromise or arrangement between the company and such persons as are mentioned in section 425 of the Companies Act 1985

(iv) a more advantageous realisation of the company's assets than would be effected on a winding up.

for the reasons stated in the affidavit of                 filed in support hereof.

6. The petitioner(s) propose(s) that during the period for which the order is in force the affairs, business and property of the company be managed by

(j) Insert full name(s) and address(es) of proposed administrator(s)

(j) _____

_____

_____

who is (are) to the best of the petitioner's knowledge and belief qualified to act as (an) insolvency practitioner(s) in relation to the company. The petitioner(s) therefore pray(s) as follows:—

(k) Insert full name of company

(1) that the court make an administration order in relation to (k) _____

_____

(l) Insert name(s) of proposed administrator(s)

(2) that (l) _____

be appointed to be the administrator(s) of the said company

(m) Insert details of any ancilliary orders which might be sought

(3) (m)

or

(4) that such other order may be made in the premises as shall be just.

Note:

It is intended to serve this petition on _____

_____

_____

_____

This petition was issued by _____

_____

_____

(n) Insert here name, address, tel no, and references of a solicitor acting for the petitioner

_____(n) (solicitor for)

the petitioner(s) whose address for service is:

_____

___ _____

_____

# Consent of Administrator(s) to Act
(TITLE)

[I] [We] _____

of _____

_____

hereby certify that [I am] [we are] authorised under the provisions of Part XIII of the Insolvency Act 1986 to act as (an) insolvency practitioner(s).
[I] [We] consent to act as administrator(s) of the above company for the purposes specified in the petition of _____

_____

dated _____ 19_____

Signed

Dated

# Affidavit of Service of Petition for Administration Order

(TITLE)

(a) Insert full name, address and description of deponent

I (a) _____

of _____

_____

Make oath and say as follows

1. That I did on _____day the _____ day of _____ 19  ,
serve the above-named company with a copy of the petition duly sealed with the
seal of the court and its supporting documents by leaving the same at the

(b) Insert the address stated in the petition to be the company's registered office

registered office of the said company at (b) _____

_____

**OR** by posting the same on _____ day the _____ day of
_____ 19  , by ordinary post first class mail in an envelope
duly pre-paid and properly addressed to the said company at its registered office
at (b) _____

_____

2. That I did on _____day the _____ day of _____ 19  ,

(c) Insert name

serve (c) _____ a person who has appointed or is [or may be] entitled
to appoint an administrative receiver of the said company with a copy of the
petition duly sealed with the seal of the court and its supporting documents by

(d) Insert address where served

leaving the same at his proper address at (d) _____

_____

**OR** by posting the same on _____ day the _____ day of
_____ 19  , by ordinary post first class mail in an envelope
duly pre-paid and properly addressed to the said (c) _____
at (d) _____

_____

3. That I did on _____day the _____ day of _____ 19  ,
serve (c) _____ the administrative receiver of the said
company with a copy of the petition duly sealed with the seal of the court and its
supporting documents by leaving the same at his proper address at
(d) _____

**OR** by posting the same on _____ day the _____ day of
_____ 19  , by ordinary post first class mail in an envelope
duly pre-paid and properly addressed to the said (c) _____
at (d) _____

_____

_____

4. That I did on _____day the _____ day of _____ 19__,
serve (c) _____ who has presented a petition to wind up the said
company with a copy of the petition duly sealed with the seal of the court and its
supporting documents by leaving the same at his proper address at (d) _____

_____

_____

**OR** by posting the same on _____ day, the _____day of
_____ 19____, by ordinary post first class mail in an envelope
duly pre-paid and properly addressed to the said (c) _____
at (d) _____

_____

_____

5. That I did on _____day the _____ day of _____ 19 ,
serve (c) _____ the provisional liquidator of the said company with a
copy of the petition duly sealed with the seal of the court and its supporting
documents by leaving the same at his proper address at (d) _____

_____

_____

**OR** by posting the same on _____ day the _____day of
_____ 19 , by ordinary post first class mail in an envelope
duly pre-paid and properly addressed to the said (c) _____
at (d) _____

_____

6. That I did on _____day the _____ day of _____ 19 ,
serve (c) _____ the person proposed to be the adminis-
trator of the said company with a copy of the petition duly sealed with the seal of
the court and its supporting documents by leaving the same at his proper address
at (d) _____

_____

_____

**OR** by posting the same on _____ day the _____ day of
_____ 19 , by ordinary post first class mail in an envelope
duly pre-paid and properly addressed to the said (c) _____
at (d) _____

_____

_____

A sealed copy of the petition and its supporting documents are now produced and
shown to me marked "A"

SWORN

# Administration Order

(TITLE)

(a) Insert name and   UPON THE PETITION OF (a) _____
address of petitioner

_____

_____

(b) Delete where   (b) (a                                    of the above named company hereinafter
company itself is   called "the company") presented to the court on _____
petitioner OR insert   19___
status of petitioner ie
director, creditor etc   And upon hearing counsel for the petitioner
(c) Insert details of any   and for (c) _____
other parties (including
the company)   _____
appearing and by
whom represented   _____

_____

and upon reading the evidence

_____

_____

_____

_____

_____

_____

IT IS ORDERED that during the period for which this order is in force the affairs,
business and property of the company be managed by the administrator
hereinafter appointed pursuant to the provisions of section 8 of the Insolvency Act
(d) Set out the   1986 for the following purpose(s) (d) _____
purpose(s) which the
order is likely to   _____
achieve
_____

_____

_____

(e) Insert full name(s)   AND it is ordered that (e) _____
and address(es) of
administrator(s)   _____

_____

be appointed administrator(s) of the company

AND it is ordered that

(f) Insert particulars of
any further order made
by the court

(f) _____

_____

_____

And it is ordered that the costs of the said petition

(g) Insert terms of
order for costs

(g) _____

_____

_____

Dated

## Notice of Administration Order
## (For Newspapers)

The Insolvency Act 1986

In the matter of    _____

_____

_____[Limited]

Nature of business _____

_____

Administration Order made _____ 19 ____

_____

Administrator/Joint administrator

**The Insolvency Act 1986**

## Notice of Administration Order **R.2.10**
Pursuant to Rule 2.10(3) of the
**Insolvency Rules 1986**

To the Registrar of Companies

**For official use**

Company Number

Name of Company

Insert full name of
company

                                                                            Limited

I/We _____

of   _____

     _____

     _____

give notice that an administration order was made against the above company on:

Insert date

Signed _____  Dated _____

Joint/Administrator(s)

Presenter's name,
address and reference
(if any):

**For Official Use**

Insolvency Section          Post Room

Rule 2.10

Form 2.7

**The Insolvency Act 1986**
## Administration Order
**Pursuant to Section 21(2) of the
Insolvency Act 1986**

# S.21(2)

**For official use**

To the Registrar of Companies

Company Number

Name of Company

Insert full name of
company

Limited

I/We _____

of _____

_____

_____

administrator(s) of the company attach a copy of the administration order.

Signed _____ Dated _____

Presenter's name,
address and reference
(if any):

**For Official Use**

Insolvency Section    Post Room

# Notice Requiring Submission of
# Administration Statement of Affairs

(TITLE)

(a) Insert full name of administrator

TAKE notice that I (a) _____

(b) Insert full name of person required to submit statement

require you (b) _____
to submit a statement as to the affairs of the company within    days.

The statement must be in the prescribed form and must show:

(i)   particulars of the company's assets, debts and liabilities
(ii)  the names and addresses of its creditors
(iii) the securities held by them respectively
(iv)  the dates when the securities were respectively given

(c) Insert details of further information if required

(c)
_____

Dated this _____ day of _____ 19_____

Signed _____

**Warning**

If without reasonable excuse you fail to comply, you will be liable:

(i) On summary conviction to a fine not exceeding the statutory maximum and, for continued contravention, to a daily default fine not exceeding one-tenth of the statutory maximum.

(ii) On conviction on indictment to a fine.

**Rule 2.12**                                                    **Form 2.9**

# Statement of Affairs

In the                           No.              of 19

Statement as to the Affairs of

_____

On the                           19          The date of the administration order.

## Affidavit

This affidavit must be sworn before a solicitor or commissioner of oaths or an officer of the court duly authorised to administer oaths when you have completed the rest of this form.

(a) Insert name and occupation

I (a) _____

_____

(b) Insert full address

of (b) _____

_____

make oath and say that the several pages exhibited hereto and attached marked _____ are to the best of my knowledge and belief a full, true and complete

(c) Insert date of administration order

statement as to the affairs of the above named company as at (c) _____ the date of the administration order and that the said company carried on business as

_____

_____

_____

Sworn at     _____

Dated        _____

Signature(s) _____

Before me    _____

A solicitor or Commissioner of Oaths or duly authorised officer

**The Solicitor or Commissioner is particularly requested, before swearing the affidavit, to make sure that the full name, address and description of the Deponent are stated, and to initial any crossings out or other alterations in the printed form. A deficiency in the affidavit in any of the above respects will mean that it is refused by the court, and will necessitate its being resworn.**

A—Summary of Assets

| ASSETS | Book Value £ | Estimated to Realise £ |
|---|---|---|
| **Assets specifically pledged:—** | | |
| | | |
| **Assets not specifically pledged:—** | | |
| | | |
| **Estimated total assets available for preferential creditors** | £ | |

Signature _____ Date _____

# A1—Summary of Liabilities

| | Estimated to realise £ |
|---|---|
| Estimated total assets available for preferential creditors (carried from page A) £ | |
| **Liabilities** Preferential creditors:— £ | |
| Estimated deficiency/surplus as regards preferential creditors £ Debts secured by a floating charge:— £ | |
| Estimated deficiency/surplus of assets available for non-preferential creditors £ | |
| Non-preferential claims:— £ | |
| Estimated deficiency/surplus as regards creditors £ Issued and called up capital:— £ | |
| Estimated total deficiency/surplus as regards members £ | |

Signature _____     Date _____

## COMPANY CREDITORS

**Note.** You must identify creditors under hire-purchase, chattel leasing or conditional sale agreements *and* customers claiming amounts paid in advance of the supply of goods or services *and* creditors claiming retention of title over property in the company's possession.

| Name of creditor or Claimant | Address (with postcode) | Amount of debt £ | Details of any security held by creditor | Date security given | Value of security £ |
|---|---|---|---|---|---|
| | | | | | |
| | | | | | |
| | | | | | |
| | | | | | |
| | | | | | |
| | | | | | |
| | | | | | |
| | | | | | |
| | | | | | |
| | | | | | |
| | | | | | |
| | | | | | |
| | | | | | |

Signature _____

Date _____

**Form 2.10**

## Notice to Directors and Others to Attend Meeting of Creditors
(TITLE)

(a) Insert name(s) of administrator(s)

Notice is hereby given that I/We (a)

_____

_____

administrator(s) of the company require you

(b) Insert name

* Delete as appropriate

(b) _____

a director*/officer/former officer of the company to attend a meeting of creditors to be held at

_____

_____

on the _____ day of _____ 19____

at _____

Signed _____

Dated _____

## Notice of Meetings in Administration Proceedings

(TITLE)

[Paragraph 2 only—Notice to members of meeting of members]

\* Delete as appropriate

Notice is hereby given that a meeting of creditors\*/members in the above matter is to be held at _____

_____

_____

On the _____ day of _____ 19_____

at _____

Delete whichever is inapplicable

(1) To consider my proposals under s.23(1) of the Insolvency Act 1986 and to consider establishing a committee of creditors

(2) under s.14(2)(b) of the Insolvency Act 1986

(3) at the request of creditors under s.17(3)(a) of the Insolvency Act 1986

(4) at the direction of the court under s.17(3)(b) of the Insolvency Act 1986

[(2)–(4) only] for the purposes of _____

_____

_____

A proxy form is enclosed which should be completed and returned to me by the date of the meeting if you cannot attend the meeting and wish to be represented. In order to be entitled to vote at the meeting you must give to me, not later than 12.00 hours on the business day before the day fixed for the meeting, details in writing of your claim.

Signed _____
        Administrator

[(1) only] A copy of my proposals may be obtained from

_____

_____

_____

# Report of Meeting of Creditors
### (TITLE)

I _____
administrator of the company hereby report that a/[an adjourned] meeting of
creditors in the above matter was held at _____

_____

_____

on the _____ day of _____ 19_____
at which:

(1) Proposals [Revised proposals] in the form hereto annexed were approved

(2) _____

_____

_____

_____

were nominated to act as members of the committee of creditors

(3) The meeting declined to approve the proposals [revised proposals]

Dated this _____ day of _____ 19_____



The Administrator

| Resolution number | Assenting Creditor's signature | Amount of Claim | Resolution number | Dissenting Creditor's Signature | Amount of Claim |
|---|---|---|---|---|---|
| | | | | | |

**Note**
When a resolution is not passed unanimously and a division is taken, all creditors and proxy holders voting should sign opposite in respect of each resolution

# Certificate of Constitution
# [Amended Certificate] of
# Creditors' Committee

(TITLE)

(a) Insert name    I, (a) _____

the administrator of the above company certify that the creditors' committee has
been duly constituted and that membership is as follows:—

(b) Insert names and    (b) _____ of [address] _____
addresses of members
of committee    _____

_____

_____

_____

_____

_____

(c) Delete as    (c) [This certificate amends the certificate issued by me on (d) _____]
necessary
(d) Insert date of    Dated _____
previous certificate

Signed _____

Administrator

# Notice by Administrator of a
# Change in Committee Membership
### (TITLE)

(a) Insert full name    I, (a) _____

the administrator of the above named company certify that the membership of the
creditors' committee has altered as follows:—

**Appointed:** _____

_____

_____

**Resigned/Removed** _____

_____

_____

_____

- - - - - - - - - - - - - - - - - - - - - - - - - - - - - - - - - - - - - - - -

(b) Insert date    And that the committee's membership as from (b) _____ is as follows:—

_____

_____

_____

_____

_____

Dated _____

Signed _____

                                        Administrator

**Form 2.15**

**The Insolvency Act 1986**
## Administrator's Abstract of Receipts and Payments
**Pursuant to Rule 2.52(1) of the Insolvency Act 1986**

# R.2.52

To the Registrar of Companies

To the Court

To members of the creditors' committee

**For official use**

Company Number

Name of Company

Insert full name of company

Limited

I/We _____

of _____

_____

administrator(s) of the company present overleaf for the period

from

Insert dates

to

Number of continuation sheets (if any) attached

Signed _____ Date _____

Presenter's name,
address and reference
(if any):

**For Official Use**
Insolvency Section      Post Room

## Abstract

| Receipts | | |
|---|---|---|
| Brought forward from previous Abstract (if any) | £ | p |
| | | |
| | | |
| | | |
| | | |
| | | |
| | | |
| | | |
| | | |
| | | |
| | | |
| | | |
| Carried forward to [continuation sheet]* [next Abstract] | | |

* delete as appropriate

| Payments | | |
|---|---|---|
| Brought foward from previous Abstracts (if any) | £ | p |
| | | |
| | | |
| | | |
| | | |
| | | |
| | | |
| | | |
| | | |
| | | |
| | | |
| | | |
| Carried forward to [continuation sheet]* [next abstract] | | |

* delete as appropriate

# Notice to Court of Resignation of Administrator Under Rule 2.53 of the Insolvency Rules 1986

(TITLE)

(a) Insert full name and address of administrator

I, (a) _____

_____

_____

the administrator of the above company give notice that I am resigning from the

(b) Insert date   said office of administrator with effect from (b)

_____

(c) See Rule 2.52(1)   for the following reason(s): (c) _____

_____

_____

_____

Signed _____

Dated _____

(d) The date must be at least 7 days before that stated at (b) above

I confirm that on (d) _____
I gave notice to:

(i) _____

(ii) _____

(iii) _____

being persons who under section 13(3) of the Insolvency Act 1986 are entitled to apply for a vacancy in the office of administrator to be filled.

# Notice of Resignation by Administrator Pursuant to Rule 2.53(2) of the Insolvency Rules 1986

(TITLE)

(a) Insert full name and address of administrator

I, (a) _____

_____

(b) Insert date

the administrator of the above company give notice that on (b) _____

19____, the court gave me leave to resign.

Signed _____

Dated _____

Form 2.18

The Insolvency Act 1986

Notice of Order to Deal with **S.15(7)**
Charged Property
**Pursuant to Section 15(7) of the
Insolvency Act 1986**

To the Registrar of Companies

**For official use**

Company Number

Name of Company

Insert full name of
company

Limited

I/We _____

of _____

_____

_____

administrator(s) of the company obtained an order for the disposal of charged
property*/goods in possession of the company under a hire-purchase agreement
on

*delete whichever is
not applicable

insert date

An office copy of the said Court order is attached.

Signed _____ Dated _____

Presenter's name,
address and reference
(if any):

**For Official Use**
**Insolvency Section      Post Room**

Form 2.19

The Insolvency Act 1986

## Notice of Discharge of Administration Order

Pursuant to Section 18(4) of the Insolvency Act 1986

# S.18(4)

To the Registrar of Companies

For official use

Company Number

Name of Company

Insert full name of company

Limited

I/We _____

of _____

_____

_____

_____

administrator(s) of the company hereby give notice that on

Insert date

the administration order was discharged. An office copy of the said order of discharge is attached

Signed _____ Dated _____

Presenter's name, address and reference (if any):

For Official Use

Insolvency Section          Post Room

**The Insolvency Act 1986**

## Notice of Variation of Administration Order

Pursuant to Section 18(4) of the
Insolvency Act 1986

# S.18(4)

To the Registrar of Companies

**For official use**

Company Number

Name of Company

Insert full name of
company

Limited

I/We _____

of   _____

_____

_____

administrator(s) of the company hereby give notice that on

Insert date

an order varying the administration order was made. An office copy of the said
order of variation is attached

Signed _____ Date _____

Presenter's name,
address and reference
(if any):

**For Official Use**

Insolvency Section    Post Room

Form 2.21

**The Insolvency Act 1986**

**Statement of Administrator's Proposals**

**S.23(1)(a)**

**Pursuant to Section 23(1)(a) of the Insolvency Act 1986**

To the Registrar of Companies

**For official use**

Company Number

Name of Company

Insert full name of company

Limited

I/We

of

administrator(s) of the company attach a copy of my [our] proposals for achieving the purposes set out in the administration order filed herein. A copy of these proposals was sent to all known creditors on:

Insert date

Signed _____ Dated _____

Presenter's name, address and reference (if any):

**For Official Use**

Insolvency Section        Post Room

**Section 25(2)(a)**

**The Insolvency Act 1986**
## Statement of Revised Proposals and Notice of Meeting to Consider Them
(TITLE)

Notice is hereby given that a meeting of creditors of the above named company is to be held

at _____

on the _____ day of _____ 19____ at

_____ to consider revisions of the proposals which

were approved by its creditors on the _____ day of

_____ 19____

The revisions I propose are:

_____

_____

_____

The reasons for these revisions are:

_____

_____

_____

A proxy form is enclosed which should be completed and returned to me by the date of the meeting if you cannot attend the meeting and wish to be represented. In order to be entitled to vote at the meeting you must, if you have not already done so, give to me, not later than 12.00 hours on the business day before the day fixed for the meeting, details in writing of your claim.

Signed _____
                        Administrator

Form 2.23

The Insolvency Act 1986
## Notice of Result of
## Meeting of Creditors
**S.24(4)/25(6)**

**Pursuant to Section 24(4)/25(6) of the
Insolvency Act 1986**

To the Registrar of Companies

**For official use**

**Company Number**

Name of Company

Insert full name of
company

Limited

I/We

of

administrator(s) of the company attach a copy of my [our] report to the Court
dated

Insert date

detailing the resolution(s) passed at a meeting of creditors held on

Insert date

Signed _____ Dated _____

Presenter's name,
address and reference
(if any):

**For Official Use**
**Insolvency Section      Post Room**

# Notice Requiring Submission of Administrative Receivership Statement of Affairs

(TITLE)

(a) Insert full name of administrative receiver

**Take notice** that I (a) _____

(b) Insert full name of person required to submit statement

require you (b) _____

to submit a statement as to the affairs of the company within    days.

The statement must be in the prescribed form and must show:

(i) particulars of the company's assets, debts and liabilities
(ii) the names and addresses of its creditors
(iii) the securities held by them respectively
(iv) the dates when the securities were respectively given

(c) Insert details of further information if required

(c) _____

_____

Dated this _____ day of _____ 19_____

Signed _____

**Warning**

If without reasonable excuse you fail to comply, you will be liable:

(i) On summary conviction to a fine not exceeding the statutory maximum and, for continued contravention, to a daily default fine not exceeding one-tenth of the statutory maximum.
(ii) On conviction on indictment to a fine.

## Statement of Affairs

Statement as to affairs of

_____

On the _____ 19__ the date of the Administrative Receiver's Appointment

### Affidavit

This affidavit must be sworn or affirmed before a Solicitor or Commissioner of Oaths when you have completed the rest of this form.

I _____

of _____

Swear/affirm that the several pages attached marked _____ are to the best of my knowledge and belief a full, true and complete statement as the affairs of the above named company as at _____ the date of the appointment of the administrative receiver and that the said company carried on business as

_____

_____

_____

_____

Sworn/affirmed at _____

Date                 _____

Signatures           _____

Before me            _____

_____

A Solicitor or Commissioner of Oaths

**The Solicitor or Commissioner is particularly requested, before swearing/ affirming the affidavit, to make sure that the full name, address and description of the Deponent are stated, and to initial any crossings-out or other alterations in the printed form. A deficiency in the affidavit in any of the above respects will mean that it is refused by the court, and will necessitate its being re-sworn/re-affirmed.**

## A—Summary of Assets

| Assets | Book Value £ | Estimated to Realise £ |
|---|---|---|
| **Assets specifically pledged:—** | | |
| | | |
| **Assets not specifically pledged:—** | | |
| | | |
| **Estimated total assets available for preferential creditors**     £ | | |

Signature _____     Date _____

A 1–Summary of Liabilities

|  | Estimated to realise £ |
|---|---|
| **Estimated total assets available for preferential creditors (carried from page A)** | £ |

**Liabilities**

Preferential creditors:— £

**Estimated deficiency/surplus as regards preferential creditors** £

Debts secured by a floating charge:— £

**Estimated deficiency/surplus of assets available for non-preferential creditors** £

Non-preferential claims:— £

**Estimated deficiency/surplus as regards creditors** £

Issued and called up capital:— £

**Estimated total deficiency/surplus as regards members** £

Signature _____     Date _____

## B
## Company Creditors

**Note** You must identify creditors under hire-purchase, chattel leasing or conditional sale agreements *and* customers claiming amounts paid in advance of the supply of goods or services *and* creditors claiming retention of title over property in the company's possession.

| Name of creditor or claimant | Address (with postcode) | Amount of debt £ | Details of any security held by creditor | Date security given | Value of security £ |
|---|---|---|---|---|---|
| | | | | | |
| | | | | | |
| | | | | | |
| | | | | | |
| | | | | | |
| | | | | | |
| | | | | | |
| | | | | | |
| | | | | | |
| | | | | | |
| | | | | | |
| | | | | | |

Signature _____

Date _____

**Rule 3.8**                                                                    **Form 3.3**

The Insolvency Act 1986

## Statement of Affairs in    R.3.8(4)
Administrative Receivership
Following Report to Creditors

Pursuant to Rule 3.8(4) of the
Insolvency Rules 1986

To the Registrar of Companies                              **For official use**

                                                           Company Number

Name of Company

Insert full name of
company

                                                                    Limited

I/We _____

of _____

   _____

   _____

administrative receiver(s) of the company attach a copy of the statement of affairs
of the company.

Signed _____ Dated _____

Presenter's name,
address and reference
(if any):

                          **For Official Use**
                          **Insolvency Section     Post Room**

**Rule 3.17**                                                    **Form 3.4**

**The Insolvency Act 1986**
Certificate of Constitution
[Amended Certificate] of            # R.3.17(4)
Creditors' Committee
**Pursuant to Rule 3.17(4) of the
Insolvency Rules 1986**

To the Registrar of Companies                          **For official use**

                                                        Company Number

|  |
|--|
|  |

                                                Name of Company

(a) Insert full name of    | (a)                                          |
company                    |                                    Limited   |

(b) Insert full name(s)    I/We (b)
and address(es)

                           administrative receiver(s) of the above company certify that the creditors'
(c) Insert names and       committee has been duly constituted and that the membership is as follows (c)
addresses of members
of committee

(d) Delete as necessary    (d) This certificate amends the certificate issued by me on (e)
(e) Insert date of
previous certificate

                           Signed                            Date

. Presenter's name,
address and reference                          | **For Official Use** |
(if any)                                       | **Insolvency Section     Post Room** |

**The Insolvency Act 1986**
Administrative Receiver's Report
as to Change In Membership of
Creditors' Committee

**R.3.17(5)**

**Pursuant to Rule 3.17(5) of the
Insolvency Rules 1986**

To the Registrar of Companies

**For official use**

Company Number

Name of Company

(a) Insert full name of
company

(a)

Limited

(b) Insert full name(s)
and address(es)

I/We (b)

administrative receiver(s) of the above company report that the membership of the
creditors' committee has altered since the last certificate dated (c)

(c) Insert date

(d) Insert details of
changes in
membership

as follows (d)

Signed

Date

Presenter's name,
address and reference
(if any)

**For Official Use**
**Insolvency Section**      **Post Room**

# M

Form 3.6

**Rule 3.32**   The Insolvency Act 1986

## Receiver or Manager or Administrative Receiver's Abstract of Receipts and Payments

# S.38/R

**Pursuant to section 38 of the Insolvency Act 1986**
**Rule 3.32(1) of the Insolvency Rules 1986**

To the Registrar of Companies

**For official use**

*Administrative Receivership only

*To the company

*To the members of the creditors' committee

Company Number

*To the appointor of administrative receiver

Name of Company

Insert full name of company

Limited

I/We _____

of _____

_____

_____

*Delete as appropriate   appointed [receiver] [manager] [receiver and manager] [administrative receiver]* of the company on

Insert date

present overleaf [my] [our]* abstract of receipts and payments for the period from

to

Number of continuation sheets (if any attached)

Signed _____ Date _____

. Presenter's name, address and reference (if any)

_____

_____

_____

_____

**For Official Use**
**Insolvency Section**     **Post Room**

**Note**
The receipts and
payments must
severally be added up
at the foot of each
sheet and the totals
carried forward from
one abstract to
another without any
intermediate balance
so that the gross
totals shall represent
the total amounts
received and paid by
the receiver since he
was appointed

# Abstract

| Receipts | | |
|---|---|---|
| Brought forward from previous Abstract (if any) | f | n |
| | | |
| | | |
| | | |
| | | |
| | | |
| | | |
| | | |
| | | |
| | | |
| | | |
| | | |
| | | |
| Carried forward to [continuation sheet]*[next Abstract] | | |

*delete as appropriate

| Payments | | |
|---|---|---|
| Brought forward from previous Abstract (if any) | £ | p |
| | | |
| | | |
| | | |
| | | |
| | | |
| | | |
| | | |
| | | |
| | | |
| | | |
| | | |
| | | |
| Carried forward to [continuation sheet]*[next Abstract] | | |

*delete as appropriate

**Rule 3.34**                                                    Form 3.7

**The Insolvency Act 1986**
## Notice of Administrative
## Receiver's Death
**Pursuant to Rule 3.34 of the
Insolvency Rules 1986**

# R.3.34

To the Registrar of Companies

For official use

Company Number

Name of Company

Insert full name of
company

Limited

Mr

of

administrative receiver of the above company died on:

Signed _____     Dated _____

For and on behalf of appointor

Presenter's name,
address and reference
(if any):

**For Official Use**
**Insolvency Section        Post Room**

Form 3.8

**The Insolvency Act 1986**

**Notice of Order to Dispose** **S.43(5)**
**of Charged Property**
**Pursuant to section 43(5) of the**
**Insolvency Act 1986**

To the Registrar of Companies

For official use

Company Number

Insert full name of
company

Name of Company

Limited

I/We _____

of _____

administrative receiver(s) of the company obtained an order under section 43(1) of
the Insolvency Act 1986 to dispose of property which is subject to a security on

An office copy of the said court order is attached

Signed _____ Date _____

Presenter's name,
address and reference
(if any):

**For Official Use**
**Insolvency Section     Post Room**

## Notice of Resignation of Administrative Receiver Pursuant to Section 45(1) of the Insolvency Act 1986

(TITLE)

(a) Insert full name and address of administrative receiver

I, (a) _____

_____

_____

(b) Insert date to be at least 7 days ahead

the administrative receiver of the above company give notice that I am resigning from the said office of administrative receiver with effect from (b)

_____

Signed _____

Dated _____

(c) Person who made the appointment

To: (c)

(d) Company or, if in liquidation, the liquidator

(d)

Form 3.10

**The Insolvency Act 1986**

Administrative
Receiver's Report

# S.48(1)

**Pursuant to section 48(1) of the Insolvency Act 1986 and Rule 3.8(3) of the Insolvency Rules 1986**

To the Registrar of Companies

**For official use**

Company Number

Name of Company

*Insert full name of company*

Limited

I/We _____

of   _____

  _____

  _____

administrative receiver(s) of the company attach a copy of my [our] report to creditors and a copy of the statement of affairs of the company

Signed _____ Dated _____

*Presenter's name, address and reference (if any):*

**For Official Use**

**Insolvency Section     Post Room**

**Rule 8.1**   **Insolvency Act 1986**

# Proxy (Company or Individual Voluntary Arrangements)

(TITLE)

Please give full name and
address for communication

Name of creditor/member _____

Address _____

_____

Please insert name of
person (who must be 18 or
over) or the ''chairman of
the meeting'' (see note
below). If you wish to
provide for alternative
proxy-holders in the
circumstances that your first
choice is unable to attend
please state the name(s) of
the alternatives as well

Name of proxy-holder _____

1 _____

_____

2 _____

_____

3 _____

_____

Please delete words in
brackets if the proxy-holder
is only to vote as directed ie
he has no discretion

I appoint the above person to be my/the creditor's/member's proxy-holder at the meeting of
creditors/members to be held on _____ , or at any adjournment of that
meeting. The proxy-holder is to propose or vote as instructed below [and in respect of any resolution
for which no specific instruction is given, may vote or abstain at his/her discretion]

## Voting instructions for resolutions

*Please delete as
appropriate

1. For the acceptance/rejection* of the proposed voluntary arrangement [with the following
   modifications:—]

Any other resolutions which
the proxy-holder is to
propose or vote in favour of
or against should be set out
in numbered paragraphs in
the space provided below
Paragraph 1. If more room
is required please use the
other side of this form.

_____

_____

_____

_____

_____

_____

This form must be signed

Signature _____ Date _____

Name in CAPITAL LETTERS _____

Only to be completed if the
creditor/member has not
signed in person

**Position with creditor/member or relationship to creditor/member or other authority for
signature** _____

_____

Remember: there may be resolutions on the other side of this form.

**Rule 8.1    Insolvency Act 1986**

# Proxy (Administration)

(TITLE)

**Notes to help completion
of the form**

Please give full name and
address for communication

Name of creditor _____

Address _____

_____

_____

Please insert name of
person (who must be 18 or
over) or the "chairman of
the meeting". If you wish to
provide for alternative
proxy-holders in the
circumstances that your first
choice is unable to attend
please state the name(s) of
the alternatives as well

Name of proxy-holder _____

1 _____

_____

2 _____

_____

3 _____

_____

Please delete words in
brackets if the proxy-holder
is only to vote as directed ie
he has no discretion

I appoint the above person to be my/the creditor's proxy-holder at the meeting of creditors to be
held on _____ , or at any adjournment of that meeting. The proxy-holder is
to propose or vote as instructed below [and in respect of any resolution for which no specific
instruction is given, may vote or abstain at his/her discretion].

## Voting instructions for resolutions

\*Please delete as
appropriate

1. For the acceptance/rejection\* of the administrator's proposals/revised proposals\* as circulated.

_____

_____

_____

2. For the appointment of _____ of _____

_____

_____

representing _____

as a member of the creditors' committee

**This form must be signed**    **Signature** _____ **Date** _____

**Name in CAPITAL LETTERS** _____

Only to be completed if the
creditor has not signed in
person

**Position with creditor or relationship to creditor or other authority for signature**

_____

Remember: there may be resolutions on the other side of this form.

**Rule 8.1  Insolvency Act 1986**

# Proxy (Administrative Receivership)

(TITLE)

**Notes to help completion
of the form**

Please give full name and
address for communication

Name of creditor _____

Address _____

_____

_____

Please insert name of
person (who must be 18 or
over) or the "chairman of
the meeting" If you wish to
provide for alternative
proxy-holders in the
circumstances that your first
choice is unable to attend
please state the name(s) of
the alternatives as well.

Name of proxy-holder _____

_____

_____

_____

_____

_____

_____

_____

_____

Please delete words in
brackets if the proxy-holder
is only to vote as directed if
he has no discretion

I appoint the above person to be my/the creditor's proxy-holder at the meeting of creditors to be
held on _____ , or at any adjournment of that meeting. The proxy-holder is
to propose or vote as instructed below [and in respect of any resolution for which no specific
instruction is given, may vote or abstain at his/her discretion]

## Voting instructions for resolutions

for the appointment of _____

of _____

representing _____

as a member of the creditors' committee

This form must be signed

Signature _____ Date _____

**Name in CAPITAL LETTERS** _____

Only to be completed if the
creditor has not signed in
person

**Position with creditor or relationship to creditor or other authority for signature**

_____

Remember: there may be resolutions on the other side of this form.

# Appendix 5

## Powers of an Administrator or an Administrative Receiver

These powers are set out in Sch. 1 to the Insolvency Act 1986 which reads as follows:

## SCHEDULE 1

## POWERS OF ADMINISTRATOR OR ADMINISTRATIVE RECEIVER

**1.** Power to take possession of, collect and get in the property of the company and, for that purpose, to take such proceedings as may seem to him expedient.

**2.** Power to sell or otherwise dispose of the property of the company by public auction or private contract or, in Scotland, to sell, feu, hire out or otherwise dispose of the property of the company by public roup or private bargain.

**3.** Power to raise or borrow money and grant security therefore over the property of the company.

**4.** Power to appoint a solicitor or accountant or other professionally qualified person to assist him in the performance of his functions.

**5.** Power to bring or defend any action or other legal proceedings in the name and on behalf of the company.

**6.** Power to refer to arbitration any question affecting the company.

**7.** Power to effect and maintain insurances in respect of the business and property of the company.

**8.** Power to use the company's seal.

**9.** Power to do all acts and to execute in the name and on behalf of the company any deed, receipt or other document.

**10.** Power to draw, accept, make and endorse any bill of exchange or promissory note in the name and on behalf of the company.

**11.** Power to appoint any agent to do any business which he is unable to do himself or which can more conveniently be done by an agent and power to employ and dismiss employees.

**12.** Power to do all such things (including the carrying out of works) as may be necessary for the realisation of the property of the company.

**13.** Power to make any payment which is necessary or incidental to the performance of his functions.

**14.** Power to carry on the business of the company.

**15.** Power to establish subsidiaries of the company.

**16.** Power to transfer to subsidiaries of the company the whole or any part of the business and property of the company.

**17.** Power to grant or accept a surrender of a lease or tenancy of any of the property of the company, and to take a lease or tenancy of any property required or convenient for the business of the company.

**18.** Power to make any arrangement or compromise on behalf of the company.

**19.** Power to call up any uncalled capital of the company

**20.** Power to rank and claim in the bankruptcy, insolvency, sequestration or liquidation of any person indebted to the company and to receive dividends, and to accede to trust deeds for the creditors of any such person.

**21.** Power to present or defend a petition for the winding-up of the company.

**22.** Power to change the situation of the company's registered office.

**23.** Power to do all other things incidental to the exercise of the foregoing powers.

# Appendix 6

## Badges of Unfitness for Directors

The various badges of unfitness for directors are set out in Sch. 1 to the Company Directors Disqualification Act 1986, as follows:

## SCHEDULE 1

## MATTERS FOR DETERMINING UNFITNESS OF DIRECTORS

### PART I

### MATTERS APPLICABLE IN ALL CASES

**1.** Any misfeasance or breach of any fiduciary or other duty by the director in relation to the company.

**2.** Any misapplication or retention by the director of, or any conduct by the director giving rise to an obligation to account for, any money or other property of the company.

**3.** The extent of the director's responsibility for the company entering into any transaction liable to be set aside under Part XVI of the Insolvency Act (provisions against debt avoidance).

**4.** The extent of the director's responsibility for any failure by the company to comply with any of the following provisions of the Companies Act, namely –

(*a*) section 221 (companies to keep accounting records);
(*b*) section 222 (where and for how long records to be kept);
(*c*) section 288 (register of directors and secretaries);
(*d*) section 352 (obligation to keep and enter up register of members);
(*e*) section 353 (location of register of members);
(*f*) sections 363 and 364 (company's duty to make annual return);
(*g*) section 365 (time for completion of annual return); and
(*h*) sections 399 and 415 (company's duty to register charges it creates).

**5.** The extent of the director's responsibility for any failure by the directors of the company to comply with section 227 (directors' duty to prepare annual accounts) or section 238 (signing of balance sheet and documents to be annexed) of the Companies Act.

## PART II

## MATTERS APPLICABLE WHERE COMPANY HAS BECOME INSOLVENT

**6.** The extent of the director's responsibility for the causes of the company becoming insolvent.

**7.** The extent of the director's responsibility for any failure by the company to supply any goods or securities which have been paid for (in whole or in part).

**8.** The extent of the director's responsibility for the company entering into any transaction or giving any preference, being a transaction or preference –

(*a*) liable to be set aside under section 127 or sections 238 to 240 of the Insolvency Act, or

(*b*) challengeable under section 242 or 243 of the Act or under any rule of law in Scotland.

**9.** The extent of the director's responsibility for any failure by the directors of the company to comply with section 98 of the Insolvency Act (duty to call creditors' meeting in creditors' voluntary winding-up).

**10.** Any failure by the director to comply with any obligation imposed on him by or under any of the following provisions of the Insolvency Act –

(*a*) section 22 (company's statement of affairs in administration);

(*b*) section 47 (statement of affairs to administrative receiver);

(*c*) section 66 (statement of affairs in Scottish receivership);

(*d*) section 99 (directors' duty to attend meeting; statement of affairs in creditors' voluntary winding-up);

(*e*) section 131 (statement of affairs in winding-up by the court);

(*f*) section 234 (duty of any one with company property to deliver it up);

(*g*) section 235 (duty to co-operate with liquidator, etc.)

# Case Table

*All references are to paragraph numbers*

**Paragraph**

**A**

A.B.C. Coupler & Engineering Limited (No. 3), Re [1970] 1 WLR 702 ...................................... 510; 1115

Aboussafy v Abacus Cities Limited [1981] 4 WWR 60 .................... 407

Airlines Airspares Limited v Handley Page Limited and Another [1970] 1 Ch. 193 ..................... 406; 409

Aluminium Industrie Vaassen BV v Romalpa Aluminium Limited [1976] 1 WLR 676 .................. 407

American Cyanamid Co. v Ethicon Ltd [1975] AC 396 .................. 307; 506

American Express International Banking Corporation v Hurley (1986) 2 BCC 98, 993; [1985] 3 All ER 564 .............................. 404; 416; 502; 1120

Anchor Line (The), Re [1937] Ch. 483 ..................................... 302

Andrabell Limited (in liq.), Re [1984] 3 All ER 407 ................. 407

Anglo-Moravian Hungarian Junction Railway Company, ex parte Watkins, Re [1875] 1 Ch. 130 .... 1003; 1019

Anson v Anson [1953] 1 QB 636 ... 608

Antione; A.-G. v (1949) 31 TC 213 804

Apex Leisure Hire v Barratt [1984] 1 WLR 1062 .......................... 515

Arcedeckne, Re (1883) 24 ChD 709 608

Arctic Engineering, Re [1986] 1 WLR 686; (1985) 1 BCC 99, 563 710

Armagh Shoes Ltd, Re [1984] 4 BCLC 405 ............................. 305

A.-G. v Antione (1949) 31 TC 213 804

**B**

Bacal Contracting Limited v Modern Engineering (Bristol) Limited and Others [1980] 2 All ER 655 ....... 412

**Paragraph**

Bank of Baroda v Panessar and Others (1986) 2 BCC 99, 288; [1986] 3 All ER 751 ................. 307; 308; 313

Barclays Bank Limited v Quistclose Investments Limited [1970] AC 567 ..................................... 407

Barclays Bank plc v Willowbrook International Ltd (1987) *The Times*, 5 February ................... 305

Barker (George) (Transport) Limited v Eynon [1974] 1 WLR 462 . 407

Barleycorn Enterprises Limited, Re [1970] 1 Ch. 465 ..................... 709

Barrows v Chief Land Registrar (1977) *The Times*, 20 October.... 516

Batchelor v Premier Motors (Romford) Ltd (Case No. 1729/82/LN) 515

Beni-Felkai Mining Co., Re [1934] 1 Ch. 406 .............................. 1304

Berridge v Berridge (1890) 44 ChD 168 ..................................... 608

Berry (Herbert) (Associates) Ltd v IRC [1977] 1 WLR 1437; 52 TC 113 ..................................... 809; 904

Boardman v Phipps [1967] 2 AC 46 1005

Bond Worth Limited, Re [1980] Ch. 228 ..................................... 407

Borden (UK) Limited v Scottish Timber Products Limited [1981] Ch. 25 .................................... 407

Botibol, Re [1947] 1 All ER 26 ..... 406; 510; 512

Bradford v Gammon [1925] Ch. 132 608

Brightlife Limited, Re [1987] 2 WLR 197; (1986) 2 BCC 99, 359 303; 304; 305; 602

British Eagle International Airlines Ltd v Compagnie Nationale Air France [1975] 1 WLR 758 ......... 1007

Brittain v Lloyd [1845] 14 M & W 762 ..................................... 608

Brook's Wharf and Bull Wharf Limited v Goodman Bros [1937] 1 KB

**Paragraph**

534 .......................................    608

Brown v Cork and Another [1984],
(unreported) ............................    609

Brown (S.) & Co. (General Ware-
houseman) Limited, Re [1940] 1
Ch. 961 ..................................    404

Brush Aggregates Ltd, Re (1983) 1
BCC 98, 904 ...........................    305

Bunbury Foods Pty Limited v
National Bank of Australasia Limited (1984) 54 ALJR 199 ...........    308

Business Computers Limited v
Anglo-African Leasing Limited
[1977] 1 WLR 578 ...................    407

Butler Machine Tool Co. Ltd v Ex-
Cell-O-Corpn (England) Limited
[1979] 1 WLR 401 ...................    407

Byblos Bank SAL v Rushingdale
Limited SA and others (1986) 2
BCC 99, 509 ..........................    302; 307;
                                        313; 410

**C**

Campbell (Archibald James); R v
[1984] BCLC 83 .......................    415

Carreras Rothmans Limited v Freeman Mathews Treasure Limited
[1985] Ch. 207; (1984) 1 BCC 99,
210 .......................................    407

Carrington Viyella plc [1983] 1 BCC
98, 951 ..................................    1109

Carter v Carter [1896] 1 Ch. 62 .....    1122

Centrebind Ltd, Re [1967] 1 WLR
377 .......................................    903

Chelsea Cloisters Limited, Re [1981]
41 P & CR 98 .........................    407

Christonette International Limited, Re [1982] 1 WLR 1245 ......    709

Clarks of Hove v Bakers' Union
[1978] 1 WLR 1207 .................    515

Clayton's case (1816) 1 Mer 572 ....    1016

Cleadon Trust Limited, Re [1939]
Ch. 286 .................................    608

Clifton Place Garage Limited, Re
[1970] 1 Ch. 477 .....................    412

Clough Mill Ltd v Martin [1985] 1
WLR 111; [1984] 1 WLR 1067 ...    407

Compania Merabello San Nicholas
SA, Re [1973] 1 Ch. 75 ............    903

Company No. 00175 of 1987, Re
(1987) 3 BCC 124 ....................    904

—— No. 00477 of 1986, Re (1986) 2
BCC 99, 171 ..........................    1109

—— No. 00475 of 1982, Re [1983]
Ch. 178 .................................    1109

**Paragraph**

Condon, ex parte James, Re (1874)
Ch. App 609 ...........................    1004

Coope v Twynam (1823) Turn & R
426 .......................................    608

Courts (Emergency Powers) Act
(1939), Re 65 TLR 141 .............    404

Craven-Ellis v Canons Limited
[1936] 2 KB 403 ......................    608

Craythorne v Swinburne (1807) 14
Ves. Jun 160 ...........................    608

Cripps (R.A.) & Sons Ltd v Wickenden [1973] 1 WLR 944 .........    307; 311;
                                        313

Cuckmere Brick Co. Limited &
Another v Mutual Finance Lim-
ited [1971] Ch. 949 ..................    307; 416;
                                        501

Cutts, Re [1956] 1 WLR 728 .........    1016

**D**

Davies v Humphreys (1840) 6 M &
W 153 ...................................    608

Davies and Hedley-Cheney v
Directloans Ltd [1986] 2 All ER
783 .......................................    1016

Debtor, Re [1937] Ch. 156 ...........    608

Deering v The Earl of Winchelsea
(1787) 1 Cox Exch Cas 318 ........    608

Denton's Estate, Re [1904] 2 Ch.
178 .......................................    608

Denton Sub-Divisions Pty Ltd (in
liq.) (1968) 89 WN (Pt. 1) (NSW)
231 .......................................    1115

Department of Health and Security
v Evans and Others [1985] 2 All
ER 471 ..................................    415

Diesels & Components Property
Ltd, Re [1985] 9 ACLR 825 ......    407; 512

Dorchester Finance Ltd v Stebbings
(1977), (unreported) ................    415

Duncan, Fox & Co. v North and
South Wales Bank [1880] 6 App.
Cas. 1 ...................................    608

**E**

Ellesmere Brewery Co. v Cooper
[1896] QB 75 .........................    608

Emmadart Ltd, Re [1979] Ch. 540.    302

English, Scottish and Australian
Chartered Bank, Re [1893] 3 Ch.
385 .......................................    1109

Evans (C.) & Sons Limited v
Spritebrand Limited & Another
[1985] 1 WLR 317; (1985) 1 BCC
99, 316 ..................................    507

**Paragraph**

**F**

F.L.E. Holdings Ltd, Re [1967] 1
WLR 1409 ............................ 1016
Fenton, Re [1931] 1 Ch. 85 ......... 608
Fosters & Rudd, Re (1986) 2 BCC
98, 955 ............................. 307; 709
Four Point Garage Limited v Carter
[1985] 3 All ER 12.................. 407
Fox v Jolly [1916] 1 AC 1 ........... 308
Freelove v Mitchell [1913] 1 Ch. 201   608
Freevale Limited v Metrostore
(Holdings) Limited [1984] 1 Ch.
199 .................................. 406
Furniss v Dawson [1984] AC 474 ... 808

**G**

Gertzenstein Ltd, Re [1937] Ch. 115    1005
Goldblatt; IR Commrs v [1972] Ch.
498 .................................. 603
Gomba Holdings UK Limited and
Others v Homan and Anor (1986)
2 BCC 99, 102; [1986] 3 All ER 94   401; 402
403; 412; 416; 710
Gooch's case (1871) 7 Ch. App. 207    1004;
1005
Gosling v Gaskell & Grocott [1897]
AC 575................................ 404; 409
Gough's Garages Limited v Pugsley
[1930] 1 KB 615 .................... 412
Grantham; R v [1984] QB 675 ...... 510; 904
Greycaine Limited, Re [1946] Ch.
269 .................................. 610
Griffin Hotel Company Limited, Re
[1941] Ch. 129 ...................... 304

**H**

Habib Bank Limited v Habib Bank
AG [1981] 1 WLR 1265............ 313
Hall (William) (Contractors) Lim-
ited (in liq.), Re [1967] 1 WLR
948 .................................. 605
Hanak v Green [1958] 2 QB 9 ...... 407;
1113
Hand v Blow [1901] 2 Ch. 721 ...... 509
Hardwick Game Farm Limited v
SAPPA [1969] 2 AC 31 ............ 407
Helstan Securities Limited v Hert-
fordshire County Council [1978] 3
All ER 262............................ 408
Hemlata Lathia v Dronsfield
Brothers Limited and others,
[1987] BCLC 321 ................... 406; 416

**Paragraph**

Hendy Lennox (Industrial Engines)
Limited v Graham Puttick Lim-
ited [1984] 1 WLR 485 ............ 407
Herbert Berry Associates Ltd v IRC
[1977] 1 WLR 1437................. 809; 904
Hillman v Crystal Bowl Amuse-
ments Ltd [1973] 1 WLR 162..... 1005
Holders Investment Trust Ltd, Re
[1971] 1 WLR 583 ................. 1109
Houghton Co. v Nothard, Lowe &
Wills Ltd [1928] AC 1 ............. 308
Howe, Re [1871] 6 Ch. App. 838 .. 608

**I**

Illingworth v Houldsworth [1904]
AC 355................................ 304
Ince Hall Rolling Mills Co. Ltd v
Douglas Forge Co. (1882) 8 QBD
179 .................................. 1113
Income Tax Commissioner v Chat-
ani [1983] STC 477 ................ 801
IR Commrs v Goldblatt [1972] Ch.
498 .................................. 603
——v Thompson (Receiver for John
A. Wood Limited) (1936) 20 TC
422 .................................. 804
Industrial Development Auth-
ority v William T. Moran [1978]
IR 159................................ 410
Introductions Ltd, Re [1970] Ch. 199   1012

**J**

James, ex parte (1874) 9 Ch. App.
609 .................................. 1004
Johnson (B.) & Co. (Builders) Limited, Re [1955] 1 Ch. 634 ......... 401; 402;
406; 416; 1005

**K**

Kasofsky v Kreegers [1937] 4 All ER
374 .................................. 407
Kayford Limited (in liq.), Re [1975]
1 WLR 279 ......................... 407
Keenan Brothers Ltd [1986] 2 BCC
98,970 ............................... 305
Kestongate v Miller [1986] ICR 672   515
Knit 'N Wool Centre Pty Ltd, Re
[1969] VR 244....................... 904
Knowles v Scott [1891] 1 Ch. 717 .. 1019
Kruppstahl AG v Quitmann Prod-
ucts Limited [1982] 1 LRM 551 .. 407
Kushler (M.) Ltd, Re [1943] Ch. 248   1016

**Paragraph**

**L**

Lamplugh Iron Ore Co. Ltd, Re [1927] 1 Ch. 308 ...................... 508

Lawson v Hosemaster Co. Limited [1966] 1 WLR 1300 ................. 406; 416

Lee v Roundwood Colliery Company [1897] 1 Ch. 373 .............. 809

Lister (Ronald Elwyn) Ltd v Dunlop Canada Ltd [1982] 1 SCR 726 .... 307

Liverpool Commercial Vehicles Limited, Re [1984] BCLC 587.... 806

Liverpool Corporation v Hope [1938] 1 KB 751 ...................... 508; 510; 804

London Pressed Hinge Co. Ltd, Re [1905] 1 Ch. 576 ...................... 307

London Wine Company (Shippers) Limited, Re [1986] PCC 121 407

Lowe v Dixon (1885) 16 QBD 455 . 608

**M**

Mace Builders (Glasgow) Ltd v Lunn [1986] Ch. 459 ................ 309

Mancetter Developments Limited v Garmanson Limited [1986] QB 1212; (1986) 2 BCC 98, 924 ....... 507

Mareva Compania Neviera SA v International Bulk Carriers Limited [1975] 2 Lloyd's Rep. 509.... 407

Marriage, Neave & Co., Re [1896] 2 Ch. 663 .............................. 508

Marshall v Cottingham [1981] 3 WLR 235 .............................. 610

Meigh v Wickenden [1942] 2 KB 160 507; 1115

Melon v Hector Powe Limited [1981] 1 All ER 313 ......................... 515

Memco Engineering Ltd, Re [1985] 3 WLR 875; (1985) 1 BCC 99, 460 904

Mesco Properties Ltd, Re (1979) 54 TC 238 ............................... 404; 1301; 1304

Mitchell, Re [1913] 1 Ch. 201 ....... 608

M'Myn, Re [1886] 33 ChD 174 ..... 608

Morel (E.J.) (1934) Limited, Re [1962] Ch. 21 ......................... 605

Morris v Kanssen [1946] 1 All ER 586 ........................................ 313

Moss Steamship Co. Ltd v Whinney [1912] AC 254 ...................... 401

**N**

N.F.U. Development Trust Ltd, Re [1972] 1 WLR 1548 ................. 1111

**Paragraph**

Newdigate Colliery Limited, Re [1912] 1 Ch. 468 ...................... 406

Newhart Developments Limited v Co-operative Commercial Bank Limited [1978] 1 QB 814 .......... 412

Nicoll v Cutts (1985) 1 BCC 99, 427 401; 502; 510; 511

**O**

Oceanic Steam Navigation Co. Ltd, Re [1939] Ch. 41 ...................... 1111

Olley v Marlborough Court Limited [1949] 1 KB 532 ...................... 407

Opera Limited, Re [1891] 3 Ch. 260 407; 1004

**P**

Palmer Marine Surveys Ltd, Re [1986] 1 WLR 573; (1985) 1 BCC 99, 557 ................................. 904

Parsons v Sovereign Bank of Canada [1913] AC 160 ......................... 407

Peachdart Limited, Re [1984] Ch. 131; (1983) 1 BCC 98, 920 ........ 407

Permoid Limited, March 1986, (unreported) ........................... 515

Pitman (Harold M.) & Co. v Top Business Systems (Nottingham) Ltd (1985) 1 BCC 99, 345 ......... 1018

Plant Engineers (Sales) Ltd v Davis (1969) 113 SJ 484 ................... 1003

Potters Oils Limited (No. 2), Re (1985) 1 BCC 99, 593; [1986] All ER 890 ............................... 307; 610

Pound (Henry), Son and Hutchins, Re (1889) 42 ChD 402 .............. 307

Predeth v Castle Phillips Finance Co. Ltd Estates Gazette, 27 September 1986 ........................... 416

Premier Motors (Medway) Limited v Total Oil Great Britain Limited [1984] 1 WLR 377 ................... 515

**Q**

Quest Cae Limited, Re [1985] BCLC 266 ....................................... 606

**R**

R v Archibald James Campbell [1984] BCLC 83 ...................... 415

—— v Grantham [1984] QB 675.... 510; 904

Ratford & Another v Northaven District Council (1986) 2 BCC 99, 242 ........................................ 508; 1115

**Paragraph**

Rendell v Doors & Doors (in liq.) [1975] 2 NZLR 191 .................. 407; 505

Reynolds v Wheeler (1861) 10 CBNS 561 ....................... 608

Rhyl Urban District Council v Rhyl Amusements Ltd [1959] 1 WLR 465 ...................... 1122

Richards v Overseers of Kidderminster [1896] 2 Ch. 212 .......... 508

Robbie (N.W.) & Co. Ltd v Witney Warehouse Co. Limited [1963] 1 WLR 1324 ........................... 406; 407; 409; 508

Robson v Smith [1895] 2 Ch. 118... 407

Rolled Steel Products (Holdings) Limited v British Steel Corporation and Others [1986] 6 Ch. 246; [1985] 2 WLR 908 ................. 309; 313; 906; 1012; 1016

Rother Ironworks Limited v Canterbury Precision Engineers Limited [1974] 1 QB 1 ................... 407

Roundwood Colliery Co., Re [1897] 1 Ch. 373 ...................... 509; 809

Roxburghe v Cox [1881] 17 ChD 520 407

Royal British Bank v Turquand (1855) 5 ECB 248 ................... 309

**S**

Said v Budd [1920] 3 KB 497 ........ 406

Saunders (G.L.) Limited, Re [1986] 1 WLR 215 .......................... 603; 604

Save (Acoustics) Limited v Pimms Furnishing Limited, 11 January 1985, (unreported) ................... 313

Savoy Hotel Ltd, Re [1981] Ch. 351 1111

Saxton (E.V.) & Sons Ltd v R. Miles (Confectioners) Ltd [1983] 1 WLR 952; (1983) 1 BCC 98, 914 ....... 903

Scammell (G.) & Nephew Limited v Hurley and Others [1929] 1 KB 419 ...................... 406

Secretary of State for Employment v Spence & Others [1986] 3 WLR 380 ...................... 515

Shamji and Others v Johnson Matthey Bankers Ltd & Others [1986] 2 BCC 98,910 ....................... 307; 406

Sharp v Jackson [1899] AC 419 ..... 1016

Sherratt (W.A.) Limited v John Bromley (Church Stretton) Limited [1985] QB 1038 ................. 407

Siebe Gorman & Co. Ltd v Barclays Bank Limited [1979] 2 Lloyd's Rep. 142 .......................... 305

**Paragraph**

Sims, ex parte Trustee [1934] 1 Ch. 1 ...................... 313

Smith v Chichester (1842) 2 Dr & War 393 ...................... 407

Smiths Ltd v Middleton [1979] 3 All ER 842 ...................... 416; 710

Snow (John) and Co. Ltd v DBG Woodcroft & Co. Ltd [1985] BCLC 54 ...................... 407

Sovereign Life Assurance Company v Dodd [1892] 2 QB 573 ........... 1111

Sowman and Others v David Samuel Trust Limited and Another [1978] 1 WLR 22 ...................... 412; 516

Specialised Mouldings Ltd, Re 13 February 1987 (unreported) ....... 512; 1119

Specialist Plant Services Limited v Braithwaite Limited [1987] BCLC 1 ...................... 407

Spurling v Bradshaw [1956] 1 WLR 461 ...................... 407

Standard Chartered Bank Limited v Walker and Another [1982] 3 All ER 938 ...................... 416; 1018

Stanford Services Ltd and Others, Re (1987) 3 BCC 326 .............. 1304

Stanton (F. & E.) Ltd, Re [1929] 1 Ch. 180 ...................... 1016

Steel v Dixon (1881) 17 ChD 825 .. 608

Stirling v Burdett [1911] 2 Ch. 418. 608

Stuart v Bell [1891] 2 QB 341 ....... 415

**T**

T.C.B. Limited v Gray [1986] Ch. 621; (1986) 2 BCC 99, 044 ........ 309

Taylors Fashion Limited v Liverpool Victoria Trustees Co. Limited [1982] 2 QB 133 ...................... 313

Teeside Times Ltd v Drury [1980] ICR 338 ...................... 515

Telemetrix plc v Modern Engineers of Bristol (Holdings) plc and Others [1985] BCLC 213 ........... 406

Thomas v Todd [1926] 2 KB 511 ... 404

Thompson (Receiver for John A. Wood Limited); IR Commrs v (1936) 20 TC 422 ................... 804

Thornton v Shoe Lane Parking Limited [1971] 2 QB 163 ................ 407

Trustee, ex parte [1934] 1 Ch. 1 .... 313

**Paragraph**

Tse Kwong Lam v Wong Chit Sen and Others [1983] BCLC 88 ......    416

**U**

Unit 2 Windows Limited (in liq.), Re [1985] 1 WLR 1383; (1985) 1 BCC 99, 489 ..........................    605

**V**

Vosper Shiprepairers Ltd, Re 17 February 1987, (unreported) ......    1104

**W**

Warlow v Harrison [1858] 1 El & El 295 ........................................    608
Watkins, ex parte [1875] 1 Ch. 130    1003
Watts and Another v Midland Bank plc and Others [1986] 1 BCLC 15; 2 BCC 98,961 ..........................    307; 412; 416; 423
Welsh Irish Ferries Ltd (in liq.), Re [1986] Ch. 471; (1985) 1 BCC 99, 430 ......................................    305
Wendelboe & Others v L.J. Music ApS [1986] 1 CMLR 476 ..........    515
Westminster Corporation v Haste [1950] 1 Ch. 442 ......................    603

Wheeler v Patel and J. Golding Group of Companies [1987] IRLR 211 ........................................    515
White Rose Cottage, Re [1965] Ch. 940 ........................................    516
Whyte (G.T.) & Co. Ltd, Re [1983] BCLC 311 .............................    1016
Willment (John) (Ashford) Ltd, Re [1980] 1 WLR 73 ....................    307; 510; 804; 806
Wood, Re [1941] Ch. 112 .............    404
Woodroffes (Musical Instruments) Limited (in liq.) [1985] 2 All ER 908 ............................    303
Woods v Winskill [1913] 2 Ch. 303    603; 606
Wood's Application, Re [1941] 1 Ch. 112 ..........................................    404
Woodstead Finance Ltd v Petrou *The Times*, 23 January 1986 .......    1016

**Y**

Yeovil Glove Co. Ltd, Re [1965] Ch. 148 ........................................    1016
Yorkshire Woolcombers' Association Limited, Re [1903] 2 Ch. 284    303
Yourell v Hibernian Bank Ltd [1918] AC 372 ................................    606

# Legislation Finding List

*References are to paragraph numbers*

| Provision | Paragraph |
|---|---|
| **Australian Companies Act 1981** | |
| 349(5) | 1115 |
| **Capital Gains Tax Act 1979** | |
| 23(2) | 804 |
| **Companies Act 1948** | |
| 147 | 416 |
| 293 | 903 |
| **Companies Act 1981** | |
| 106 | 903 |
| **Companies Act 1985** | |
| 35 | 309 |
| 127(4) | 1109 |
| 151 | 309 |
| 196 | 304; 602; 603 |
| 245 | 412 |
| 322 | 1016 |
| 369 | 903 |
| 375 | 1106 |
| 380, 382 | 1005 |
| 395 | 309; 407; 412 |
| 405(1) | 312 |
| 405(2) | 701; 702; 704; 705 |
| 405(4) | 705 |
| 425 | 902; 903; 1109; 1110; 1111; 1112 |
| 459, 459(1) | 1109 |
| 497 | 710 |
| 561 | 414 |
| 588 | 903 |
| 602 | 414 |
| 604 | 709 |
| 614(2)(*b*) | 304 |
| 615 | 309; 1016 |
| 617 | 1016 |
| 637 | 907 |
| 725 | 308 |
| 727 | 1005; 1018 |
| Pt. XXVI | 903 |
| 735(1) | 903 |
| 744 | 308 |
| Sch. 19 | 802 |
| Sch. 19, para. 2 | 810 |
| Sch. 19, para. 7 | 508 |

| Provision | Paragraph |
|---|---|
| **Companies (Floating Charges and Receivers) (Scotland) Act 1972** | 303 |
| **Companies (Floating Charges) (Scotland) Act 1961** | 303 |
| **Companies (Tables A – F) Regulations 1985** | |
| para. 12 | 410 |
| **Companies (Winding-up) Rules 1949** | |
| r. 154 | 1107 |
| r. 163 | 1107 |
| r. 195(1) | 1304 |
| **Company Directors Disqualification Act 1986** | |
| 1(1) | 415 |
| 6, 6(1)(*a*) | 415 |
| 6(2), (4) | 415 |
| 7 | 415 |
| 7(1)–(3) | 415 |
| 9 | 415; 1106 |
| 9(1) | 415 |
| 22(5) | 415 |
| Sch. 1 | 415 |
| Sch. 1, para. 10 | 1106 |
| Sch. 1, para. 10(*g*) | 414; 415 |
| **Copyright Act 1956** | |
| 1(2) | 507 |
| 17(2), 18(2) | 507 |
| **EEC Council Directive** | |
| 77/187 | 515 |
| **Employment Protection Act 1975** | |
| 99–101 | 515 |
| **Employment Protection (Consolidation) Act 1978** | |
| 57(3) | 515 |
| 83, 84 | 515 |
| 94 | 515 |
| 122 | 515 |
| 127(1)(*c*) | 515 |
| Sch. 13, para. 17(2) | 515 |
| **European Communities Act 1972** | |
| 2 | 515 |

| Provision | Paragraph |
|---|---|
| Factories Act 1937 | 507 |

**Finance (No. 2) Act 1975**

| | |
|---|---|
| 69 | 802; 805 |

**Finance Act 1980**

| | |
|---|---|
| 43 | 802 |

**Finance Act 1983**

| | |
|---|---|
| 27 | 805 |

**Finance Act 1985**

| | |
|---|---|
| 31 | 806 |

**Finance Act 1986**

| | |
|---|---|
| 44 | 805 |
| 115 | 305 |

**Financial Services Act 1986**

| | |
|---|---|
| 33, 74 | 903 |

**Income and Corporation Taxes Act 1970**

| | |
|---|---|
| 53 | 805 |
| 54 | 804; 805 |
| 89 | 805 |
| 94 | 805 |
| 114(1), (4) | 804 |
| 137 | 808 |
| 156, 157, 159 | 805 |
| 177(1) | 808 |
| 204 | 802; 805 |
| 238 | 1301 |
| 243(3), 244 | 1301 |
| 247 | 808; 1301 |
| 247(3), (7) | 1301 |
| 252 | 504; 808 |
| 252(1)(a) | 805 |
| 252(1)(b), (3A) | 808 |
| 253 | 805 |
| 272, 273 | 808 |
| 278 | 808; 1306 |
| 380 | 805 |
| 391 | 805 |
| 482 | 519 |
| 483 | 504; 808 |
| 526(5) | 808 |
| 532(1)(b) | 808 |

**Income Tax (Sub-Contractors in the Construction Industry) Regulations 1975** .. 802

**Insolvency Act 1976**

| | |
|---|---|
| 8(3)(b) | 1302 |
| 387(3) | 1302 |

**Insolvency Act 1986**

| | |
|---|---|
| 1–7 | 902 |
| 1(1), (2), (3)(a) | 1111 |
| 2 | 1111 |
| 2(1), (2), (4) | 1111 |

| Provision | Paragraph |
|---|---|
| 3(2) | 1111 |
| 4(1)–(3) | 1111 |
| 4(4) | 1111; 1302 |
| 4(6), (7) | 1111 |
| 5(2)–(4) | 1111 |
| 5(2)(b) | 1111 |
| 6 | 1109; 1111 |
| 7(3) | 1111 |
| 7(4)(b) | 903; 1111 |
| 8(1) | 902 |
| 8(1)(a) | 901 |
| 8(2) | 901; 902; 1005; 1014 |
| 8(3) | 902 |
| 8(3)(d) | 1113 |
| 9 | 903 |
| 9(1) | 903; 904 |
| 9(2) | 903 |
| 9(2)(a) | 903 |
| 9(3) | 903; 904 |
| 9(3)(a) | 905 |
| 9(3)(b) | 906 |
| 9(4) | 903; 904; 906; 1110 |
| 9(5) | 903 |
| 10(1) | 902 |
| 10(1)(a) | 904 |
| 10(1)(b) | 904; 1104 |
| 10(1)(c) | 904; 1307 |
| 10(2), (3) | 904 |
| 10(4) | 904; 908 |
| 11(1) | 908 |
| 11(1)(a) | 904; 1204 |
| 11(2) | 705; 908 |
| 11(3) | 706; 902; 908; 1109 |
| 11(3)(b) | 905 |
| 11(3)(c) | 908; 1104 |
| 11(3)(d) | 1115; 1118; 1204; 1307 |
| 11(4) | 706 |
| 11(5) | 705; 904 |
| 12(1), (2) | 907 |
| 12(5) | 415 |
| 14(1) | 411; 1009 |
| 14(2) | 1010 |
| 14(2)(b) | 1011; 1106; 1108 |
| 14(3) | 1011; 1106; 1113 |
| 14(4) | 904; 1010 |
| 14(5) | 1003 |
| 14(6) | 1012 |
| 15 | 905; 1007; 1008; 1122 |
| 15(1) | 1008; 1122 |
| 15(2) | 1122 |
| 15(3) | 706; 1122 |
| 15(4) | 1008; 1104; 1122 |
| 15(5) | 1122 |
| 15(9) | 1122 |
| 17(1) | 810; 1006; 1101 |

| Provision | Paragraph |
|---|---|
| 17(2) | 1014; 1101 |
| 17(2)(a) | 1113; 1115 |
| 17(2)(b) | 1115 |
| 18(1), (2) | 902; 1204 |
| 18(2)(a) | 1113 |
| 18(3) | 1106; 1204 |
| 18(4), (5) | 1204 |
| 19 | 1115 |
| 19(1) | 1109; 1205; 1206 |
| 19(2) | 1205 |
| 19(3)(a) | 1106 |
| 19(4) | 1115; 1209 |
| 19(5) | 1101; 1115; 1119; 1209 |
| 20 | 1211 |
| 21 | 907 |
| 22 | 419; 1011; 1111 |
| 22(1), (3)–(6) | 1011 |
| 23 | 1103 |
| 23(1) | 902; 1103; 1106 |
| 23(1)(b) | 1106 |
| 24(2), (4) | 1106 |
| 25 | 1105 |
| 25(2) | 1105; 1106 |
| 26 | 1107 |
| 27 | 1301 |
| 27(1) | 708; 1109; 1118 |
| 27(2) | 1110 |
| 27(3)(b) | 1110 |
| 27(4) | 1110 |
| 27(5) | 1109; 1122 |
| 29(2) | 301 |
| 31(2) | 1111 |
| 33, 33(1), (1)(b) | 311 |
| 34 | 313; 706 |
| 35 | 421; 422; 512; 604; 609 |
| 36 | 307; 610 |
| 36(2) | 610 |
| 39 | 312; 418 |
| 40 | 304; 602; 603; 810 |
| 41 | 416; 710 |
| 41(2), (3) | 710 |
| 42, 42(1) | 411 |
| 44 | 513; 515 |
| 44(1)(a) | 302; 401; 404 |
| 44(1)(b) | 401; 510; 511; 512; 804; 1119 |
| 44(2) | 511; 512 |
| 45(1) | 702; 703 |
| 45(2) | 705 |
| 45(3) | 706 |
| 45(4) | 701; 702; 704; 705 |
| 45(5) | 705 |
| 46(1), (2), (4) | 312 |
| 47, 47(1) | 419 |
| 48, 48(1) | 420 |
| 48(2) | 420; 421 |

| Provision | Paragraph |
|---|---|
| 48(3) | 420 |
| 48(4) | 421 |
| 48(5), (6), (8) | 420 |
| 49 | 421 |
| 49(2) | 422 |
| 51 | 301 |
| 62 | 810 |
| 98 | 903 |
| 107 | 404 |
| 108 | 1205 |
| 115 | 709; 1115; 1209 |
| 122 | 1204 |
| 123 | 903; 1016 |
| 123(1), (2) | 903 |
| 124 | 1204 |
| 124(1) | 903 |
| 129 | 1204 |
| 129(2) | 1204 |
| 133 | 1211 |
| 140 | 1204 |
| 140(1) | 1208 |
| 156 | 709 |
| 165 | 1009 |
| 166 | 903 |
| 167 | 1009 |
| 173, 174 | 1211 |
| 175 | 602; 1209 |
| 175(2)(b) | 304 |
| 188 | 907 |
| 212 | 1005; 1018; 1211 |
| 212(1)(b) | 416 |
| 212(3) | 1005 |
| 212(4) | 1005; 1211 |
| 212(5) | 1005 |
| 213 | 401; 509; 904 |
| 214 | 901; 903; 904 |
| 214(6) | 1016 |
| 216 | 519 |
| 218(6) | 1104 |
| Pt. V | 903 |
| 230–246 | 414 |
| 231 | 310; 903; 1013; 1111 |
| 231(2) | 413 |
| 232 | 313; 909 |
| 233 | 414; 1003; 1011; 1117 |
| 234(1) | 1011 |
| 234(2) | 414; 1006; 1011 |
| 234(3), (4) | 501; 506; 1006; 1115 |
| 235 | 415; 416; 1011; 1106 |
| 235(2)–(5) | 414 |
| 235(2)(b) | 414 |
| 236 | 414; 1011 |
| 236(2)–(6) | 414 |
| 237 | 414; 1011 |
| 238 | 309; 905; 906; 1016; 1111 |

**Provision**      **Paragraph**
**Insolvency Act 1986**—continued
238(2), (4), (5) ..................................1016
239.......................309; 905; 906; 1016; 1111
239(2), (3) ....................................1016
239(4)(b)...........................................1016
239(6), (7) ......................................1016
240......................... 905; 906; 1016; 1204
240(1)(a), (c) ...................................1016
240(2)............................................1016
240(3)..................................... 1016; 1204
240(3)(a) ................................. 1016; 1208
241...............................................1016
244................................................1111
244(1)–(4)........................................1016
245.......................309; 412; 906; 1016; 1111
245(2)–(6)........................................1016
245(3)(a) ........................................1016
246...............................................1011
247(2)..................................... 1016; 1204
248(6)........................... 706; 908; 1111
251.......................301; 304; 311; 405; 602;
                      903; 1005; 1007
386........................... 601; 802; 810
Pt. XIII...............................102; 205
388(1)........................................ 201
388(1)(b)........................................1111
389............................................ 201
389(1)........................................ 705
390............................................ 909
390(1), (2) ................................. 202
390(3)........................................ 206
390(4)........................................ 202
391............................................ 203
392..................................202; 204
392(2), (4) ................................. 204
393(1), (2), (4), (5) ..................... 205
394(2)........................................ 205
395............................................ 205
396(2), (3) ................................. 205
397............................................ 205
423...............................................1016
423(2), (3), (5) ...............................1016
424(1)(a) .......................................1016
425...............................................1016
436...............................................1104
Sch. 1 ..................................... 411; 1009
Sch. 1, para. 8..................................1009
Sch. 1, para. 15, 16 ...........................1114
Sch. 4, para. 7.................................1009
Sch. 6 ..................................... 601; 802; 810
Sch. 6, para. 11, 14(2) ........................ 601
Sch. 7, para. 1.................................. 205
Sch. 11, para. 1(1) ........................... 903
Sch. 11, para. 27................................ 803
Sch. 13, Pt. 1 ................................. 603

**Provision**      **Paragraph**
**Insolvency Practitioners (Recognised Professional Bodies) Order 1986**............ 203

**Insolvency Practitioners Regulations 1986**
reg. 4–6...........................................205
reg. 7............................................ 204
reg. 8............................................ 205
reg. 10 .......................................... 206
Sch. 2 .......................................... 206

**Insolvency Rules 1986**
r. 1.3–1.5, 1.9................................1111
r. 1.9(2)(b), (3) ..............................1111
r. 1.10(1)(b)...................................1111
r. 1.11, 1.11(1)(b) ...........................1111
r. 1.12(1), (2), (5) ..........................1111
r. 1.13–1.15...................................1111
r. 1.13(1).......................................1111
r. 1.16(2).......................................1111
r. 1.17(2)–(9)..................................1111
r. 1.18, 1.18(2) ..............................1111
r. 1.19(b).......................................1111
r. 1.19(2)–(4) .................................1111
r. 1.19(3)(b), (4)(c) ..........................1111
r. 1.20(2), (3) .................................1111
r. 1.21, 1.21(6) ...............................1111
r. 1.22(1), (3) .................................1111
r. 1.23(1)–(5) .................................1111
r. 1.24..........................................1111
r. 1.24(3)–(5)..................................1111
r. 1.26–1.30....................................1111
r. 2.1 .......................................... 903
r. 2.2(1), (2) ................................. 903
r. 2.3(1) .......................................1108
r. 2.3(6) ...................................... 903
r. 2.4 .......................................... 903
r. 2.4(3), (6) ................................. 903
r. 2.4(6)(c)..................................... 903
r. 2.5(1)–(3) ................................. 903
r. 2.5(4) ...................................... 904
r. 2.6, 2.6(2)(a) ............................. 903
r. 2.7 .......................................... 903
r. 2.7(1) ................................903; 904
r. 2.8 .......................................... 903
r. 2.9(1) ...................................... 906
r. 2.9(2) ...................... 903; 906; 1115; 1201
r. 2.10......................................... 907
r. 2.11–2.15............................... 419; 1011
r. 2.11(3), (4) .................................1011
r. 2.15(1).......................................1115
r. 2.15(3).......................................1011
r. 2.16..........................................1103
r. 2.16(f) .......................................1115
r. 2.17..........................................1103
r. 2.18(1), (3), (4) ...........................1106
r. 2.19(2), (3)..................................1106

| Provision | Paragraph |
|---|---|
| r. 2.19(4) | 1103; 1106 |
| r. 2.19(5)–(7) | 1106 |
| r. 2.20–2.22 | 1106 |
| r. 2.21(1)(e) | 1106 |
| r. 2.23 | 1111 |
| r. 2.23(2), (4), (6) | 1106 |
| r. 2.24, 2.25 | 1106 |
| r. 2.26, 2.27 | 1106; 1111 |
| r. 2.28(1) | 902; 1106 |
| r. 2.28(2), (3) | 1106 |
| r. 2.30 | 1106; 1210 |
| r. 2.31(2)–(6) | 1108 |
| r. 2.32–2.40 | 1107 |
| r. 2.41(2), (3) | 1107 |
| r. 2.42, 2.43 | 1107 |
| r. 2.44(1), (2) | 1107 |
| r. 2.45(1) | 1107; 1115 |
| r. 2.45(2) | 1107 |
| r. 2.46 | 1107 |
| r. 2.47(2)(b) | 1202 |
| r. 2.47(3)–(6) | 1202 |
| r. 2.48–2.50 | 1203 |
| r. 2.51 | 1122 |
| r. 2.52 | 1210 |
| r. 2.52(1), (3) | 1210 |
| r. 2.53 | 1206 |
| r. 2.53(2), (3) | 1206 |
| r. 2.56 | 807 |
| r. 3.1 | 311 |
| r. 3.2(2)–(4) | 312 |
| r. 3.3–3.7 | 419 |
| r. 3.3(1) | 419 |
| r. 3.5 | 704 |
| r. 3.8 | 420 |
| r. 3.9–3.30 | 421 |
| r. 3.16–3.30 | 422 |
| r. 3.18, 3.19 | 422 |
| r. 3.28 | 422 |
| r. 3.29(1) | 510 |
| r. 3.32 | 416; 710 |
| r. 3.33 | 705 |
| r. 3.33(1) | 703 |
| r. 3.33(3) | 705 |
| r. 3.34 | 704 |
| r. 3.35 | 701; 705 |
| r. 3.37 | 807 |
| r. 4.170 | 1107 |
| r. 4.218 | 709 |
| r. 4.226–4.230 | 519 |
| r. 7.55 | 1106; 1111 |
| r. 8.1–8.7 | 1111 |
| r. 8.1 | 1106 |
| r. 8.1(1), (4), (5) | 1106 |
| r. 8.2(1), (3) | 1106 |
| r. 8.3–8.7 | 1106 |

| Provision | Paragraph |
|---|---|
| r. 8.3(3) | 1106 |
| r. 12.4 | 703; 904 |
| r. 12.4(1) | 1106 |
| r. 12.8(2) | 421; 422; 1107 |
| r. 12.8(3) | 1115 |
| r. 12.9 | 1106; 1110 |
| r. 13.3 | 703 |
| r. 13.6 | 903; 1107 |
| r. 13.13(4) | 907 |

**Insolvent Companies (Report on Conduct of Directors) No. 2 Rules 1986** ............ 415

**Law of Distress (Amendment) Act 1908** .... 509

**Law of Property Act 1925**
| | |
|---|---|
| 1 | 406 |
| 74(1) | 309 |
| 74(3) | 516 |
| 101 | 307 |
| 101(1)(iii) | 610 |
| 109(1) | 307 |
| 109(2) | 401 |
| 109(6) | 610 |
| 109(8) | 606; 609; 610; 804 |
| 109(8)(i) | 508 |
| 172 | 1016 |
| 196 | 308 |
| 205(1)(xxi) | 309 |

**Mental Health Act 1983**
| | |
|---|---|
| Pt. VII | 202 |

**Mental Health (Scotland) Act 1984**
| | |
|---|---|
| 125(1) | 202 |

**Mercantile Law Amendment Act 1956**
| | |
|---|---|
| 5 | 608 |

**Sale of Goods Act 1979**
| | |
|---|---|
| 12 | 513 |
| 18, r. 4 | 512 |
| 19 | 407 |
| 25(1) | 407 |

**Social Security Act 1975**
| | |
|---|---|
| Sch. 1, para. 4, 5 | 805 |

**Stamp Act 1891**
| | |
|---|---|
| 59(1) | 808 |

**Taxes Management Act 1970**
| | |
|---|---|
| 61 | 809 |
| 62 | 809; 810 |
| 108 | 801 |

**Transfer of Undertakings (Protection of Employment) Regulations 1981**
| | |
|---|---|
| reg. 4 | 515 |
| reg. 5(1)–(3) | 515 |

**Provision**        **Paragraph**

**Transfer of Undertakings (Protection of Employment) Regulations 1981—**
continued

reg. 7 ............................................... 515

reg. 8, 8(2), 8(2)(b) ............................. 515

**Treaty of Rome**

Art. 100, 117 ..................................... 515

**Unfair Contract Terms Act 1977** ............ 513

**Value Added Tax Act 1983**

22, 22(3)(*b*) ...................................... 807

31 ................................................... 806

Sch. 7, para. 4(4), (10) ......................... 806

**Value Added Tax (Bad Debt Relief) Regulations 1986**

reg. 8–10 .......................................... 807

**Provision**        **Paragraph**

**Value Added Tax (General) Regulations 1977**

reg. 56 ............................................. 806

**Value Added Tax (General) Regulations 1985**

reg. 11 ............................................. 806

reg. 11(1) .................................... 510; 804

reg. 58 ............................................. 803

reg. 58(1) .......................................... 802

reg. 58(3) .................... 802; 803; 806; 1303

reg. 63 ............................................. 806

reg. 65 ............................................. 809

**Value Added Tax (Special Provisions) Order 1981**

reg. 12 ............................................. 808

# Index

*References are to paragraph numbers*

**Paragraph**

## A

**Accounting period**
. corporation tax .............................1301

**Accounts**
. administrative receiver, abstract of
  receipts and payments................... 710
. administrator.................................1210

**Administration order**
. affidavit...................................... 903(6)
. application
. . company, meaning ..................... 903(1)
. . debts, inability to pay ................. 903(2)
. . details of ..................................... 903
. . hearing of.................................... 906
. . legal consequences ..................... 904(1)
. . practical consequences ............... 904(2)
. . secured creditors, attitudes of........... 905
. charges – see Charges
. consequences of order...................... 908
. definition....................................... 901
. discharge of ................................1204
. notice of....................................... 907
. petition ...................................... 903(4)
. . contents ................................... 903(5)
. . filing........................................ 903(7)
. . notice of.................................... 903(8)
. . practical aspects........................903(10)
. . time of service........................... 903(9)
. statutory purposes ....................... 903(3)

**Administrative receivers**
. accounts, abstract of receipts and
  payments................................... 710
. agency
. . conflict of interest .......................... 402
. . effect of liquidation ........................ 404
. . nature and extent........................... 401
. . responsibilities............................... 403
. appointment
. . acceptance of, rules regarding .......... 311
. . after presentation of petition ............ 904
. . checklist...................................... 309
. . confirmation of acceptance......311(4)–(7)

**Paragraph**

. . construction of loan and security
  documentation.......................... 307(3)
. . contractual and statutory powers... 307(1)
. . demands generally.......................... 308
. . formalities subsequent to ................ 312
. . form of ................................... 310(1)
. . invitation of borrower................. 307(2)
. . limited duties of mortgagee ......... 307(4)
. . notice of.................................... 312
. . occurrence ................................... 306
. . 'on demand'............................. 307(5)
. . right to appoint ............................ 307
. . specimen appointment ............... 310(2)
. assets, realisation of – see Realisation of
  assets and property
. charges
. . fixed charges ............................. 304
. . floating charges.............................. 303
. . future book debts........................... 305
. . general outline ............................ 302
. . mortgages.................................... 304
. . definition..................................... 301
. duties
. . cooperation with official receiver... 416(3)
. . creditors' committee ...................... 422
. . distributions................................. 417
. . enforcement of ............................. 423
. . fulfilment of transactions ............. 416(4)
. . meetings of creditors ..................... 421
. . notification ................................. 418
. . proper price or market value........ 416(1)
. . provision of information ............. 416(2)
. . reasonable care in realisation ....... 416(1)
. . report on unfit directors ................. 415
. . report to creditors.......................... 420
. . sales delay because of market
  conditions.............................. 416(2)
. . specialist advice on valuation........ 416(4)
. . statement of affairs........................ 419
. . trading – see Trading
. employees
. . adoption, meaning ......................... 512
. . personal liability ............................ 511
. invalid appointments
. . effect of invalidity ...................... 313(1)

## Adm

**Paragraph**

**Administrative receivers**—continued
. . indemnities ............................... 313(3)
. . statutory validity ....................... 313(2)
. payments and distributions
. . contribution between co-guarantees – see
    Co-guarantees
. . order of payments ......................... 606
. . preferential creditors – see Preferential
    creditors
. position as agent ............................. 409
. powers
. . additional statutory powers ............. 411
. . contractual provisions .................... 410
. . joint appointments ........................ 413
. . limitations ................................. 412
. . office holder................................ 414
. preferential creditors – see Preferential
    creditors
. property
. . covered by appointment – see Property
. . realisation of – see Realisation of assets
    and property
. realisation of assets and property – see
    Realisation of assets and property
. receivership expense ........................ 510
. remuneration ................................ 610
. responsibilities.............................. 403
. specific penalty sum......................... 206
. taking control
. . establishment of procedures ............ 502
. . preliminary steps.......................... 501
. tax liabilities – see Tax
. termination of office
. . accounts, abstracts of receipts and
    payments................................... 710
. . death .................................... 704
. . dismissal, court order..................... 702
. . duty to cease to act ...................... 701
. . indemnities – see Indemnities
. . repayment of secured debt.............. 701
. . resignation................................. 703
. . vacation of office ......................... 705

**Administrators**
. administrative receiver vacating office,
    relationship with ......................... 708
. administration order – see Administration
    order
. agency
. . nature and extent......................... 1003
. . officer of the company ................... 1005
. . officer of the court ...................... 1004
. appointment
. . comparison with other office-holders.1001
. . outline of procedure ...................... 902

**Paragraph**

. . property covered by – see Property
. . purposes of ............................... 1002
. . rationale of the administration
    process............................,,,,,, 901
. breach of duty/trust.................... 1005(5)
. care and skill, duty to show ......... 1005(4)
. comparison with other office-holders...1001
. creditors' meetings – see Creditors' meetings
. death of .................................... 1207
. duties
. . company .................................. 1018
. . creditors and members ................. 1019
. . fiduciary ................................. 1005(3)
. . investigating antecedent transactions – see
    Antecedent transactions
. miscellaneous ............................. 1017
. . outline.................................... 1014
. . reporting on unfit directors ............ 1015
. employees, payment of .................. 1119
. fiduciary duties .......................... 1005(3)
. fines, liability ........................... 1005(1)
. hiving-down .............................. 1114
. information and powers as office-
    holder.................................... 1011
. invalid appointment........................ 909
. investigating antecedent transactions – see
    Antecedent transactions
. joint appointments, exercise of
    powers.................................... 1013
. liabilities
. . officer of the company ................. 1005
. . tort .................................... 1116
. negligence .............................. 1005(5)
. powers
. . directors of the company .............. 1010
. . joint appointments ..................... 1013
. . limitations ............................. 1012
. . office-holder............................ 1011
. . statutory list.......................... 1009
. property
. . covered by appointment – see Property
. . realisation of assets and property – see
    Realisation of assets and property
. proposals
. . court orders and time limits ........... 1110
. . examples of possible .................... 1104
. . formal requirements .................... 1103
. . revision of .............................. 1105
. . statement of............................ 1103
. remuneration ......................... 1107(10)
. . application to court ..................... 1203
. . creditors' committee ................... 1202
. . pre-order................................ 1201
. report on unfit directors ................ 1015
. resignation............................... 1206

**Paragraph**

. schemes – see Voluntary arrangement
    schemes
. statement of affairs.....................1011(1)
. supplies of utilities .....................1117
. taking control
. . establishing procedures .................1102
. . preliminary steps.........................1101
. tax – see Tax
. termination of office
. . accounts....................................1210
. . death.........................................1207
. . discharge of administration order .....1204
. . expenses paid out of floating charge
    assets........................................1209
. . floating charges, expenses paid out
    of...............................................1209
. . general considerations....................1208
. . release of discharge from liability .....1211
. . resignation.................................1206
. . vacation of office by court order ......1205
. trading – see Trading
. unfairly prejudicial management and
    acts ..........................................1109

**Affidavit**
. administration order .................... 903(6)

**Agency**
. administrative receiver
. . conflict of interest ......................... 402
. . effect of liquidation ....................... 404
. . nature and extent.......................... 401
. . responsibilities............................. 403
. administrator
. . nature and extent..........................1003
. . officer of the company ..................1005
. . officer of the court ......................1004

**Annual payments**
. income tax.................................... 805

**Antecedent transactions**
. administrator investigating ................1016
. . avoidance of floating charges.......1016(7)
. . court orders ............................1016(4)
. . defrauding creditors...................1016(8)
. . extortionate credit transactions ....1016(6)
. . preferences ...................... 1016(3), (5)
. . transactions at an under
    value ........................... 1016(2), (5)

**Anti-avoidance measures**
. hive-downs ................................... 808

**Arrangements** – see Voluntary arrangement
    schemes

**Paragraph**

**Arrears of tax**
. seizure of goods and chattels.............. 810

**Articles of association**
. administrative receiver's powers        410

**Assets**
. fixed charges................................. 305
. realisation of – see Realisation of assets and
    property

**Assignment**
. prohibition on charging .................... 408

**Attorney**
. administrative receiver, power of ........ 516

**Avoidance of floating charges**
. administrator investigating ...........1016(7)

**B**

**Bad debt relief**
. value added tax .............................. 807

**Bankrupts**
. insolvency practitioner prohibition....... 202

**Banks**
. credit balances, book debts............... 305
. cross guarantees............................. 607

**Bills of exchange**
. creditors' meetings, evaluation of
    debts .....................................1106(5)
. voluntary arrangement schemes .....1111(6)

**Bonding**
. insolvency practitioners .................... 206

**Book debts** – see also Debts
. charges ........................................ 302
. . future book debts........................... 305

**Books**
. surrender to administrative receiver . 414(2)

**Breach of duty**
. administrative receiver's liability ..... 507(3)
. administrator's liability................1005(5)

**Business letters**
. appointment of receiver to be
    stated .............................312(5), 418

**C**

**Capital losses**
. taxation....................................... 808

**Centrebinding**...............................903(10)

**Paragraph**

**Chairman**
. creditors' meetings ......................1106(2)
. members' meetings.........................1108
. voluntary arrangement schemes,
   meetings................................1111(5)

**Charged property**
. administrator................................1008
. . power to deal with .......................1122

**Charges**
. fixed charges ................................. 304
. floating charges – see Floating charges
. future book debts........................... 305
. general outline ............................. 302
. mortgages....................................... 304

**Chartered Association of Certified
Accountants**
. recognised professional body.............. 203

**Chattel leasing agreements** ...................1007
. creditors' meetings, evaluation of
   debts ...................................1106(5)

**Chose in action**
. prohibition on charging ..................... 408

**Claims**
. value added tax bad debt relief........... 807

**Class rights**
. unfairly prejudicial management and
   acts ......................................1109

**Co-guarantors**
. contribution between
. . co-sureties ............................... 608(2)
. . general outline ........................... 607
. . indemnity from principal debtor.... 608(1)
. . receiver's power and duty to allocate
     funds ...................................... 609
. . subrogation to creditors' security... 608(3)

**Committee of creditors** – see Creditors'
   committee

**Competent authorities** ......................... 204
. authorisation to act as insolvency
   practitioner.......................... 202; 205

**Company**
. meaning................................... 903(1)
. petition for administration order .... 903(4)
. property – see Property
. purchase of own shares ................. 309(5)

**Company seal**
. administrative receiver
. . power to use ................................ 411
. . valid appointment ...................... 309(1)

**Paragraph**

**Compulsory liquidation** .......................1204

**Conditional sale agreements**
. creditors' meetings, evaluation of
   debts ...................................1106(5)

**Construction industry**
. contractors in, preferential payments ... 802
. income tax.................................... 805

**Contracts**
. charge on contingent right to payments under................................. 305
. prohibition on charging ................... 408
. realisation of assets and property .... 515(5)

**Contractual rights**
. third party rights............................ 406

**Conveyancing**
. administrative receiver ..................... 516
. administrator.................................1121

**Copyright royalties**
. income tax.................................... 805

**Cork Report**
. floating charges.............................. 303
. insolvency practitioners bonding ......... 206
. nefarious conduct........................... 101

**Corporate capacity of borrower**
. appointment of administrative
   receiver................................... 309(2)

**Corporation tax**
. administration expense.....................1304
. before administration order..............1301
. existing liability ............................ 801

**Counterclaims**
. set-off...................................... 407(2)

**Courts**
. administrative receiver
. . request for property and documents to be
     passed over............................. 414(2)
. . summons for persons to appear
     before.................................. 414(4)
. administrator
. . as officer ..................................1004
. . discharge of administration order .....1204
. . remuneration, application for
     increase...................................1203
. . vacation of office by order .............1205
. hearing of petition for administration
   order ....................................... 906
. notice of administration.................... 907
. protection of creditors and members...1110

**Paragraph**

. transactions at an under value/pref-
  erences ...............................1016(4)
. unfair prejudice, application.............1109

**Credit**
. administrative receiver obtaining..... 510(4)

**Creditors** – see also Preferential creditors
. administrative receiver, report to ........ 420
. administrator
. . duties owed to.............................1018
. . statement of proposals ...................1103
. committee – see Creditors' committee
. meaning of ...............................1111(7)
. meetings – see Creditors' meetings
. petition for administration order ..... 903(4)
. protection of
. . court orders and time limits ............1110
. . unfairly prejudicial management and
    acts .........................................1109
. rights of execution........................ 407(5)
. transactions defrauding, administrator
    investigating...........................1016(7)
. unfair prejudice ...........................1109
. . court orders and time limits ...........1110

**Creditors' committee**
. accounts to ................................... 710
. administrative receivers' duties ........... 422
. administrator's remuneration...... 1107(10);
                                          1202
. certificates ................................1107(3)
. conflict of interest ......................1107(9)
. expenses...................................1107(8)
. functions ..................................1107(1)
. meetings....................................1107(4)
. membership ...............................1107(2)
. proceedings...............................1107(6)
. resignation and vacancies..............1107(5)
. resolutions ................................1107(7)
. travelling expenses ...................... 510(3)

**Creditors' meetings**
. administrative receiver's duties ........... 421
. chairman ..................................1106(2)
. conduct of ................................1106(7)
. committee, establishing – see Creditors'
    committee
. creditors' right to call..................1106(3)
. evaluation of secured and other
    debts .....................................1106(5)
. general rules .............................1106(1)
. minutes....................................1106(8)
. notice of results ........................1106(9)
. proxies.....................................1106(6)
. voting entitlement ......................1106(4)

**Paragraph**

**Credit transactions**
. extortionate, administrator investi-
    gating ...................................1016(5)

**Criminal offences**
. administrative receiver, notice of
    appointment............................ 312(2)
. insolvency practitioner acting when
    unqualified................................. 201
. non-payment of value added tax ......... 804

**Crown**
. preferential creditor, set-off .............. 605

**Crystallisation**
. floating charge............................. 303(4)
. distress, levy ................................. 809
. local authority rates...................... 508(1)
. preferential creditors, payment out of
    assets......................................... 602
. third party property......................... 406
. third party rights, execution
    creditors................................. 407(5)

**Customs and Excise**
. powers, distress ............................. 809

**D**

**Damages**
. administrative receiver's liability ......... 501
. invalid appointment of adminis-
    trative receiver ......................... 313(1)

**Death**
. administrative receiver ..................... 704
. administrator.................................1207

**Debenture holder**
. administrative receiver, notice of
    appointment of......................... 312(1)
. payment local authority rates ............. 508
. receiver, appointment of .................. 307

**Debts** – see also Book debts; Preferential debts
. charges on ................................... 305
. composition in satisfaction of – see Vol-
    untary arrangement schemes
. creditors' meetings, evaluation.......1106(5)
. inability to pay, administration order – see
    Administration order
. set-off..................................... 407(2)
. tax ............................................. 802

**Deed of release** ............................ 516(3)

**Definitions and meanings**
. administration order ........................ 901
. administrative receiver ..................... 301

**Paragraph**

**Definitions and meanings**—continued
. adoption.........................................512
. company ................................. 903(1)
, creditor............................ 1111(7)
. floating charge..............................304
. officer.......................................1005
. on demand ...................................307
. ordinary share capital ......................808

**Demands for repayment of borrowings**
. method of service............................308

**Directors**
. administrator
. . power to appoint and dismiss ..........1010
. . report on unfit.............................1015
. creditors' meetings ......................1106(1)
. disqualification .............................. 415
. notice of abuse of powers in creating
    charge, appointment of administrative
    receiver................................. 309(3)
. petition for administration order .... 903(4)
. powers........................................ 412
. unfit, administrative receiver's report ... 415
. voluntary arrangement schemes,
    meetings...............................1111(5)

**Dismissal**
. administrative receiver ..................... 702

**Disqualification orders**
. insolvency practitioner prohibition....... 202
. unfit directors............................... 415

**Distress**
. Revenue powers ............................. 809

**Distributions**
. administrative receiver's duties ........... 417
. contribution between co-guarantors – see
    Co-guarantors
. preferential creditors – see Preferential
    creditors

**Documents**
. administrator's name to appear........... 907
. method of service............................308
. realisation of assets and property,
    sale contract................................ 513
. surrender to administrative receiver . 414(2)

**E**

**EEC**
. employees' rights, unfair dismissal... 515(5)

**Electricity supplies**
. administrative receiver's rights........ 414(1)
. administrator's rights ...............1003; 1117

**Paragraph**

**Employees**
. administrative receiver's appointment .. 502
. adoption, meaning .......................... 512
. information to............................. 414(3)
. personal liability ............................ 511
. realisation of assets and property .... 515(1)
. Redundancy Fund, payments out
    of......................................... 515(4)
. right to redundancy ...................... 515(3)
. unfair dismissal............................ 515(5)
. wages ...................................... 510(6)
. administrator
. . hiving-down ...............................1114
. . liability for payment of...................1119

**Employment Protection Act 1975**........ 515(1)

**Entertainers**
. foreign, income tax ......................... 805

**Equitable assignment**
. set-off...................................... 407(2)

**Equitable charge**
. local authority rates...................... 508(2)

**Equities**
. set-off...................................... 407(2)

**Estoppel**
. invalid appointment of administrative
    receiver................................. 313(1)

**Execution creditors**
. third party rights.......................... 407(5)

**Expenses**
. administrative receiver ..................... 510
. administrator
. . payment out of floating charges .......1209
. . trading.....................................1115
. corporation tax as an administration
    expense....................................1304
. creditors' committee ...................1107(8)
. creditors' meetings .....................1106(3)
. voluntary arrangement schemes ... 1111(12)

**Extortionate credit transactions**
. administrator investigating ............1016(5)

**F**

**Fading blue chip** ............................... 901

**Fees**
. application to act as insolvency prac-
    titioner...................................... 204
. repayment, invalid appointment of
    administrative receiver .............. 313(1)

**Paragraph**

**Fiduciary duty**
. administrator..............................1005(3)

**Fines**
. administrative receiver, report to
    creditors....................................420
. administrator's liability for............1005(1)

**Fixed charges** ....................................304
.. future book debts............................305
. surplus of realisations ........................604

**Floating charges**................................303
. administrator, expenses paid on termin-
    ation of office.............................1209
. advantages..................................303(1)
. avoidance, administrator invest-
    igating ...................................1016(6)
. crystallisation .............................303(4)
. definition.......................................304
. disadvantages .............................303(2)
. elements of................................303(3)
. third party property.........................406

**Foreign entertainers and sportsmen**
. income tax.....................................805

**Foreign dividends**
. income tax.....................................805

**Fraudulent preferences** – see Preferences

**Furniss v Dawson**
. rule in........................................808(2)

**Future book debts** ..............................305

**G**

**Gas supplies**
. administrative receiver's rights........414(1)
. administrator's rights ...............1003; 1117

**Groups of companies**
. contribution between co-guarantors .....607
. taxation........................................808

**H**

**Hire purchase agreements**
. creditors' meetings, evaluation of
    debts .....................................1106(5)
. realisation of assets and property ....515(3)
. third-party property.........................1007
. voluntary arrangement schemes .....1111(6)

**Hive-downs**
. administrative receiver ......................504
.. tax liabilities ................................808

**Paragraph**

. administrator................................1114
.. tax liabilities ..............................1306

**Holiday pay**
. preferential debt .......................... 601(5)

**I**

**Identification**
. reservation of title........................ 407(3)

**Income tax**
. liability, general rule........................ 801
. obligation to deduct......................... 805
. preferential debt ................601(1); 802(1)

**Incorporation**
. reservation of title........................ 407(3)

**Indemnities**
. administrative receiver
.. administrator, relationship with ........ 708
.. appointor, relationship with ............ 707
.. co-guarantor's rights ................. 608(1)
.. invalid appointment............. 313(1), (3)
.. liquidator, relationship with ............ 709
.. statutory provisions ....................... 706

**Information**
. administrative receiver's require-
    ments ..................................... 414(3)
. administrator as office-holder ...........1011

**Inland Revenue**
. powers, distress .............................. 809

**Insolvency legislation**............................ 102

**Insolvency practitioners**
. acting when unqualified.................... 201
. bonding........................................ 206
. competent authorities ...................... 204
.. authorisation by............................ 205
. educational qualifications and practical
    experience ................................. 205
. prohibitions ................................. 202
. qualifications ............................... 202
. recognised professional bodies........... 203
. specific penalty sum........................ 206

**Insolvency Practitioners Association**
. recognised professional body ............. 203

**Insolvency Practitioners Tribunal**
. authorisation to act as practitioner re-
    fused or withdrawn....................... 205
. members ..................................... 205

**Institute of Chartered Accountants in England
and Wales**
. recognised professional body ............. 203

**Paragraph**

**Institute of Chartered Accounts in Ireland**
. recognised professional body .............. 203

**Institute of Chartered Accountants in Scotland**
. recognised professional body .............. 203

**Insurance**
. administrative receiver's cover ............ 501

**Interest**
. income tax ..................................... 805

**Interest in property**
. third party property ......................... 406

**Intra vires transactions**
. appointment of administrative
　receiver ................................. 309(2)

**Invalid appointments**
. administrative receiver ..................... 313
. administrator ................................. 909

**Invoices**
. appointment of administrative receiver
　to be stated on ........................ 312(5)

**J**

**Joint appointments**
. administrative receiver ..................... 413
. administrator ................................. 1013

**L**

**Land Registry**
. administrative receiver conveyancing ... 516

**Law of Property Act 1925**
. administrative receiver, power to
　appoint ..................................... 307

**Law Society**
. recognised professional body .............. 203

**Law Society of Scotland**
. recognised professional body .............. 203

**Leased equipment**
. realisation of assets and property .... 515(3)

**Leasehold premises**
. realisation of assets and property .... 515(4)

**Leases**
. prohibition on charging .................... 408

**Liability**
. administrative receiver
. . employees .......................... 502; 515(1)
. . hiving-down ................................. 504
. . PAYE ...................................... 802
. . statutory and tortious ..................... 507

**Paragraph**

. . tax – see Tax
. . tort ......................................... 501
. administrator
. . tort ........................................ 1116

**Licensing requirements for insolvency
practitioners**
. acting when unqualified ..................... 201
. bonding requirements ...................... 206
. competent authorities ...................... 204
. . authorisation by ........................... 205
. Cork Report ................................. 101
. legislation ................................... 102
. prohibitions ................................. 202
. recognised professional body .............. 203

**Liens**
. charges on debts ......................... 305(2)
. third-party rights ........................ 407(1)

**Liquidation**
. administrative receiver's agency, effect
　of .............................................. 404

**Liquidator**
. administrative receiver, relationship
　with ........................................... 709

**Loan document**
. appointment of administrative receiver . 307

**Local authority rates**
. payment ..................................... 508

**London Gazette**
. administrative receiver
. . appointment, notice of ............... 312(3)
. administrator
. . appointment, notice of ............... 907(2)
. . proposals, notice of ...................... 1103

**M**

**Mareva injunctions** ......................... 407(5)

**Meetings**
. creditors – see Creditors' meetings
. members' ................................... 1108
. voluntary arrangement schemes ..... 1111(5)

**Members**
. administrator
. . duties owed to ............................ 1019
. . proposals ................................... 1103
. creditors' committee ................... 1107(2)
. Insolvency Practitioners Tribunal ........ 205
. meetings ................................... 1108
. unfair prejudice ............................ 1109
. . court orders and time limits ........... 1110

Paragraph

**Mental Health Act patients**
. insolvency practitioner prohibition ....... 202

**Mines and quarries**
. rents, income tax ............................ 805

**Minutes**
. creditors' meetings ..................... 1106(8)

**Misfeasance**
. administrative receiver's liability ..... 507(3)

**Mortgages** ......................................... 304

### N

**National Insurance contributions** ........... 805

**Negligence**
. administrative receiver ...................... 501

**Nominee**
. voluntary arrangement schemes – see Voluntary arrangement schemes

**Non-resident landlords**
. income tax .................................... 805

**Notices**
. administration order ........................ 907
. . petition for ............................... 903(8)
. administrative receiver, appointment of ............................................. 312
. creditors' meetings ..................... 1106(1)
. . results of ............................... 1106(9)

### O

**Occupational pension schemes**
. contributions, preferential debt ....... 601(4)

**Office-holder**
. administrative receiver as ................. 414
. administrator
. . comparison with other .................. 1001
. . powers as ................................. 1011

**Official receiver**
. administrative receiver duty to co-operate with ........................... 416(3)

**Ordinary share capital**
. meaning ...................................... 808

### P

**Patent royalties**
. income tax .................................... 805

**PAYE**
. income tax, obligation to collect ......... 805
. preferential payments ...................... 802

Paragraph

**Payments and distributions** – see also Distributions
. accounts ...................................... 710
. co-guarantors – see Co-guarantors
. order of ...................................... 606
. preferential creditors – see Preferential creditors

**Petitions**
. administration order ..................... 903(4)
. . contents ................................. 903(5)
. . filing .................................... 903(7)
. . hearing of ................................. 906
. . legal consequences ...................... 904(1)
. . notice of ................................. 903(8)
. . practical consequences ................. 904(2)
. . practical aspects ....................... 903(10)
. . time of service .......................... 903(9)
. winding-up ................................. 1204

**Preferences**
. administration order ........................ 905
. administrator investigating ........... 1016(3)

**Preferential creditors**
. categories summarised ...................... 601
. Crown set-off ............................... 605
. fixed charge, surplus of realisations ..... 604
. obligation to pay ........................... 603
. payment out of assets ...................... 602

**Preferential debts**
. categories ................................... 802
. list ......................................... 601
. tax ......................................... 1302
. voluntary arrangement schemes, effect on rights .............................. 1111(2)

**Preferential payments** ....................... 802

**Premises**
. leasehold, sale of ....................... 515(4)

**Professional body** – see Recognised professional body

**Promissory notes**
. creditors' meetings, evaluation of debts .................................... 1106(5)
. voluntary arrangement schemes ..... 1111(6)

**Property**
. administrative receiver
. . contractual position .................... 405
. . liens .................................... 407(1)
. . prohibitions on charging ............... 408
. . reservation of title .................... 407(3)
. . rights of execution creditors ......... 407(5)
. . set-off .................................. 407(2)

Pro

**Paragraph**

**Property**—continued
. . third party property and contractual
    rights ......................................... 406
. . third party rights, specific ............... 406
. . trusts .................................... 407(4)
. administrator
. . charged property............................1008
. . directors, power to appoint and
    dismiss .....................................1010
. . duties owed to company ................1018
. . duties owed to creditors and
    members ...................................1019
. . information and powers as office-
    holder......................................1011
. . investigating antecedent transactions.1016
. . joint appointments, exercise of
    powers .....................................1013
. . limitations on powers and their exer-
    cise .......................................1012
. . miscellaneous requirements.............1017
. . powers, statutory list .....................1009
. . purposes of appointment ................1014
. . report on unfit directors ................1015
. . 'right to possession' ......................1006
. . third party property......................1007
. realisation of – see Realisation of assets and
    property

**Proposals** – see Voluntary arrangement
    schemes

**Protection of creditors and members** ......1109
. court orders and time limits ..............1110
. voluntary arrangement schemes ... 1111(11)

**Protective awards**
. employees ................................. 515(5)

**Proxies**
. creditors' meetings ......................1106(6)
. voluntary arrangement schemes,
    meetings.................................1111(5)

**Public lending rights income** .................. 805

**R**

**Ramsay principle** ............................... 808

**Ranking of charges**
. administrative receiver,
    appointment............................ 309(9)

**Rates**
. payment ...................................... 508

**Realisation of assets and property**
. administrative receiver
. . charged property to sell.................. 517
. . common areas of concern ............... 515

**Paragraph**

. . contracts ................................. 515(5)
. . conveyancing.............................. 516
. . employees ................................ 515(1)
. . hire purchase and leased equip-
    ment..................................... 515(3)
. . leasehold premises ..................... 515(4)
. . negotiating the deal...................... 514
. . price, valuation and apportionment ... 518
. . purchasers, list of considerations ...... 519
. . sale documentation....................... 513
. . title ..................................... 515(2)
. administrators
. . charged and third party property,
    power to deal with .....................1122
. . considerations ...........................1120
. . conveyancing.............................1121

**Receivership expense** ...................... 510

**Recognised professional bodies** .............. 203
. insolvency practitioner qualification to
    act ....................................... 202
. petition for administration order ..... 903(4)

**Recognised self-regulating organisation**
. petition for administration order ..... 903(4)

**Redundancy Fund** ......................... 515(4)

**Registrar of Companies**
. accounts to be delivered to ............... 710
. administrative receiver
. . notice of vacation of office.............. 701
. . report to creditors....................... 420
. administrator, statement of proposals..1103
. discharge of administration ..............1204
. notice of administration order ........ 907(6)

**Registration of charges**
. appointment of administrative
    receiver.................................. 309(6)

**Remuneration**
. administrative receiver ..................... 610
. administrator........................... 1107(10)
. . application to court ......................1203
. . creditor's committee .....................1202
. . pre-order................................1201

**Rents**................................... 509
. mines and quarries, income tax........... 805
. non-resident landlords, income tax ...... 805

**Reports**
. administrative receiver
. . conduct of directors...................... 415
. . creditors................................. 420
. administrators
. . company's affairs ...................... 903(6)

**Paragraph**

. . unfit directors..............................1015
. . voluntary arrangement schemes . 1111(10)

**Reservation of title** ........................ 407(3)
. trading.......................................... 506

**Resignation**
. administrative receiver ...................... 703
. administrator................................1206

**Resolutions**
. creation of security, appointment of
    administrative receiver .............. 309(4)
. creditors' committee ....................1107(7)
. creditors' meetings ......................1106(7)

**Retention of title**
. administration order ......................... 905
. agreements ..................................1007
. creditors' meetings, evaluation of
    debts ...................................1106(5)
. voluntary arrangement schemes .....1111(6)

**Romalpa clauses**........................... 407(3)

**Rule in Furniss v Dawson** .................... 808


**S**

**Sale of assets and property** – see Realisation of
    assets and property

**Sale of business as a going concern** ......... 515

**Schedule C income tax** ........................ 805

**Schemes** – see also Voluntary arrangement
    schemes
. under s. 425 of Companies Act 1985...1112

**Seal** – see Company seal

**Secretary of State**
. insolvency practitioner authorisation to
    act ........................................... 202

**Secured creditors**
. administration order ......................... 905
. voluntary arrangement schemes, effect on
    rights....................................1111(2)

**Secured debts**
. creditors' meetings, evaluation.......1106(5)

**Security document**
. administrative receiver's
. . authority .................................... 302
. . charges on debts ........................... 305
. . covenant to repay loan on demand .... 307
. . form of appointment.................... 310(1)
. . powers....................................... 411

**Paragraph**

. . remuneration ........................... 610(2)
. . right to appoint ........................... 307

**Self-regulating organisation** – see Recognised
    self-regulating organisation

**Set-off**........................................ 407(2)
. Crown, preferential creditor.............. 605
. trading........................................ 505

**Shadow directors**
. administrator, report on unfit ............1015

**Social security contributions**
. preferential debt .......................... 601(3)

**Specific penalty sum**........................... 206

**Sportsmen**
. foreign, income tax ......................... 805

**Stamping of charges**
. appointment of administrative
    receiver...................................309(10)

**Statement of affairs**
. administrative receiver ...................... 419
. administrator.............................1011(1)
. voluntary arrangement schemes .....1111(3)

**Statement of proposals**
. administrator................................1103

**Stationery**
. administrative receiver, appointment
    to be stated......................312(5); 418
. administrator's name to appear.......... 907

**Sub-contractors in the construction industry**
. preferential payments ...................... 802

**Subrogation**
. creditors' security......................... 608(3)

**Supervisor**
. voluntary arrangement schemes – see Vol-
    untary arrangement schemes


**T**

**Tax**
. corporation tax
. . administration expenses.................1304
. . before administration order.............1301
. general rule ................................. 801
. hive-downs ..................... 504; 808; 1306
. income tax, obligation to deduct ......... 805
. incurred during receivership.............. 804
. preferential debts in administration ....1302
. preferential payments ...................... 802
. Revenue powers ...........................1307
. . distress..................................... 809

Tax

**Paragraph**

**Tax**—continued
. . priority of claim for tax ................... 810
. value added tax .........................803; 806
. . accruing ......................................1303
. . after administration order ..............1305
. . bad debt relief............................. 807

**Telecommunication services**
. administrative receiver's rights........ 414(1)
. administrator's rights ..............1003; 1117

**Third-party rights**
. administrative receiver
. . execution creditors ..................... 407(5)
. . general principles ...................... 406(1)
. . judicial consideration ................. 406(3)
. . liens ....................................... 407(1)
. . property and mere contractual
     rights ..................................... 406(2)
. . reservation of title.................... 407(3)
. . rights of execution creditors ........ 407(5)
. . set-off..................................... 407(2)
. . specific.................................... 407
. . trusts ..................................... 407(4)
. administrator...............................1007
. . power to deal with .......................1122
. . trading considerations ..................1113

**Title**
. administrative receiver
. . power of attorney ........................ 516
. sale of....................................... 515(2)
. administrator................................1121

**Tort**
. administrative receiver's personal liab-
     ility ........................................... 501
. . trading ..................................... 507
. administrator's liability....................1116

**Trading**
. administrative receiver
. . considerations for and against........... 503
. . hiving-down ............................... 504
. . local authority rates....................... 508
. . receivership expenses..................... 510
. . rents........................................ 509
. . reservation of title....................... 506
. . set-off...................................... 505
. . statutory and tortious liabilities........ 507
. administrator
. . administration expenses..................1115
. . considerations ...........................1113
. . employees .................................1119
. . existing contracts ........................1118
. . hiving-down ...............................1114
. . liability in tort ...........................1116

**Paragraph**

. . suppliers of utilities .......................1117

**Trading stock**
. valuation, taxation ........ 808

**Transactions at undervalue**
. administration order .................... 905(5)
. administrator investigating ...... 1016(2), (5)

**Tribunal** – see Insolvency Practitioners
     Tribunal

**Trustees**
. administrative receiver's report to cre-
     ditors....................................... 420

**Trusts**
. charged debt held for chargee ............ 305
. third party rights......................... 407(4)

**Turquand's case rule**
. appointment of administrative
     receiver.................................. 309(4)

**U**

**Uncalled capital**
. administrative receiver's power to call.. 411

**Unfair dismissal**
. employees ................................. 515(5)

**Unfair prejudice**...............................1109
. court orders and time limits ..............1110
. voluntary arrangement schemes ....1111(2),
                                                    (11)

**Unpaid tax**
. distress........................................ 809
. seizure of goods and chattels.............. 810

**Unsecured creditors**
. administrative receiver's report .......... 420

**V**

**Validity**
. invalid appointment
. . administrative receiver ............... 313(2)
. . administrator.............................. 909
. reservation of title....................... 407(3)

**Valuation**
. trading stock and work-in-progress, tax-
     ation........................................ 808

**Value added tax** ............................... 806
. accruing ............................... 803; 1303
. after administration order .................1305
. bad debt relief............................. 807
. existing liability ........................... 801
. preferential debt ............... 601(2); 802(3)

**Paragraph**

**Voluntary arrangement schemes**
. administrator's proposals
.. content of ............................... 1111(4)
.. preparation ............................. 1111(3)
. creditor, meaning ...................... 1111(7)
. general outline ........................ 1111(1)
. implementation ....................... 1111(8)
. meetings ................................. 1111(5)
. protection of creditors ............... 1111(11)
. remuneration of nominee .......... 1111(12)
. reports .................................. 1111(10)
. supervisor, position of ................ 1111(9)
. termination ............................ 1111(12)
. types of schemes ..................... 1111(2)
. voting ................................... 1111(6)

**Voting entitlement**
. creditors' meetings .................... 1106(4)

**Paragraph**

voluntary arrangement schemes ..... 1111(6)

**W**

**Wages**
. employees ............................... 510(6)
. preferential debt ...................... 601(5)

**Water supplies**
. administrative receiver's rights ........ 414(1)
. administrator's rights ............... 1003; 1117

**Wayleave rents**
. income tax .................................. 805

**Winding-up by the court** ..................... 1204

**Work-in-progress**
. valuation, taxation ......................... 808